ALICE MORSE EARLE
AND THE
DOMESTIC HISTORY OF
EARLY AMERICA

A VOLUME IN THE SERIES

Public History in Historical Perspective

Edited by Marla R. Miller

ALICE MORSE EARLE
AND THE
DOMESTIC HISTORY OF
EARLY AMERICA

Susan Reynolds Williams

UNIVERSITY OF MASSACHUSETTS PRESS
Amherst and Boston

ISBN 978-1-55849-988-1 (paper); 987-4 (hardcover)

Designed by Sally Nichols
Set in Adobe Caslon Pro
Printed and bound by Thomson-Shore, Inc.

Library of Congress Cataloging-in-Publication Data

Williams, Susan, 1948–
Alice Morse Earle and the domestic history of early America / Susan Reynolds Williams.
pages cm. — (Public history in historical perspective)
Includes bibliographical references and index.
ISBN 978-1-55849-988-1 (pbk. : alk. paper) — ISBN 978-1-55849-987-4 (hardcover : alk. paper)
1. Earle, Alice Morse, 1851-1911. 2. Historians—United States—Biography. 3. Women historians—
United States—Biography. 4. United States—Social life and customs—To 1775—Historiography.
5. New England—Social life and customs—To 1775—Historiography. 6. Material culture—United
States—Historiography. 7. Home economics—United States—Historiography. I. Title.
E175.5.E14W55 2013
974'.0207202—dc23
[B]
                                        2012039636

British Library Cataloguing in Publication data are available.

Publication of this book and other titles in the series
Public History in Historical Perspective
is supported by the
Office of the Dean, College of Humanities and Fine Arts,
University of Massachusetts Amherst.

In memory of
Susan Powers Urstadt
and
Donald J. Post Jr.

CONTENTS

PREFACE

ESPITE HER LARGE READERSHIP and widespread popularity, little is actually known about Alice Morse Earle. As a young ceramics curator at a large history museum, I first encountered Earle through her book *China Collecting in America*, which I found to be reliable but dated, and rich in anecdotal material. I came to appreciate her significance later in my career when, as a graduate student, I was required to reread *Home Life in Colonial Days* for a colonial history seminar, this time with a far more critical eye. The analysis and assumptions that underlay the research narrative intrigued me, and I realized that Earle's work offered an important avenue into the world of late nineteenth-century American culture, particularly that of women.

I initially approached this project with the intention of discovering how Earle's private history had shaped her published work—her public history. The most comprehensive biography of Earle, an article published in 1947 by the New England writer Esther Averill, laid out the essential details about her birth, family, and career, along with a tantalizing reference to "nearly fifty boxes of notes and material unearthed and partly used in her writings."[1] Averill's research notes for that article, which have survived in the collections of the American Antiquarian Society, reveal that her sources included some family papers and photographs from the estate of Earle's sister, Frances C. Morse. Unfortunately, the fifty boxes of research material seem to have disappeared.

The quest for those fifty boxes, however, led me to pursue Earle in many different directions. I went to her house in Brooklyn Heights— only to find that it has been converted into condominiums. I canvassed many historical societies and archives in New York and New England— to no avail. Eventually I tracked down a great-grandson in Connecticut, who had family photographs and leads to other family members. I located a family compound of Earle's descendants in Vermont, who had family artifacts that had belonged to her, as well as portions of her personal library, including her own annotated copies of her books. In keeping with family tradition (albeit unconsciously), her great-granddaughter was a literary agent and her great-grandson a publisher. Writing seems to run in the blood—but still no fifty boxes.

The absence of a large body of personal papers forced me to begin my task of reconstructing Earle's life and work with her published texts, which are full of assumptions, stories, pictures, and veiled but enticing personal references. Because historical writing was for Earle a vehicle of self-definition as well as a means of educating her audience, I found that close readings of her texts provided much in the way of autobiographical detail. Nothing that she wrote, however, was explicitly autobiographical; Earle was so ambivalent about publicity that she granted only one biographical interview during her entire writing career. Yet her desire to establish an emotional link with her readers, as well as confirm her authority, percolated beneath the surface of her many books and articles, yielding snippets of revelation about her own past and present.

Genealogical investigation proved another path to evidence about Alice Morse Earle, especially because transmission of family experiences from generation to generation was a central issue in her work. I reconstructed both the Morse and Earle families back to the original emigrants—a task in which I was greatly assisted by an existing family genealogy, created by Earle's daughter in the 1920s and built on Earle's own genealogical research.[2] Family letters going back three generations—especially those between Earle's mother and father prior to their marriage—and assorted family photographs provided yet another set of clues to the family value system and the set of life experiences that Earle inherited, as well as those she wished to transmit to her own children.

Only fragments have survived of the material environments in which Earle spent her childhood and lived and worked as an adult. Her parents' home in Worcester, Massachusetts, which was subsequently occupied by her sister, Frances, was razed in 1934. Although there is no documentation of the house and its furnishings during the years when Earle lived there, several photographic illustrations in Frances Morse's book *Furniture of the Olden Times* depict the interior of the house at the turn of the twentieth century.[3]

The house where Earle lived from the mid-1870s until she died in 1911 still stands on Henry Street in Brooklyn Heights, although the interior has been considerably altered for current residents. Nonetheless, the exterior finish, architectural details, and overall plan, as well as the topography of the neighborhood, are all useful evidence of Earle's urban world and the social strategies that she and her upper-middle-class family employed to buffer themselves from it.[4]

Although Earle was an avid letter writer, surprisingly little of her personal correspondence remains; insights into her relationships with her husband, children, parents, in-laws, sister, and friends must be gleaned from other sources. Her professional identity, however, can be discovered from the many letters between Earle and her editors and publishers, which have survived in the papers of Charles Scribner's Sons at Firestone Library, Princeton University, and the Macmillan Company papers at the New York Public Library. Other small pockets of letters exist at the Massachusetts Historical Society, the University of Virginia, Northwestern University, the American Antiquarian Society, the Boston Public Library, the Old York Historical Society, the Library of Congress, the Historical Society of Pennsylvania, the Sophia Smith Collection at Smith College, Historic Deerfield, the Pocumtuck Valley Memorial Association, and in the hands of Earle's descendants.[5] These letters, when considered collectively, offer the strongest remaining evidence about Earle's personality and literary agenda.

In the absence of a large body of personal papers, the next best source for Earle's own voice remains her published works. These I have examined both for their explicit literary and historical content and for more cryptic statements that might reveal fleeting glimpses of the inner Alice Morse Earle. I analyzed her historical narratives for evidence of personal narrative, and have searched her texts and the artifacts they featured for metaphoric and structural components that could shed light on her mentality.

Although Earle's few surviving letters contain some information about her research methods and historical sources, these too remain essentially locked in the matrix of her texts. The process of unlocking that information involves examining her work within the framework of broader cultural and intellectual currents, particularly the context of the rapidly emerging historical profession, as well as piecing together a picture of her intellectual methods from textual clues, the type of historical evidence she chose to use—material and archival—and her mode of presentation. This involves direct analysis of Earle's books as cultural artifacts as well as texts—their design, format, structure, illustrations, and linguistic conventions. Fortunately, Earle's personal copies of many of her books still exist, annotated throughout with pasted-in clippings and handwritten notations, in anticipation of future editions.

ACKNOWLEDGMENTS

During the twenty years I have been working on this book, many people have aided me, in terms of my research and writing as well as my personal well-being. For wise guidance in the earliest stages of this project at the University of Delaware, I thank David Allmendinger, Anne Boylan, Bernie Herman, and Richard Bushman. Thanks for your patience—I know that some of you have been waiting a long time to see this book come to print

I received invaluable assistance from numerous research libraries and archives. The Macmillan Company, Firestone Library at Princeton University, and the Division of Rare Books and Manuscripts at the New York Public Library permitted me to reproduce portions of Alice Morse Earle's correspondence, as did Northwestern University Library, the American Antiquarian Society, Boston Public Library, the Sophia Smith Collection at Smith College, the Small Special Collections Library at the University of Virginia, the Historical Society of Pennsylvania, Syracuse University Library, Memorial Hall Museum and the Pocumtuck Valley Memorial Association, and the Old York Historical Society. I also thank Dun & Bradstreet and the Baker Library at Harvard Business School for permission to cite sections of the R. G. Dun & Company papers.

Thanks also to the Morris Library at the University of Delaware, Forbes Library in Northampton, Mass., Rush Rhees Library at the University of Rochester, Schlesinger Library, the DAR Library in Washington, the

Massachusetts Historical Society, Worcester Historical Museum, the McGilvrey Room of the Peterborough (N.H.) Library, Worcester Public Library, the Worcester Art Museum, and the Division of Prints and Photographs of the Library of Congress. Special thanks to Neville Thompson and Winterthur Museum; archivist and dear friend Sandra Markham; Ann Lanning at Historic Deerfield; Suzanne Flynt and David Bosse at the Memorial Hall Museum and Library; and Kathy Bell, librarian at the Tower Hill Botanic Garden. At my home institution, Fitchburg State University, helpful librarians, past and present, assisted me, especially Kathryn Wells, Lisa Field, Sara Marks, Linda LeBlanc, Jenny Fielding, Mark Melchior, Jason Simon, and always, Bob Foley.

Early on, both Marilyn Williams and Jackie Goggin generously shared their own research on Alice Morse Earle with me. Thanks also to Jane Nylander, Mary Anne Caton, Kevin Murphy, Laura Sprague, Bill Hosley, Ellen Dencker, and the late Sandy Armentrout, whose interests in china collecting and the colonial revival paralleled mine, and to Jennifer Anderson Lawrence, who helped me to penetrate the mysteries of the Colonial Dames. Thanks to Beverly Gordon, whose long-ago suggestion that I find Earle's friends proved invaluable, and to Tim Cranston at the Wickford (R.I.) Town Office, who helped me track down Earle's Wickford past and Earle/Greene descendants. Patricia Hoffman facilitated my search for documents and photographs at the New Ipswich Historical Society, as well as cultivating my interest in gardens and plants. Thanks also to John Harris, archivist extraordinaire in the town of Dublin, and Mary Meath of Historic Harrisville—who lived on the site of Reuben Morse's farm—both helped me track down the early Morse family in New Hampshire. Julia Pane was kind enough to share her house in Brooklyn Heights with me. I am further indebted to the people in Andover, Vermont—Larry Sullivan, Peter Farrar, and Reino and Dotty Berquist—who welcomed me into their homes and patiently answered my questions. I also thank Andover town clerk Claudia Hazeltine for her willing assistance.

One of the great pleasures of working on this book was meeting Alice Morse Earle's great-grandchildren—Don Post, Susan Urstadt, Joshua B. Powers, and Tom Powers—who gave me free access to their family papers, photographs, genealogical materials, and hospitality, all of which I greatly appreciated. Sadly, Don and Susan did not live to see this book's completion. Matt Post, Earle's great-great-grandson, and his wife, Laura, turned up with a series of lovely watercolor paintings done by Alice and her sister, Frances, one of which is reproduced here. I have fond memories of a Post family reunion of sorts at Tower Hill celebrating Alice's 160th birthday and an exhibition of those paintings. From another branch of the family, Natalie Hamlin, an Earle/Greene descendant, helped me to understand the history of Duck Cove and "Homogansett."

Early on, Carolyn Goldstein, Michael Kucher, Julie Nicoletta, and Ruth Oldenzeil read the manuscript. Thanks also to students in my women's history and graduate historiography seminars, who read portions of the manuscript and offered their feedback. Special thanks to Marjo Kaartinen at the University of Turku, Finland, and my colleague at Fitchburg State, Edith Murphy, for their wise suggestions. Without the help of Marla Miller at the University of Massachusetts, this book would have been a very different product. Thank you, Marla, for all of your patience and incredible editorial insights.

At University of Massachusetts Press, thanks to Clark Dougan, Carol Betsch, Amanda Heller, Mary Bellino, and others for your support and talents. At Fitchburg State University, thanks for the support and friendship from my departmental colleagues and friends, especially Laura Baker, Rod Christie, Christine Dee, Sean Goodlett, Kate Jewell, Ben Lieberman, John Paul, René Reeves, Dan and Tracey Sarefield, Josh Spero, Paul Weizer, Shirley Wagner, Rala Diakite, Peter Laytin, Helen Obermeyer Simmons, and especially Karen Valeri. Thanks also for the Fitchburg State Faculty Research and Scholarship Award, which ultimately provided partial funding for this publication.

In New Ipswich, my Saturday morning walking group—Louise DelPapa, Liz Freeman, Barbara Graham, Christine Neill, Victoria Peterson, Amy Proctor, Nancy Rappaport, Betsy Rode, and the late Suzan Schafer Meiszner—has helped keep me happy and healthy. I love you all. Newbie Carolyn Dick Mayes introduced the idea of an ongoing Friday afternoon tea, something Alice Morse Earle would have understood, which grew to include dear friends and Bank Village neighbors Gwyn Baldwin, Laurel Blaine, Gail Ford, Nancy Haas, Marcia Ober, and Susie Ulfelder. Other friends have nourished me in innumerable ways, including Greg Hanselman, Woody Meiszner, Stan Zabierek, Kim Rode, Doug Ford, Clark Baldwin, Roland Coates, Ken and Pat Mogensen, Dixie Rhoades, Danielle LeBris Friedman, Shannon and Regina Stirnweis, Bea Bearden and David

Wells, and Federica DiRossi. Deepest thanks to my Northway friends—
Susan Coe Adams, Dee Dee Booth, Judy Prewitt Brown, Mary Herman
(and honorary NWL groupie Angus King), Mary Susanne Lamont, Fran-
ny Wells, Mary Polacheck, and Mary Roudebush. You are the best!

Sadly, neither of my parents lived long enough to see the book come to
fruition, but my sisters, Mary McLaughlin and Ann Chiara, along with
their spouses and children, as well as cousins Susan Meyer Call and Barbara Williams Galbraith, and my sister-in-law Marlene Nicholson—all
remind me continually of the importance of family. My dear friends Hugh
Van Dusen and Wendy Wolf, who know all too well the trials and tribu-
lations that plague writers, have quietly kept me moving forward since the
beginning. They are family as much as my actual family.

My husband, Harvey Green, muse and life companion, has fed me, tol-
erated my periods of detachment, made me coffee, and fed the dogs in the
morning. During the course of this book project, he built me a screened
porch—where I spent much time writing and revising—a new kitchen,
and a new staircase (among other things), all while doing his own significant scholarly work. Without his love, encouragement, and intellectual
sustenance, this would not have been possible.

ALICE MORSE EARLE
AND THE
DOMESTIC HISTORY OF
EARLY AMERICA

Alice Morse Earle, 1905.
Collection of Donald J. Post Jr.

INTRODUCTION
Hunting for Alice Morse Earle

※

T HE AUTHOR, COLLECTOR, AND HISTORIAN Alice Morse Earle
(1851–1911) was among the most influential writers of her day, but
for contemporary readers she is surprisingly elusive. She operated
within the context of a dramatic growth in popular history at the end of
the nineteenth century. Between 1891 and 1904 Earle generated seventeen books, as well as numerous articles, pamphlets, and speeches about
the life, manners, customs, and material culture of colonial New England.
These writings coincided with a surge of interest in colonial history, genealogy, and antique collecting. More than a century after the publication of
her first book, *The Sabbath in Puritan New England* (1891), the historical
writing of Alice Morse Earle still resonates in the minds and hearts of
her readers.

Although academic and other professional historians have not always
agreed with her assumptions, Earle's work influenced popular perceptions of the American past for most of the twentieth century and beyond.
Given that extraordinary influence, she needs to be better understood
today. An Amazon.com reader review of Earle's *Home Life in Colonial
Days* praised the book as "excellent early social history" and commented,
"This hundred-year-old work retains its vitality and usefulness." Another
reader, commenting on *Customs and Fashions in Old New England*, wrote,
"Alice Morse Earle's work should be considered a national treasure." A
third comment praised that book as "a widely referenced, widely consulted

classic."[1] Scholars studying the American past have regarded her as an authority on the material culture of the colonial home and family, if occasionally somewhat dismissively. Early historians of women tended not to address her as a subject of their study, although they clearly used her scholarship to support their arguments and included her books in their bibliographies. In *America through Women's Eyes* (1933), for example, Mary Ritter Beard cited Earle's *Colonial Dames and Goodwives* as a reference, although she did not discuss Earle's work directly.[2]

In 1950, almost forty years after Earle's death, in his massive *Society and Thought in Early America* the historian Harvey Wish praised Earle's *Colonial Days in Old New York,* as well as her work on childhood, calling it a source of "considerable social history in a simple narrative form."[3] By the 1980s, when women's history began to gain momentum as a scholarly enterprise, Earle appeared with increasing frequency, both as a resource *and* as a subject. Elizabeth Stillinger mentioned Earle as an important figure in the world of American collectors and collecting. Laurel Thatcher Ulrich paid tribute to Earle in the preface to *Good Wives,* a title that, she explained, "consciously echoes Alice Morse Earle's *Colonial Dames and Good Wives* . . . , honoring an early generation of women's historians who skillfully practiced what later scholars dismissed as 'pots-and-pans history.'" Eight years later, however, Linda Kerber dismissed the work of Earle and her early peers as "descriptive and anecdotal."[4]

Only later did Earle's work come to be treated in critical terms, evidence in itself of late-nineteenth and early-twentieth-century ideas about history, memory, class, domesticity, and gender. Karal Ann Marling's *George Washington Slept Here* (1988) positioned Earle as a prominent figure in the colonial revival movement. Marling cited *Home Life in Colonial Days,* Earle's 1898 "treatise on seventeenth- and eighteenth-century American households," as having "exerted an enormous influence on what the American home of the next several decades would look like." In his 1990 study *Rudeness and Civility,* John Kasson referred to Earle as an authority on pre-nineteenth-century manners. A year later, Michael Kammen's *Mystic Chords of Memory* traced the rise of the American passion for all things colonial in the 1890s, noting, "The key individual in this entire surge . . . was unquestionably Alice Morse Earle[,] . . . who became the most frequently consulted authority on American antiques." Kammen offered as further evidence of her impact that several of her books had "passed through countless printings and did much to make the colonial revival a genuinely popular phenomenon during the last years of the nineteenth and first decade of the twentieth centuries."[5]

Among more recent historians to assess Earle's significance, Joseph Conforti described Earle as "the most popular, productive, and influential interpreter of the 'old-times,'" as well as "a prolific custodian of regional identity." He acknowledged her role as a dominant force in the emergence of the colonial revival, into which she breathed both local color and moral imperative. For Conforti, Earle's most important contribution, however, was her resurrection of "homespun" domesticity as a resource for cultural and social renewal, through the agency of historical women from "Old New England." Ellen Fitzpatrick positioned Earle prominently in her discussion of the changing parameters of the historical profession in the decades between 1875 and 1900, arguing that despite Earle's status as an amateur historian, her studies of everyday life were at the forefront of a trend toward modern social history.[6]

In 1890, when Earle embarked on her career as a writer of history, history itself was in the process of redefinition as a professional discipline. Once the purview of genteel amateurs—mostly men—who wrote heroic narratives about war and politics, history was transformed by the formation of the American Historical Association in 1884, which set new standards for its practice. To be a historian was to have a Ph.D. and to work in an academic setting, publishing scholarly work that was "scientific" and adhered to the principles of rigorous research and objective analysis. The opening of Johns Hopkins University in 1876 and the inauguration of the seminar method of training in America, as well as the founding of the American Historical Association in 1884, initiated a new era of historical professionalism. The idea of professionalism was propelled by a widespread cultural and intellectual ambivalence over what had become an increasingly conflicted and unpredictable society.[7] By 1895 the AHA had launched the *American Historical Review,* a journal that proclaimed the new organizational mission—one that had little room for women or amateurs. Despite these hindrances, women historians did prevail, albeit often on their own terms. Julie Des Jardins has argued that Earle was part of a "collective biography" movement that "allowed women to disseminate their prescriptions for national manhood to mass audiences as never before," as well as to construct a defining role for women's historical agency.[8]

To be sure, Earle's writings as a collective entity presented a vision of an ideal society, a golden age that had reached its zenith during the years surrounding the drafting of the Constitution, and that had been waning ever since. She created a historical depiction of early America that was appealing, emotionally compelling, and supportive of a progressive social vision. Her major contribution to American culture was to provide that social vision a material form with which her readers and subsequent users of her work could readily identify. Earle believed that history, and particularly the intimate mix of material and local history that she promulgated, had a twofold value. In a paper delivered before the Daughters of the American Revolution in 1899, she argued, first, that history "may combat and dispel that local ignorance and indifference which has made the political boss and his henchmen so powerful a promoter and controller in our present afflicted and afflictive city politics," a sentiment that would have evoked in her listeners' minds images of corrupt immigrants, adding to the urgency of her message. Second, she perceived that local issues—those associated with "our own town, and above all our own family and kins-folk"—provided the strongest incentive to further research. She warned her audience of the danger, however, of a strictly myopic historical perspective. Unless local history was further interpreted as part of a national and international context, she argued, it might engender among students "an exaggerated notion of the importance of [their] surroundings."[9]

In Earle's attempts to write the history of early American social and cultural life, her interests carried her far beyond the watershed of American Independence, despite the modern interpretations of her work as part of the "colonial revival." *China Collecting in America, Old-Time Gardens, Sun-Dials and Roses,* and *Two Centuries of Costume in America* all encompassed a period that extended, in some cases, up to Earle's present. *Stage Coach and Tavern Days* too drew heavily on the material life of nineteenth-century America. For Earle, America's golden age encompassed not only the seventeenth and eighteenth centuries but also the postcolonial era, after the Revolution, when American culture (in the hands of her grandparents' generation), released from its colonial bonds, had flowered. It was an age of intimate scale, when people traveled by stagecoach, stopping at taverns whose hospitality was warm and welcoming, even to strangers. This was an age when women served tea from English earthenware teapots graced with a vision in blue and white of the marquis de Lafayette standing reverentially at the tomb of George Washington, an age when trade signboards represented a form of commerce that was conducted face-to-face, based on family networks and local or regional production rather than a national rail system and anonymous managers. The massive scale and rapid pace of life in the late nineteenth century, with its crowded cities, high-speed railroad travel, fashionable hotels, and bureaucratic structure, stood in stark counterpoint to this nostalgic vision and makes more comprehensible the underlying anxiety about the present and future that Earle and her reading public must have felt. Paradoxically, Earle depended on the amenities of modern life, and probably enjoyed her visits to spas and vacation resorts, as well as the ability to conduct her research away from home—in Philadelphia, Worcester, Washington, or Boston—easily and comfortably. Her work should be viewed not entirely as an antimodern rejection of the present but rather as a desire to curb its less positive aspects by reinvigorating elements of the past that had helped to shape what she perceived as the American character.

Born Mary Alice Morse in 1851, Earle was reared in a comfortable middle-class milieu in Worcester, Massachusetts. Her parents, Edwin and Abigail Clary Morse, had only recently arrived from northern New England, but were carving out a place for themselves in the new industrial economy. Essentially rural people adjusting to the pace and customs of the modern urban world, Edwin and Abby instilled in their daughter the combined values of family, community, industry, ambition, and service.

As she was emerging into young womanhood, Alice lived through the turbulence of national dissolution during the Civil War. Her brother Edwin served his country in the Union Army. For her, as for many others of her generation, the assassination of President Abraham Lincoln in 1865 was a defining event. In 1874, when she was twenty-three years old, Alice met and married Henry Earle, and the couple made their own foray into the new industrial economy, moving to Brooklyn Heights, New York. There they reared four children, while Henry worked as a commodities broker on Wall Street. In 1890, on the brink of her fortieth year, Earle began to write.

Her career took off. She wrote feverishly for the next fourteen years, producing seventeen books and numerous magazine articles. She became a best-selling author for Charles Scribner's Sons, then Houghton Mifflin, Herbert S. Stone, and Macmillan. Her work also appeared continually in popular magazines, including *New England Magazine,* the *Atlantic Month-ly, Scribner's Magazine,* the *Journal of American Folklore, The Dial, The Chau-tauquan, Chap Book, Outlook,* and (posthumously) *Century Magazine.* She was reviewed widely and positively in the *Atlantic Monthly,* the *London Quarterly Review,* the *American Historical Review,* and elsewhere. Earle and her publishers had identified a niche in historical writing—one that em-phasized the material world of ordinary people. Her books have remained in print in various editions up to the present, further testament to her wide appeal and continuing significance.

During the brief period when she was writing, Alice Morse Earle con-structed herself as an authority on the domestic sphere of early America. Her books and articles introduced her readers to the material settings that, she argued again and again, shaped the course of family, community, and nation. As a best-selling author, Earle influenced the emerging field of what we would today call material culture. She demonstrated and pro-moted a systematic method for considering artifacts as part of a larger social and cultural context. By virtue of her popularity, she was in a posi-tion to select the evidence that would both support and reshape the main-stream story about America's colonial past.

Earle's reconstructions of colonial life configured Puritanism in a new way: she offered a vision of community without harshness. Her books and articles responded to a mounting desire among many late-nineteenth-century Americans for an infusion of art and intimacy into the existing American historical narrative of piety and austerity in seventeenth-century New England. This new historical interpretation reverberated widely, af-fecting not only her immediate readers but also a much wider audience: the creators and viewers of exhibitions of early American life in museums and historical societies; the producers of, participants in, and onlookers at his-torical pageants and other forms of patriotic, educational, or celebratory presentations; and those charged with furnishing and interpreting historic and contemporary household interiors, as well as those who lived in, vis-ited, or worked in such environments. The picture that emerged after 1890 of ordinary life in the days before the dramatic social, political, technologi-cal, and economic transformations of the nineteenth century corresponded to Earle's assumptions about the past.

The centrality of domesticity was a key component of Alice Morse Earle's historical vision. She assumed that women had played a key role in the historical pageant; that they had been instrumental in creating community, in nurturing family and friends, in constructing households that both served and shaped their families. Relying on female skills and personal influence rather than direct legal authority, Earle's women of the past extended their reach well beyond the confines of the domestic realm. While this home-centered view of women's roles may have put her at odds with some of her more strongly pro-suffrage sisters, Earle cannot easily be written off as a staunch anti-suffragist. Her own life serves as an expression of her politics, demonstrating her belief that women were capable of filling any number of important roles, public and private. Although she never aligned herself strongly with either side of the suffrage debate, she clearly understood the importance of women as historical actors, past and present.

Earle also assumed that social class was important in "colonial days." She perceived that world as essentially hierarchical, and admired the leaders of that society, but she also valued the lives and contributions of ordinary people. Although she sometimes adopted a sentimental tone in her writings, she worked hard not to romanticize her subjects. She knew that life was difficult in the seventeenth and eighteenth centuries; she proclaimed in several of her books that she would not have wanted to be a child in colonial America. Despite the hardships, though, she viewed that world as inherently better than her own. Work was more honest, craftsmanship finer, family life more stable and continuous. Above all, Earle assumed the existence of a shared national ideology about patriotism, virtue, and gender in colonial America that now seemed elusive. In this book I identify and address those assumptions, offering suggestions as to their origins, their broader applicability, and their impact.

Viewing Earle's life and work through the analytical lenses of family, class, ideology, race, and gender enables her to emerge in sharp focus as a cultural product and as a cultural producer. The first lens, that of family, reveals a social and economic pattern more easily characterized as one of motion than of persistence and stability. Earle came from a large and long-established New England family that had settled in Massachusetts during the Puritan Great Migration. Despite their seventeenth-century roots, however, the family proceeded to move out from its original home in the towns surrounding Boston, farther and farther into the hinterlands of New Hampshire, Vermont, and Maine. The relative instability of the

Morse family (like many other New England families) raises questions about strategies for continuity and family security. What was the impact of her forebears' historical experience of constant geographical mobility on Earle's generation, and on Earle herself, particularly given that the historical vision Earle presented in her books and articles was one of long-term stability and persistence? The extent to which that pattern of social and geographic dislocation characterized other American families may account in part for the broad appeal of Earle's work.[10]

Furthermore, she was writing during a period when the American family as an institution was in flux. The "demographic transition" of the nineteenth century had reduced the number of children born to American couples of white, Anglo-Saxon, and northern European extraction from an average of 7.04 in 1800 to 3.56 in 1900. The causes and impact of this event have long been the subject of scholarly speculation, but certainly the decline in family size led to an alteration of gender relations, as well as a heightened emphasis on children and child rearing.[11] Moreover, during the early twentieth century, increasing numbers of women received an education and entered the labor force. Although these were largely single women who tended to leave the workforce upon marriage, their growing numbers, coupled with the decreased numbers of children to replenish the Anglo-Saxon stock, posed an implicit threat to the sanctity of the nuclear family as a fundamental social institution.[12]

Earle was in so many ways an ordinary woman—a woman of comparative privilege, to be sure, but nonetheless a product of mainstream American culture. It is that quality of ordinariness that made—and still makes—Earle and her story so interesting. Her life and work were like or akin to those of many others of her class and generation; an increasingly dispersed but culturally cohesive body of white, middle-class Americans shared her ideas and values. Earle's life and works thus offer a window into the past that can enhance our understanding of modern American society.

In terms of ideology, Earle and her work were part of a broad middle- and upper-class cultural enthusiasm in the United States. The rise in interest in the American past began as early as 1800 and gained momentum throughout the nineteenth century, culminating in a full-blown "colonial revival" by the 1890s.[13] For Earle, however, the colonial revival was a progressive enterprise, although that was not a label she ever applied to herself or her work. Her mid-century birth date affiliates her with contemporaries such as Jane Addams, Frank Lloyd Wright, Charles Ives, John Dewey, Charlotte Perkins Gilman, William Allen White, and other well-known progressives, all engaged in a painful struggle to find meaningful alternatives to religious vocation in a world where devout Protestantism had lost much of its potency and relevance. Their resultant career choices tended to focus on journalism, settlement work, higher education, law, and politics, arenas through which they could invest their activities with moral significance. Earle viewed her writing as an instrument for social reform, an effective yet palatable means of restoring to America the values that had defined its early glory.[14]

Despite, or perhaps because of, her early literary success and her comfortable upper-middle-class life, Alice Morse Earle shared a cultural tension over gender with many of her female peers: What should the proper role of women be in modern American society? Middle-class women had begun to exercise their female authority in new ways by the end of the nineteenth century. Both the settlement house movement and the clubwoman's movement offered new arenas for women to effect social change. Although the right to vote still eluded women, the suffrage movement had achieved major successes in individual states by 1890. Women, on the verge of the new century, found multiple ways to express their gendered identities, including through the power of the pen.[15]

For Earle, this gender tension emanated from the nineteenth-century faith in the power of possessive individualism—an ideology with which she was inculcated by her middle-class parents—struggling with a competing faith, shared by many early feminists, in the necessity of collective action to cure the social ills she saw around her. Both of these ideas competed with more traditional notions about "woman's proper sphere." The idea of individualism had emerged in the eighteenth century as a product of the Enlightenment, challenging existing notions of destiny and hierarchical social order. By the late nineteenth century, individualism as a political, social, and philosophical concept was firmly engrained in the American consciousness and was generally linked to the idea of progress. American historical narratives focused on success in overcoming great odds—the wilderness, the British, technological handicaps, lack of civilization. Usually success came through some sort of individual agency—heroism, industry, inventiveness, and, particularly where women were involved, virtue.[16]

Individualism was, however, a problematic concept for women of Earle's generation, who were in many ways free to express their individuality, but in many others—most notably politically—unfree. Most historians now agree that individual consciousness among middle-class white women began to emerge around the time of the Revolution and led to two crucial developments during the nineteenth century: the rise of a distinctly female mentality within this group and dramatic changes in gender relations, as is suggested by the changing size and structure of American families.[17] Earle's assumption of female agency expressed itself abundantly in her writings. Throughout her work she emphasized the roles of women as agents of family, church, and community, imbued with the power to shape the individual character and habits of others. Domesticity, education, and child-rearing techniques, as well as personal presentation, were all instruments that could help bring about a society and a nation of orderly, industrious people and good citizens.

In contrast with earlier constructions of individualism, which stressed an independent, atomistic self, Earle's conception of individualism devolved from the more feminine notion of *individuality,* which emphasized uniqueness as a social and economic strategy, but placed that unique individual clearly within the context of a social group.[18] Earle's constant emphasis on authenticity established uniqueness as a dominant value throughout her work, whether in reference to others or to herself. Through elaborate genealogical machinations, as well as contrived historicisms and self-consciously antiquated language, Earle fashioned herself as an individual power, drawing heavily on authentic devices from the past for confirmation. Her sense of herself as an individual power, however, existed firmly within the boundaries of broader group identities, circumscribed by class and gender.

Earle's gender set her belief in individual power at odds with an implicit faith in the collective power and responsibility of women to shape society. Her assumptions about appropriate social roles for women were shaped by an ideology of domesticity that had dominated her class throughout her lifetime and most of the nineteenth century. That ideology defined women, particularly middle-class women like Earle, as a separate group, invested with special powers to influence society through the exertion of moral suasion. The perpetuation of the social order required that women fulfill that mission, whether or not it had a legitimate historical basis.[19] By the 1890s, however, when Earle was beginning her career as a writer of history, the domains thought appropriate for middle-class women had expanded considerably beyond the private realm of home and family. Since the end of the Civil War, American women's consciousness of their inferior status had grown considerably, as had political activism to change that condition. Lucy Stone, Julia Ward Howe, and others founded the American Woman Suffrage Association in 1869, when Earle was only eighteen, and by 1890, when she was nearly forty, women in the Wyoming and Utah territories, as well as Michigan, Minnesota, Colorado, New Hampshire, Oregon, Massachusetts, Mississippi, New York, Vermont, Arizona, Montana, New Jersey, North Dakota, South Dakota, Oklahoma, and Washington, had won full or partial suffrage. Women's colleges including Vassar, Wellesley, Smith, Spelman, and Bryn Mawr all opened during this period, expanding the possibilities of higher education for women. Women had grown increasingly active and visible in public arenas, ranging from the financial world, medicine, and the law to education and social work. Within this context of changing gender opportunities, many women sought new outlets for socializing with other women, in the process expanding their minds and their opportunities. Earle was active in at least five different organizations that were run either exclusively or largely by and for women, and she seems to have been quite familiar with the (albeit indirect) social and political potential of women operating in concert.[20] She clearly supported women's reform activities, but the extent to which she saw suffrage as crucial to the success of those activities is less clear. Like many women of her generation, she may have felt ambivalent about the impact of women's full equality on their domestic responsibilities. She could not have been unaware of the benefits of complete political access for women and their causes, but she hesitated to express her own political opinions openly.

The powerful impact of women on society, despite their lack of suffrage, was a recurrent theme in Earle's many books and articles. The scale and pace of life in late-nineteenth-century America, especially urban America, seemed to her to supersede the power of any individual to effect social or cultural change. The collective notion of woman-powered social engineering that Earle wanted to harness in the present was built on a legacy that had originated a century and a half earlier, with the increasingly child-centered focus of American families. By about 1750, rising levels of geographic mobility had begun to transform expectations about kinship, community, and family authority over children. Traditional assumptions

FIGURE 1. Candle dipping, from *Home Life in Colonial Days*, 1898. Earle frequently employed images of reenactment in her books. Here, a costumed woman dips candles. The spinning wheel lurking in the background, a universal symbol of female industry by the late nineteenth century, was technically obsolete but had been reborn as an object of decorative charm. The gentility of this woman is expressed in her clothing, her fashionable hairstyle, and the two fancy chairs that support her rack of freshly made candles. Earle and her readers would have understood the lessons embedded in these fanciful reconstructions of a golden age of domesticity.

about maintaining order into the future through intergenerational proximity had been washed away by the lack of available land close to settled communities. Increasingly, behavioral and material systems from gentility to family affection, education, domestic architecture, clothing, and gender roles were invested with new symbolic significance as vehicles of social and cultural continuity.

The topics Earle addressed—religious ritual, ceramic table and tea wares (a traditional means of expressing gentility and status), social customs, the household and its furnishings, modes of travel, child rearing, gardens, and clothing—were important symbolic devices that had helped transmit collective standards involving family and community at least since the middle of the eighteenth century (fig. 1).[21] I would argue that the symbolic order Earle created in her historical writings—one that drew heavily on notions of gender and community—was intended to replace a waning order that had drawn its authority largely from an ideology of individualism.

The immediate context in which Earle lived and worked should not be ignored as a formative influence on her mentality and her writing. Throughout her career—in fact for her entire life—Earle lived in urban environments. Worcester was a booming city during her childhood and adolescence. After her marriage in 1874 and her move to Brooklyn Heights, she spent the rest of her life immersed in metropolitan culture. Her urban context had a powerful impact on her vision of society. Like many Americans, she accepted growth as inevitable, a natural result of human progress. Her writings, however, demonstrate a profound ambivalence about the impact of that growth and progress.

Generally, I argue in this book that Alice Morse Earle's interest in discovering a usable past stemmed from her culturally determined ambivalence about the present. Her popularity suggests that her writings struck a cultural chord—that she served a larger need for historical references that could help lead Americans into the future. She, like many middle- and upper-class American men and women of her generation, believed that the past could provide those ideological and emotional moorings as well as new directions. By 1890, when Earle began writing professionally, national events had brought into high relief the same discontinuous patterns that characterized her family history, her domestic context, her social experiences, and her expectations about her role as a woman. The search for a usable past that stimulated Earle to write so prolifically about the culture and society of those who had preceded her was two-pronged. It was a personal quest for new symbols that would help redefine her individual identity and provide historical continuity in what seemed to her and many like her an increasingly incoherent world. And it was also a moral quest for new behavioral modes and sources of authority that could ultimately lead to broad social reform.

Earle's work grew directly from her own family's experiences in early New England. In chapter 1 I begin the examination of Earle's personal history, looking for events that would ultimately affect the form and message of her public history. In chapter 2 I continue that examination, focusing specifically on Earle's urban world, family life, and gender assumptions as a stimulus for her reformist ideology. The Puritan world, as envisioned by Earle in her first book, *The Sabbath in Puritan New England* (1891), and the changing cultural interpretations of Puritanism form the focus of chapter 3. For Earle, as for many Americans in 1891, the history of her own family in New England no longer seemed to fit the Puritan myth, and the twin assumptions about destiny and the leadership of "great men" that had long dominated American notions of social order and cultural change seemed in need of revision.[22] Chapter 4 marks Earle's entry into the world of material culture with the publication of *China Collecting in America,* positioning her as a key figure in the new literature of collecting and antiquarian pursuits. Chapter 5 probes Earle's choice of writing as a mechanism for change; her career as an author reflected shifting conceptions about appropriate social roles and a new belief in the collective power of women and intellectuals to reform society. In chapter 6 I explore Earle's materialist emphasis on ordinary domestic life as expressive of this new collective orientation, particularly in terms of its implications about gender and reform. Chapter 7 extends this emphasis out into the garden and landscape. Earle wrote two books explicitly about gardening, and numerous other essays and articles that emphasized the significance of landscape, gardens, and plant materials as vehicles for historical memory. Chapter 8 explores the importance of ancestry and genealogical connections for Earle and her readers as a scientific endorsement of class supremacy. Ancestry offered a means of countering the seemingly random character of modern society, of maintaining some degree of continuity with Puritan notions of destiny, and of mediating between the inclusive premises of assimilation and a class-based desire for social exclusion. The final chapter assesses Earle's legacy as the creator of a new kind of democratized history of American life. She provided a formula that purveyors of history on a popular scale could follow, a template that facilitated the reinvention of American domestic life and social relations. Her version of history emphasized material life and ordinary people, employing notions of authenticity, color, quaintness, art, and intimacy to heighten the emotional appeal and hegemonic power of her social message.

This book is not strictly a biography of Earle but rather a biographically grounded study of her intentions, her methods, and her significance as a writer of history. The chapters are not strictly chronological; often they are shaped more by my cultural and intellectual analysis of her work than by sequential events. I have tried, however, to show how her ideas and historical methods progressed from book to book, as well as how her books clustered around certain epistemological assumptions.

Alice Morse Earle changed our vision of the American past. She introduced a new kind of authoritative voice to the study of American family and social history, a voice that integrated the intimacy of domesticity with the scholarly objectivity required by the historical profession. The continuing power of that voice is evident in the extent to which scholars today still try to find ways to rely on the enormous body of detail that Earle assembled during her brief career. It is not my intention to verify Earle's historical facts here; I am more concerned with her historical vision. There is much, I would argue, that is usable in Earle's writings, but we have to know where to look. This work offers a guide.

CHAPTER 1

Family Matters

❧

I N 1834 ALICE MORSE EARLE's father, Edwin Morse, left his family
home in rural Vermont at the age of nineteen. He headed for New England Village, a textile-manufacturing center near Grafton, Massachusetts. New England Village, with its proximity to Worcester—one of the
fastest-growing cities in the state—could offer an ambitious young man
opportunities unavailable in the dying hill town of Andover. Within fourteen years, Edwin Morse had established himself as a machinist, moved to
Worcester, and married his first cousin, Abigail Clary, of Jackson, Maine.[1]

As with many Americans who migrated from country to city during
the nineteenth century, the lives of the Morses were profoundly affected
by the experience—and that move ultimately shaped their daughter's
worldview and literary agenda as well. Abigail and Edwin, cut off from
their traditional support networks of family and community, had to invent
new modes of behavior for both work and play. In turn, their daughter
Alice would leave her family home in Worcester for the even larger and
more alien urban environment of Brooklyn, New York. This daughter of
country people who had moved to a small city had to devise yet another
set of coping strategies to ease the transition to and make sense of a vast
urban environment. This she did through a careful investigation of the
customs, fashions, and even the gardens of her New England ancestors.

Edwin Morse and thousands of other young men like him who joined
the industrial workforce in the second quarter of the nineteenth century

entered a world that was dramatically different from the one they left behind. Apprenticeship, which might have provided continuity with the authority of family and community, had eroded by the 1830s. Apprentices no longer lived with their masters but found shelter in more independent settings, typically boardinghouses. A work relationship that was based on cash wages rather than a more paternalistic contractual arrangement broadened their independence but also increased the risk of failure and raised the requisite level of personal responsibility.[2]

Edwin Morse further established his new, independent life away from his family when he married Charlotte Hooker Smith, of Grafton, in 1841. She died in childbirth a year later, leaving Edwin a twenty-seven-year-old widower with a newborn son, Edwin Augustus (fig. 2). The following summer, Edwin and his brother John met for the first time their Clary cousins in Maine, including twenty-three-year-old Mary Clary and her thirty-one-year-old sister, the recently widowed Abigail Clary Goodhue. John Morse, a student at Union Theological Seminary in New York City, recalled that meeting in a letter of condolence to Abby a year later, shortly after Mary died. "Most vividly now return to my mind the events and scenes of my delightful visit with you but a year ago," he wrote, "my meeting for the first time with unknown and yet well known cousins, the week of gladness, the journey to Boston, to Walpole, the meeting at Father's and the sad parting."[3] By the time Abigail received this letter, John, too, had died, of typhus. These deaths would bring the surviving cousins closer together.

The twin bonds of family connection and bereavement initiated a four-year correspondence between Edwin and Abigail. In their letters they normally exchanged personal and family news but also, increasingly, served as each other's confidant. Because they were both widowed, they felt comfortable discussing such intimate subjects as the trials of finding a new mate, as well as their shared feelings of loneliness. Abby in particular complained about the isolation of her life in rural Maine. As a widow who had known a small degree of freedom in her marriage, she felt constrained by her reversion to the role of daughter. She shuttled back and forth between her parents' house and the houses of her sisters and brothers, looking for a place where she would fit in comfortably and with some degree of independence. As a childless woman, Abby did not always wish to have to act as a surrogate mother to her nieces and nephews or even tolerate them.

FIGURE 2. Edwin Morse (1815–1891) with Edwin Augustus Morse (1842–1890), about 1845. Edwin's first wife died in childbirth, leaving him a widower with a young son. Although Edwin still turned to his parents in Vermont for support when he could, he had by now moved away, to southern New England. As a single parent, he was focused during this period of his life on finding a wife and mother for Edwin Augustus. Collection of Donald J. Post Jr.

"There has been a great change with us since last year," she complained in 1845. "Brother Daniel has come home to live with all their children, & however fond I may be of *good* children, I cannot endure the greater part with whom I come in contact."[4] That same summer she taught school "for want of better employment," but the recent loss of her sister had thrown her into a depression from which she was struggling to emerge. "O Edwin, you cannot imagine what a blank her death has made in my life," she wrote; "no one for an associate, no one to whom I can speak wholly without reserve."[5] No one, that is, except Edwin.

With Edwin, Abby could discuss her romantic prospects candidly. Pondering the topic of marriage in general, she wrote: "I suppose you will think of me (as I do of you) that I am too particular. Perhaps I am so, yet I cannot think of dragging myself into bondage. I rather go willingly." She had considered doing so with "a gentleman whose name has figured largely in our legislature for a few years past, . . . but finally I concluded that I never could have that regard for him that I ought to." Besides, she added, "he has four or five children." After tallying up his merits for Edwin to consider, Abby admitted with some embarrassment that "as a *wooer he was altogether* too much your humble Scot to—"; and here she cut herself off and dropped the subject, asking Edwin to excuse her for discussing "the silly part."[6]

A year later, Abby—still unmarried—wrote to Edwin that she had no news at all for him. "I spend my time about as usual," she complained, adding that she would like to move away from rural Maine. Specifically, she had directed her thoughts toward Massachusetts. "My folks think it would be folly," she continued wistfully, "yet I can't help longing almost to do something that will give me employment & a home for which I pine." Not wishing to appear ungrateful, Abby assured him that she appreciated all of the kindness extended her by her friends, "& I have very kind friends indeed, yet their home is not my own."[7]

Abby's interest in a home of her own suggests the care with which she would construct her household when she had the opportunity to do so, as well as the fact that it would be nuclear. Furthermore, it would be in the city, not the country. Abby contrasted Edwin's life in the city, a life that seemed full of excitement and intellectual stimulation, with her own country life, which seemed stifling by comparison. "Do pray send me some news papers to read," she begged Edwin, in the postscript to her letter. "I don't get half so much to read as I want."[8] Both Edwin and Abby had already explored the alternatives and knew that the city, not the country, offered the possibilities they desired. Their daughter Alice Morse Earle would later incorporate her parents' values into her own domestic ideology.

Although he seems not to have been suffering as much as his cousin, Edwin also was searching for a mate. Early in their correspondence he confided to Abby "of myself so far as getting married is concerned I have not advanced a single step since I saw you. The truth is," he admitted, "I love my little boy so well that it is hard, nay almost impossible to tender my affections on another."[9] The task of bringing up Edwin Augustus by himself apparently did not burden Edwin greatly; although he never mentioned to Abby specifically how he accomplished it, he may have relied on his in-laws in Grafton for child care. He reported on one visit to his own parents' home in Andover with three-year-old Edwin Augustus, noting that the journey to Vermont went smoothly and that the boy's grandparents doted on him throughout the entire visit. "Mother was very much interested with him and as Grandmothers are prone to do, indulged him in everything he desired," he wrote, adding that young Edwin had not lost his ability to obey, despite his grandmother's indulgences.[10]

Edwin apparently came close to matrimony when he courted a Miss Rice during the fall and winter of 1846. He discovered, however, after generating high expectations for the relationship, that she had a serious health problem, and he subsequently backed out of the relationship. Abby chastised him severely for being so negligent: "I could have wept for that unfortunate girl for no doubt she loved you deeply." Nevertheless, she added, "I do not certainly blame you for not wanting to marry a person afflicted with that disease," advising, "You must find out the particulars of their health before you begin the *courting business* again."[11]

In November 1848 Edwin and Abby, tired of looking elsewhere for companionship, recognized the value of their friendship and married each other. Edwin by that time was working as a machinist for a prominent Worcester firearms manufacturer, Ethan Allen. He probably first became acquainted with Allen at New England Village, where Allen had been manufacturing guns and shoe cutlery (tools used by shoemakers to cut out leather soles and uppers) as early as 1832.[12] Worcester, a lively inland trading city since the late eighteenth century, had benefited tremendously from the internal improvements of the second quarter of the nineteenth century. The completion of the Blackstone Canal in 1829, and two rail lines in the 1830s and 1840s, propelled Worcester's economy, transforming the town into a major manufacturing center by the 1860s.[13] Between 1840 and 1855 the population of Worcester increased dramatically, from 7,497 to 22,286 inhabitants. In 1845, the year Edwin Morse arrived there, about half the population consisted of immigrants (mostly from Ireland), as well as young, usually unmarried native-born men and women. During the 1850s, when the Morses were settling down to raise their family, approximately 100,000 people moved into Worcester but did not remain.[14]

The size and demographic turmoil of Worcester must have seemed both thrilling and intimidating to Abby Morse when she arrived in 1848, newly married and suddenly stepmother to her husband's six-year-old son. For the first few years of their marriage, the Morses lived in a house at 33 Pleasant Street, not far from the old commercial center of the city. The social geography of Worcester during this period of rapid growth paralleled that of other American cities, and was still characterized by high levels of heterogeneity. People of diverse income levels and occupations lived side by side in the same neighborhood, although a distinct downtown and separate manufacturing sections were beginning to emerge, as were class-defined residential areas.[15] The Morses shared their house with another family, that of William Billings, a twenty-seven-year-old boot maker; his wife, Mary; their five-year-old son; William's sister Martha; and fifty-two-year-old Martha Huntley, who may have been Billings's mother-in-law.[16] Both William and Mary Billings had migrated to Worcester from New Hampshire; the Billingses may have had some personal connection with the Morse family, although they may just as easily have been complete strangers.

A survey of the Morse family's other neighbors confirms the inclusive character of their immediate community. A survey of forty-eight individuals and families who lived within a two-block radius of 33 Pleasant Street reveals a diverse mixture of occupations, income levels, and household size.[17] The value of real estate ranged widely. Thirty-two families owned nothing. Edwin Morse held $200 worth of real property, while Alfred D. Foster, who lived a block and a half north on Chestnut Street, owned real estate valued at $78,500. Stephen Salisbury, one of the wealthiest men in Worcester with property valued at $210,000, lived only one block away from the Morses.

Most of the Morses' neighbors had been born in Massachusetts (forty-three); others, like the Morses, had moved to Worcester from Maine (seven), New Hampshire (four), Vermont (three), and Connecticut (four), but scattered neighborhood residents had also emigrated from Rhode Island, New York, New Jersey, and as far away as Kentucky, Illinois, Mississippi, and Georgia. Some—typically servants or laborers—were not native born. Fourteen residents came from Ireland, one from England, and one from Nova Scotia. Two people in the neighborhood were of African American descent.[18]

In this Worcester neighborhood the Morse family first encountered an array of people far more diverse than they had known in northern New England, though far less diverse than their daughter Alice would later know in Brooklyn. The neighborhood's mixture of occupations was as varied as its economic and geographic arrays. Just as the Morses shared their house not with family but with an unrelated boot maker, two other machinists and their young families shared the house next door. Other occupations represented in the immediate vicinity included merchant, painter, laborer, dentist, tanner and shoe manufacturer, publisher, grader, farmer, lawyer, and inn holder; there was also a boardinghouse accommodating assorted young, unmarried working people.[19] For some residents, such as the tanner, who shared his house with a shoe manufacturer, shoe trader, and two shoemakers, or the publisher, whose household included another publisher and three printers, the work premises may have been part of the residence.

Far from her family and friends in Maine, Abby Morse attempted to reconstitute a kinship network in Worcester. By 1850 two of her nieces, Persis Thorndike, aged twenty-seven, and Olive Snow, aged twenty-two, had arrived in Worcester and moved into the Morse household.[20] The presence of Abby Morse's nieces in her household attests to the magnetic lure of Worcester for unmarried young people of both sexes. Like their aunt Abby, Persis Thorndike and Olive Snow could not envision a satisfying future for themselves in the languishing hill towns of rural Maine. In Worcester they would re-create as best they could a remnant of the country kinship network that Alice Morse Earle would later venerate. These two young women, as well as neighbors such as Grace Oliver, who had also migrated to Worcester from Maine, must have been a comfort to Abby, whose first child, a son, died at birth in 1850. Within a year, however,

FIGURE 3. Abigail Morse with Alice and Edwin Augustus, 1852. Edwin married his first cousin Abigail Clary in 1848. Two years later Abby bore her first child, who died in infancy. A second child, Mary Alice, was born in April 1851. Collection of Donald J. Post Jr.

she became pregnant again, and gave birth to a daughter, Mary Alice, on April 27, 1851 (fig. 3).[21]

Young Alice thus began her life in a household that was far more reminiscent of the country society her parents had left behind. The arrival in Worcester of Edwin Morse's recently widowed mother, Betsey, in 1853 furthered the replication of a country household in the city: extended, intergenerational, and fluid. This early family context, especially the presence of her grandmother in the household, shaped young Alice's assumptions about the ideal family and community. Her later historical constructions envisioned family cohesion and interdependence as a source of great strength—as had been her own family's experience.

The death of Alice's paternal grandfather, Benjamin Morse, represented a crucial juncture for thirty-eight-year-old Edwin and his growing family. It confirmed his commitment to the urban world of Worcester rather than rural Vermont, as well as providing some financial means to pursue that commitment.[22] Worcester offered great opportunity for an ambitious machinist, and Morse took full advantage. By the time his father died, he was in partnership with two other machinists, Russell S. Shepherd and Martin Lathe. Shepherd, Lathe & Co., and Edwin Morse along with it, was riding the prosperity that had been stimulated by the growth of railroads and the accompanying demand for tools; appropriately, given its name, the firm specialized in the manufacture of lathes and planers.[23]

In 1856, perhaps owing to the birth of Alice in 1851, the arrival of Betsey Morse in 1853, and the birth of a second daughter, Frances Clary, soon known as Fanny, in January 1855, as well as their increasing prosperity, the Morse family moved into more commodious quarters at 23 Chatham Street.[24] There they stayed until Frances, the last remaining family member, died in 1933.[25] The Chatham Street location, house, and grounds testi-fied to the Morses' changing consciousness of themselves as members of a distinct middle class—and provided their young daughters with a new urban, middle-class outlook.

Much has been written about the formation, character, and identity of the American middle class, and the Morse family's domestic strategies at this point in their history fit many of the broad patterns that have been sketched out as the identifying features of a middle-class mentality.[26] Their purchase of the house on Chatham Street represented a significant but not surprising departure for the Morses, removing them from the inclusive, heterogeneous world of their Pleasant Street accommodations. As one social commentator remarked in 1857, "Time was when it was sufficient for a comfortable liver to have half a house," as the Morses had on Pleasant Street. "Now, the same man must have a whole house, and the first story must be thrown into parlors."[27] Like many other middle-class Americans who had recently made the transition from country to city, Edwin and Abigail Morse no doubt wanted their children to grow up in a household that would not only provide economic security but also nurture strong character and a sure sense of well-being. This desire was reflected in their choice of the large frame structure on the southeast corner of Chatham and Oxford streets, a fashionable four blocks away from Main Street, the

Common, City Hall, and the commercial center of the city. The Friends' Meeting House stood diagonally across Chatham Street, on the northwest corner of Chatham and Oxford. One block south on Oxford was the Goddard, Fay, & Stone Shoe Company, and the Bay State Shoe and Leather Company was three blocks away, on the corner of Austin and High streets. The notion of intermingling manufacturing establishments with residences did not surprise the Morses; the rural villages where they were born followed the same pattern, as did the Pleasant Street neighborhood where they had lived until recently. In the densely populated urban environment of Worcester, however, middle-class Americans like the Morses began to draw more conscious distinctions between the realm of home and family and that of business and industry.[28] Increasingly, the old pattern of mixed social and economic use came to be replaced by subcommunities of people grouped by class. Alice Morse Earle embraced this newer pattern in her own adult life, but her writings betrayed a sense of regret at the loss of the old organic neighborhoods.

In 1853 Chatham Street, particularly the Morses' block between Oxford and Irving, was lined with maples and elms and comfortable homes. Their lot was slightly more than twice as deep as it was wide, with about seventy-five feet of frontage. F. W. Beers's 1870 map of Worcester identifies the exact location of the "E. Morse" property, and a slightly later map confirms that there was a stable or shed at the rear of the lot.[29] Beers's map also reveals a hierarchy of residential patterns, beginning with the largest houses and park-like lots on Elm Street—Mrs. Levi Lincoln, G. W. Richardson, Mrs. Burnside—and descending southward by degrees. Between Elm and Pleasant streets, the houses seem to have been generally smaller—though still substantial—and between Pleasant and Chatham smaller yet. The smallest houses and lots were south of Chatham, closer to the shoe factories, although their lot sizes indicate that most of these were still middle-class houses.[30]

The Morses had located themselves spatially in a neighborhood that would buffer their family against abrupt changes, protect themselves and their children from the more disorderly parts of the city, and provide a sense of continuity with older country values. Their choice of a single-family house on a relatively homogeneous block reflected a mentality characteristic of the urban middle class. Although both Edwin and Abby Morse had embraced Worcester for its opportunities, the disorderly aspects of life in the city compelled them to turn their attention increasingly toward their own nuclear family, and especially toward the creation of a home that would nurture and protect their children.[31]

Young Mary Alice Morse, then, grew up in a house that, in plan and decoration, affirmed her parents' developing domestic vision. The new house was three stories high, with a mansard roof, a porch or "veranda" across the front, and a wooden fence around the property. The mansard roof, a feature of the newly fashionable Second Empire style, boldly expressed the family's sophistication and culture. With its explicit allusions to French taste in architecture, as well as in furniture, modes of dining, clothing, and even language, the house expressed the Morse family's newly acquired genteel sensibilities. Edwin and Abby had "arrived" in society, and their children were promised a future firmly planted in Worcester's burgeoning middle class.[32]

Inside the house where Alice spent her childhood, the array of rooms included a dining room with attached conservatory, a music room, and four bedrooms. Each of these types of rooms had special significance for the urban middle class. The dining room, a relatively new social space for most Americans, enabled the Morse family to entertain guests and visiting relatives graciously. This room also confirmed a family's commitment to gentility, providing a dedicated space for the family meal, a daily socializing event.[33] The attached conservatory enabled nature, in its most highly cultivated form, to become part of that ritual, in the process instilling a love of plants and gardens into the Morse daughters.

Edwin and Abby's decision to allocate an entire room to music (in name anyway) reveals yet another self-conscious middle-class stratagem for social advancement.[34] Here, young Mary Alice and her sister, Frances, could receive the education in art and music considered necessary for respectable young women to succeed in polite society. Upstairs, the four bedrooms on the second floor, and probably more on the third, would have enabled each of the three Morse children to have a separate room. This feature of the Morse house corresponded to yet another defining feature of the middle class: the emphasis on childhood and the education of children.[35]

Alice Morse Earle, describing her early childhood memories, wrote that once the family was settled at Chatham Street, her parents began to enhance the outdoor areas of their new home by creating a garden. With this act they initiated overlapping spheres of family connectedness which would link them to their own pasts and parents and extend that linkage through their children to their children's children. Earle firmly believed in the power of a garden to perpetuate family continuity, and especially to resurrect the specific past of childhood and family relationships. "Who," she asked, "garden-bred, can walk in the springtime through the garden of her childhood without thought of those who cared for the garden in its youth, and shared the care of their children with the care of their flowers, but now are seen no more?"[36]

The vision of Edwin and Abigail Morse laying out the plan for their garden—sweet-scented flowers near the house; a central path leading from the rear of the house to the stable and back fence, flanked along its length by beds of flowers; a small orchard of apple and pear trees near the rear boundary; and the whole landscape defined and contained within a wall— would emerge as a powerful image in their daughter's later writings. For Alice Morse Earle, plants and gardens functioned metaphorically, channeling family memory and intergenerational connectedness.[37]

The Morse garden also served an important social purpose, connecting the family, especially Abigail, with other families in Worcester. One family in particular, the Edwin Fawcetts, retained a position of importance in Earle's mind as a source of inspiration, as well as of plant materials, for the Morses. The Fawcett family lived one block east of the Morse house on Chatham, at the southwest corner of Chatham and Irving streets. "In my childhood," Earle reminisced, "this home was that of flower-loving neighbors who had an established and constant system of exchange with my mother and other neighbors of flowers, plants, seeds, slips, and bulbs."[38]

When Alice was nine years old, the outbreak of the Civil War profoundly shook the world of Chatham Street, as it did the nation at large. On April 19, 1861, her half brother, Edwin Augustus, enlisted in the Twenty-fifth Regiment of the Massachusetts Volunteers and went off to fight for the Union. On December 21, 1861, she and Fanny received a Christmas letter from Eddie, as they called him, describing his life and doings at Camp Hicks in Annapolis. He particularly noted the camp's Christmas decorations, commenting that the regiments "decorate their camps with trees between the tents & large arches over the head of the street, eagles, wreaths, stars, &c in the centre. We are building a fine one over our street, worked on it all the afternoon." He added a note for his father, the machinist, about the regiment's inferior rifles: "Tell Father that we have tried our rifles & they are not as good as they might be. They miss fire don't

snap the caps. The 24th Reg had the same, did not like them & now have
the Springfield guns." Eddie offered his sisters other bits of news about
family friends in the Washington vicinity whom he had seen recently, and
then signed off, "from your affectionate brother."[39]

As the war heated up during the spring and summer of 1862, all of the
Morses left behind in Worcester must have worried about Eddie's where-
abouts and fate. In between letters, the daily newspaper accounts had to
serve the family's anxious desire for information. Only the constancy of
a regular routine of school, friends, and family activities helped sustain
the sisters and their parents. Ultimately, Edwin was seriously wounded in
1864. He wrote home to his parents to report on the incident: "My wound
is in the shoulder & neck, going in & just missing the shoulder blade &
coming out just missed the jugular vein in the neck. Another bullet hit me
on the hip bone taking the skin off two or three inches leaving it black &
blue & very lame. Ain't I a lucky boy this time?"[40] He was indeed lucky,
though the severity of his injury left a lasting impression on his young
sisters. Life was not to be taken for granted.

Alice entered the Worcester Classical and English High School on
Walnut Street just as the war was ending. Classical and English had
opened as a new institution in 1845, merging the previously all-male Latin Grammar School and all-female English High School. The merger was
hotly debated at the time, but ultimately, arguments for "the refining influence that the girls will have on the boys" won out.[41] By 1858, the year
when Alice's stepbrother Edwin graduated, his class included eighty-one
students. Alice's class of 1869, by contrast, revealed the effects of the recent
war, with only fourteen graduates, most of them female. It took until 1881
before class sizes regained their prewar numbers.[42]

At Classical and English, the curriculum for the academic course of
study required proficiency in natural philosophy, algebra, geometry, trig-
onometry, physiology, chemistry, botany, astronomy, political economy,
bookkeeping, Latin, and the history of the ancient and modern worlds,
as well as that of the United States and Massachusetts. Of her history
coursework Alice commented much later in life that she had thought it
dry, dull, and full of dates.[43] "I have seen within a few days the American
history I studied when I was a child," she reported to an audience in 1899,
discussing the merits of modern history teaching, "and it was worse than
all the others, and as I tried to read the ill-balanced facts in its dull pages,

I looked back and distinctly pitied that poor tortured child, who, it is strange to think, was myself." She had much preferred *The Child's History of England* by Charles Dickens to any history book she had read in school. Dickens's language and use of wit made history come alive for her in ways that her school textbooks never could.[44]

An examination question in grammar given to Alice and the rest of her class required her to analyze the structure and language of the famous "With malice towards none" passage in Lincoln's Second Inaugural Address.[45] She was asked to identify the infinitives that modify the word "strive," for example, and what was being modified by the phrase "among ourselves" and "with all nations." That she was later able to pursue a career in writing is not surprising: the examination questions suggest that she was well grounded in the mechanics of literary expression. Bronson Alcott, father of Louisa May Alcott, had apparently remarked on her early literary abilities. Writing much later, she recalled him as "a sweet philosopher whom I shall ever remember with deepest gratitude as the only person who in my early youth ever imagined any literary capacity in me." Alcott, an important progressive educator in Massachusetts, may have had connections with the administration of Worcester Classical and English. Earle's mention of him suggests that he was also an acquaintance of the Morse family, although he did not correctly predict Alice's future literary career as a writer of history. "He was sadly mistaken," she wrote, "for he fancied I would be a poet."[46]

The final question on the examination asked students to identify the author of the "With malice towards none" passage. For Alice and her peers, this passage would have been very familiar in 1869, in the midst of Reconstruction after the Civil War. Lincoln's plan for reuniting the nation, as expressed in this address, had been cut short by an assassin's bullet in 1865, the year when Alice's class entered high school. The experience of national tragedy must have shaped her outlook profoundly, in ways that persisted well beyond her teenage years. Lincoln's death influenced many Americans of her generation to pursue careers that would enable them to build a better world—as it certainly did Earle herself.[47]

At her graduation exercises on May 3, Mary Alice Morse appeared twice in the program, first taking part in a musical presentation, and then presenting a paper titled "Woman as an Artist."[48] Her choice of subject suggests that she was already thinking about issues related to women's roles in society, in addition to revealing a fondness for artistic endeavor. Her thesis likely engaged prevailing ideas about woman's proper sphere, in contrast to the growing cries for radical reform of women's roles. Much domestic advice literature of the day argued that a woman's nature suited her best to serve society through domestic influence rather than political or other public callings.[49] Creating an artistic home could help civilize children, husbands, and society at large—and female education functioned to intensify that process. Author, domestic advice writer, and early historian of women Elizabeth Ellet, in particular, may have piqued young Alice's interest in the linkage between women, art, and domesticity. Ellet's two-volume work *The Women of the American Revolution* (1848) and its companion, *Domestic History of the American Revolution* (1850), presented American women for the first time as part of history. Ellet drew on letters, documents, and other archival sources to document the stories of both famous and ordinary eighteenth-century women. For a young woman curious about history and women's place in society, these works would have been almost the only books in print that addressed the important role of women as shapers of America's past.[50]

After graduating from Classical and English, Alice went off to Boston to a fashionable finishing school operated by the Reverend George Gannett. The Gannett Institute claimed to offer its students "the same freedom and thoroughness which was then enjoined in our principal [male] colleges."[51] Such schools offered small classes and individualized attention. In 1883 *King's Dictionary of Boston* commented:

> Private finishing schools for girls in their teens abound in the city. Many of these schools limit the number of pupils to 50, and even less; while the maximum with this class of schools does not exceed 100. This limitation of numbers is generally due to the desire of many parents to have their children receive the direct and individual attention of the teachers, which they think cannot so well or so satisfactorily be secured by the large class system in larger schools. At these schools modern languages are taught, and various accomplishments, besides the branches which are classed under the general term of a finished English education. They are situated in the old and the new West End, and in the best parts of the South end. Among the oldest of these schools is Rev. George Gannett's, No. 69 Chester Square, South End.[52]

The choice to send their daughter to Gannett's finishing school furnishes another piece of evidence about Alice Morse and the woman she would become. While young women who were her social peers were beginning to attend newly established women's colleges (Vassar College opened in 1865, and closer to home, Mount Holyoke had been operating for almost thirty years by that time), Alice's education ended in a significantly more traditional manner. Edwin and Abby Morse may well have been influenced by the debate that swirled around the issue of educating girls. Edward Clarke's *Sex in Education* (1873) proclaimed that women were physiologically unsuited to higher education, and that too much brainwork might jeopardize their reproductive capabilities.[53] Her parents must certainly have believed that Alice had intellectual promise that deserved further nurture, but they no doubt also wanted to "finish" her by enhancing her social accomplishments. Their decision says as much about their own social aspirations—that they wanted their daughter to have a "finished English education"—as it does about their educational goals for young Alice. At this school they could be assured that she would meet other young women (and ideally some eligible men) who would become lifelong social companions. The son and daughter of New England farmers wanted more for their children than they had had. By the time Alice entered the Reverend Gannett's school, Edwin Morse had built up a highly successful business, the Lathe & Morse Machine Tool Company, which grew dramatically during the Civil War. In 1869, aged only fifty-four, he had been financially able to turn the business over to his son and retire. When Edwin Morse died in 1892, his probate inventory offered evidence of his success. He had amassed all of the trappings of a genteel lifestyle, including a personal library, elegant household furnishings, horses, carriages, sleighs, cash, stocks, and real estate, both residential and commercial. His estate was valued at almost $63,000, at a time when the average annual salary for a factory worker (the occupation in which he began his career) was $439, and five pounds of sugar cost thirty-five cents.[54]

Alice's education, both at Worcester Classical and English High School and during her tenure at Gannett's school, prepared her well for the disparate social roles she was to enact for the rest of her life. Within four years of entering finishing school, she "finished" by marrying Henry Earle, a prosperous young man from an old Providence family. She entered into her adult life shaped by competing cultural messages. Women, on the one hand, were a valuable national resource, worthy of higher education. Some, such as Lucy Stone (1818–1893), Susan B. Anthony (1820–1905), Elizabeth Cady Stanton (1815–1902), or even Worcester's own Abby Kelley Foster (1811–1887), would even argue that women could be a powerful political resource as well. Worcester itself had been a scene of women's activism at least since 1850, when the first National Woman's Rights Convention was held there. Alice's high school had admitted its first black student in 1845, an indication of its progressive inclinations.[55] On the other hand, women's powers, as Gannett himself would certainly have agreed, were best implemented in the domestic sphere—as wives, mothers, and creators of artistic environments in which to influence and civilize their families.

CHAPTER 2

Parlor Culture, Public Culture

O N THE EVE OF HER TWENTY-THIRD BIRTHDAY, Alice Morse (fig.
4) married Henry Earle, a New York City stockbroker with distinguished roots and access to many useful business connections,
but little money. The couple settled in Brooklyn Heights, where Henry
was already living, and there they remained for the rest of their lives. For
the newly married Mrs. Earle, the move to Brooklyn located her in an
urban social environment that must have made Worcester seem placid by
contrast. In Brooklyn she conducted an active social life and established
herself as a highly regarded clubwoman and noted writer.

Motherhood arrived quickly and in rapid—if orderly—succession.
Within two years of their wedding, Alice and Henry's first daughter, Alice
Clary Earle, was born in April 1876 (fig. 5), and their second, Mary Pitman
Earle, was born two years later, in May 1878. After two more years a third
child—this time a son, Henry Earle Jr.—was born, and a year and a half
later, in 1881, Alexander Morse Earle, their final child, arrived.[1] Being a
wife and mother was a demanding job, one that Alice always took very
seriously. During the early years of her marriage, she devoted herself to a
mix of social activities with Henry, educational and family-related activities with the children, and parlor-centered female social engagements and
club activities on her own.[2] These activities ultimately prepared her for her
second career, as a writer of historical prose. At the same time, however,
they created conflicting priorities for her as she sought to fulfill her wifely

FIGURE 4. Mary Alice Morse, 1873. At twenty-two, Alice appears to be a serious, poised, and refined young woman. Her sumptuous velvet and lace-trimmed silk gown and gold necklace create an impression of maturity and respectability. One year later she married New York City stockbroker Henry Earle and moved to Brooklyn Heights.

duties in support of Henry's career as a stockbroker, her maternal duties, and her personal need to express herself, as well as to do cultural work in a more public way.

Henry Earle came from a Providence family whose roots stretched back into the seventeenth century.[3] His father, however, died young, and Henry and his siblings were reared in the home of their maternal grandfather, John

Alice / *1876*

FIGURE 5. Alice Morse Earle with baby Alice, 1876. Within two years of her marriage, Earle became a mother. Her firstborn, also named Alice, would pass the name along to her first daughter, Alice Earle Hyde. Collection of Donald J. Post Jr.

Pitman, a prominent federal judge in Rhode Island. At the time of his marriage, Henry was a partner in Putnam & Earle, a stock brokerage firm in New York. He and his partner, Nathaniel D. Putnam, were highly regarded in the business community. In 1874, the year of his marriage, credit analysts at R. G. Dun & Co. reported, "The firm stands well on the street," nevertheless noting that Henry Earle "has but little means."[4] Henry and his partner had been able to parlay their Rhode Island family and social connections into a potentially lucrative venture—one that would not realize much of its potential, however, until the 1880s. Henry cut his teeth in the brokering trade working for his uncle Randall H. Greene, who ran a thriving business importing drugs and later indigo, madder, and rubber.[5]

The Earle family first settled in a house at 277 Henry Street in Brooklyn Heights, between State and Joralemon streets, in 1877.[6] Henry could commute easily across the river from there on the Fulton ferry—a pattern that typified the lives of many middle- and upper-class Brooklynites, and that was made even easier with the opening of the Brooklyn Bridge in 1883.[7] George T. Lain, in 1880, described the level of anticipation that he and his fellow Brooklyn residents felt about the impact of the bridge: "Brooklynites know they have but a short time to exercise their patience ere 'The Bridge' will be completed and Rapid Transit fully established, this eliminating the only objection to 'Our Side,' and repaying such patience by its healthful atmosphere and its many natural and artistic beauties."[8] As publisher of the *Brooklyn City Directory,* Lain certainly must have been a Brooklyn booster, but by comparison with the "Other Side," Brooklyn probably did seem less crowded and more healthy. According to another observer, who employed statistics to support his assertions, "the marvelous contrast between Brooklyn and New York," which were still separate cities, "is the contrast in the number of tenement houses and the contrast in rents. New York has 244,000 families, 160,000 of whom (or two-thirds in all) live in tenement houses." In Brooklyn, by contrast, only a quarter of the population lived in tenements. His concluding assessment, however, that "high rents in New York are driving merchants and working-people to Brooklyn" did not bode well for Brooklyn's ability to maintain its healthful atmosphere forever.[9]

In 1880, as Henry's stock brokerage prospered, the family moved across Henry Street to number 242, a three-story Greek Revival style brick row house near the southwest corner of Joralemon Street. The house, with its pilastered doorway and commanding front stoop, embellished with curved frontal blocks and sweeping iron railings, quickly communicated to potential visitors a social message of prosperity and power, tempered by classical restraint.[10] In plan the house resembled many others in the neighborhood, with its three-story, side-passage layout, front and back parlors, and added "tea room" on the first floor. The kitchen and family dining room lay below, bedrooms above.[11] The Earle household at the time included four-year-old Alice, two-year-old Mary, and baby Harry. To help with demands of housekeeping, the Earles employed four servants.[12] Kate Sheridan and Bridget Vaughn, both forty-five and born in Ireland, would have brought considerable domestic experience—in cooking, housekeeping, and the care of small children—to the Earle household. The two younger servants, Jennie Gilligan and Kate Brennan, were both in their early twenties, born in New York of Irish parents. They probably helped with the more menial chores: laundry, cleaning and dusting, washing up, assisting with food preparation in the kitchen, cleaning the grates, and maintaining the coal fires in each room. The presence of these four women made it possible for their employer to have an active social life, in and outside her house, as well as to find time to travel, study, read, and write. Their presence also suggests a very comfortable level of wealth for the young couple. At this point in his career, Henry Earle's business was thriving. Although many families on their block employed one, often two, and occasionally three servants, only one other family engaged such a large household staff. That family, the tea merchant Max Sand and his twenty-five-year old wife, Alice, had four children and lived down the block at number 276.[13]

The prospects of the Earle family seemed quite secure in 1882, the year after Alexander's birth. Henry's firm, Putnam & Earle, had lately been thriving, and he and his partner were reportedly worth over $100,000. On the brink of his fortieth year, Henry Earle, with his safe, conservative business style, could guarantee his wife and children social respectability and a predictable future (fig. 6). Since the beginning of his career, he had been part of a network of family and friends from Rhode Island. His uncle Randall Greene had employed his three sons, as well as his nephew Henry, and quite possibly his sons-in-law. Although he was doing business in New York, Greene retained and relied on his business connections from Rhode Island, primarily in the textile trade. When Henry Earle went into business for himself, he formed a partnership with someone who had another extensive family network, one involved heavily in banking and investments in New York. Putnam & Earle had been financed by bankers David M. Morrison and Albert E. Putnam, who had each invested $25,000 in the partnership. These two very wealthy men, also brothers-in-law, were closely connected to Henry's new partner, Nathaniel Putnam. David Morrison's father had been president of the Manhattan Bank, and Albert E. Putnam was married to Morrison's sister. Putnam's nephew Nathaniel D.

FIGURE 6. Henry Earle, 1886. At the time Alice married him, Henry was thirty-one years old and already successfully established in business on Wall Street. Henry was born to a prominent Providence family, but his father died young, leaving a widow and family without much support. Henry learned to fend for himself early in life, although the profession he chose sometimes put his own family at risk of financial insecurity. Collection of Donald J. Post Jr.

Putnam had been a clerk for the firm of Morrison & Putnam and, according to R. G. Dun & Co.'s credit reporter, Putnam & Earle "succeed[ed] to the bus[iness] of Morrison & Putnam."[14]

Henry's two younger brothers, Joseph and William, had begun their own business as rubber brokers, following in the footsteps of Randall H. Greene & Sons. Crude rubber had been made increasingly important as a commodity by Charles Goodyear's invention of a new process for hardening or "vulcanizing" liquid rubber in the 1840s. Rubber quickly became an essential material for the production of tubing, footwear, tires, sports equipment, life preservers, and many other goods. Initially, raw rubber was imported from South America, but by the late 1870s, the British were setting up a plantation system in Asia to produce rubber, which only increased the opportunities for investors to reap enormous profits—or losses.[15] Smyth, Earle & Co., with Joseph P. Earle as one of its principals, led the investment community in the brokering of crude rubber between 1873, when the firm was founded, and 1877, when it dissolved.

Business for Henry Earle was conducted as a gentlemen's club, revolving around a network of family and old friends, and his firm, Putnam & Earle, provided an important banking and investment link in that network. Personal loyalties, however, sometimes overrode financial judgment. Henry Smythe, the other principal in Smythe, Earle & Co.'s rubber brokerage, appeared to be "rather intemperate" to R. G. Dun's credit reporters. By 1877 Smythe had left the Earle brothers and gone off on his own. Joseph and William Earle then formed Earle Brothers. Within two years of establishing the partnership, Earle Brothers prospered greatly, quadrupling its net worth as a result of its timely presence in a booming rubber market. A peek into William Earle's credit history offers a glimpse of the comfortable lifestyle possible for a rubber broker. His worth in 1882 was estimated at $200,000. He owned stock in several different rubber companies, "a nice residence near Newport worth $35,000 clear," a half interest in the yacht *Gracie,* and assorted stocks.[16]

Henry Smythe was less successful. In 1877 the Williamsport Rubber Company of Williamsport, Pennsylvania, failed, nearly wiping him out. By 1882 he had lost everything.[17] Putnam & Earle failed the same year. According to Nellie Greene, Henry's cousin and the daughter of Randall Greene, his business mentor and first employer in New York, "Putnam & Earle was failed by a friend they helped."[18] No evidence remains to connect the failure of Henry Smythe with the failure of Putnam & Earle, but it is probable that Henry Earle's decision to help Smythe, a family friend, led to his own financial downfall.

Henry, aided by family and friends, regained his financial security. After 1882 he returned to the rubber business, probably joining up with his brothers. The family remained in their house at 242 Henry Street, and life resumed its normal pace. For Alice Morse Earle, however, this financial setback surely undermined her faith in a predictable future, especially where her family was concerned. If she could not fully entrust her family's financial security to her husband, she needed to develop resources of her

FIGURE 7. The even spacing of Earle's children is apparent in this photograph of her brood, taken in 1887. Standing beside Alice Clary Earle is Mary Pitman Earle, named for Henry Earle's maternal grandmother. Alexander Morse Earle, the firstborn son, is next in line, and finally the youngest, Henry Earle Jr. Earle has dressed her children up in matching dark velvet belted jackets and straw hats, perhaps for some holiday celebration. Collection of Donald J. Post Jr.

own—and at some point, writing must have seemed an appealing, even compelling, means to that end.

Throughout the 1880s, she spent much of her time and energy rearing her children and running the household in Brooklyn Heights. The regular spacing of her children (evident in fig. 7), and the fact that she stopped having children altogether when she was thirty, indicate that Henry and Alice Earle, as products of their middle-class culture, employed their understanding of family planning and child rearing as a critical social strategy. With fewer children than their forebears had to attend to, more individual attention could be given to each—a notion that corresponded to the prevailing idea that children, as malleable beings, needed to be nurtured and cultivated into civilized adults and perfect citizens.[19]

The values Earle sought to instill in her children, particularly concerning their role in the family and their responsibilities to their community, found expression in various amusements she devised for them. These activities, in turn, foreshadowed her later literary interests, suggesting that the experience of child rearing influenced what would become her philosophy about the function of history in education. She made frequent summer trips with her children to Worcester to visit their grandfather Edwin Morse and their aunt Fanny, Earle's sister Frances Morse. These visits maintained family connections that had been disrupted by Earle's move to Brooklyn, enabling her children to experience some of the formative aspects of her own childhood. During the summer of 1887, their visit was documented by a series of photographs of the children. Most of these photographs depicted the Earle children at play—in a hammock, all tucked together into a large four-poster bed, or in the garden.[20]

Many of the images have a staged quality which suggests that Earle had some purpose in having them taken beyond the simple documentation of her offspring's childhood. The care with which she planned and accessorized these photographs makes it appear that she intended them as much for publication as for display, although she had not yet begun to write. Beverly Gordon has suggested that this act of "playing" with one's collections is a gendered female way of enhancing personal connections between friends and among family members. In dressing up her children in their ancestors' (or someone's ancestors') clothing and positioning them among family heirlooms, Earle established an intimate romantic narrative in which she and her family were important actors.[21]

One photograph, which shows a brass warming pan hanging on the wall, banister-back and Windsor chairs, and an ornately carved bedstead, captured all four Earle children in their aunt Fanny's bed (fig. 8). The image countered the contemporary expectation that children would have separate rooms, instead presenting the Earle children more in the manner of olden times, when children shared beds. Other photographs depicted the children in historical dress. Nine-year-old Mary was photographed sitting in an upholstered armchair in her grandfather's parlor, wearing an old-fashioned dress and lace gloves, holding a small book in her lap. Another showed Mary wearing the same dress but with added bonnet, lace shawl, and beaded bag, this time seated in an eighteenth-century banister-back chair, apparently ready for tea. In a third photograph, Mary appeared in Dutch costume (fig. 9). Twelve-year-old Alice was photographed in costume in the garden, seated on the same banister-back chair—apparently a favorite prop—with her five-year-old brother Alex on her lap, similarly costumed in bonnet and dress.

FIGURE 8. Earle's children in their aunt Fanny's bed in Worcester, 1887. Earle made frequent visits to her sister, Frances Morse, who lived in the family home in Worcester. During those visits she recorded her children's adolescence, immersed in the material culture of their ancestry. Collection of Donald J. Post Jr.

FIGURE 9. Mary Pitman Earle in Dutch costume, 1887, F. H. Rice, Worcester, photographer. Earle's purpose in having her daughter photographed in historical dress is unclear but may be an early indication of her intention to use her children as models for illustrations in her later books. Collection of Donald J. Post Jr.

Earle's dress-up photographs of her children fall into the larger context of romanticized historical paintings and photographs that had emerged during the later nineteenth century, one of the many visible manifestations of a growing colonial revival. In the paintings of artists such as Edward Lamson Henry and Eastman Johnson, or the photographic images of Frances and Mary Allen, Emma Lewis Coleman, Clifton Johnson, Emma D. Sewall, and later Wallace Nutting, Americans could observe the past lovingly reenacted through the haze of memory. These images were both charming and useful, with their explicit embodiment of the values of patriotism, gentility, and the nobility of honest work. They also offered an implicit commentary on the deficiencies and problems of the present through their allusions to piety, class, community, gender roles and relations, environmental degradation, and even education.[22]

A series of photographs depicted all four Earle children at contrived play in the garden. One, titled "Playing 'horse' in Grandpa's Garden, Worcester," pictured a harnessed Alice pulling her younger brothers and sister in a wagon (fig. 10). Another showed them apparently working in the garden: Alice displaying a potted plant to Mary, with Henry digging (in the grass) and Alex observing. This photo, which was later used by Earle in *Old-Time Gardens* to illustrate the benefits of a garden-based education for children, clearly expressed the connection between her own child-rearing experiences and her philosophy of education.[23]

Earle perceived play, and especially guided play, as an important aspect of childhood. As had Catharine Beecher before her, Earle understood the benefits of gardening—both physical and spiritual. In *The American Woman's Home*, written by Beecher and her sister Harriet Beecher Stowe, published just four years prior to Earle's marriage, Beecher and Stowe advised their readers about suitable domestic amusements and recreations. "One of the most useful and important, is the cultivation of flowers and fruits," they wrote, adding that this activity would promote health as well as good habits such as early rising, benevolence, self-discipline, and community spirit.[24]

The importance to Earle of what she termed "garden experiences" (by which she meant non-urban or rural experiences) was underscored years later in a letter to the garden writer George Ellwanger in 1901. "To my own children I could only give summers in a garden—since our winter lot was cast in a city," Earle lamented, apparently discounting as a garden the small plot of land behind her Brooklyn Heights row house.[25] Summers in

FIGURE 10. "The Children's Garden," inscribed on reverse "Alice Clary Earle, Mary Pitman Earle, Henry Earle, Jr., Alexander Morse Earle, Playing 'horse' in Grandpa's garden, Worcester, July 1887." Earle believed firmly in the power of historical play as a shaping force in childhood development. The photograph, possibly taken by Earle's sister, Frances, was made during a summer visit to the family home on Chatham Street. Earle later used it as an illustration in *Home Life in Colonial Days* (1898). Collection of Donald J. Post Jr.

a garden, however, made up for the lack of a winter garden, and Earle made certain that her children were provided with that opportunity. In addition to their visits to Worcester, the family spent part of each summer, probably during July and certainly during August, at Duck Cove Farm, the country home of the Pitmans—Henry Earle's mother's family—on Narragansett Bay in Wickford, Rhode Island.[26] Earle's later literary descriptions of Wickford offer a sense of the pace and texture of the family's summer visits, as well as the components of that experience which she perceived as particularly beneficial to her children. Once there, the Earle children (and, no doubt, the Earle parents) enjoyed a wealth of amusements—the seashore, the garden, excursions across the bay to Newport, and visits with their grandmother Mary Pitman Earle (who lived in Providence but summered in Wickford), as well as numerous Pitman aunts, uncles, and cousins.[27]

During this period of intensive mothering, a few of the seeds of Earle's later career as a writer began to germinate. Part of what motivated her to write was a desire to endow her children with a sense of their own history—which she did through continual reinforcement of family ties with the past, as well as through artifactual, architectural, horticultural, and behavioral ties to prior generations. Her children were exposed to the memory of their great-great-grandmothers and -grandfathers every time they sat in the family's eighteenth-century banister-back chair or inhaled the fragrance of century-old boxwood at Duck Cove. Earle believed furnishings to be an important indication of an individual's or family's worth, both economic and social. In 1895, evaluating the belongings of the Reverend John Pitman (her husband's ancestor, and thus her children's as well), Earle noted "silver, china, glass, and furniture," which she found to be "good, the latter even handsome." They were "much treasured to this day by his grandchildren and their children," she noted, adding, "Two of his handsome harp-backed mahogany chairs are in constant use in my own home to-day."[28] Earle's descriptions of material objects reinforced her assumptions about the moral utility of artifacts from the past, assumptions that would shape her literary efforts for years to come. In Earle's worldview, informed by Darwinian theories about the genetic transmission of traits, objects, though inanimate, could convey the power and heritage of their owners across time and distance down to the present. They could also shape the future through their influence on successive generations of children.

Within this broader intellectual context, Earle significantly chose Wickford as one of her earliest literary subjects, one with a direct bearing on her children's family history. In one of her first published articles she described it as "a quiet little village" set in a landscape featuring "the green woods and hills of Narragansett and the blue water and white sails of the ocean."[29] Her writings about Wickford, however, contained a motif that recurred continually throughout her career—that of decline. By the early 1890s, she noted, the fertility and prosperity that had characterized this part of Rhode Island during the seventeenth and eighteenth centuries had vanished. "All now has changed in Narragansett," she wrote, "and few of the old mansions that remain standing show the presence of wealth." She attributed this state of decline not to any lapse of character on the part of the original settlers but rather to the failure of a system that depended on the institutions of slavery and primogeniture for its survival. Furthermore, outmoded farming techniques had worn out the land. Earle's summation, however, revealed her romantic preference for a decayed past over the fruits of progress, both for herself and as a therapeutic experience for her urban children: "Few of the old farms are now owned or occupied by descendants of the original settlers. The fields are sterile and barren, and the only trace remaining of the extraordinary early fertility of the Narragansett soil is seen in the luxuriant growth of wild flowers along the edges of the road,— perhaps because by the roadside there has been no close succession of exhaustive crops to impoverish the ground. . . . Never have I seen elsewhere in New England such variety and rich abundance of wild flowers as glorify the edges of the old Narragansett roads in midsummer."[30] For Earle, the wildflowers confirmed the power and persistence of nature, providing her children with a hopeful image of the future—perhaps even instilling in them a sense of their individual potential to overcome adversity. Here, in her description of the old village, lay a moral purpose that infused much of her later literary output.

In contrast to the roadsides of Wickford, the grounds at Homogansett—the more formal name of the family estate at Duck Cove—had been carefully cultivated by successive generations since the 1850s. Earle would include an unidentified photograph of that garden in *Old-Time Gardens* in 1901. She revealed its identity to the renowned horticulturist George Ellwanger in a letter following that book's publication: "The garden on page 35 is our Farm-garden—on our family country place on Narragansett Bay," wrote Earle. "The farm is Homogansett," she continued. "We have owned it a century and a half. Daniel Webster and Chief Justice [Joseph] Story planted the box in that garden," she proclaimed proudly.[31] Earle was using the term "we" loosely here; in fact the farm belonged to her husband's uncle and aunt, Randall H. and Harriet Pitman Greene. In addition, although Joseph Story was indeed a Supreme Court justice, he was never chief justice.

Harriet and her sister Mary Pitman Earle had inherited the farm from their father, John Pitman. Mary remained in the original cottage, while the Greene family built a large Victorian summerhouse nearby. Subsequently the Earle family acquired another cottage on the property, overlooking the beach and Narragansett Bay. The Earle house connected with the Greene and Pitman houses by means of a narrow lane, by which all the families had access to the beach. The compound at Duck Cove promised Earle and her children a future of summers on the water, surrounded by relatives and nurtured by the remnants of a long family history.[32]

By the late 1880s, Earle had devoted a dozen years to raising her children. When the youngest, Alex, turned seven in 1888 and Earle herself turned thirty-seven, she must have begun to think about new directions for herself. It seems clear that motherhood, particularly the approaching end of it, served as a direct impetus for Earle's sudden immersion in the life of a writer. By 1890 she had published her first four articles, beginning in January with "A Pickle for the Knowing Ones," for the *Christian Union*. The following year she published her first book, *The Sabbath in Puritan New England*, and eight more articles. A year later she published her second book, *China Collecting in America*, as well as five articles. Her career as a writer was successfully launched.[33]

Writing for Earle was a solitary pursuit, but she did not isolate herself from society in order to accomplish it. Throughout the 1890s, her membership in various women's clubs reinforced her literary agenda, frequently serving as a preliminary sounding board for ideas or works in progress. Club activities also doubtless offered some welcome relief from the burdens of research and writing. Club memberships conferred status as well and helped Earle anchor herself in the urban environment that surrounded her. During the course of their marriage, Henry and Alice Earle participated actively in the social world of Brooklyn Heights. Private clubs formed the nexus for most of their activities. In the highly fluid and rapidly changing context of Brooklyn, club memberships offered a comfortable haven from the increasingly diverse urban milieu outside, affording people living among strangers a means of replicating the small-scale community life they had left behind when they moved to the city. *Brooklyn Life* reported in its society pages that Henry was a member of five of Brooklyn's and New York's best clubs. He served as secretary of the Brooklyn Club, located on the corner of Pierrepont and Clinton streets, a place where "one will find the leading men of affairs in this borough—representatives of the judiciary, the prominent lawyers, political magnates and men of influence in finance and mercantile life." Moreover, "its cuisine is proverbial for its excellence, and the atmosphere of old-fashioned club comfort pervades the house."[34]

In addition to the Brooklyn Club, Henry belonged to the Crescent Athletic Club and the Marine & Field Club, both of which owned extensive property in the country and at the beach. Crescent Athletic, "organized by university men," had 1,500 members and was "known for the uncommonly high social quality of its membership." The club owned two houses and a large parcel of land in the suburbs of Brooklyn. Marine & Field, located at Bath Beach, was considered "the country club of Brooklyn," offering its members boating, tennis, and golf.[35]

The Earles also belonged to two other social clubs that were dedicated to more intellectual pursuits, the Twentieth Century Club and the Barnard Club. Here Henry and Alice had the opportunity to hear lectures and discuss important events of the day in the company of their social peers in Brooklyn Heights. The Twentieth Century Club, which had as its members "men and women of social position and influence," held meetings at which speakers addressed current issues in politics and the arts. The Barnard Club, formed ostensibly to promote Barnard College, was a "semi-literary club of men and women of intellectual tastes" and, of course, "high social position."[36] The *Brooklyn Daily Eagle* reported: "The Barnard club is unique. Papers are not read at its meeting, though many of its members are well known contributors to literature. Philanthropy is not its object, notwithstanding the fact that the club's supports include the most liberal donators to charity in the city. Lastly, civic interest did not inspire its birth, though loyal lawmaking citizens make up its roll call. The Barnard club is purely social. But, most unique of all, its members are composed of men and women."[37]

Club culture, traditionally dominated by an all-male mentality, was changing, perhaps an indication of the growing demands of women for more public roles in society. This list of club memberships offers a suggestive picture of Alice and Henry Earle's social activities as a couple. While Henry would have spent time at the Brooklyn Club on his own, in the company of other men, he and Alice could have participated in cultural pursuits together at the Barnard and Twentieth Century clubs. For physical fitness or pure relaxation, the Marine & Field offered the entire Earle family the opportunity to participate in sporting events—tennis, golf, or swimming at the beach. Participation as a family also ensured that their children would grow up surrounded by "the right people," so that when the time came for them to find mates, they would have appropriate options.

Alice was also deeply involved in clubs of her own, where she spent a great deal of time in the company of other women who shared her interests in literature, artistic enlightenment, and history. Her memberships ranged from Mrs. Field's Literary Club to the Brooklyn Woman's Club, the National Society of New England Women, and the City History Club, as well as two hereditary-patriotic organizations, the Daughters of Revolution (which merged with the Daughters of the American Revolution in 1895) and the National Society of Colonial Dames. Some of her clubwomen friends were published authors too, although most were simply interested in the combination of intellectual stimulation and socializing.

Many of Earle's social activities revolved around Mrs. Field's Literary Club, of which she became a member in 1892. Founded in 1884, the club had as its mission the goal of bringing together its members "for literary culture and social intercourse." Its beginning as a reading group in the late 1870s under the tutelage of Mary J. Field suggest a rising interest among women for intellectual companionship outside the home. One member recalled in a published history of the club: "When I was first married and came to Brooklyn to live, Mrs. Bowen asked me to join a small reading class, which met once a week. After a couple of years, a desire to give a thorough study to the English language possessed us, and Mrs. Charles Phelps and I were asked to find a teacher. We were fortunate to find Mrs. Field and this class began with ten pupils in 1882." The study group proceeded from philology to literature, "from the ancient Epics to the latest novel, and this took several years." At that point the group decided to become a club, one that would offer a literary forum for its members. Mrs. Field's objective was "to develop the literary ability of the members, and often the best work was done by women who declared they could never write upon a given subject."[38]

By 1892, when Alice Morse Earle was first listed as a member, the club had grown to include 125 members. The admission process was exclusive, requiring nomination in writing by four different members, although Alice's sister-in-law Mary Louise Earle, William's wife, who was a club member, may well have been her most effective sponsor. Since by that time Earle was already a published author—with two books and seven magazine articles to her credit—she was surely eligible for inclusion in the club's membership rolls. During her first year as a member, the club's monthly programs included a paper presented by Mrs. Sturgis Coffin titled "Photography in Medicine." Coffin's husband, a perfume manufacturer, had lived two doors away from the Earle family in the early 1880s, and presumably the families were acquainted. At another meeting that year, members heard Edith B. Southard present her paper "Musical Notes," and the following year author Esther Singleton enlightened the members in a talk titled "Antique Dances," with musical accompaniment on the piano. Most of the papers, however, typically focused on literature. In 1895 the club selected a theme for its papers, "What Are the Elements of Popularity in the Novel of Today?" One of the respondents, Mrs. Alice Morse Earle, surveyed "Novels of the Year," while Mrs. Leech discussed George du Maurier's recently published *Trilby,* a sensational novel about the tone-deaf diva Trilby O'Ferrall, hypnotized to perform brilliantly by her wicked mentor, Svengali. *The Bookman: A Literary Journal* had begun publication that year and included a new feature, a regional lists of best-sellers, which noted *Trilby* as a top-selling work.[39]

In subsequent years Earle became more and more active in the club. From 1895 on, Earle, by then a well-respected author, was a regular presenter to the club on a wide-ranging array of subjects. She hosted a social meeting in 1896 at her house on Henry Street. Members heard papers on English, French, and Russian literature, with discussion led by Earle and a Mrs. Bellamy. In 1897 she appeared again on the program, this time with "The Songs of Shakespeare," as part of a general consideration of Shakespeare's lyrics and historical context. In 1898 the club considered "New York City from a Historical Point of View as a Factor in American Civilization," to which end members presented papers about New York's political, economic, and legal history, including one by Earle titled "The City History Club."[40]

The club's focus on New York City history reflected a growing interest in the power of history as a civilizing agent. The City History Club, about which Earle spoke, was a reform organization founded in 1896 by Mrs. Robert Abbe "for the purpose of familiarizing New Yorkers with the history of their city, just as Boston's history is familiar to all New Englanders." Catherine Amory Bennett Abbe was an important philanthropic force for municipal reform in New York, and founding the City History Club was part of that larger agenda.[41] According to Anna Ware Winsor, one of the club's teacher-mentors and author of an article about the club in 1898, history education could confer "the mental poise and calm judgment necessary to wise political thinking [which] cannot exist without that sense of men's growth and change, their weakness, their ignorance and their power, which comes only with the backward look and a familiarity with the lapses of generations." Winsor pointed to New York's "heterogeneous population" as the source of the problem: with no common ancestry or history, she believed, New Yorkers tended toward a fragmented political vision. The club's activities included history classes about colonial New York taught to schoolchildren by volunteers, public lantern slide lectures about historical topics, historical walking and bicycle tours of the city, and publication of the *Half Moon Series,* a collection of articles about New York history. Winsor noted that the *Half Moon* papers were all written and edited by club members, and the first article published, Earle's "Stadt Huys of New Amsterdam," Winsor considered "a most instructive and interesting paper" as well as "a valuable addition to the histories of New York."[42]

Earle's City History Club activity confirms her belief in the reforming power of history, as well as her own active role as an instrument of that reform. The club had been created within the larger milieu of a city whose politics had been corrupted by Tammany Hall and whose population had been transformed by massive immigration. Like many other reformers, Earle saw education as a means of reshaping society, and history education as a means of improving civil life through Americanization.

Earle was also a member of the Brooklyn Woman's Club, another prestigious social organization dedicated to fostering women's intellectual and cultural achievement. The club, founded in 1869 by Mrs. Anna C. Field and Mrs. Cecilia Burleigh, was similar in purpose and political makeup to Sorosis, which had been founded a year earlier in Manhattan (and of which Earle was not a member). Both organizations sought to create a place where women could meet and discuss literature, the arts, and social issues. According to the minutes from the Brooklyn club's first meeting, "its object shall be the improvement of its members, and the consideration of the various important questions growing out of the relations of individual to society and the effect of social institutions upon individual development. It shall be independent of sect, party and social cliques. The indispensable conditions of membership are earnestness of purpose, love of the truth and a design to promote the best interests of society."[43]

The club, which grew from its original membership of a hundred women to 199 members by 1898, recognized the power of collective action from its start, petitioning the mayor of Brooklyn to appoint a woman to the Board of Education in 1871. Earle's activities as a member may have included working on the establishment of free kindergartens in Brooklyn, an activity that culminated in the establishment of the Froebel Academy.[44]

Like Mrs. Field's Literary Club, the Brooklyn Woman's Club was organized into standing committees that reflected the interests of the members, including literature, music, drama, art, science, and philanthropy.
Each committee would develop programs for the entertainment and edification of the members. In 1893 the *New York Times* reported: "The Brooklyn Woman's Club, a splendid body that is only a trifle younger and smaller
than the New-York Sorosis, has had a most successful initial meeting. It
was Literature Day, and Mrs. Alice Morse Earle, author and essayist, was
most appropriately Chairman." For that meeting Earle devised a program
titled "Fads and Fashions in Literature," presented by fellow member
Alice T. Bartram.[45]

Like many white middle-class women of her generation, Earle believed
that women had a cultural mission to perpetuate civilization through the
nurture and education of their families. This theme had its origins in the
early years of the American republic, embodied in the notion of the republican mother, whose responsibility it was to foster the growth of her
children, overseeing their transformation into good citizens. To this end,
women sought both to educate themselves—that they might be better
teachers—and to create domestic environments that would reinforce republican cultural values of industry, frugality, and simplicity. Earle's own
mother, Abigail Clary Morse, born in Jackson, Maine, in 1812, was doubtless reared in a culture steeped in this republican rhetoric of "true womanhood," and would certainly have sought to inculcate into young Alice the
values of her generation.

Earle embraced domesticity as a means of maintaining social order,
both in her life and in her writing. Her books and articles carried on a
female literary tradition begun in the advice literature and magazine writing of the antebellum era, as Sarah Leavitt has shown.[46] What views she
did express about "the woman question" reflected ambivalence. On the
one hand, she lamented in *China Collecting in America* (her second book)
that women were proscribed from the adventure of driving a tin peddler's
cart: "Such happy peaceful joys are forbidden to me, not because of the
lack of inclination or capacity, but—thrice bitter thought—because I am
a woman. Tin-peddlaring is not for me, it is not 'woman's sphere.'"[47] This
statement suggests that Earle, who had already embarked on a career as
a writer that would increasingly impinge on her responsibilities as wife

and mother, felt constrained by the traditional gender roles and the social vision of separate spheres.

On the other hand, Earle was avowedly reluctant to align herself with voices calling for radical social change. In this she was hardly alone. The woman suffrage movement had been gaining momentum gradually since the late 1860s, when Congress accorded equal rights to all men, black or white, but declined to give women those same rights. Squabbles over strategy had divided the movement into two camps by 1870. Members of the American Woman Suffrage Association (AWSA) supported the Fourteenth and Fifteenth Amendments to the Constitution and felt that the battleground for suffrage should be moved to individual states, while members of the National Woman Suffrage Association (NWSA) opposed the two amendments and sought full and immediate equality with men. In 1871 the NWSA declared that women were already entitled to suffrage on the basis of the Fourteenth Amendment, which stated, "All persons born or naturalized in the United States . . . are citizens." Under this logic, termed the "New Departure," women had the right to vote, and no constitutional amendment was necessary. When NWSA leader Susan B. Anthony voted in Rochester, New York, however, as a test of this assumption, she was arrested.

By 1890, when Earle began her career as a writer, the NWSA and AWSA had reconciled and formed the National American Woman Suffrage Association (NAWSA). Three years later the International Council of Women and the United States National Council of Women emerged as umbrella organizations for women's issues, indicating a new solidarity among women. As a sign of inclusiveness, the U.S. National Council even included in its membership anti-suffrage groups, which had been gaining supporters among a population of largely upper-class women in the early 1890s. Their main argument was that the taint of politics would undermine the "natural" moral authority of women and their ability to influence the behavior of men.[48] Many anti-suffrage women viewed their domestic duties through the lens of religion, believing that God had created woman's sphere for a special purpose. They listened eagerly to Theodore L. Cuyler at a Brooklyn anti-suffrage rally in May 1894. "Your creator has laid heavy loads on woman's head and hand and heart, and the wisest of your sex are seeking more of divine grace to bear them," Cuyler preached.

"Beware how you rashly clamor for new burdens which would be light only to those who are too weak to understand them, or too wicked to respect their sacred responsibility. Let the high endeavor of every good woman be to do her full duty to God, to society, to her family and to the commonwealth in that great sphere in which God has placed her," urged Cuyler, concluding, "Woman must do her work for her country as a woman and not as a counterfeit man."[49]

Within Earle's own social circle, the debate disrupted the harmony of at least two of her clubs. The Brooklyn Woman's Club, which had initially been pro-suffrage, agreed in 1874 not to discuss the subject anymore, at which point pro-suffrage members broke away and formed the Woman's Suffrage Society, a separate organization—although many members belonged to both groups.[50] As Karen J. Blair has noted in her study of women's clubs, many of these organizations were inherently conservative, even on the issue of suffrage. Their major purpose was to implement women's power through what has been termed "domestic feminism," the ability of women to influence social and cultural change by cultivating their traditional, home-centered female authority.[51]

Twenty years later, in 1894, Earle's chapter of the Daughters of Revolution held a symposium about the woman suffrage question, with speakers from both sides. Supporters argued passionately that suffrage would help alleviate "the misery caused among women by the drunkenness of men." Children would benefit as well, proponents argued, when money currently spent on liquor could be diverted to education.[52] Other pro-suffrage speakers at the meeting pointed to Wyoming and Utah, which, prior to achieving statehood, had given women the vote in 1869 and 1870, respectively. For their part, the anti-suffrage speakers countered that "it might be a dangerous experiment" to permit a woman to vote, "because it would place on her the power and responsibility of government." Mrs. William A. Putnam (the daughter-in-law of Henry Earle's former business partner) argued that "if the women were in politics, they would require political leaders," adding, "I do not know any women whom it would be safe or desirable for us to have as our leaders in great political movements." Putnam's logic reflected her political conservatism and, most likely, that of many of her family and friends. Other anti-suffrage critics resorted to outright fearmongering, suggesting that suffrage would mean the end of marriage as an institution and that a suffrage supporter desired to "render herself entirely independent of man."[53]

The Outlook, a religiously oriented "family paper," reported on the symposium, terming it an anti-suffrage rally and commenting favorably on its spontaneity, its all-female makeup, and its objective tone, which "makes no appeal to sentiment; none to feeling; none even to tradition."[54] The magazine provided explicit reasons for opposing imposition of "the obligation of suffrage," including the argument that "because the energies of women are engrossed by their present duties and interests, from which men cannot relieve them, . . . it is better for the community that they devote their energies to the more efficient performance of their present work than to divert them to new fields of activity."[55]

For *The Outlook,* the fact that the anti-suffrage women in particular had overcome their distaste for publicity to speak out against suffrage provided further proof of the sincerity of their commitment. The magazine concluded its report with a call to arms: "The woman's suffrage movement has not heretofore been treated seriously. The time has come when it must be treated seriously. Every woman is under sacred obligation to herself and her children to ponder it carefully and weigh well the arguments pro and con." *The Outlook,* doubtless expected its readers to arrive at a conclusion on the "con" side of the suffrage question.[56]

Earle's name was not on the list of attendees, but the symposium included a number of her friends and neighbors, people who might have constituted her audience, if not necessarily her political peers. The meeting took place seven blocks from her Henry Street house, and twelve of the twenty-one anti-suffrage activists lived in Earle's Brooklyn Heights neighborhood. Furthermore, fourteen of the twenty-one who attended were among the guests at the wedding of Earle's daughter eight years later.[57]

The level of political commitment Earle herself may have felt for or against the suffrage cause must remain a matter of speculation, although she seems to have been proximally involved on several different levels. She and her family socialized with a number of people whose political ideology—at least with regard to "the woman question"—was anti-suffrage. It would be hard to envision her siding with Susan B. Anthony or Elizabeth Cady Stanton on the subject of female emancipation, given the evidence of her published works. Earle's veneration of the Puritan family as the ideal social unit would have put her at odds with Stanton's call for social and economic independence for women. In fact, she sounds much closer to Catharine Beecher in her ambivalence about the issue of suffrage.

Beecher, in her *Woman's Profession as Mother and Educator with Views in Opposition to Woman Suffrage* (1872), had argued that suffrage should be limited to women who were financially independent, and that women in general should not rely on the ballot to improve their situation but should focus instead on education and collective action.[58]

In fact, after she had become an established authority on colonial life, Earle engaged in a rather public war with Elizabeth Cady Stanton, one of the leading figures in the suffrage movement, over an article Stanton had written about Christmas celebrations among the Pilgrims for *St. Nicholas Magazine.* According to Earle, Stanton had misrepresented her facts, and she wrote a letter to the editors to say so. In their response to her, the editors assured Earle that they had already printed a note "explaining that Mrs. Stanton's article is not to be taken as true," but rather that Stanton herself had deemed it "half fact, half fiction." Because of an editorial oversight, this had been omitted from the article.[59] A year later the magazine asked Earle to write "a serious account" of Pilgrims and Christmas as a refutation of Stanton's article. Earle expressed reluctance to do so, referring to Stanton as "that past-mistress of Women's Rights and Colonial History" and worrying that such an article might "attract to myself all the bitter words of Mrs. Stanton's many strong-minded friends."[60]

Through her City History Club activities, however, Earle was directly associated with the club's founder, Mrs. Robert Abbe, a suffrage activist. According to the *New York Times,* "Abbe, who is a leader in the most exclusive social set in New-York, was among the first of the society women to take up the movement," and her home was "one of the rallying points for the Sherry campaign," which enlisted upper-class women to work to amend the state constitution and accord women the right to vote. Abbe called the Sherry effort "the most earnest movement I have ever known in New-York," adding: "There is no thoughtlessness or flippancy about the people who have taken it up. They are earnest and intellectual women, and the whole movement is a dignified one, and should be treated as such." Abbe's emphasis on earnestness and dignity reflected the group's desire to work quietly, distancing itself from the more vocal mainstream suffrage movement. "I think that if the woman suffragists have done anything wrong in their work," Abbe commented, "it has been in antagonizing and talking against men. We owe everything to them. If it had not been for

them we should not now own our own property or make our own wills."
Moreover, Abbe asserted: "Do I think having the franchise would take
women away from their homes? How much time do men give to the ballot? It does not take them away from their homes. I think women have
more leisure than men, and that they would take up the study of politics
conscientiously. There is no doubt that they could serve on juries, as well
as they do on large committees, with men."[61]

The fundamental differences between Earle's social vision and that of
her more radical suffragist sisters can be made readily apparent by considering the parallels and differences between the messages of her book *Margaret Winthrop*, published in 1895, and Charlotte Perkins Gilman's *Women
and Economics*, published three years later. Both Earle and Gilman were
responding to changes in American society, focusing their attention particularly on the institutions of marriage and family. Gilman, however,
found those institutions ill-equipped to cope with the conditions of contemporary society and called for broad institutional changes. Earle, by
contrast, invoked the power of hegemony, urging her readers to embrace
the life of Margaret Winthrop, wife of John Winthrop, seventeenth-century governor of Massachusetts, as a social model. "Throughout her life,"
Earle wrote, Winthrop "ever displayed traits of character, disposition, and
faith that were most noble and beautiful." Within the context of this
model, Earle defined a role for herself as a facilitator of change. Although
Winthrop's ilk "belongs to an existence that has forever passed from this
earth," she wrote, "it has an immortal soul which still lives, and speaks to
us with clear voice [that of Earle] down through the centuries."[62] The lesson of Margaret Winthrop was clearly not one of emancipation—a point
driven home by Earle in a chapter on Anne Hutchinson, a moral tale about
the destructive power of woman unleashed. The mania around Betsy Ross
that emerged during the 1890s created a much more palatable model of
women in the American Revolution, as her lauded contribution involved
sewing, not fighting or voting.[63] Earle continually emphasized domesticity as a positive virtue for women, stressing "the beauty in woman's life
of home-loving, home-keeping, home-influencing."[64] Like Gilman and
other radical feminists, Earle was critical of the current state of American
social institutions, but unlike them, she resorted to a constructed vision of
the past for amelioration rather than to an uncertain future. Whereas

Gilman sought systemic change, reform of the institution of marriage it-self, Earle celebrated individual character as the change agent.[65]

Whether or not Earle favored suffrage, her women's club activities indicated that, like Beecher, she understood the collective potential of her gender and valued the opportunity for female self-education. Literary activities, a means to improve both self and society, were an essential part of women's club culture. Members produced and presented reviews, es-says, poetry, plays, pageants, and other intellectual or artistic efforts for one another, as well as for the general public. In 1894, the twenty-fifth anniversary year of the Brooklyn Woman's Club, Earle joined several other members in writing "stories, sketches, essays, and poems" for a commemorative album.[66] Another of Earle's clubs, the National Society of New England Women, also engaged its members in creative activities, staging "notable entertainments . . . typifying old New England customs, such as 'The Quilting Bee,' . . . 'The Husking Bee,'" held at the Waldorf in 1896, and "'The Carnival of American History' given at the Metro-politan Opera House on November 30 and December 1, 1897."[67] Events such as these not only provided Earle with yet another outlet for her tal-ents, validating her sense of individual worth through peer affirmation, but also may have served as a supportive forum for her early literary efforts.

The debate about the proper role for women in American society ex-tended deep into women's club culture. An article published in *Brooklyn Life* in 1898 offered a history of women's clubs with insights into the mis-sion of several of them, of which Earle was a member. The author, identi-fied only as G.H.H., "one of the best known club women in Brooklyn," began by asserting that "the first ones that were founded in this coun-try—the New England Women's Club, the Women's Club of Orange, the Brooklyn Woman's Club, and Sorosis—had for their purpose the broad-ening of woman's outlook on life in general, the raising of her intellectual standard, and the cultivation of her ethical nature." She quickly turned to an underlying agenda, however, to argue that women's proper sphere was naturally the home. The fact that these four clubs, after thirty years in existence, had never built clubhouses seemed to be "proof" that "the idea of their founders and members has not been social enjoyment away from home." She continued:

It is not, and it seems to me that it never will be, natural for the normal woman to find her social recreation away from the home. Even women who are misled into over-doing club activities and philanthropic efforts are essentially home-loving women. They seem simply to be betrayed by transitory errors of judgment into assuming responsibilities which unfold unduly and make it necessary for them to be much abroad.

As soon as women realized that women made the home itself, in its broadest ideals, it was the one object of their coming together in clubs. Nearly every woman's club of which I know has a committee which devotes its energy to discussions of questions bearing on the home, and as soon as women began to feel the force which came through their organization, their special objects of educational, moral, and social reform began to have a large part in their club discussions.

"In short," the anonymous G.H.H. concluded, "as women's clubs tend towards home life rather than away from it, . . . they do not as a rule, and probably never will depend upon individual buildings for social enjoyment."[68] Although this argument did not explicitly mention the issue of woman suffrage, it offered a popular counterargument to it: that women were naturally inclined toward the private sphere of home and family, a sphere that seemed threatened somehow by the possibility of full citizenship for women.

How to explain Earle's seeming ambivalence about suffrage in particular and radical feminism in general? Timing and ensuing personal motives may ultimately have shaped her political stance. When she began writing, she was already thirty-nine years old, and she was fifty-four when she published *Two Centuries of Costume in America,* her last book. While it is difficult to quantify the impact or significance of life experience on creative output, her age may provide a partial explanation for Earle's prescriptive and inherently conservative tone. During this period her children became adults, married, and began bearing their own children—all of which could have contributed to Earle's progressive desire to shape the future—not for herself but for her progeny. The methods she chose relied heavily on her faith in the power of environment and material culture both to confirm and to facilitate the social function of heredity. Objects for Earle, as we have seen, provided a tangible link with the past. They operated as a point of access to underlying social and institutional structure; through their agency, the past could achieve embodiment in the present.

The final piece of Earle's club activities revolved around the newly formed hereditary-patriotic organizations that began to develop in the early 1890s to celebrate ancestral links to America's heroic past. The earliest, the Sons of the American Revolution, founded in 1889, did not admit women as members. Within a year, a group of women in Washington, D.C., had met to organize a sister organization, the Daughters of the American Revolution (DAR). Chapters formed in cities around the country, beginning with the Martha Washington chapter in Washington and quickly followed by the New York chapter. Earle filed her application for DAR membership on February 6, 1895, citing her descent from Captain the Honorable Richard Heard of Sudbury, Massachusetts, Ensign Reuben Morse, Captain Josiah Hoar, and Lieutenant Jonathan Hoar as evidence of her acceptability. She became a member that year and was elected regent of her chapter in 1896.[69] She also belonged to the New York Chapter of the National Society of Colonial Dames and the National Society of New England Women, two other heredity-based patriotic organizations. These groups, like many women's clubs that had appeared during the 1890s, claimed the education of women as one of their chief objectives.[70] The specific objectives of the DAR, as proclaimed at the inaugural meeting in 1890, were aimed as much at the general public as at individual members: to "teach patriotism by erecting monuments and protecting historical spots, by observing historical anniversaries, by promoting the cause of education, especially the study of history, the enlightenment of the foreign population, and all that makes for good citizenship."[71]

Membership in these organizations required a certain amount of historical research to verify the existence of a colonial ancestor who had fought on the American side during the Revolutionary War, in the case of the DAR, or who fought in the war *and* had been eminent, in the case of the Colonial Dames. The Colonial Dames initially required candidates for membership to fill out the application form by hand, perhaps reflecting a traditional faith in handwriting as evidence of character. This rule was soon abandoned, however, whether because of the new availability of typewriters or the opposition of wealthy women who preferred to hire professional genealogists to prepare their application papers is not clear.[72]

As was the case with the Brooklyn Woman's Club, Mrs. Field's Literary Club, and other organizations to which Earle belonged, self-improvement formed a major agenda item for both the Daughters of the Revolution and the DAR. Member Jane Meade Welch presented a paper, "American History for American Women," at the First Continental Congress of the DAR, stating that historical research and writing would be good for women, asserting, "Mental growth and character growth will result to the Daughters of the American Revolution from such a study and writing of American history, and an increasing self-respect with a corresponding growth of power."[73]

Earle's involvement with the DAR, in particular, refined and further legitimized her research interests and enabled her to present papers to her colleagues on a regular basis. These papers, as well as those presented to Mrs. Field's Literary Society, would form the groundwork for many of her published writings. Although it is tempting to argue that Alice Morse Earle's club activities led directly to her subsequent literary career, in fact her literary career began in 1891, before she became a member of Mrs. Field's Literary Club. Her clubs, however, certainly reinforced Earle's writing career, offering her a forum for her research, as well as a place where she would find affirmation and support for her published works. The underlying philosophy of her clubs was that a woman had not only a right but also an obligation to improve herself. Club meetings facilitated that self-improvement. They also functioned as a sort of public parlor, in the sense that Earle and her friends were essentially performing for one another, but safely within the confines of their parlors rather than in a truly public venue. Earle, however, had stepped well beyond these boundaries in pursuit of her very public career as a professional historian and writer.

After 1901 Earle retreated from active club membership, attending meetings less and less frequently. Her experience and organizational wisdom, however, persisted. In 1904 she emerged briefly as a founding adviser to a new club being organized in London. The Lyceum Club was to be a "common meeting ground for women throughout the world who are workers in literature, art, or science, including medicine," offering facilities for "refreshment, recreation, work," and possibly even a place to stay. To qualify for membership, a woman had to be a published author, composer, artist, or scientist, with university qualifications (which Earle did not have), or the wife or daughter of a man so distinguished. The Provisional Committee was described as being composed of "America's leading club-women," including Alice Morse Earle, representing literature and journalism.[74]

CHAPTER 3

New England Kismet

✤

WITH HER DECISION TO ENTER THE WORLD of professional writing, Earle chose to disrupt the comfortable sanctuary of her home for a career that intruded on her social obligations, sometimes put her at odds with her family, and even jeopardized her health. Earle's early focus on her own ancestors and the instructive value of Puritan society suggests a mission that was both personal and progressive. Her club activities instilled in her a strong sense of obligation to improve society at large by improving herself. Through those activities, or perhaps in part because of them, she had come to view history as a mechanism for effecting larger social changes, as demonstrated by her City History Club activities. In the modern urban context in which she lived and worked, her own family history as well as her children's future seemed to be at risk in the wake of massive immigration, political corruption, and a tempo of life that often overwhelmed genteel convention. By writing about the past—her own as well as that of the nation—Earle felt that she could potentially influence the future of the country by educating its populace. She had chosen Puritan New England as her first topic, believing, as did many other Americans at that time, that traditional narratives served as the most effective remedy for the problems of the present. Earle's interpretation of Puritan society and culture, however, was shaped as much by her own family history as by the scholarly resources to which she had access. She needed the assurance of history as much as her audience did. As her first book and subsequent books and articles reveal, Alice Morse Earle used historical narrative to counter her own anxieties about the future. She needed to know that her Puritan ancestors would serve *her* well, and to ensure that, she needed to make them more accessible.

As the demands of child rearing lessened, Earle may have turned to writing as an activity to fill a void. She may also have been waiting for many years for the opportunity to write. In an interview published in 1900 in the *New York Times,* allegedly "the first semi-biographical words . . . put into type about her," she modestly claimed that she had entered the field of writing quite unexpectedly, and that "a dozen years ago she had no idea of authorship."[1] A quick review of Earle's life "a dozen years ago" would put us back in the late 1880s, for her a period of intensive mothering. In 1888 her eldest child was twelve, her youngest seven. Henry Earle's financial difficulties seem to have been resolved by then, and the family enjoyed a comfortable life shuttling between home in Brooklyn Heights and family visits to Worcester and Wickford.

Earle claimed to have begun writing at the urging of her father, who enlisted her to write about the old church in Chester, Vermont, next door to Andover, where his father and mother had lived. According to the interview, "the material for this was so abundant, and Mrs. Earle spun it so interestingly together that her father encouraged her to make another essay." She did so, and submitted her results to Thomas Bailey Aldrich, editor of the *Atlantic Monthly,* who accepted her article for publication.[2] Unfortunately for her, Aldrich stepped down as editor a month later, and the new editor, Horace Elisha Scudder, had reservations about the piece. Earle later recalled: "I soon got a letter from him saying that he did not think he could make use of the manuscript. I wrote him to send it back. In reply I got another letter stating that he had changed his mind and would keep it, after all." In fact, this article seems never to have been published, although its contents may have served as fodder for Earle's future writings. Encouraged by Scudder's endorsement, Earle had sent him a book proposal for *The Sabbath in Puritan New England*—which he ultimately rejected, stating, Earle remembered, "that he did not see how there could be any sale at all for such a book."[3] His response is puzzling in light of a recent spate of other books about Puritanism, including Brooks Adams's *Emancipation of Massachusetts* (1886), as well as two notable books from Houghton Mifflin: *Puritan Age and Rule* (1888) and *Beginnings of New*

England (1890). Perhaps Scudder felt that the market was saturated. His claim that Earle's manuscript had limited sales potential may also have been influenced by her gender (such a serious study, written by a woman?) or, more likely, her status as an unknown author (in contrast to Brooks Adams).

Despite these mixed messages from Scudder, Earle was undaunted. When the book was completed, though, she sent it to Charles Scribner's Sons. "There soon came back word from Mr. W. C. Brownell approving it highly," Earle recounted, adding, "I afterward learned that they had sent it to Dr. Van Dyke to read, and that he had spoken very favorably of it." Henry Van Dyke, a well-known clergyman and author of several religious books published by Charles Scribner's Sons, would have been an excellent referee for Earle. Brownell gave the project his go-ahead, and Earle's career took off. *The Sabbath in Puritan New England* sold some ten thousand to twelve thousand copies during its first year of publication, a commendable record by any standards for a history book, especially one from an unknown author.[4]

The success of Earle's book reflects a general interest in Puritanism in the 1880s and 1890s, as authors, both popular and scholarly, undertook a reconsideration of the character of the Puritans and Pilgrims and the utility of their history for modern Americans.[5] Moses Coit Tyler had begun the process in 1878, with his pathbreaking two-volume *History of American Literature, 1607–1765*. During the late 1880s, when Earle would have been thinking about *The Sabbath in Puritan New England,* several dozen works appeared that would have aided her research, including the English historian John Andrew Doyle's study *The English in America: The Puritan Colonies* (1887), John Richard Green's *History of the English People* (1888), John Fiske's *Beginnings of New England, or, The Puritan Theocracy in Its Relation to Civil and Religious Liberty* (1889), and William Babcock Weeden's *Economic and Social History of New England, 1620–1789* (1890). These scholarly works were supplemented by several other studies that focused on particular aspects of the Puritan past that would have appealed to Earle, including William Chapman's *Notable Women of Puritan Times* (1887), Herbert Mortimer Luckock's *Studies in the History of the Book of Common Prayer* (1889), and especially *Music in America* (1890) by Frédéric Louis Ritter. Earle may or may not have read novels such as *The Puritan Lover* by Laura Dayton Fessenden (1887), *The Fair Puritan: An Historical*

Romance of the Days of Witchcraft by Henry William Herbert (1890), or *The Puritan's Daughter* by Thomas C. DeLeon (1891), sequel to *Creole and Puritan: A Romance of Two Sections* (1889). She was surely familiar, however, with the local-color fiction of Sarah Orne Jewett, which had been published in the *Atlantic Monthly* continuously since 1869, as well as the New England novels of Harriet Beecher Stowe. Her own later stories in *New England Magazine* seem to have drawn inspiration from some of them.

A strong common thread ran through this published work: all of it focused on the Puritan past, whether using that past as an instrument for better understanding the evolution of modern ideas and values, as a romantic lure into historical study, or as a trope through which to comment on the conditions of the present. Earle's use of the term "backsliding" to describe modern-day descendants of Puritans suggests that she too sought more than just hagiographic thrills from learning about her ancestors and their world.

Ten years into her successful career as a professional writer, Earle's version of the beginnings of that career, as conveyed to the *New York Times* reporter, would imply that she had played only a limited and largely passive part in its initiation. She claimed that she had not had any personal aspirations to write for the public, that she had done so only at the request of her father. Once given his permission, and even his encouragement, she then felt less constrained about moving outside the traditional strictures of her gender and class. Despite her claims to have fallen into a writing career, in fact Earle began to work on it deliberately. Her article on New England meetinghouses, which was published in the *Atlantic Monthly* in February 1891, had been preceded in 1890 by six previous articles; she published five more articles in 1891—two in the *Atlantic,* two in *New England Magazine,* and one in *Scribner's Magazine.*[6] The publication of her first book in 1891 suggests that Earle's writing career must have been in its incipient stages for some time prior to 1890, perhaps as early as 1887, when she was posing her children for photographs in historic costume.

Even though the social stigma against professional women had diminished considerably by 1890, Earle still seemed conflicted about the propriety of what she was doing: hence the published myth. Her interviewer quite clearly stated that Earle continued to maintain a sharp distinction between the public Alice Morse Earle, author, and the private Mrs. Henry Earle, to the extent of refusing to give interviews and suppressing all details about her family circumstances.[7] According to the interviewer, "the story of how and why she came to write, how these early successes were made, how Mrs. Earle gathered her material, has never been told," because "Mrs. Earle the author and Mrs. Earle of private life are kept intentionally very far apart."[8]

Earle had turned down at least one previous request for a personal interview, from E. W. Morse, who wanted a photograph for *The Book Buyer,* a magazine owned by Charles Scribner's Sons.[9] In what must have been something of a coup for the *Times,* Earle for some reason decided to submit to the interview—possibly at the request of her publishers to promote book sales. As it turned out, the interview caused Earle great embarrassment. After its publication, Scribner's wrote to Earle, denying that her manuscript had been sent to Van Dyke. "We assume that you will be glad to receive this assurance from us," the letter noted, "in order that you may cooperate with us in preventing the error from gaining further circulation." Earle responded that she had agreed to the interview "most unwillingly," and that she had a well-known "desperate aversion to anything of the sort." She added, however, that Van Dyke himself had told her that he had read her manuscript prior to its publication. Whether she had been embellishing her personal history, or whether Van Dyke had indeed read her manuscript, perhaps informally, remains a question.[10]

Earle, like many of her female peers who chose writing as a career, experienced residual conflict about assuming responsibilities that challenged her traditional obligation to preside over the private realm of home and family. Throughout the nineteenth century, women writers expressed their ambivalence about public performance. The most common prescriptions for female happiness, from the colonial period into the twentieth century, revolved around marriage and motherhood, not professional activities.[11]

Earle's decision to turn to a career in writing was reinforced by a powerful sense of a woman's mission to apply professional reformist standards both to the education of her children and to society at large, a sense of purpose hardy enough to sustain her through any hesitancy she may have felt. Earle viewed her writing as a pleasant instrument for social reform, a palatable means to restore to America the values that had defined its early glory. "It is curious to see how completely social ethics and relations have changed since olden days," she wrote in 1898. "Aid in our families in times of stress and need is not given to us now by kindly neighbors as of yore; we now have well-arranged systems by which we can buy all that assistance, and pay for it, not with affectionate regard, but with current coin," she concluded, indicting contemporary urban society for its lack of humanity.[12] Modern reforms seemed to Earle to be not only inhumane but also frequently ineffective and shortsighted, especially where education was concerned. "It is surprising and pathetic, too, to hear in a public primary or parochial school the children of German, Italian, or Irish parentage chanting 'Green gravel, green gravel, the grass is so green,' within the damp and dingy yard walls or in the basement playrooms of our greatest city," she remarked disdainfully.[13] In an era that was generally characterized by rising levels of professionalism in many different spheres, women as well as men sought to define and achieve new kinds of professional standards. This was particularly evident in the application of scientific principles to the domestic sphere, as well as in the realm of education. In Earle's case, this purpose was to be executed by means of a prolific literary output over the next fourteen years.

Despite her strong sense of female mission, as we have seen, Earle was ambivalent about the subject of woman's suffrage, an ambivalence she expressed in a letter to her editor, William C. Brownell, at Charles Scribner's Sons. Discussing the gendered focus of her current books in progress, *Colonial Dames and Goodwives* (published in 1893) and the biography of Margaret Winthrop (1895), she informed him of "an urgent offer from another publishing house, asking me for a book which I felt might not exactly conflict but run perhaps concentric with the Margaret Winthrop." She cited the subject matter of her books as well as the rival offer as evidence that "the air is full of feminine literary meteors, and some planets of considerable light seem to be coming above the horizon," adding, "I think the firm of Charles Scribner's Sons had best hasten to shed its brilliant rays before any other house starts out upon the 'woman question' in early days." But she concluded this exhortation with a political disclaimer: "I am not so over fond of the woman aspect of everything that I should ever, of my own choice, care for any book specially on any woman."[14]

This last remark is puzzling in light of the fact that *Colonial Dames and Good Wives* focused *entirely* on women. Earle structured the book around the biographies and explicitly female worlds of seventeenth- and eighteenth-century women. Her perception of a women's culture was particularly interesting, expressed in a discussion of "Boston Neighbors." She wrote, "in order to present clearly a picture of the social life of women in the earliest days of New England, I give a description of a group of women, contiguous in residence, and contemporary in life." This strategy, Earle believed, would yield far more useful information about women's lives than what she termed "an account of some special dame of dignity or note."[15]

Earle laced *Colonial Dames and Good Wives,* published in 1893, with commentary about women's roles and their relation to the prevailing male power structure. In a chapter titled "Women of Affairs," Earle celebrated activist women, women in business, women who founded towns, women publishers, and other women who contributed prominently to the public sphere. She tempered her message, however, by including examples of women who successfully combined their activism with housewifery rather than abandoning their domestic duties in the process. Jane Colden, "the most distinguished female botanist of colonial days," seemed to her a woman worthy of esteem. Colden, daughter of New York governor Cadwallader Colden, loved science and had collected and recorded more than four hundred American plants using the Linnaean system. One admirer, Walter Rutherford, wrote of her: "She has discovered a great number of Plants never before described and has given their Properties and Virtues, many of which are found useful in Medicine and she draws and colours them with great beauty. Dr. [Robert] Whyte of Edinburgh is in the number of her correspondents." As an aside, however, Rutherford noted, "N.B. She makes the best cheese I ever ate in America." Earle revealed her own feminist sympathies, commenting wryly on this remark, "The homely virtue of being a good cheese-maker was truly a saving clause to palliate and excuse so much scientific knowledge."[16]

The conclusion to *Margaret Winthrop* provides a clear example of Earle's sense of social mission, as well as her view of ideal womanhood. Earle characterized Winthrop as "the emblem and personification of what I have learned to believe is one of the purest types of womanhood—Puritan wife and mother." In her recounting of Winthrop's story, with all of the attendant detail about daily patterns, domestic arrangements, clothing, courtship, and marriage, Earle intended to provide her readers with a model for living in late-nineteenth-century America. That model embodied "the true dignity which comes from . . . simplicity in dress, in home-furnishing, in hospitality, in all social and domestic relations."[17]

The destiny of New England, a vision dominated for almost three centuries by the legacy of Puritanism, no longer seemed certain to Earle at the outset of her writing career. The small-scale, closely knit community and family life she fancied that both her mother and father had known as children had been swept away by a tide of progress. Earle herself knew that she lived in a world her grandmothers and grandfathers had never even imagined. Her conception of destiny, or "kismet," as she quaintly termed it in a short story published in 1892, demanded a departure from the Puritan concept of a society that functioned according to God's will within a clearly defined social hierarchy.[18] That older ideal had been thoroughly demolished by a new mentality of individualism and by the seemingly irresistible destiny of industrial capitalism. By the last decade of the nineteenth century, Earle sought new ways of understanding the changes that had occurred during her life. Although her own family history confirmed the value of progress, Earle believed that growth and change also undermined traditional rural values and historical continuity.[19] Her faith in orderly transformation had been seriously challenged by the new industrial and urban order. Blind obedience to divine agency and Calvinist notions of determinism and destiny no longer seemed adequate as an explanation for change; human agency was possible and indeed required. Earle joined a growing body of cultural critics, as well as a venerable literary tradition, when she chose to write about the New England past as a means of countering the deficiencies of the present. Through her books and articles, she offered her readers a New England pastoral, shaped by the urgent demands of her life in the city. Historical narratives about colonial America, particularly those that elaborated on the specific material settings in which those forebears lived and worked, would serve Earle's present as a form of therapy for the trials of modern living.[20]

Puritanism, however, needed revision before it could be useful to Earle and her contemporaries. The dominant historical narratives about Puritanism in 1890 suggested an inevitable weakening of traditional family and community in the face of progress. The twin themes of human impotence before powerful new material forces and the ensuing cultural loss resonated through all of Earle's work. These themes were particularly evident in her characterization of rural New England and New Englanders. She depicted the society of her own rural contemporaries as typified by isolation, poverty, and cultural decline; the old Puritan values of industry, frugality, and simplicity had not proved sufficiently resilient to accommodate the demographic and economic transformations of the nineteenth century. Even more depressing, the Puritan family—large, cohesive, and for so many generations the glue that held the society together—seemed to have scattered forever across the nation. That is not to say, however, that the Puritan myth had no currency for Earle and her contemporaries. Its narrative merely needed to be reshaped to conform to the social conditions of late-nineteenth-century America, which is what Earle attempted to do through her books and articles. In She challenged the old model of Puritanism by reworking the Puritan personality. She characterized her Puritan forebears as people with humor, idiosyncrasies, and human empathy that offset their stern, cold, repressive, blindly, and by late nineteenth-standards slavishly, devout demeanor.

Her first book to that end, *The Sabbath in Puritan New England*, began with the assumption that religious orthodoxy had dominated all aspects of seventeenth-century life. Puritans were "patient, frugal, God-fearing, and industrious, cruel and intolerant sometimes, . . . sternly obeying the word of God in the sprit and the letter."[21] Orthodoxy, according to Earle, was constantly reinforced through the material culture of Puritanism. She analyzed the structure, floor plans, and seating arrangements of meeting-houses, as well as much more obscure artifacts—communion tokens, for example—for evidence about social hierarchy, attitudes about family and children, authority, and particularly about deviance.

The beginnings of this idea of the social and cultural power of physical artifacts can be ascribed to the New England theologian Horace Bushnell.[22] Bushnell's *Christian Nurture* (1847) introduced the notion that children could be shaped by their environments and that it was the task of mothers to construct domestic realms that would nurture their children along the paths of piety and virtue. In 1851 Bushnell gave an address celebrating the centennial of Litchfield, Connecticut, in which he dismissed the traditional heroic historical narrative as "a fiction," arguing instead that "spinning wheels have done a great deal more than these" to shape the nation. He went on to praise cloth making and "an economy of homespun," instead of the work of eminent ministers and other distinguished men, as the underlying basis for American progress. According to Laurel Thatcher Ulrich, "By shifting attention from political narrative to the unseen workings of ordinary life, Bushnell paved the way for later studies of the relationship between economy and culture."[23]

Later in the nineteenth century, John Richard Green, an amateur historian, produced his best-selling *Short History of the English People* (1874), another study that laid the groundwork for Earle's approach. Green, in contrast to the rapidly professionalizing academic historians who preferred to emphasize great men and constitutional development, embraced popular culture as well as traditional political and military narratives, as the inclusion of the work "people" in his title suggests.[24]

Earle clearly shared both Bushnell's ideology of environmental agency and Greene's populist framework, making the leap backwards with these two visions all the way to the seventeenth century. She saw material evidence of Puritan attempts at social control everywhere she looked. Communion tokens—lead or pewter disks stamped with the initials "L.D." (for Lord's Day) and issued to communicants to ensure that only the worthy partook.[25] In Puritan meetinghouses, social deference was maintained through strictly controlled seating arrangements, supposedly reflecting God's view of an orderly society. Her social vision embraced humor, and she seemed particularly eager to dispel the notion that Puritan society was above reproach—as evidenced by the presence of naughty boys, illiterate printers, and sleeping parishioners. According to the Reverend Daniel Rollins, who reviewed Earle's book in the *New England Historical and Genealogical Register,* "the writer is thoroughly in sympathy with her subject, and, though of Puritan descent, does not hesitate to criticise some features of the Puritan belief and of the customs and habits of its people."[26]

Throughout *The Sabbath in Puritan New England,* Earle offered examples of irrepressible human behavior that tested the relevance of Calvinist determinism. Her work countered traditional scholarly interpretations of Puritan life, which emphasized orthodoxy and unquestioning compliance, demonstrating that even Puritans had difficulty accepting unyielding authority. She began this critique in her opening chapter of *Sabbath,* which focused appropriately enough on the physical and spiritual center of Puritan society, the New England meetinghouse. Her discussion traced the evolution of these structures, from the early rude log buildings to the more polished square wooden churches, as exemplified by the "Old Ship," a church erected in 1681 at Hingham, Massachusetts. Earle noted the gradual incursion of pride and vanity into Puritan piety through changes in the appearance of meetinghouses. At first they were austere, with no ornamentation of any sort. By the eighteenth century, however, new ideas about church design had spread across New England, resulting in large structures with painted exteriors, interior galleries, and three-tiered glass windows. As Earle put it, "the early meeting-houses in country parishes were seldom painted, such outward show being thought vain and extravagant." Within one or two generations, however, "paint became cheaper and more plentiful, and a gay rivalry in church-decoration sprang up. One meeting-house had to be as fine as its neighbor."[27]

The townspeople of Pomfret, Connecticut, painted their meetinghouse bright yellow, which stimulated a flurry of painting in the surrounding Connecticut towns of Windham, Killingly, and Brooklyn. The first two towns followed Pomfret's example, but Brooklyn, not wanting to be outdone, voted to paint its church "bright orange; the doors and 'bottom boards' a warm chocolate color; the 'window-jets,' corner boards, and weather-boards white." The roof would be crowned by an "Eleclarick Rod," making this church "the newest, biggest and yallowist" in the area. Earle, speaking through the voice of a contemporary critic of this excess, commented on "the spirit of envious emulation, extravagance, and bad taste that spread and prevailed from the example of the foolish and useless 'colouring' of the Pomfret meeting-house." Puritans, like their modern counterparts, were clearly vulnerable to human foibles.[28]

This excess left parishioners susceptible to distraction, especially children. "The study of the knots and veins in the unpainted wood of which the pews and galleries were made" offered them a respite from the tortures of lengthy sermons. According to Earle, "the children, and perhaps a few of the grown people, found in these clusters of knots queer similitudes of faces, strange figures and constellations," and "the dangling, dusty spiders' webs afforded, too, an interesting sight and diversion for the sermon-hearing, but not sermon-listening young Puritans." In the same passage, Earle rooted out the paradox of Puritan theology in her dismissal of the sermon as a "dreary exposition and attempted reconciliation of predestination and free will."[29]

Earle discovered numerous other instances in which the material and behavioral realities of Puritan life did not match the severity of its theological ideals. During the midday break between services, worshippers gathered in the "noon-house," where there was a fire and usually food. Earle characterized the noon-house conversation as operating on two levels. "The men talked in loud voices of the points of the sermon, of the doctrines of predestination, pedobaptism and antipedobaptism, of original sin, and that most fascinating mystery, the unpardonable sin," she commented dryly. Meanwhile, those same men talked "in lower voices" about the doings in their secular lives, "of wolf and bear killing, of the town-meeting, the taxes, the crops and cattle."[30] Here Earle hinted at the Puritans' resistance to Calvinist dogma while affirming the positive values of Puritan community. Although she did not mention her own family explicitly in any of these accounts, the intimate tone of her description of this culture of resistance suggests that Earle could hear the voice of her grandfather Benjamin Morse echoing among those other voices in the noon-house.

No Puritan virtue was exempt from Earle's subtle critique. "Surely they had no traits to shame us," she concluded, "to keep us from thrilling with pride at the drop of their blood which runs in our backsliding veins"; and yet when Earle probed beyond the façade of orthodoxy, she found much to contest.[31] She countered the perception of piety, simplicity, and freedom from vanity with descriptions of a Puritan wedding custom whereby the bride and groom "rose, in the middle of the sermon, from their front seat in the gallery and stood for several minutes, slowly turning around in order to show from every point of view their bridal finery to the eagerly gazing congregation of friends and neighbors."[32]

In this, as in many of her descriptions of Puritan customs, Earle injected evidence of human vanities and desires, sympathetically portrayed. She clearly thought it foolish to assume that the arbitrary standards and conventionality of Puritan culture could contain human urges. She argued against orthodoxy either by reducing it to the realm of quaintness or by exposing it as a sham.

In her discussion of changing attitudes toward music in colonial churches, Earle's central intention surfaced. She explained the establishment of "singing schools"—a product of the new custom of singing "by rule" rather than "by line." The singing school, she asserted, provided an "outlet for the pent-up, amusement-lacking lives of young people in colonial times." Furthermore, "what that innocent and happy gathering was in the monotonous existence of our ancestors and ancestresses, we of the present pleasure-filled days can hardly comprehend."[33]

The following year Earle again voiced a lament about the current state of New England, this time more explicitly, in "A New England Kismet," published in *Scribner's Magazine* and again that same year as a portion of the closing chapter of her new book, *China Collecting in America*.³⁴ The story chronicles the visit of an urban New England "china hunter" to an ancestral homestead in the country in pursuit of old porcelain, blue and white china, or any other remnants of the past that might catch her fancy. The protagonist and a companion leave their homes in the city, setting out by "steam-car" for the fictitious Wheelton, a small manufacturing town whose dreariness is accentuated by its newness, as confirmed by the "hideous carpets and marble-topped bureaus" in the hotel where they spend their first night. The next morning the china hunters set out for Rindge (a remote village in southwestern New Hampshire) to find the home of Anthony Hartington, allegedly "the oldest and most china-hiding house around."³⁵ The plot, like those of Earle's other country stories, constructs a dreamlike past—one in which her readers would not want to live, but which they felt the lack of nonetheless.

The beauty of the New England countryside—fringed gentians blooming prolifically across the land—adds to the poignancy of Earle's description of Hartington, "an elderly man with bowed head, ragged clothes, slouching gait, and a general appearance of extreme depression and sadness."³⁶ The pervasive aura of expectations unrealized turns the narrator's eager anticipation about the potential treasures contained inside the noble brick mansion into a melancholy reverie. "A heavy gloom settled on us as we walked from room to room," she relates, "and I was additionally overwhelmed by the uncanny, unreasoning sense that I had been there before, had lived there."³⁷ Although these feelings of déjà vu are not grounded in reality—the Hartingtons are not ultimately revealed to be distant relations of the narrator—they serve to set up a bond between Earle and her readers, that of a common New England heritage and its loss. Throughout the story Earle juxtaposes images of ruin, decay, and death with those of childhood innocence, eager optimism, and high ideals, heightening the emotional quality of that bond. Her protagonist describes an overgrown garden and "the well-tenanted family graveyard with its moss-grown and chipped slate headstones, with their winged cherubs' heads and crossbones," noting, "I had often gathered flowers in that garden, I remembered it well, and had walked and played among the gravestones."³⁸

Ruin pervades the interior of the house as well, as it does the entire Hartington family. Most of the furnishings are stained, tattered, chipped, cracked, broken, or in some other way deficient—a legacy of use without replenishment.[39] Hartington's wife died the previous June, and all nine of his children have been lost to consumption. Despite this, Earle's relentless china hunter manages to find a number of objects to "rescue": bits of English china and earthenware, some brass candlesticks, "a really beautiful but broken candelabra of Sheffield plate," and the bottom half of a high chest of drawers (the top of which "had been gnawed by rats and whittled by knives until it was useless"). The most desirable treasure, a graduated set of fifteen pewter porringers, the old farmer refuses to sell, clinging to the memory of his wife, a memory those particular artifacts transmit to him.[40]

By contriving to have her narrator discover a hidden letter in a drawer of the chest after returning home, Earle constructed a historical context for the story and an intergenerational explanation for the decline. This letter, written in 1810 by one George Hartington (father of the current occupant of the house) to his mother, Madam Janet Hartington, discusses George's recent marriage to a woman named Oriana. Madam Hartington has apparently voiced some objection to Oriana because of rumors that her father made his fortune "in the African Slave Trade." George reassures his mother that Oriana is "quite ready to become a most dutifull and obedient daughter to you, and I trust, my Dr Mother, the fact of her being an orphan will open your heart to her." Besides, she has "much good furniture and china which will grace well our home."[41]

George also reveals that because of family debts, coupled with his college debts, he has given up his intention "to practice as a lawyer, and have decided to return to manage your Farm," hoping ultimately to "carry out my Grandfather's plans to make our house and name one of the most powerful in the State."[42] But that was not to be. George, it turns out, died shortly after his marriage, and his wife followed him eight years later. Although Madam Hartington survived into her ninety-second year, the farm languished, never regaining its eighteenth-century glory. "And this is the end of all Madam Hartington's ambitions," Earle concludes, "a broken-down, broken-hearted, childless old man. It is the New England Kismet."[43] Her choice of "kismet" for her title—an exotic word with faraway associations—not only romanticized the story, suggesting a link between New England history and a larger world, but also hinted at the tragic consequences of fate, from which there seemed to be no escape.

The New England kismet, as Earle interpreted it, promised a destiny of decline for those who did not actively resist it. The success of the Puritan

experiment had hinged on the willingness of the entire community to adhere to common values, never challenging the authority of the covenant.
Although Earle loved the old ways, she also realized that the present posed
challenges that could potentially overwhelm the diminishing resources left
from the past. Future salvation lay in individual action rather than placid
acceptance of modernity. Earle seemed to be suggesting in this story that
had George Hartington not yielded to his mother's wishes to return to the
farm to carry out his grandfather's ambitious dreams—had he instead
struggled to complete his studies in the law—perhaps the life course of
the Hartington family might have been different. And Anthony Hartington, the last hope for the family, seems totally incapable of resisting his sad
fate, although it is hard to imagine what individual action on his part
could possibly have deterred the twin forces of westward expansion and
industrialization.

Earle's decision to use a first-person narrative voice suggests an autobiographical dimension to this story, and a personal inspiration for this elegiac
vision of the New England past. Although her own ancestors had not followed exactly the same course as the Hartingtons, there were many parallels, and Earle could easily have constructed the Hartingtons of Rindge
from her own family history. The gaps between expectation and realization,
between optimism and pessimism, seem to have been the result both of the
industrial presence represented by Wheelton and the inability of individual families to cope with social and economic change. Unlike the Hartingtons, however, who remained on the farm in Rindge, Edwin Morse and
Abigail Clary—Earle's mother and father—made decisions that sent the
life course of their families in a different direction. Around 1840, a decade
before Earle's birth and during her grandparents' waning years, Edwin and
Abby had left their homes in the dying countryside and moved to the city.
The consequences of this choice, positive and negative, would not have
been lost on Earle. Because of it, she was reared in an urban environment.
Although she never lived in the country, the direct memory of a rural past
remained close at hand throughout her childhood, only one generation
removed from Earle herself.[44] Her father had been born in Andover, a tiny
village in southern Vermont; his father, Benjamin, had moved to Andover
from Dublin, New Hampshire, when he was about twenty-five.[45] In 1815,
the year of Edwin Morse's birth, Andover had been in existence as a geographic entity for only fifty-four years. It had been created out of 23,500

acres of land initially granted by George III to Benning Wentworth, the first royal governor of New Hampshire (1741–1766). The township was divided into seventy-two shares of 250 acres each; sixty-six of those shares were granted to settlers and two, in the northeast corner of the town, were reserved for Governor Wentworth and henceforth known as the Governor's Lot.[46]

The presence of this country past in her immediate family history would also have endowed Earle with an understanding of power relationships based on family connections and hierarchy. In 1798 Reuben Morse (1742–1810) of Dublin, New Hampshire, bought three hundred acres of the Governor's Lot for $400.[47] Morse, the son of Thomas Morse—one of the original proprietors of Dublin and a friend of Benning Wentworth—had served in the Revolutionary Army.[48] After the war he returned to Dublin, and with his wife, Abigail Mason, he built a farm overlooking Mount Monadnock.[49] As a member of a prominent Dublin family, Morse was undoubtedly a highly esteemed citizen, and his stature was further enhanced by his marriage to the daughter of Benjamin Mason, a master carpenter who had framed most of the early houses in Dublin.[50]

By the time Reuben purchased the Governor's Lot in 1798, he and his wife had reared ten children, five of whom had recently married. For this country family, however, the patriarchal ideal of continuity through family proximity was about to be disrupted by the incursion of new economic factors outside their control. The recently opened fulling and finishing mills in nearby Harrisville increased the competition for land to supply wool to the mills; that fact, coupled with the poor, rocky soil of New Hampshire, meant that Morse was not able to maintain family order by providing land in Dublin for all of his children.[51] Patty, the eldest, married Robert Muzzy and moved to Oswego, New York. Reuben Jr. left for nearby Sullivan, New Hampshire, after his marriage in 1793. Third-born Hannah and her husband, Darius Gassett, settled in Andover, as did Benjamin and his wife, Betsey Hoar. Persis and Abigail married Daniel and John Clary, cousins from nearby New Ipswich, New Hampshire, and both moved to central Maine. Ebenezer went to Dartmouth College and became a physician. After his marriage to Esther Crafts, daughter of John Crafts, a prosperous tavern owner in Walpole, New Hampshire, he settled there. Only sons Bela and Asa remained in Dublin after their marriages, and Bela inherited his father's farm.[52]

The purchase of the Governor's Lot coincided exactly with the marriage of Benjamin to Betsey Hoar in 1798. The lot seems to have been intended, however, not as a wedding gift but rather as provision for the future. In 1803 Reuben Morse sold 155 acres of the lot to his son Benjamin for $200; he also sold a smaller portion of the lot to his son-in-law Darius Gassett for $50 and retained the rest as an investment.[53] His decision to sell rather than give the land to his children suggests both a reluctance to "spoil" the children and a desire to maintain some degree of control through property, if not proximity.[54] Morse, a devout member of Dublin's Congregational church, doubtless believed in the power and social value of frugality and industry; his conception of appropriate parental responsibilities would have transmitted the stern legacy of Puritanism, with its emphasis on order and conformity, to yet another generation. His great-granddaughter's sense of the country past, then, had its basis in family reality, passed down from one generation to the next. Although the Calvinist ideals of her Puritan ancestors were probably fairly well diluted by the 1890s, some remnant of that legacy expressed itself in Alice Morse Earle's simultaneous endorsement and rejection of country values.

Earle's grandfather Benjamin Morse, "like all the early settlers . . . had the forest to subdue, his land to clear, and a small house to build, seed to put into the ground—the preparatory work of civilization."[55] The early years in Andover undoubtedly required all the resources that Benjamin and Betsey Morse could muster just to ensure the survival of their family. The Morses were amply rewarded for their efforts; by 1814 they owned four hundred acres of land. Not all was a success, however. Between 1806 and 1814, five of their first nine children died before reaching the age of four. When Earle's father, Edwin, and Edwin's twin brother, Edward, were born in 1815, in the wake of their brother John's death a year earlier, twin babies must have seemed a hopeful sign of change for the better. From that date the family appears to have stabilized; at least the pattern of childhood deaths ceased, although the births did not. Betsey Morse bore another son, Reuben, in 1817, and her final child, John, in 1821.[56] In reviewing her family history, Alice Morse Earle must have perceived these nineteenth-century children of Puritans to have embarked on a promising revival of country life, purified, in her retrospective vision, of a blind adherence to destiny.

A brief account of the Morse family history conveys some of the complex social and cultural aspirations of Earle's grandparents, as well as the

competing worlds of traditional Puritanism and emerging industrial opportunities that shaped her father, Edwin's, mentality. Edwin and his siblings grew up as Andover was developing into a small industrial village.
By the time Edwin was ten years old, Andover had eight school districts.[57]
In 1840 the census reported three gristmills, three sawmills, a carding machine, a fulling machine, two stores, two taverns, and a tannery.[58] Life in
Andover revolved around the burgeoning New England textile industry—to which Andover's farmers supplied wool—and the production of
flour, lumber, leather, and wood products. The town's location at the base
of Markham's Mountain, near the headwaters of the Williams River, affirmed its pastoral character, while waterpower, one of its most valuable
resources, assured its future. By the 1840s, however, as steam was beginning to supplant water-driven turbines, that resource lost its value, and
Andover entered a period of economic and demographic decline from
which the town never reemerged.[59] Andover remained on the periphery
of industrialization, and it began to lose its young people as a result. Abby
Maria Hemenway, the town historian, commented mournfully in 1886
that "the clearings of the first settlers in many places have grown up again
to woods. The town has been hard drained by the emigration of its young
men."[60] Edwin Morse, Earle's father, had been among that group of young
men who left Andover in pursuit of a future elsewhere. His departure,
replicated endlessly across New England, was an exercise of free will that
contested the traditional Puritan script.

Earle's mother, Abigail Mason Clary (1812–1881), had experienced a
similar small-town childhood in a close-knit family environment, with
some significant similarities and differences. The most significant similarity was that Abigail's grandfather was Reuben Morse—who was also
Edwin Morse's grandfather. Her mother, Persis Morse Clary (1779–1837),
was Edwin's aunt. Through her mother's Morse heritage, Abby assimilated the same set of Puritan values with regard to family, community, and
work as her husband. But Abby's father, Daniel Clary, who was born in
New Ipswich, New Hampshire, a small hill town on the Souhegan River
fifty miles northwest of Boston, injected a different social heritage into
the family mix. Unlike the Morses, who had emigrated to Massachusetts
during the seventeenth century, the Clary (originally McClary) family
had emigrated from Ireland during the early eighteenth century.

Earle learned about her mother's ancestors from Frederic Kidder's and Augustus Gould's *History of New Ipswich,* published in 1852 to celebrate one hundred years of progress in the town. According to Kidder and Gould, New Ipswich initially had been granted in 1735 to a group of proprietors from Ipswich, Massachusetts; actual settlement began in 1738, and the town grew slowly over the next ten years.[61] When Catherine McClary, widow of Daniel McClary of Lunenburg, Massachusetts, arrived in New Ipswich in 1751 with her two sons Daniel and William, the town was still a sparse cluster of rough houses and primitive roads. By 1763 the population had increased from about 140 to 350 people. The McClarys appeared on the Minister's Rate List that year, Catherine in the tenth or bottom decile, Daniel in the ninth, and William in the fourth.[62] The McClarys shared a lot in the western part of the town, a geographic location that, according to Kidder and Gould, implied a different social and economic condition from that of residents who had settled in the northern and eastern sections, where "seldom has more than one family located on a lot; in the southern and western parts, however, two persons frequently settled on the same lot."[63] In contrast to the Morse family in Dublin and even in Andover—where they had arrived as proprietors and had always had access to prime land and a certain degree of social and economic security—the McClarys came to New Ipswich as outsiders, part of a large community of transients for whom the margin between success and disaster was very slim. They tried hard to fit in. (Both brothers served in the Revolutionary army and dropped the "Mc" from their name at that time.)

The McClarys left few traces of themselves, other than Kidder and Gould's observation that they had emigrated from Northern Ireland via Lunenburg, that they "had all the propensies for fun and jokes that are so characteristic of their countrymen," and that "they did much to amuse the town, and no doubt were useful in other ways."[64] In fact, Daniel's propensity for amusing people led to his death in 1780, when he was killed at a barn-raising after he "undertook to stand on his head, on the ridge-pole, as he had often done at such times."[65] This anecdote about her great-grandfather's death, falling while trying to stand on his head on the frame of a barn, with the community gathered below, must have charmed Earle on some level. It provided her with a direct ancestral connection to a culture that was neither Puritanical nor orderly. The folk culture that she found so invigorating, and that emerged frequently in her books and articles, had its roots firmly planted in the pastoral and offered a persistent counter-vision to the authoritarian rigidity of Puritanism.

When he died, Daniel McClary left his wife, Catherine Taggert, with six young children. Once again country culture, with its emphasis on networks of family and kin, would have shaped her options, although it is unclear which course she chose. She may have remained in New Ipswich after her husband's death; having lived there since her marriage, she no doubt had strong bonds to the community. Her chief source of emotional and financial support in New Ipswich—her sister Margaret, who had married Daniel's brother William—had recently moved away, however, to Belfast, Maine.[66] Catherine and her children may have joined them there, but it is also possible that she returned to her family of origin in nearby Peterborough. Whatever her course, she retained strong connections with south-central New Hampshire, strong enough that her son Daniel Clary (1774–1856) married a young woman from the neighboring town of Dublin. This marriage, in 1799, established the link between the Clary and Morse families: Daniel's bride was Persis Morse, the sister of Benjamin Morse, Alice Morse Earle's paternal grandfather.

Family stories, passed from one generation to the next, served to inculcate family values and beliefs in subsequent generations. Earle, as her family's historian, would have been the natural recipient of many of these stories. In the 1890s she received a letter from one of her Clary aunts recounting an event that had occurred shortly after the marriage of Daniel and Persis Clary. Finding the opportunities in New Hampshire increasingly limited, the Clarys had moved to rural Maine, yet again reviving a family network on the frontier. They settled near Daniel's uncle in the town of Jackson, farming there and ultimately rearing eight children— one of whom was Abigail Mason Clary, mother of Alice Morse Earle.[67]

As the story suggested, the rigors of life in Jackson came to be seen by the Clarys as a formative element in their family identity. According to the letter, one of Persis's sisters, a mother of four, had left her children alone and gone to borrow something from a neighbor three miles away. She was caught in a sudden snowstorm and lost her way. When their mother did not return from her errand, the children, frightened by the severity of the storm and thoughts of their mother's peril, elected to send six-year-old Levi out on the family's horse to search for her. Forced to abandon the horse, Levi continued "bravely" on foot through snow two feet deep until he finally reached his father, a carpenter, at work two miles away. After an extensive search of the surrounding countryside, the missing woman was located, miraculously alive but "utterly exhausted and only half conscious at the foot of a tree." The men in the search party made a rough litter of branches and carried her home. As she recovered, she told of her terrible experience, of her mental suffering when she thought of her children, of her moments of hope followed by darkest despair, and of her prayers and confused dreams. She had composed and recited verses in the dark and lonely silence.[68]

As family memory, this legend fit the larger pattern of an American, and especially a New England, narrative: the power of faith, bolstered by individual spirit, to overcome the wilderness. For Earle, the courage, sense of adventure, and willingness to persevere which she understood to be qualities that had shaped her grandparents' lives were important aspects of her personal vision of an ideal society. These were the qualities that propelled families onward; without them, as in the case of the Hartingtons, the future promised only stagnation and oblivion. Her own family had overcome such a destiny: they would not be victims of a darker New England kismet. On her journeys around the countryside, however, Earle saw numerous signs of economic and moral decline, which she wove into many of her books and articles as cautionary tales, usually in the guise of humor.

Her reappraisal of Puritanism, then, was grounded in a need for new social models to counter the ubiquitous evidence of its failure, both in individual New England families and in American society at large. Earle did not intend to reject her Puritan heritage, but rather wished to diminish the negative aspects of its influence. She could not embrace the historical precedent of total regulation that characterized early Puritan society; nor could she accept the idea of Calvinist determinism. She valued evidence that individual action, and perhaps a tradition of disorder, had also played a part in the formation of the American national character. She was preceded in this endeavor by a growing body of American intellectuals, including Hawthorne, Emerson, Melville, and Harriet Beecher Stowe. Lucius E. Chittenden, in an 1876 Fourth of July address, "The Character of the Early Settlers of Vermont—Its Influence upon Posterity," had stated: "Surely it will be to our advantage if we can find out the causes of [the settlers'] success. In those causes we may find the secrets of some of our failures."[69]

As Chittenden's words suggest, the American past was assuming increasing importance as a predictive source about the future. Puritanism, a significant part of that past, needed revising, however, before it could be useful as a model for the present. Puritan ideas were thought to be at once inspirational and intolerant, to nurture community values at the same time that they repressed individual will, to be a source of moral order as well as a mechanism for social control, to stimulate economic growth and economic ruthlessness simultaneously.[70] On balance, the negative aspects of Puritanism seemed to have a greater destructive potential than its positive elements could counteract, particularly with regard to economic behavior and the Protestant ethic. By the 1890s, evidences of greed and culturally destructive capitalist excess were present in the everyday landscape of most Americans. Earle's early work on Puritan culture must be viewed as part of a broader intellectual consensus that it was time to challenge the power of Puritanism, to discover new social and cultural dimensions to the Puritan past that could serve as more humane, more culturally beneficial models for the present.[71]

In a review of Earle's third book, *Customs and Fashions of Old New England,* published in 1893 as a companion volume to *The Sabbath in Puritan New England,* the Boston genealogist and legal scholar Daniel Rollins commented, "There will be a difference of opinion in regard to the value set by the author on the influence of Puritan belief and action on the history of our native land. While evidently meaning to be just in her estimate," Rollins continued, "there yet permeates her writings a spirit altogether too common at present among many of our writers, a spirit of depreciation of the grand work wrought by our Puritan ancestors in laying the foundations of our great Republic here in the wilds of the new world."[72]

Rollins's comments confirm the existence of a cultural struggle for control of the story of Puritanism. The traditional historical view, perpetuated by amateur and academic historians alike, emphasized great works and profound thoughts. The new attitude respected the Puritans' spiritual and intellectual contributions but also emphasized their physical vigor and their humanity, even their human frailties—a more compelling historical model for the new century. This reinterpretation of Puritanism was especially appealing to New Englanders, who had been experiencing a gradual cultural and demographic decline since the 1840s. Much of the new scholarship sought to reinstate New England, the cultural hearth of Puritanism, to its rightful place in the national order.[73]

The inscription on the title page of *Customs and Fashions of Old New England* confirmed the ambivalent tone detected by Rollins. Earle's ambivalence was born out of her progressive faith in the power of ancestry to interact productively with the opportunities of the present, and a consequent reluctance to dwell exclusively in the past. "Let us thank God," she wrote, "for having given us such ancestors; and let each successive generation thank him not less fervently, for being one step further from them in the march of ages."[74]

For Earle, the process of making the past useful for the present involved revising notions of Puritan personality and the facts of Puritan life to conform to her late-nineteenth-century understanding of human nature. For Earle and her peers, the austerity and country simplicity of Puritanism provided an antidote to the luxury of modern life. Puritanism could serve contemporary cultural needs without endangering the tradition of nineteenth-century individualism, and without imposing culturally unacceptable conceptions of destiny. This construct enabled Earle to embrace Puritanism as easily as she embraced her own family history, to use it as a corrective for the problems of her modern society without having to forgo the benefits of advanced civilization. The dismal lesson of "New England Kismet"—the tragedy of Puritan repressiveness gone awry—did not have to end inevitably in decay and decline, as Earle's own family history had demonstrated.

CHAPTER 4

The China Hunter

❦

THE SUCCESS OF ALICE MORSE EARLE'S FIRST BOOK, which sold more than ten thousand copies during its first year in print, and her growing popularity as a magazine writer led to the publication of a rapid succession of books and articles. Increasingly Earle's writings began to focus on the material culture of early America—an emerging trend. *China Collecting in America*, published in 1892, was her first attempt at categorization and contextualization of the artifacts of the past. Subsequently she became highly skilled at enhancing her historical narratives through the social and cultural analysis of artifacts. As reviews and book sales demonstrated, this approach resonated strongly with an audience of antique collectors; creators of historical societies, period rooms, and house restorations; as well as architects and designers of household furnishings and amateur and professional historians alike (fig. 11).

Moreover, in her new book, Earle extolled the personal benefits of china collecting, claiming that it heightened her emotional sensibilities. China hunting, she declared, offered "insights into human nature, love of my native country, knowledge of her natural beauties, acquaintance with her old landmarks and historical localities," and "admiration of her noble military and naval heroes."[1] This view of collecting as a therapeutic endeavor was shared by many middle-class men and women at the turn of the century as part of a larger antimodern outlook, which sought to remedy the

HOME DECORATION. [*Page* 420.

FIGURE 11. William Cowper Prime used this image as the frontispiece for *Pottery and Porcelain of All Times* (1878). The image suggests a cultural resonance for china far beyond its function as a container for liquids or a surface for eating. Earle's *China Collecting in America* would have resonated with a widespread desire to use ceramic objects to saturate family spaces with new kinds of visual complexity. Author's collection.

problems of industrialization and the breakdown of traditional institutions with authentic or historical activities and experiences.[2]

Briann Greenfield has argued that the rise of antiques collecting, period rooms, house restorations, and museum exhibitions of American artifacts served a desire to counter the perceptions of material and moral decline resulting from unfettered capitalism by constructing a new national narrative of restrained progress from a traditional "homespun" past, a goal Earle certainly shared. This phenomenon followed a defined trajectory, from artifacts serving on a symbolic level as "memory markers," embellishing historical pageants and house restorations, and reappearing as reproductions, to their ultimate transformation into national aesthetic treasures that formed the basis of an active consumer marketplace for antiques. The World's Columbian Exposition in 1893 stimulated a national desire to reconfigure the image of the United States as a world power, and along with that, to construct a new cultural identity of national superiority.[3] By 1900, cultural indications of this revival abounded. Americans could learn about colonial life in numerous magazine articles and books, including popular fiction that utilized the literary device of a colonial setting. They could also observe colonial life re-created in pageants, at the theater, and in the period rooms, historic houses, and gardens that had been appearing since the mid-century restoration of George Washington's headquarters at Hasbrouck House in Newburgh, New York. Washington's home at Mount Vernon opened to the public just before the Civil War. Both of these sites reflected the popular fascination with historical associations and environments. The power of place at Mount Vernon was sufficient to save it from destruction during the war. The antiquarian and Washington scholar Benson Lossing reported that although the Civil War had "raged at times with destructive energy in the vicinity of Mount Vernon, the most profound and reverential respect for the HOME OF WASHINGTON was shown by the soldiery of both parties."[4]

During the Civil War, generically "colonial" room settings became the focus of so-called sanitary fair exhibitions. The first of these, a New England kitchen, was constructed in Brooklyn for the Brooklyn and Long Island Sanitary Fair of 1864.[5] The organizing committee for the Brooklyn exhibition was composed of a number of people who, like Earle after them, were transplanted New Englanders. The Brooklyn kitchen was furnished with objects on loan from personal collections as well as artifacts collected in New England specifically for the fair.[6]

The hundredth anniversary, in 1876, of the signing of the Declaration of Independence stimulated widespread patriotic celebrations, the most notable being the International Centennial Exhibition in Philadelphia. For Earle personally, 1876 marked a pivotal moment in her life, with the birth of her first child. As a twenty-five-year-old wife and mother living in Brooklyn Heights, she was undoubtedly preoccupied with more immediate affairs, but the massive publicity about the events and exhibits in Philadelphia can hardly have escaped her notice. She later identified the Centennial Exhibition as "that turning-point in household art decoration in America."[7] Antiques—objects that embodied both age and heritage—began to coexist alongside newly fashioned household furnishings that looked "antique." In terms of her own life, her interest in history and the material culture of colonial America, as well as her later career as a historian and professional writer, stemmed, at least in part, from the events of 1876.

At the fair, the prevailing message offered to Centennial Exhibition visitors contrasted America's progress with the nation's past, expressed through numerous historical exhibits. Many of these offered a new historical perspective, one that focused on the domestic elements of the American past. At the Centennial Exhibition, the U.S. Patent Office presented George Washington's life as a collection of relics: his uniform, his sword and pistols, his camp kit, a table and chair, and other household items from Mount Vernon. The presence of these artifacts, which had once been held, worn, and valued by Washington himself, humanized him in ways that resonated with the fair's visitors far more than dry biographical accounts of his military campaigns. Their very ordinariness gave visitors a tangible way of relating the great hero to their own lives.[8]

Earle may well have attended the Philadelphia Centennial Exhibition in 1876, where colonial life in New England was re-created in the "New England Farmer's Home and Modern Kitchen." This exhibit constructed an entire house, with parlor, kitchen, and bedroom all furnished with New England antiquities donated for the purpose, according to one visitor's description.[9] The catalogue welcomed visitors to "Ye Olden Time" and detailed the exhibit's contents, categorizing the objects into five groups: kitchen, Revolutionary relics, dresser, bedroom, and a list of books. The kitchen, with its grand hearth, was equipped with "the first candle-mould used in Maine, 165 years ago"; an "old settle, always found in old-fashioned kitchens, home-spun garments hung on the back"; a "historic quilt" made of printed chintz that depicted "the Goddess of Liberty crowning Washington, and presenting at the altar of Liberty medallions of her illustrious sons"; a "kitchen cupboard, 150 years old, used at Cape Cod, Mass., and furnished with ancient crockery"; a "very small churn, used for goat's cream 200 years ago"; and a number of other curiosities.[10]

The Revolutionary relics on exhibit included an array of powder horns, the spurs of General John Stark, a sword that Nathan Barrett had used at the Battle of Concord, and other military memorabilia, including an "Indian Bow, taken from the Chief 'Little Bear,' Concord, 1760."[11] The Dresser, described in the catalogue as being "adorned with blue dishes, Lowestoft China, and ancient pewter platters and porringers," contained eleven items, some with associations to Lafayette, Paul Revere, and Mary Kendall (a *Mayflower* emigrant), as well as "a silver tankard which has been in the family of one of the ladies of the 'Log House' over 100 years."[12]

The bedroom seems to have been furnished as a colonial parlor—the more formal room in a hall and parlor house, which typically would have contained the bedstead as well as other important pieces of furniture. The array of items spanned two centuries, and in its arrangement suggested little attempt to maintain any standard of chronological purity. A "Pilgrim's Wall Pocket" coexisted with an eighteenth-century china cupboard, complete with an "old China Tea and Coffee pot and Tea Caddy," a "Glass Tumbler 125 years old," and the "First pair of Shoes made in Lynn, Mass." The shoes carried added significance for many of the visitors because, as one of the earliest American manufactured products, they implicitly expressed the massive changes wrought by industrialization in the nineteenth century, the contrast between "then" and "now."[13] Several of the items carried their genealogies with them to the exhibition, such as John Alden's desk, "brought over on the May Flower, 1620," owned by Dr. Samuel Alden of Bridgewater, Massachusetts, the seventh-generation descendent of John and Priscilla Alden. A linen sheet "spun and woven by Mrs. Betheah Southwick, 200 years ago" was also exhibited, with the identifying caption that it was "now owned by her granddaughter, Mrs. Boyce, of Lynn, Mass."[14]

The inclusion of books reinforced the didactic purpose of the exhibit. They ranged in content from religious tracts such as "Synopsis of Papism, 1634" and "The Gospel Way of Escaping the Doleful State of the Damned, 1729," to "Letters Writ by a Turkish Spy, 1770," William Penn's *No Cross,*

No Crown, and *The History of America from Its Discovery to the Death of Washington.*[15]

Unlike the exhibits at predecessor sanitary fairs, the New England kitchen at the Philadelphia Centennial was viewed by hundreds of thousands of visitors. After the fair closed, the momentum it had generated continued to spawn interest in the domestic artifacts and social customs of colonial New England. A similar exhibit was constructed in Chicago in 1893 on the Midway Plaisance of the World's Columbian Exposition. It offered visitors the same combination of relics, contexts, and costumed interpreters serving food and demonstrating colonial crafts which had proved so successful in Philadelphia. One wonders how Earle, who visited the White City in May after its opening, responded to the exhibit, which she surely must have seen.[16]

For those who could not make it to Philadelphia, the press reported on and illustrated the exhibits widely, especially the popular "New England Farmer's Home and Kitchen." Readers could absorb the specific details of the furnishings from these illustrations: gourds hanging on the chimney; a broad hearth strewn with iron pots, grills, toasters, and other implements, at which a kneeling woman prepared food over an open flame; women spinning wool, churning butter, and rolling out pie dough; and on the back wall a dresser laden with plates, cups, pitchers, and pots.[17]

Within a year, the sense of the historical moment implicit in 1876 coupled with a growing nationalistic interest in American-made rather than imported goods ultimately resulted in a new style for interior furnishings as well as a desire to reclaim the indigenous goods of the past before they disappeared forever. "Antiquing" in general had become a popular activity for wealthier Americans beginning around 1850, and china—whether rough pottery or highly refined porcelain—became an object of desire for collectors after the Centennial. By the end of the century, the interest in antiques had blossomed into a full-blown colonial revival, fed by the establishment of historical societies, museum exhibitions, historic preservation societies, and an active network of antique dealers, merchants who specialized in procuring and marketing the stuff of the past.[18] Antiquarians, at least since the Renaissance, had collected artifacts for both their aesthetic value and their political associations. It was not until the nineteenth century, however, and particularly under the spell of the 1876 Philadelphia Centennial Exhibition, that antiquarians began actively studying

American objects for their value as "antiques."[19] The first books about collecting American antiques were published in the 1870s, and the first store featuring American antiques opened during that same decade. According to the popular women's magazine *Godey's Lady's Book* in 1878, antiquing had become "the latest mania." By 1893, in the preface to *Through Colonial Doorways,* author Anne Hollingsworth Wharton could write, "The revival of interest in Colonial and Revolutionary times has become a marked feature of the life of to-day."[20]

Robert and Elizabeth Shackleton expressed the importance of collecting to the development of the colonial revival in their popular book *The Quest of the Colonial,* first published in 1906. The authors traced the beginnings of their personal interest in colonial America to the acquisition of a copper kettle, a pair of brass candlesticks, and a Shaker chair.[21] "There is, as yet," they reported to their readers, "no essential scantiness of supply of the delightful and desirable old! There is just enough of scantiness to render the quest alluring."[22] The Shackletons were part of a widespread community of collectors who scoured the American countryside looking for antiques. Earle had detailed her own jaunts through New York and New England in pursuit of "old blue," Chinese porcelain, and innumerable other scarce ceramic treasures in *China Collecting in America.* Stories of her successes, such as the six Chinese ginger jars she found "in a hen house on an inland farm on Long Island," must have both tantalized and encouraged her readers. The jars, "after being pumped upon for a long season at the horse-pump, and swept off vigorously with a birch broom, . . . revealed their original glories of color." Finally, "after a thorough cleansing and disinfecting," the prizes, fully expunged of their recent rusticity, "now grace teak-wood cabinets in New York homes."[23]

The dynamics of collecting those antiques, however, could prove challenging to middle-class morality, particularly with regard to the social relations implicit in the act of collecting. In *Sun-Dials and Roses of Yesterday* (1902), Addy Dean, a Connecticut Valley farmer's wife, observed to Earle that although she came from a long tradition of self-sufficient housewifery, she had become far "shrewder than her grandmother." As Earle noted, "to raise eggs to sell is far less work to the farm-wife than to make butter; and selling antiques is more profitable than either." Dean had been "clever enough ten years ago to discover, even on that isolated farm, through the queries of the collectors for antique dealers, that there was an opening for her to make money." She set up a showroom in the village, in the house of a friend, "where she can display any unusual piece of furniture or china which she has found ... to catch the eye of the summer visitor, and thus tole him or her to the isolated Dean Farm and further purchases." Earle confirmed the success of this strategy with the observation that "we are apt to fancy that we secure great treasures if we purchase them from lonely farmhouses."[24]

Although Earle's book poked fun at herself and her urban collecting community, her relations with Dean were different from those she had experienced with the New England farmwives whose pantries she had been raiding ten years earlier. Dean was an active member of Earle's trading network, as well as a kind of "living informant" who could provide Earle with direct access to a disappearing culture; for that, Earle accorded her a level of respect that her earlier victims had not received.[25] Earle's observations about Dean, however, ignored the circumstances that made Dean's antique dealing possible and necessary. Although Earle was sympathetic to Dean and greatly admired her ambition and perseverance, her easy relegation of Dean to the realm of the "picturesque" reveals that Earle had little or no direct knowledge of the realities of farming in early-twentieth-century New England. By objectifying her, Earle in a sense collected Dean along with her treasures, transforming her into a literary metaphor that could be integrated into Earle's own urban social agenda.

Earle's antique-hunting successes were not limited to the countryside, however, as she demonstrated with her story about a rare Bow goat cream jug, found by a young woman collector in a New York City antique shop for a dollar.[26] By 1900, New York, Boston, Philadelphia, and other large cities were full of antique dealers. The Manhattan Antique Store, at 394 Fourth Avenue, advertised its 1901 stock as including "Colonial Furniture, Historical Blue and White China, Old Arms, Bronzes and Bric-a-Brac, Old Chelsea Figures, Paintings, and Engravings."[27] Another Manhattan dealer, Arthur True, had died recently, and the ensuing estate auction, conducted by W. S. Macy, his surviving partner, listed 2,900 lots, a full litany of desirable collectibles, including "Colonial Furniture, Hall and Mantle Chime Clocks, Mirrors, Old English Silver, Antique Jewelry, Sheffield Plate, Paintings, Old Engravings, Relics, Autograph Letters, Brass, Copper and Pewterware, Andirons, Fenders, Banjo Clocks, a renowned offering of Old China; also the most remarkable collection of rare Old Historical Blue and White Plates and Platters in Existence."[28]

The Boston Antique China Exchange, at 3½ Bromfield Street, published a photograph of the interior of its shop in its advertisement, enticing customers with visions of sprig ware, Bohemian glass, pressed glass decanters—some in the desirable "Ashburton" pattern—as well as molded English stoneware jugs, Astral lamps, Liverpool pitchers, and the ubiquitous blue and white transfer-printed earthenware plates, hanging on the wall in plate holders (fig. 12).[29] Another Boston dealer, Albert J. Hill, advertised that he had been doing business since 1860 at 8 and 9 Hamilton Place.[30] Frederick Forehand, who had recently moved to Boston from Worcester, announced in his advertisement that he offered certain "rare and valuable pieces, illustrated in Frances C. Morse's new book on Colonial Furniture."[31] Forehand's reference to the book by Earle's sister, Frances, effectively embellished the pedigree of the items he was trying to sell. In the hierarchy of objects, those deemed worthy enough on some level to be elevated to the realm of print (if only by virtue of their accessibility to the author) were ranked above more anonymous objects. Books about collectibles, then, could provide yet another level of validation for the legitimacy of a particular object, and many new publications appeared after the turn of the century to accommodate that cultural need.

Macmillan had published *Furniture of the Olden Time* in 1902, after a great deal of lobbying by Earle on behalf of her sister. Earle apparently envisioned her literary mission as a family enterprise. As early as 1900 she had proposed to Scribner's that Morse write a book on historical china, which Earle envisioned as a complement to her own *China Collecting in America*. Morse's book would be illustrated with halftone photoengravings, augmenting some of the images already made for *China Collecting* with new photographs of recently discovered rare examples; it would retail for no more than a dollar and a half. Earle cited Dodd, Mead's recently published *Pictures of Early New York on Dark Blue Staffordshire Pottery* by R. T. Haines Halsey as an example of the existing literature on the subject. Halsey's book, as Earle noted, was "very costly"; at fifty dollars a copy, the distribution would necessarily be extremely limited. Earle also mentioned Edwin Atlee Barber's book *Anglo-American Pottery*, which she termed a "miserable little list," also available at a dollar and a half, as the most direct competition. Morse, Earle claimed, "is known everywhere as a collector and authority upon china. She writes well, and is far more competent to do the book than I should be," though Earle assured Scribner's, "I should

FIGURE 12. Advertisement for the Boston Antique China Exchange, from *Old China* magazine (December 1901). Customers browsing through the shop could easily envision an array of blue and white plates hanging on their own parlor or dining room walls.

of course work with her, advise, assist, &c."[32] Scribner's responded negatively to Earle's proposal, reminding her that her own book—which they had published—was still in print, and "a considerable portion, you will remember . . . dealt with historical china and we should hardly care to bring out another book which covered this same ground even if it did treat the subject more fully."[33]

Earle next approached Macmillan, her current publisher, about another project for her sister. "For some time past," she wrote in 1901 to Macmillan president George Brett, "I have been urging my sister, Miss Frances Morse of Worcester, to write a book upon colonial furniture. She had been solicited to write upon Historic Homes of New England," Earle noted, "but refused," adding, "Then we heard that Doubleday Page and Co. were to bring out a book 'Furniture of Our Forefathers'—by Esther Singleton." Earle expressed serious doubts about Singleton's competence to write such a book, having read some of her magazine articles. These, Earle felt, "displayed much ignorance." The advertising for Singleton's book had borne out Earle's reservations, featuring "a piano-forte—far from an old one, shown as a *spinet*—which is a very different instrument." The error was compounded by the fact that the book had been published in New York, "a city which has the very best collection of musical instruments in the world, the one at the Metropolitan Museum of Art given by Mr. and Mrs. Crosby Brown."[34]

The Furniture of Our Forefathers and Dr. Irving Whitall Lyon's *Colonial Furniture of New England: A Study of the Domestic Furniture in Use in the Seventeenth and Eighteenth Centuries,* which had been published in 1891, were, according to Earle, the only published sources on colonial furniture.[35] Lyon's book, however, was expensive: it had initially cost ten or twelve dollars (Earle was uncertain which) and was currently for sale on the out-of-print market for fifty dollars.[36] And Singleton's book, as Earle pointed out repeatedly to Brett, was also expensive (it retailed for sixteen dollars), as well as unwieldy in its eight-book structure and haphazard topical arrangement.[37] Most damning, however, was its unreliability. A friend of Earle's, who was "not an expert, nor did she pretend to any profound knowledge, just a lover of old furniture," had found "16 errors and absurdities in the first part alone" and had demanded a refund from Doubleday.[38] "The fact is Miss Singleton has written the book too hurriedly," wrote Earle dismissively—an ironic complaint from her, given the rate of her own production. "It needs *years* to prepare for such a book. Dr. Lyon was 12 years making ready for his limited book."[39]

This exchange reveals much about Earle's sense of herself as a professional and an expert. Through her denunciation of Singleton, Earle was further establishing her own expertise. Professionalism, whether among historians, authors, or antiquarians, demanded an aggressive adherence to "standards" as a means of maintaining both personal and group authority. In her relationship with her publishers especially, Earle rarely relaxed her insistence that she be accorded the degree of professional deference that she expected.

Earle assured Macmillan that her sister was well qualified to write about furniture and that the book would be organized according to a strictly functional scheme. Macmillan editor W. S. Booth reported to Brett Earle's conception that the book "be divided into subject rather than into periods," and listed wall furniture, floor furniture, hall furniture, dining room furniture, withdrawing room furniture, and bedroom furniture as possible subjects. "Miss Morse is a first rate woman for this book," he added. "She is widely travelled & a capital writer & has a very exact and intimate knowledge of the subject." Furthermore, to assuage any hesitation on account of Morse's lack of authorial experience, Booth noted: "Mrs. Earle & her sister are almost joint writers of this book. They are planning it together." The book was to be about three or four hundred pages in length, approximately the same height and width as Earle's *Stage Coach and Tavern Days,* and would sell for "a popular price." In terms of its market position, "it is to be as far as possible from the Singleton book: every page of which has several childish blunders," reported Booth, noting that Doubleday had had to reset much of the first two parts "and are dejected about the whole thing. . . . Miss Singleton is a tyro at furniture."[40]

Brett apparently agreed with Booth's recommendations, and within a week, Morse had a contract for the furniture book. The publication of *Furniture of the Olden Time* in November 1902 added significantly to the existing literature on colonial American furnishings and, by providing yet another roadmap to the past, must have further stimulated the growing urge to collect. An advertisement in *Old China* identified several more books that could be added to the collector's shelf: Frederick Litchfield's *Pottery and Porcelain: A Guide to Collectors* and *History of Furniture,* W. P. Jervis's *Encyclopedia of Ceramics,* William Chaffers's *Marks and Monograms,* and Llewellynn Jewitt's *Ceramic Art of Great Britain.*[41] As the decade progressed, N. Hudson Moore focused on collectible metal wares in his *Old Pewter,* published in 1905, and also on furniture, in his *Old Furniture Book.*[42]

Other works in print that catered particularly to collectors included Edwin Atlee Barber's *American Glassware, Old and New,* published in 1900, and Luke Vincent Lockwood's *Colonial Furniture in America,* first published in 1901.[43] Surprisingly, Earle never mentioned the existence of Lockwood's book to her publisher, although she must have been aware of it. Lockwood lived in Brooklyn, and her old publisher, Charles Scribner's Sons, published his work. Perhaps she found less to criticize in

Lockwood's work—which employed the same topological organization as Morse's book—or perhaps because Lockwood was a more prestigious scholar, she felt reluctant to engage him in a contest of expertise.

A flurry of magazine articles further educated collectors during this era, appearing in specialty magazines such as *Old China* as well as in more general-interest magazines. *Country Life in America* advertised its "Collector's Exchange" column as "a well established and very attractive feature" of the magazine. The column provided readers with information about such topics as old china, jewelry, antique silver, old furniture, rare books, and "Art Curiosities of Every Sort."[44] *Country Life* also printed numerous articles about restoring old houses—rescuing them from degradation, as well as decorating to achieve a "colonial" look.

In the early twentieth century, interest in antiques had begun to spawn specialized collecting organizations, an impulse that gained momentum during the ensuing years.[45] Earle and other writers about colonial antiquing had constantly reminded their readers of the importance of self-education. The bucolic pleasure of searching the countryside for colonial relics could potentially be marred by an encounter with an antique dealer who was less than scrupulous about the provenance or authenticity of the objects offered. The Shackletons devoted an entire chapter to "Fakes: How to Recognize Them," advising their readers that "in learning to discriminate between the genuine and the imitation the old-furniture collector comes to see that there is much to consider and that constant watchfulness is necessary."[46] Earle had discussed the problem in *China Collecting* in 1892, relating a story about a dealer planting modern fakes in a country auction held in an old house in New Hampshire's White Mountains. In anticipation of unsuspecting summer tourists, who would presumably be lured to the sale, the dealer purchased "modern willow pattern ware, freshly imported Canton china, new copper luster and painted teasets." He then carefully "placed the crockery in the cupboards, the brand-new brass candlesticks on the mantles, and the flimsy new andirons in the old fireplaces, arranged all the furniture in judicious shadow, and had a successful auction of 'rare old colonial furniture and family china.'"[47]

The summer travelers who were duped by this ploy were, of course, the urban middle class. Earle used this story to construct a moral tale about issues of survival and entitlement, and the impact of capitalist values on the benign countryside. For her readers to be entitled to own old things, they had to make themselves knowledgeable. Her colonial prescriptions demanded authenticity, a quality that was inextricably linked to the idea of expertise. For Earle, then, expertise had both a personal and a cultural dimension: in a personal sense, she depended on expertise to confirm her professional status; in a cultural sense, expertise could provide an alternative to social decline. Even the most knowledgeable collectors, however, were not exempt from the wiles of the marketplace. Earle herself was duped by an antique dealer posing as a farmer, from whom she purchased a sundial. At the time of purchase, she had seen some china and luster-ware that aroused her suspicions, but she had no time to investigate without missing her train. "At the station I had one minute to interview a stage driver," she recounted. "'How long has Ellis lived on his place up the road,' I said. 'About a year,' was the answer. 'Hasn't he a sundial for sale?' I ventured diplomatically. 'Don't know as he has; he sold it last week.' Now if he sold his sundial last week," Earle wondered, "from whence came my dial? My friends believe the dial is an old one," she mused, "but I think Farmer Ellis is a broken-down city dealer with an attic full of new dials cast in some mold or stamped with some old die, ever ready to replace the recently sold one in the kitchen yard."[48]

The possibility of fraud and its inherent risk may have heightened the experience of collecting for some. Earle's characterization of the culprit as a "broken-down city dealer" exposes the debilitating effects of the city (in this case Boston), even in the countryside. Although stories such as these did not appear in all of Earle's books—both *China Collecting* and *Sun-Dials* were targeted at collectors—they helped to define the social and demographic composition of Earle's audience as middle-class urbanites who may have assumed themselves to be well educated and therefore incapable of being duped. It was not traditional rural New Englanders who were the problem—even if Addy Dean did stretch the truth a bit now and then. The problem stemmed, rather, from city people posing as country folk, thus necessitating the warning *caveat emptor*—let the buyer beware. While the notion of warranty had doubtless existed even in the face-to-face transactions of colonial society, Earle seemed to be implying that the facts of modern urban life had made it an essential component of any transaction.

Earle apparently did not judge her own acquisitive practices by the same standards she applied to the antique dealers. She related her exploits in the countryside quite gleefully, as she tricked, wheedled, and sometimes even bullied rural New Englanders out of their ancestral goods. Her bi-furcated view of traditional rural people, represented by Addy Dean on the one hand, ennobled by her recognition of the value of the past, and the ignorance of those who held what Earle perceived as *her* cultural inheri-tance on the other, fed into a broader cultural need to mediate between a vision of a lost Arcadia and the reality of modern urban life. Addy Dean represented an alternative to the rural New Englander's destiny: she had made herself an expert.

Moreover, Earle never indicated any concern that the act of purchas-ing antiques might be construed as an attempt to create a family heritage that was inherently false. These eagerly sought objects, after all, repre-sented *someone else's* family heritage. Several generations of urban life had strengthened the views of the middle and upper classes about the neces-sity for artifice in all forms of social presentation, and had, by the end of the nineteenth century, obviated many lingering moral concerns about the hypocrisy of that behavior.[49]

In Worcester, Alice Morse Earle's hometown (where her parents and sister still lived), a group of women with leisure time and disposable income founded the China Hunter's Club in the wake of the Centen-nial. Members included Annie Trumbull Slossen, whose brother Gurdon Trumbull was described by the Hartford collector Henry Wood Erving as "one of the very earliest real collectors of old china."[50] Slossen's artist sister Mrs. William Cowper Prime of New York City also collected china; Erving commented that she was "probably the first person in this country, certainly the first woman, to collect china systematically." In 1878 Slossen published a history of the China Hunter's Club, in which she advanced the idea that collecting china had important implications for the future of the nation. "The country home had almost always bright and beauti-ful table furniture," she wrote, "and the family must have enjoyed it and lingered around it. Probably, on that account, domestic influences, home thoughts, and family thoughts had more influence on men in those days." Slossen argued that the currently fashionable white crockery had no such influence over men. She equated "womanly characteristics of gentleness, kindness, and all kinds of loveliness" with "a pretty tea-service," conclud-ing, "Men under the influence of such women, and such cheerful home associations, are always better citizens."[51]

The same year that Slossen published her history of the China Hunters, her brother-in-law Dr. William C. Prime published a massive and authoritative history of ceramics, *Pottery and Porcelain of All Times and Nations*. Prime began with an assertion about the growing ranks of collectors who would be his audience: "Ten years ago there were probably not ten collectors of Pottery and Porcelain in the United States. To-day there are perhaps ten thousand."⁵² Among that ten thousand were certainly Alice Morse Earle and her sister Frances, although perhaps not quite as early as 1878. By 1892, however, Earle had amassed a collection of china that was sizable enough to enable her to publish her own book, *China Collecting in America*.⁵³

China Collecting in America, which Earle dedicated "To the Companion of my China Haunts, My Sister, Frances Clary Morse," departed in both style and form from her previous book, *The Sabbath in Puritan New England*. Beginning with the cover (fig. 13), which was embellished with a three-color image of a Delftware charger, the book utilized visual as well as textual evidence throughout. The first of Earle's photographically illustrated books, *China Collecting* included sixty-six images of ceramic objects—sometimes in situ, artfully installed in dressers, corner cupboards, and on the top of highboys, and sometimes alone (fig. 14). For Earle, china collecting was a gendered activity, particularly appealing to women. She opened her first chapter with a quotation from Charles Lamb's *Essays of Elia*, where he stated, "I have an almost feminine partiality for old china."⁵⁴

The idea of china collecting as a feminine pursuit was grounded in three separate cultural notions. First, the ceramic objects being collected had inherent physical characteristics that reinforced conceptions of gender. They were intricate, small in scale, fragile, pale in color, sometimes translucent, and often precious. These attributes placed most pottery and porcelain collectibles in a cultural category that would have seemed feminine to Earle and her peers. Moreover, as Beverly Gordon has argued, objects imply or demand different social distances that have gendered implications. The larger the object, the greater the social distance required for viewing, and the more masculine the gender implications. China teacups, by contrast, beg to be viewed at close range, at an intimate, and therefore feminine, social distance.⁵⁵

A second cultural notion related to the kinds of collectible objects made from pottery and porcelain, functional objects traditionally associated with

FIGURE 13. *China Collecting in America* (1892) was Earle's first photographically illustrated book. The cover alone, with this colorful design of a Delft-like plate, could have lured scores of prospective china hunters.

women's household roles. The diverse array of plates, cups, saucers, pitchers, tea caddies, coffeepots, cream jugs, and saltcellars that Earle illustrated all operated within a female domestic sphere, supporting the care, feeding, and entertainment of family and guests. Women, as users and choosers of these goods, shaped the very characteristics that made them so desirable for collectors. Beginning with Josiah Wedgwood in the late eighteenth century, manufacturers of ceramic wares had been increasingly sensitive to the demands of the marketplace, and by the era of the early American republic, that marketplace had become part of a female domain.[56]

FIGURE 14. "A Beaufet," from *China Collecting in America* (1892). Earle used an eighteenth-century term to describe this cupboard, no doubt to enhance its antiquity and value as a household furnishing. Such built-in cupboards afforded multiple opportunities for displaying gentility and taste. They were clearly part of the fabric of a room, suggesting longevity and endurance, not something newly purchased for impression. The scalloped shelves displayed a variety of ceramic, glass, silver, and pewter table and tea wares in artful arrangements, ideal for close-up viewing.

The third cultural notion that "feminized" china collecting derived from the aesthetic function of these objects and the high value placed on household environments as social devices in the nineteenth century. Exhibited as household art, ceramic plates hung on the wall or vases and pots arranged on a mantel shelf or corner cupboard seemed to have a mystical power to educate and civilize the occupants of the house (see fig. 14). Women of Earle's generation knew that the creation of aesthetically pleasing environments was a crucial domestic responsibility. Inspired by the preaching of Horace Bushnell and other ministers and educational theorists, household advice literature had begun to stress this most important function for women as early as the 1830s, and by 1890 the idea was fully integrated into cultural conceptions of gender identity. In Deerfield, Massachusetts, Frary House, created by local women and opened in 1892, contained an array of artifacts, including china, that expressed a domestic, moral agenda.[57] As Gordon has shown, women's collecting activities were invested with intimacy and aesthetically saturated experiences. In contrast to men, who collected to fulfill categories or accomplish other specific goals, women used their collections to create period room settings or enhance a social event (such as a tea or dinner party). China lent itself particularly to these food-centered social events by aestheticizing their service and settings.[58]

Both William Prime and Alice Morse Earle incorporated instructions for decorating with china into their china collecting guides, urging readers to hang their plates on the wall in a pleasing arrangement. Prime included instructions for fabricating a wall-hanging plate holder out of twisted wire, as well as an illustration. Earle, however, objected to Prime's design because "it requires for its manufacture a wire workman or a tinker, either amateur or professional, with tools of various kinds, and a neatly made spiral cylinder of wire. This places the possibility of manufacturing Mr. Prime's holder quite out of the reach of the average woman." But Earle had a solution to this problem. "I too have invented a holder," she announced, "and it can be made by any woman," using sewing scissors and "feminine materials" including dress hooks, twine, thread, or picture wire. A final advantage of her design over Prime's was that it was cheaper. She urged her readers to use these holders to hang their dark blue transfer-printed plates on the wall to enrich the interior decoration of their homes.[59]

Decorating with old china recurred as a secondary theme throughout Earle's book on china collecting, but her main purpose in writing the book was to offer a systematic overview of pottery and porcelain made or used in America, from the pre-Columbian era into the nineteenth century. She discussed the antecedents to ceramic wares and then proceeded to map the progress of ceramic production through time. She couched her interest in pottery and porcelain in terms of her own experiences as a "china hunter," interjecting personal accounts into her chronology. Lest her readers dismiss china hunting as frivolous, she offered a defense of her activities, arguing that history could be rather dull when learned from books, but the narratives depicted on china made history come alive. Important lessons could be learned from china hunting, including the history of leading figures and social lessons about the development of table manners; insights into New England country life and human nature could be intuited through the act of collecting; geographical lessons could be absorbed during the search for more china; and finally, as a plus, Americans could learn about English history, since most of the china used in America originated in England.[60]

Earle discussed the activity of china hunting extensively, advising her readers to engage in "authentic" collecting rather than purchasing their china from shops, for the emotional stimulation which she perceived as a benefit of the act of searching and negotiating would be lost otherwise.[61] She proposed numerous strategies for dealing with the New England farmers and their wives who possessed the objects of her quest: listen carefully, avoid disappointment by avoiding preconceptions, don't purchase by proxy but rather examine the object carefully in person, and prepare for the pursuit of china as if preparing for a battle. Collecting for Earle was clearly exhilarating. "For myself," she wrote, "I never hear the words 'old china' but my heart is moved, more than 'with the sound of a trumpet.'"[62]

The passion for old china moved Earle in other directions, too, away from traditional assumptions about ladylike behavior. "China hunting is not an ennobling pursuit," she admitted. She felt that the act of acquisition was a contest, one that she was "wickedly waiting" to win. To that end, she was willing to engage in trickery, mild deception, and sometimes outright lying. She urged her readers to deal with men whenever possible and to avoid their wives—who would presumably be less willing to part with their possessions than their unsuspecting husbands. Another strategy she admitted to having used was telling the owner of an object she wanted that the item was a missing link in her own family's set. Apparently this ruse persuaded more than one farmwife to part with a Chinese porcelain bowl or Spode plate. Above all, she urged her readers not to hurry. Be patient: country people do not operate at the same pace as city folk and might be put off by pressure to sell.

Once these acquisitions were brought home, Earle had advice about how to display them. "It is a matter of course that this old china should show to its best advantage in an old-fashioned house," she wrote, or at the very least "a new house built in 'American colonial' style of architecture." Two key pieces of furniture would greatly improve the display of a china collection: a corner cupboard and a dresser. Earle illustrated both in *China Collecting*, noting that the corner cupboard "seems to be, like all old-fashioned furniture, well adapted for the express purpose for which it was made." She contrasted this form with what she termed "a modern pattern combination china-closet, washstand, and refrigerator all in one," greatly preferring the former for "china holding and china showing."[63] Her implicit critique here of modern industrial production would have resonated with her readers in 1892.[64] The objectionable item to which Earle referred was perhaps the "Acme Combined Dry Air Refrigerator and Sideboard," offered by Sears, Roebuck & Company in various grades of oak and levels of complexity. Sears described it as "a combination of sideboard, refrigerator, and water cooler," claiming it was "suitable for a well furnished dining room."[65]

With the publication of *China Collecting*, Earle significantly advanced the scholarship about ceramic wares made or used in America. She included a catalogue of known designs and forms, tying sections of the catalogue to specific chapters. The catalogue began in an appropriately patriotic manner, with designs relating to George Washington as they were used on various objects. These commemorative items ranged from Liverpool pitchers, plaques, and medallions to Staffordshire transfer-printed wares, Wedgwood basalt and cameo wares, Parian wares, Continental pieces, works by Ralph Wood, and Chinese export "Canton" wares. Earle may have owned some of the items she recorded, but a large number of them came from the Huntington Collection at the Metropolitan Museum of Art in New York, as she noted in her catalogue entries. Item number one in the catalogue was "Washington Head from Stuart's Portrait."[66] This printed design, after Gilbert Stuart's portrait made for the marquis of Lansdowne, appeared on Liverpool oval plaques and pitchers. After Washington, Earle continued in the same vein, listing wares related to Franklin and Lafayette.

She devoted an entire chapter to the blue and white transfer-printed wares from the Staffordshire potteries, commenting, "No ceramic specimens are of more interest to the American china collector than the pieces of dark blue Staffordshire crockery that were manufactured in such vast variety of design, and were imported in such great numbers to America in the early years of this century."[67] She considered these wares to be highly desirable and regaled her readers with stories about her own adventures in pursuit of "old blue." The primary appeal of Staffordshire wares lay in their rich cobalt coloration and in their pictorial depictions of historic American events, people, and places. Not all Staffordshire wares, however, were created equal. Those lighter-colored designs, produced in pale blue, pink, green, brown, and lavender from around 1830 on, Earle judged to be "degraded," although they, along with "English views," could be "exceeding useful as wall decorations."[68]

China Collecting in America recorded the history of collecting as it unfolded, especially with regard to American historical wares. As a collector herself, Earle had eagerly followed the pursuit of new information about these objects. She knew that there was little information available from the potteries in England, primarily because of numerous changes of ownership. She was also aware that American historical china, so revered by American collectors, was not present in English collections, nor was it for sale in England. To remedy that, Earle mentioned "that a collection of Staffordshire ware bearing both American and English views is now being gathered in America for presentation to the Museum in Burslem, and consequent enlightenment of English collectors and manufacturers." Exhorting her fellow American collectors to "unite and form a new table of marks of 'American pieces,'" she began that process by listing all of the maker's marks in her own Staffordshire collection.[69]

As a conclusion to *China Collecting*, Earle listed and evaluated the important public and private ceramic collections in the United States. This list, which suggests the breadth of her research, included the Museum of the East India Marine Company in Salem, as well as the Essex Institute, the Bostonian Society, the Historical Society of Pennsylvania, Deerfield's Memorial Hall, the Connecticut Historical Society, and what she termed "the various societies of antiquity, and local associations throughout New England."[70] She lamented that the East India Marine Museum had been transformed in recent years by "an arranger, a labeler, and a model cataloguer" who had "ruthlessly invaded the dusty shelves and weeded out the boxes of dried-up and shriveled fruits, the skins of moth-eaten birds, and of seedy and disreputable fishes."These "iconoclasts," as she referred to the modernizing curators, "have prosaically separated each old sea-captain's relics into parcels and placed them in wonderfully well-arranged and classified cases. . . . The old-time glamour, the 'unstudied grace' of the museum was gone."[71] Ironically, Earle herself had just written an entire book that attempted to classify and make rational sense of prevailing information about ceramics; but this statement suggests the romantic core of her passion for objects from the past. Without human narrative suggested by their original historical context, for Earle the objects seemingly lost some of their innate power. That power was essential to Earle for the fulfillment of her larger cultural mission. Love of artifacts might be the bait, but understanding the emotional and social relevance of history was the goal.

In *China Collecting in America,* Earle probed the limits of an increasingly ethnographic historical methodology, which supplemented traditional archival sources with material evidence. Perhaps she was inspired by the work of the anthropologist Franz Boas, who has been credited with introducing the idea of fieldwork as a research method.[72] Moreover, studying and collecting folklore was closely associated with women's missionary work in the American South. Early folklorists were often involved in social enterprises aimed at community building and economic uplift through traditional craft production. Finally, because of the prevailing notion that women had special skills that gave them access to informants in the field unavailable to men, women were accorded greater stature in the newly emerging anthropological profession than in other disciplines.[73]

Earle was well aware of the emerging discipline of folklore through her relationship with the American Folklore Society. Her china studies coincided with the formation and early development of the society; she had written for its journal and would have been familiar with the theories and debates about research methods that it published. Modeled after the Folk-Lore Society, organized in England in 1878 "for the preservation and publication of popular traditions, legends, ballads, local proverbial sayings, superstitions, and old customs," the American Society was founded in 1888 by a group of scholars that included the pioneering anthropologists Franz Boas and Alice Cunningham Fletcher as well as the literary scholar William Wells Newell, whose work included *Games and Songs of American Childhood* (1883), a study the predated Earle's own book on the history of childhood by sixteen years. As editor of the society's journal, Newell laid out four specific scholarly areas to be covered, including "Relics of Old English Folk-Lore (ballads, tales, superstitions, dialect, etc.)," as well as the "Lore" of African Americans and Native Americans, and of French Canada and Mexico. He expressed particular concern about the first category, which included ballads, nursery rhymes, children's games, and local dialects. "If they are not gathered while there is time," he urged, "they will soon be absorbed into the uniformity of the written language."[74]

Although Earle never joined the American Folk-Lore Society, she was a member of the English Folk-Lore Society. Her documented relationship with the American organization dates from 1891, when she queried the members about several arcane linguistic usages. The following year Earle published a brief article, titled "Waste-Basket of Words," in which she discussed a collection of obscure culinary terms found in the 1656 household "receipt" (recipe) book of England's Queen Henrietta Maria. The original seventeenth-century volume, "The Queen's Closet Opened," was the subject of an article Earle had written the previous year. Subsequently her books were regularly reviewed in the journal, and she published several additional research articles.[75]

In a frenzy of fieldwork propelled by the possibility of collecting both objects and memories, Earle scoured the countryside, seeking out the material remains of seventeenth- and eighteenth-century New England. In one instance Earle, with the help of a "Yankee china dealer," concocted an intricate plan to represent herself and her sister as relatives of a Republican gubernatorial candidate in an effort to gain entry to "Farmer Rice's" and buy his wife's prized English tea set. Upon learning that Farmer Rice was in fact a "bitter Democrat," Earle commented, "This was a sharp blow, for neither he nor we knew one thing about the private life of a Democratic candidate." The sisters persevered, however, studying a newspaper for useful details, "and invented an imaginary home for the Democratic Governor," for which the coveted tea set was supposedly intended, as well as drilling each other "on the strong points on Free Trade and Protection." In the end, the plan failed. According to Earle's story of the collecting adventure, they awakened "a very deaf old lady from a very sound nap" and were given only the briefest glimpse of the prize.[76]

On the one hand, Earle's fascination with collecting might be interpreted as mere antiquarian pursuit. She was writing about the American colonial past during the last decade of the nineteenth century and the first decade of the twentieth, a time when interest in both ancestors and their material relics ran high. On the other hand, when viewed in a metaphoric sense, china collecting seems to have been emblematic of a much broader pursuit for Earle—the pursuit of her own vanishing New England past. Discussing her personal philosophy of history in a speech to the Daughters of the American Revolution in 1899, Earle pointed toward a crucial linkage between intimate familiarity with vernacular detail, which would have been provided by the hundreds of objects she had encountered in her collecting jaunts, and the generation of broader historical questions and cultural understanding.[77] This educational philosophy was clearly articulated in *China Collecting in America*, where she commented that her ongoing "study of the ancient manners, customs, and traditions of [America's] early inhabitants have all been fostered, strengthened, and indeed almost brought into existence by the search after and study of old china."[78]

Earle's first two books achieved for her a certain amount of acclaim. This was important, because the inclinations that made it possible for Earle to become a meticulous researcher and prolific writer also caused problems. Her correspondence reveals that she was frequently troubled by the conflicting demands of home and family and her career as a writer. Still, there was her success. In 1896 the historian and *Dial* reviewer Francis W. Shepardson included her in a list of authors he felt were responsible for the recent rise of scholarly interest in history, along with Henry Cabot Lodge, William Babcock Weeden, William Root Bliss, Henry M. Brooks, Anne Hollingsworth Wharton, and Maude Wilder Goodwin. He speculated that while the original impulse came, "no doubt," from John Richard Green's work in English history, it was also "greatly stimulated by the formation and growth of patriotic heredity societies."[79] This new audience, of which Earle was a part as a member of both the Society of Colonial Dames and the Daughters of the American Revolution, created a demand for all sorts of books about history, historical settings, and historical artifacts.[80]

As she evolved into a professional writer, Earle came to define herself in terms that paralleled those applied to other professional women writers. She actively maintained her relationship with her publishers, personally negotiating her own royalty arrangements, deadlines, and photography budgets, as well as actively overseeing design and promotional considerations. Her commitment to her career was total, even at the expense of her health; she periodically drove herself to the point of exhaustion. Like her female peers, she infused her writings with a strong dose of moral significance.[81] Like her contemporaries Jane Addams and Ellen Gates Starr, who were working to establish Hull House in Chicago during the decade when Earle was busy writing about history, and like the fellow members of the New York City History Club, Earle believed that society needed to be fixed, and that she, as a writer of history, had the power to do just that. Through reading history, Earle reasoned, Americans could learn much about their own society. In a discussion of a lecture titled "The Influence of American Ideas on the French Revolution" given by Cornell University president Andrew Dickson White, Earle commented, "The lesson of how this American influence on European liberty was gained, and now, alas! it has now been largely lost through disgust at the management of our great cities—notably New York—might be read by every American citizen with profit."[82]

The urban social context in which she lived and worked helped to shape her reform agenda. By the 1890s, New York was a city of immigrants, many of whom spoke little English and certainly lacked a clear grasp of American history. Earle worried that a citizenry that did not understand its own past did not bode well for the future—and she urged an appreciation of history as a prescription for the present. "We all know that our country is great," she argued, "far better than we know *why* it is great. And perhaps that is the best reason why we should love history," she continued. "It makes us love our country."[83]

CHAPTER 5

Writing the Past

❧

I
N CHOOSING TO WRITE ABOUT THE HISTORY of domestic life, Alice
Morse Earle was, in numerous ways, part of a broader literary tradition.
Since the 1820s and 1830s, many writers had focused on the American
domestic environment as an avenue to understanding the national char-
acter.[1] Earle built on the work of Washington Irving, Catharine Maria
Sedgwick, Lydia Maria Child, Nathaniel Hawthorne, Horace Bushnell,
Catharine Beecher, Harriet Beecher Stowe, Louisa May Alcott, William
Dean Howells, and Sarah Orne Jewett, writers who concerned themselves
with domestic life and the transformation of the Northeast. Her historical
studies, however, incorporated a new sense of cultural urgency characteristic
of the 1890s. She wrote for multiple audiences—popular and academic—
publishing book-length works, magazine fiction and nonfiction, and articles
for scholarly journals. Earle's distinctive form, methodology, and modes of
presentation were calculated to instill in her white middle-class readers a
clear understanding of the past while pointing to a viable path for the future
through the twin vehicles of history and domesticity.[2] Over the course of
her career, Earle came to see herself as an important voice in the reappraisal
of the culture and society of colonial America, transmitting its lessons to
ordinary readers in her many books and articles. At the same time, she confirmed her authority as a scholar through book reviews and articles in more
highbrow and academic venues such as *The Dial,* the *American Historical
Review,* the *Journal of American Folklore,* and *The Chautauquan.*

Earle's professional activities cannot be fully explained, however, simply in terms of a reformist impulse for social improvement. The extent and pace of her literary output suggest additional motivations. Her writing certainly must have supplemented her family's household income. Her high production rate throughout the 1890s may have been linked to the generally poor economic climate of that decade. Henry Earle's fortunes as a rubber broker on Wall Street were vulnerable to any economic downturn, as she well knew, and the depression of the 1890s may have created financial difficulties for him, adding to the pressure on his wife to contribute publishing income. Earle's literary earnings can be discussed only speculatively, but typical publishing contracts in the 1890s normally netted the author a royalty of 10 percent—and occasionally as much as 20 percent—of retail sales. Magazine writing was a common strategy employed by many authors to increase their income, sometimes significantly. If one of Earle's books, priced at $2.50 a copy (which was ten times the cost of a pound of butter in 1895), sold ten thousand copies, she had the potential to earn between $2,500 and $5,000 on that book alone, and income from magazine writing could have augmented that figure significantly. By comparison, the average annual wages in 1890 for men and women working as "Officers, Firm Members, and Clerks in Manufacturing Establishments" was $1,039 and $508, respectively.[3]

Following the publication of *China Collecting in America* in 1892, Earle continued writing at a feverish pace. Scribner's published her third book, *Customs and Fashions in Old New England,* in 1893, as a companion volume to *The Sabbath in Puritan New England,* and timed to capture the surge of interest in history stimulated by the World's Columbian Exposition in Chicago.[4] The following year Earle wrote *Costume of Colonial Times.* Unlike her previous publications, these two new books employed an ethnographic scheme of organization. Earle surveyed clothing, education, household furnishings, tableware, food and drink, travel, festivals and celebrations, grooming, medicine, death, and mourning customs in early America. As with her book on the Puritan Sabbath, Earle relied on primary sources, both archival and artifactual. She commented in 1899 that her research methods paralleled those developed by the German historian Leopold von Ranke and introduced to the United States in 1872 by "President Adams" at the University of Wisconsin. Earle was a bit confused here. Her reference was to an American historian, Herbert Baxter Adams, who had studied under Ranke in Germany and subsequently brought his ideas about research and the seminar method of instruction to Johns Hopkins University. He was a founder of the American Historical Association in 1884. His most famous student, Frederick Jackson Turner, later taught at the University of Wisconsin, where Charles Kendall Adams was president from 1892 to 1901.[5]

Earle used as an example a study of Indian corn to explain the new historical method to her audience, advising them, "When you have hunted in old letters, books, newspapers, in Indian histories, in diaries, and kept your notes and shaped them out, you would have done something of value; in this case made an historical record of a great food-product of this nation." To this procedural mix was added "what I call historical imagination, a power of interpretation, by a quickening of dull outlines." She stressed the value of original manuscript sources, stating, "They are penetrated with the spirit of the time in which they were written, and the spirit enters in a measure into us." But, she warned, only the original versions should be used, because much can be lost in the process of transcription and editing, particularly an original document's charm.[6]

Earle's bursts of productivity were occasionally followed by brief periods of withdrawal. Abrupt declines in her production in 1892, 1897, and after 1899 raise questions about whether other events in Earle's life might have affected her work. The loss of her twelve-year-old son Henry to cerebrospinal meningitis in 1892 was a massive blow (fig. 15). The summer after Henry's death, she commented on her loss in a letter to George Sheldon, a fellow collector, friend, and founder of the Pocumtuck Valley Memorial Association in Deerfield, Massachusetts. On black-bordered mourning stationery Earle wrote, "I enjoyed my day at Deerfield more than I can ever tell you—it shines out a bright and happy day of self-forgetfulness in a very unhappy summer." Seven years later, still grieving, she dedicated *Child Life in Colonial Days* to her own lost child: "This book has been written in tender memory of a dearly loved and loving child, Henry Earle, Junior, MDCCCLXXX–MDCCCXCII."[7] Henry's death certainly accounted for that year's drop. The ensuing productive burst in 1893–1895 was another result of her son's death, as Earle, grief-stricken, sought solace through total immersion in her work and conversations with like-minded friends like Sheldon. While in Deerfield, she had reviewed a scrapbook containing Sheldon's history of Deerfield. In the same letter to him she enclosed a copy of an article she had just written about funeral customs and mourn-

FIGURE 15. In 1892 Earle's firstborn son, twelve-year-old Henry, died of cerebrospinal meningitis. Earle's grief over this loss must have affected her writing, suppressing her output temporarily, but then stimulating a frenzied burst of writing activity in 1893 through 1895. This photograph was probably taken during the summer of 1887, during a family visit to Worcester. Collection of Donald J. Post Jr.

ing rings for Sheldon's critical review. She also included a query about "silk grass" for Sheldon to ponder.

Earle accomplished such high levels of production by maintaining a focus on the topics she commanded, and by judiciously recycling her research materials, both as chapters (with some alteration) in multiple books and as variant forms of similar articles. Her published article about New England meetinghouses, for example, became chapters one and five in *The Sabbath in Puritan New England*. She, and presumably her publishers, had identified a niche in historical writing—one that emphasized the material world of ordinary people—and she worked hard to tailor her research to fill that niche again and again.

Her work patterns and research methods can be pieced together from numerous comments she made to correspondents, from evidence embedded in her publications, and from the trends suggested by the publication dates of her periodical literature. In January 1895, for example, she wrote to Nathaniel Paine, treasurer and member of the council of the American Antiquarian Society in Worcester, inquiring about the Stephen Sewall papers in that collection. "Is it possible for me to examine these papers and make extracts from them?" she asked. "I am writing a book on the life of the woman of early days which I think I shall call *Colonial Dames and Goodwives*, and I think I might find in these manuscripts interesting suggestions of the every day life of the times."[8] Four days later she wrote again, this time inquiring about an artifact in the society's collection, a stoneware jug that had originally been owned by John Winthrop, which she wished to discuss in the text of her biography of Margaret Winthrop. A glimpse of Earle as the meticulous researcher came through in this letter. "I want to be exact," she stated. "Was it not given to you by William Winthrop—last surviving son of Prof. John Winthrop? What year was it given to you?" she persisted. "Is there any account of this in your proceedings?"[9]

She doubtless spent many hours working in the reading room at the Antiquarian Society. Her normal pattern was to spend at least part of the summer and early fall in Worcester, although much of that time was taken up with family social events. In September 1895 Earle wrote to Mrs. Morris P. Ferris, a member of one of the New York chapters of the Colonial Dames, about a monograph Ferris had written about a Mrs. Van Cortlandt. "Just at present my sister's house is full of visitors," she noted, "and I have to share her duties as hostess." Furthermore, she added, "I haven't written a word all summer, but hope soon to start at something or other."[10]

Since January (when she first wrote to Paine), however, she had completed two more books. Earle mentioned to Ferris that *Colonial Dames and Good Wives* would appear in September. She also revealed that her life of *Margaret Winthrop* was due out at the end of September, and that she had grown "very fond of her during the two months I was writing about her."[11] Earle's peak production year was 1895; that year she published two books, fifteen articles, and three book reviews. But 1893 and 1894 were hardly less productive. During each of those years she published two books and a number of articles and reviews. In order to accomplish that demanding rate of scholarly output, Earle must have had significant blocks of time in which to write, in addition to well-developed and systematic research techniques. The presence of four female servants in her household—Kate Sheridan, Bridget Vaughn, Jennie Gilligan, and Kate Brennan—made it possible for Earle to follow this idiosyncratic work schedule without entirely disrupting normal family life.

Earle's relationship with her publisher Charles Scribner's Sons deteriorated during 1896 and 1897. After a lengthy dispute over her royalty agreement for *Colonial Days in Old New York,* Earle finally agreed to 15 percent with a $750 advance, but after six successful books, she may have thought her work should command more than that amount. Later that year Earle expressed concerns about the cover design planned for the book, and the final blow came in November, when she had to write Scribner's about her advance, which was seven weeks overdue. "I should have liked it to invest at that time, with some other money of mine, and had advantage of the recent rise in prices in stocks," she commented, "and let me say too that frankly I don't like to have to write asking for it."[12] Her editor at Scribner's, W. C. Brownell, wrote her a highly conciliatory response, but within a year she had moved over to Macmillan.

Blocks of time for writing were not always easy to find. Although Earle's children were growing up, they were not yet adults. Alexander, her youngest, was only thirteen in 1895. Summers were spent at Homogansett or Worcester, where she was preoccupied with other activities. During the rest of the year her routine seems to have been intermittently broken by research trips, vacations, meetings, and family events. Her published articles, examined collectively over the course of her career, appear only between the months of January and September, with the peak occurring in April—but never in October, November, or December. If one folds publication lead time into this formula, this pattern suggests that she did most of her work during the six autumn and winter months, finishing in early spring.

Earle's daughter Alice Earle Hyde, recalling her mother's work habits, observed, "Part of the day, when social events did not interfere, Mrs.

Earle spent at the Long Island Historical Rooms, which library, for certain historical work, she considered the first in the country." The Long Island Historical Society had been established in 1863, and by 1881 it was housed in an elegant Queen Anne style building on Pierrepont Street, within a few blocks of Earle's Henry Street house. In addition, according to Hyde, Earle regularly sent messengers to fetch books for her from the Mercantile Library, also in Brooklyn Heights and now a branch of the Brooklyn Public Library. "It was not an unusual circumstance for a carrier to be sent there two and even three times a day," she remembered. The most revealing statement about her mother's daily pattern, however, related to its essentially nocturnal character. "It was rarely earlier than nine o'clock in the evening that serious work began," wrote Hyde. "Then, free from interruptions, came the all night sessions and oftener than not this indiscreet woman of genius, worked and corrected until broad daylight, when the maids began their early morning duties. A supply of apples and oranges was the only refreshments taken by Mrs. Earle." In describing Earle's research methods, Hyde implied that her mother seemed to have an intuitive sense about what she was seeking and where she might find it. In addition to the two Brooklyn libraries, Hyde named the genealogical columns of the *Boston Evening Transcript* as an important source of research data for her mother. Her mother "cut and pasted in scrap books all the data," wrote Hyde, "although it is difficult to understand where she found the time for the work."[13]

Letter writing was another crucial means by which Earle gathered information. In writing to J. Thomson Willing, editor of the journal *North American,* with whom she shared an interest in roses and sundials, she commented on the benefits of correspondence, wondering rather pointedly why anyone would fail to answer letters: "Aside from any question of civility, I would not fail to answer such letters for some most curious incidents have come to my knowledge, some very helpful things simply through my answering strangers' letters. It is true I have answered hundreds that have been great bores, unremunerative in any way—but I feel even in these cases a distinct happiness in the thought that I have helped others—and I *have* helped." A sense of the volume of her correspondence may be gained from another comment in the same letter. "My book *China Collecting in America* and a series of 3 articles on the same subject in *Ladies Home Journal* have brought me many hundred letters—probably in the 8 years at least a thousand letters." Furthermore, she added, "I could almost write another book on what I have learned from them."[14] Earle's other books most certainly generated their own significant volume of mail, in addition to the china collecting queries.

Earle organized all of the information she obtained into a series of scrapbooks. She noted to Willing that she had "many scrapbooks—one on Wild-Flowers, Table-Talk, Costume, Customs, Manners & Customs, Holidays, &c." When, for example, she needed poems about roses—as she did in 1902 when she was putting together *Sun-Dials and Roses of Yester-day*—she knew that she would be able to find appropriate verses in her "Garden" scrapbook.[15] She was apparently not alone in this practice; other collectors of information about which she was writing sometimes shared their scrapbooks with her. She referred to "a scrapbook lent to me" which included "a slip from a newspaper having a picture of the *Cross* sundial at East Laurel Cemetery."[16] Receipt of this piece of information excited her greatly, and she would not rest until she had obtained a photograph of that sundial for herself.

Her daughter again supplied a sense of exactly how Earle went about constructing her scrapbooks: "Early in her literary life Mrs. Earle acquired the habit of writing a little history or description or directions concerning an article she might be going to lay away for a long or short time. These written words were placed with the article, whether it was a package of manuscript papers, a bit of needlework, a family tree or a length of embroidery." According to Hyde, "this habit developed as time went on." For example, Earle inscribed the reverse of all pictures hanging on the walls of her home with dates and related anecdotes. Family photographs as well "were never laid aside without the name, date, place and description carefully inscribed."[17] Such discipline further confirms Earle's sense of the importance of her personal history as well as her obsession with accuracy and historical continuity.

A passing remark made by Earle to a correspondent who had invited her to review a new edition of the letters of Horace Walpole bears out this tendency toward obsession. When Earle received her review copies of the Walpole letters, she wrote back to Frederic Brown, editor of *The Dial,* noting: "I am such a creature of *habit*—of associations of memory—of regularity—that the sight of the Walpole Letters in books so much smaller than those I have always read (the old editions of the letters) that I am terribly disappointed. . . . So these new volumes look so pinched to me." She continued, recounting a story that confirmed her conservative inclinations, "My liking of 'the same thing' extends even to the binding of books—and I mourn over my old 2 volume copy of Dickens Child's History of England," explaining that she had worn out "the old red covers with much reading—and had the volumes rebound for my children." Unwittingly, she told Brown, the binder put green cloth on the cover, and "I have never opened them since."[18]

Photographs were critical to Earle's research and writing. Much of her correspondence centered on the problem of finding photographic images of places, gardens, houses, and objects that would support her research needs. With the publication of *China Collecting in America* in 1892, Earle inaugurated her practice of including photographic illustrations in her work whenever possible. Although many of her contemporaries used artists' renderings as illustrations, Earle did not take that route unless she had no alternative; perhaps she felt that it would somehow undermine her credibility as a serious historical scholar to use drawings rather than photographs. Yet after *China Collecting,* Earle's next eight books (with one exception) had no illustrations at all. There is no way to know whether this was a decision made by the author or by her various publishers, Harper & Brothers, Herbert S. Stone, Charles Scribner's Sons, and Houghton Mifflin. It may, however, have been a factor in her switch, in 1898, to the Macmillan Company. *Home Life in Colonial Days,* published that year, was the first of six books she wrote for Macmillan, and all were heavily illustrated with photographs.

For Earle, authenticity was an important issue, in part because of her educational agenda.[19] She aimed to present her readers with a comprehensive view of the ordinary details of colonial life, "the everyday life of the times," and the photographer's lens was as expedient a means to that end as the letters, diaries, court records, wills, deeds, and other primary sources that she quoted freely throughout her publications.[20] Earle understood that images greatly facilitated the imaginative reconstruction of historical events or ideas for her readers. And whether through professionally made or "snapshot" images, the eye of the camera captured "the real thing"—something that a hand-drawn sketch could not convey.

Most of the photographs she included were unattributed, perhaps because they were the work of amateur photographers, who often mailed their images of inherited or collected treasures to Earle. She also used the work of professional photographers. *Home Life in Colonial Days,* for example, contained images by Clifton Johnson of Hadley, Massachusetts,

FIGURE 16. "Making Thanksgiving Pies," used as an illustration in *Home Life in Colonial Days* (1898), was one of the most evocative images produced by Frances and Mary Electra Allen of Deerfield, Mass. The scene, photographed in the Allen kitchen, included potent Colonial Revival imagery: a Windsor rocker, a wooden bread bowl, a syrup jug, an apple basket, a reflector oven, and a tin candle mold on the mantle. The women in this kitchen offered an intergenerational prescription for modern women as they slid their pies into the bake oven in preparation for Thanksgiving. Photograph courtesy of the Pocumtuck Valley Memorial Association, Memorial Hall Museum, Deerfield, Mass.

a well-known New England photographer and essayist; that book also included forty-five images by the sisters Frances and Mary Allen of Deerfield, Massachusetts (fig. 16), as well as the work of Emma Coleman (also of Deerfield and Boston), E. D. Sewell, and Eva Newell.[21]

In contrast to the rather sparse list of photographic attributions in *Home Life in Colonial Days*, a later work, *Old-Time Gardens, Newly Set Forth*, published in 1901, included detailed credits for almost all of its photographs. Perhaps Earle (or her publishers) believed that the subject matter—landscapes and gardens—would appeal to connoisseurs of mainstream art photography, who would have been interested in the makers of the images. The inclusion of photographs as illustrations in her books would certainly have worked to expand her audience. She firmly believed in making history broadly accessible, and photography served her well to that end.

In anticipation of the publication of *Home Life*, Earle had inquired about the Allen sisters in a letter to George Sheldon. "I am going to ask you to be kind enough to write me—upon this postal card—the address of the 'Allan [*sic*] girls'—who will take photographs," she wrote. "I would much prefer to have them take them to getting a photographer from Springfield," she told Sheldon, but wondered if the Allens would "be allowed to handle the things in the cases," apparently a reference to using the collections in Memorial Hall, "so to put them in a good light &c. &c."[22] Frances (1854–1941) and Mary Electra Allen (1858–1941) had already established themselves as professional photographers by the late 1880s, and each had had photographs published in books and magazines by 1892. Their careers paralleled Earle's in many ways—tapping into a cultural desire for pictorial representations that seemed sharply focused and authentic but romantic at the same time.[23] The Allens, like other "pictorialist" photographers, were gaining acclaim as artists in their own right. Earle particularly valued the way their photographs contextualized the artifacts she wrote about, depicting them in room settings populated by women in colonial costume. (The photographs would also have offered readers a prescription for integrating the same objects into their own kitchens and parlors.)[24] After supplying so many photographs for Earle and numerous other publications, however, the Allens were apparently reconsidering their pricing structure for what Mary Allen termed "fussy tiresome . . . hack work" in a letter to her friend Frances Benjamin Johnson.[25] She had just completed almost fifty photographs for *Home Life in Colonial Days.* Even "hack work" by the Allens would have raised the overall aesthetic quality of Earle's books. Earle recognized that and sought out their images. By 1901, however, she was complaining to Sheldon that the Allens had priced themselves out of her reach. "I had much satisfaction in the photographic work Miss Allen did for me," she declared, "but now her prices have gone up to $10 a picture I do not feel I can have any more from her."[26]

In trying to understand Earle's motives for writing so explicitly about ordinary life, it would be easy to dismiss her simply as a sentimentalist longing for a lost past. The issue appears to be more complex than that, however, and requires a more careful analysis of her role as a popularizer. Earle, despite—or perhaps because of—her upper-middle-class origins, was selling her cultural heritage to a mass audience. Her photographically illustrated books provided a roadmap for collectors. Using *China Collecting in America,* for example, anyone could learn to distinguish "Old Willow" from truly old Willow. She was intentionally diluting the power of class ownership of cultural information. Why? Earle, like many other white middle-class women, believed that these artifacts, and the culture they implied, had a civilizing effect on society at large, which was perceived to have departed widely from what seemed in retrospect a comparatively homogeneous population in seventeenth-, eighteenth-, and early-nineteenth-century America. The values embedded in the material culture of the past, it was felt, would somehow facilitate the assimilation process. The period when Earle was writing so feverishly followed a decade in which America had experienced the highest levels of immigration ever. Newly arrived immigrants, however, were not Earle's intended audience. She was speaking to her own class, hoping that her work would strengthen and consolidate cultural power that she feared was being eroded by the massive social discontinuities of the era. Ultimately, though, since photographically illustrated books cost more than books without photographs, her books never functioned fully to extend that cultural information to the masses. Nor is it likely that Earle ever expected to reach a truly "mass" audience, despite her City History Club efforts and other reformist involvements. Everything about her books—their elevated scholarly tone, educational subjects, and carefully calculated artistic design—suggests she believed that control over history should remain firmly in the hands of white middle-class people like herself.

During the course of the fourteen years when she was writing, Earle's literary tone changed, perhaps as she clarified her scholarly and cultural agenda. Throughout her career she was concerned with constructing herself as a cultural power and with establishing and maintaining an authoritative voice. Her earliest articles were written in a straightforward expository style. Although she never used the apparatus of scholarly citation, Earle generally tried to make her readers aware of her sources, frequently by presenting them at the beginning—as in "The Queen's Closet Opened," which began:

> There lies before me a leather-bound, time-stained, dingy little quarto of four hundred and fifty pages that was printed in the year 1656. Its contents comprise three parts or books. First, "The Queen's Closet Opened, or The Pearl of Practise: Accurate, Physical, and Chirurgical Receipts." Second, "A Queens Delight, or The Art of Preserving, Conserving, and Candying, as also a Right Knowledge of Making Perfumes and Distilling the most Excellent Waters." Third, "The Compleat Cook, Expertly Prescribing the most ready wayes, whether Italian, Spanish, or French, For Dressing of Flesh

and Fish, Ordering of Sauces, or Making of PASTRY,"—"pastry" in capitals, as is due so distinguished an article and art.[27]

By the time her readers had gotten through this opening paragraph, they not only were well aware of the scholarly pedigree of her source—a seventeenth-century recipe book—but also were charmed by Earle's exquisite invocation of the little volume.

Earle's sense of herself as a professional and of her power as an author was apparent even in some of her earliest work, where she showed a willingness to experiment with her genre. Two pieces written for *New England Magazine* in 1891— "Ghost, Poet, and Spinet" and "Top Drawer in the High Chest"—made extensive use of the fictive voice.[28] "Ghost, Poet, and Spinet" in some ways presaged the publication of *China Collecting in America* a year later. It details the travels of two women, the author, "Anne," and her sister, "Kate," in pursuit of a spinet that they "had heard was hidden in a farmhouse in a little town in the heart of Massachusetts."[29] Anne and Kate's spinet quest to "Pardon," as the town is called, may well have been grounded in the real-life antique-hunting experiences of Earle and her sister Frances. In fact, Frances Morse discussed spinets at some length in her own book about antique furniture, noting that their presence in British North America was documented in inventories as early as 1654.[30] The association of this instrument with the founding of the country would most certainly have increased its appeal for collectors. Morse did not have a spinet in her collection; at least she did not illustrate one belonging to her or her sister in her book. She did, however, illustrate an early pianoforte, "owned by the writer, who bought it in Falmouth, Massachusetts," probably on just such an antiquing expedition. According to Morse, this "was said to be the first piano brought into Falmouth," and she exhorted her readers to "imagine the wonder and envy of the little seaport village when a whaling captain, after a successful voyage, gave the piano to his daughter."[31] Anne and Kate are not so successful in Earle's story; the spinet they seek turns out to be only a melodeon—a nineteenth-century instrument without the lineage of its seventeenth-century predecessor. As she was to do later in her book about china hunting, Earle used the motif of spinet hunting to express her disdain for the Yankee farmers of "Pardon," the present-day trustees of her New England heritage and clearly not the audience for whom she intended her message.

These degraded New England natives were part of the problem. The solution lay with her readers, middle-class men and especially women who would rescue the past from these "aliens," as she termed them.

Earle's story "The Top Drawer in the High Chest" is set, notes the narrator, "in the quiet New England seaport town in which I lived when I was a little child."[32] This town, perhaps modeled after Wickford, Rhode Island, had apparently once been prosperous; but by the time of the narrator's childhood, there were no children except herself and her sister Anna—a sure sign of a dying community. The two children amuse themselves by visiting one of their elderly relatives, a cousin, Eliza Story, who has chosen to live in strange circumstances, closeted on the second and third floors of her family homestead.[33] The plot involves many secrets, beginning with Eliza's choice of living arrangements. The children are captivated by the mystery of their cousin, who feeds their imaginations with tidbits from her past in the form of objects stored away in the top drawer of her high chest.

Earle used this story to construct a detailed vision of the past gone awry. The artifacts of Eliza's household—remnants from a much more genteel era—were lovingly described: a lacquered Chinese worktable, a box containing silhouettes of ancestors, a "forty-legged table," barberry water and seedcakes for tea. Yet this vision could exist only in a shuttered environment, isolated on the top floors of the house, wrapped up in the top drawer, too fragile to survive the scrutiny of the present. Again, Earle seemed to be lamenting, if in a fictive form, the current condition of rural New England, a lament that tapped the shared culture of individualism and progressive ideals of much of her middle-class urban readership.

In addition to fiction, Earle also experimented throughout the early years of her career with the genre of biography as a device for reconstructing the past. She believed that from a pedagogical standpoint, biography was a particularly useful form for arousing interest in history.[34] She selected her individuals as much for the broader implications of their lives as for the particular details. *Diary of Anna Green Winslow: A Boston School Girl of 1771* (1894), examined one year in the life of Anna Winslow, at the same time using her story to bring to life the world of colonial Boston. *Margaret Winthrop* (1895) was published as part of a series about notable women of the Revolutionary era. The life of John Pitman, "A Baptist Preacher and Soldier of the Last Century" (1895), was personal for Earle as well as didactic, for Pitman was her husband's ancestor. Her essay provided her readers with an exemplary model of a religious leader and a brave patriot, augmented by rich detail about his daily activities and circle of acquaintances from a surviving family diary. In each of these biographies, Earle used the lives of specific individuals to enter into the culture and society of which they were a part.

Much in the way that anthropologists look at cultural groups, Earle used aggregate data to construct these cultural biographies. Beginning with *Customs and Fashions in Old New England,* she examined the lives of her subjects collectively, "from the hour when the Puritan baby opened his eyes in bleak New England," through courtship, marriage, domestic life, travel and entertainment, intellectual pursuits, and ultimately death.[35] She used this same format in a number of books, including *Colonial Dames and Good Wives* (1895), *Colonial Days in Old New York* (1896), and *In Old Narragansett* (1897).

By 1896, when *Curious Punishments of Bygone Days* was published, Earle appears to have completed a methodological shift toward a strictly ethnographic approach (fig. 17). With this book Earle abandoned biography completely as an organizing device, shifting to an examination of human behavior and institutions—specifically deviant behaviors and the institutions of punishment. Some of her source material for this study was drawn from John Pitman's diaries, but in contrast to her earlier biography of Pitman, here Earle demonstrated her familiarity with the newly emerging disciplines of anthropology and folklore.[36] *Curious Punishments* surveyed the array of devices used for controlling members of society in early America. "In all—indeed, in nearly all—of the penalties and punishments of past centuries," she explained to her readers, "derision, scoffing, contemptuous publicity and personal obloquy were applied to the offender or criminal by means of demeaning, degrading and helpless exposure in grotesque, insulting and painful 'engines of punishment.'" These may have included stocks, bilboes, the ducking stool, branding, and, ultimately, the gallows. The ducking stool interested Earle particularly because it was generally used to punish "scolding women." She quoted a French traveler, Henri Misson, about its use. "The way of punishing scolding women is pleasant enough," he began, then went on to describe a chair supported on two long beams balanced on a fulcrum. The offending woman was placed in the chair, which could be raised and lowered into the water "as often

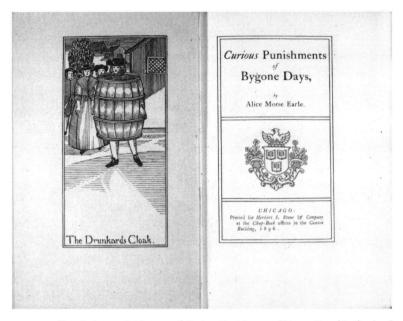

FIGURE 17. Frontispiece and title page of *Curious Punishments of Bygone Days* (1896), a book that marked a departure for Earle from the world of women at home. Her new focus on social deviance and the institutionalization of punishment suggests that she was influenced by ongoing changes in the historical profession and the emergence of scientific history. Author's collection.

as the sentence directs, in order to cool her immoderate heat."[37] Earle used a woodcut illustration to show exactly how this "pleasant" instrument worked, commenting, "The adjectives pleasant and convenient as applied to a ducking-stool would scarcely have entered the mind of any one but a Frenchman." Furthermore, she absolved her own Puritan ancestors from ever having used this device, declaring that although "many minor and some great historians of this country have called the ducking-stool a Puritan punishment. I have never found in the hundreds of pages of court records that I have examined a single entry of an execution of ducking in any Puritan community." In the South, however, the "cavalier colonies," she observed that ducking had been a common occurrence, as it had in England—a statement that hinted at a lingering post–Civil War resentment of the South, as well as at the regional identity of Earle's intended audience.[38]

All of her subsequent books—*Home Life in Colonial Days* (1898), *Child Life in Colonial Days* (1899), *Stage Coach and Tavern Days* (1900),

Old-Time Gardens, Newly Set Forth (1901), *Sun-Dials and Roses of Yesterday* (1902), and *Two Centuries of Costume in America* (1903)—reflected Earle's methodological shift toward a material culture approach to history. In these she employed an anthropological structure, with each chapter organized around a particular type of material evidence (generally involving food, clothing, or shelter), and then proceeded from ethnographic analysis of that material culture to interpretive historical narrative. With this new methodology, recently advanced by Franz Boas, who founded the first department of anthropology, at Columbia University in 1895, Earle broadened her audience considerably to include connoisseurs and collectors of artifacts as well as professional historians and readers of history. In the process, she also began to train her readers to view artifacts in new ways—as purveyors of historical culture and narrative.

The physical structure of her books reinforced their intellectual structure, and Earle was a conscious participant in the development of each one. In a letter to a correspondent in York, Maine, who had lent Earle a tinderbox to be photographed for her forthcoming *Home Life in Colonial Days,* Earle wrote: "I have a charming photograph of the old tinder box— and I now return it to you with many thanks. I have some of the most interesting and charming photographs for my book—over two hundred in all. No book has ever been published that will equal it in the curious illustrations. I only hope the text will keep close company with the pictures."[39] Her use of the word "curious" is revealing. Earle knew her audience. She knew that "curiousness" and "quaintness" were two qualities that were certain to sell books. She tried to incorporate features into each book that would charm her readers at the same time that she was instructing them. "'Quaintness,' you say—I long for it," she wrote to J. Thomson Willing in 1902, "but I have used up all my quaintness. I have written a dozen books in ten years—and each has some novelty." She referred to her use of lowered initial letters and the Renaissance cupid device on the title page of *Old-Time Gardens* as examples of specific features she considered quaint. She also expressed her fondness for "having verses for chapter headings," although she did not consider epigraphs appropriate for every book.[40]

Earle prided herself on the fact that all of her Macmillan books had indexes, although she noted that she was "a bit hurt that no reviewer has ever referred to it." She also felt that she had pioneered in the layout of photographic books. "One thing I introduced," she wrote to Willing, "and now every book of the Macmillan's is illustrated that way, *viz.:* every illustration (full page) faces the front of the book. You never turn over the pages . . . to a blank page. Formerly all books had the illustrations set in as might happen to be—half to the front—half to the back." Earle believed that consistency of layout would make it easier for readers to absorb her message. Also, Willing had apparently commented unfavorably about the quality of reproduction, which he attributed to Macmillan's use of coated paper stock in the text. "If I have illustrations among the text I *must have* shiny paper," Earle argued. Furthermore, she observed, "Many of my illustrations are not important enough to be full page," indicating that she exercised care in her selection of illustrations, placing them in a hierarchy of importance in terms of the degree to which they contributed to the text. "Besides," she added, "I can only have about 50 illustrations if I have only 'insets'—full pages." Finally, commenting on her readership and the marketability of her output, Earle noted, "Books with pictures in the text are far more popular."[41]

Fortunately for Earle, she found her relationship with her publishers to be generally satisfactory, despite her falling-out with Scribner's. She told Willing that she had "the most generous, yielding, adaptive publishers in the world" and dedicated *Two Centuries of Costume in America,* her final work, to George P. Brett, her Macmillan editor.[42] Macmillan certainly seems to have accommodated Earle's wishes on most aspects of the production of her books. All of her Macmillan books had elaborately designed covers, abundant illustrations, and a variety of typographic novelties. Macmillan also spent money advertising and promoting her books. In 1902 it sent out a prospectus for special editions of both *Old-Time Gardens* and the forthcoming *Sun-Dials and Roses of Yesterday. Old-Time Gardens* was offered in a "Large Paper Edition, Limited to 350 Copies. . . . With many full-page photogravure illustrations and half-tone reproductions. Printed on paper specially made for this edition. Enclosed in a handsome slide-case. Decorated cover, 8vo., $20.00 net." *Sun-Dials and Roses* was offered in a similarly luxurious companion edition—although this time only one hundred copies were produced, "printed on large handmade paper, profusely illustrated with photogravure plates made from original photographs and handsomely bound in silk and vellum."[43]

Earle actively shaped public perception of the artistic qualities of her books, not only through their illustrations but also by their design.

FIGURE 18. Cover, *Colonial Days in Old New York* (1896).
The entwined initials "MA" confirm that this is the work of
Margaret Armstrong, one of the best-known book designers
of the day. Although Earle did not approve of this highly
stylized design, she noted approvingly that it captured the
spirit of the Colonial Dames, with its blue and buff cover.
Author's collection.

Francis W. Shepardson, in his review of Earle's *Colonial Days in Old New
York,* mused about the new style of books on colonial history, which took
into consideration form as well as content: "The book-maker's art has
been drawn upon for dainty bindings and attractive illustrations, until a
shelf of this colonial life-portrayal has become a delightful part of a
library." Shepardson described in detail the covers of each of the books
discussed in his review. In the case of *Colonial Days in Old New York* (fig.
18), he found that "the cover of the book anticipates the delights of the
contents. It is distinctly Dutch, reproducing the design of a white and
blue cloth, and decorated with suggestive windmill, beaver, and beer keg."

That particular cover, designed by Margaret Armstrong, was the most elaborate that Charles Scribner's Sons ever produced for Earle, intricately stamped in blue and gold on a white ground and bearing Armstrong's cipher prominently on the front. Margaret Armstrong was a well-known book designer, and her association with Earle's book would have increased its appeal to bibliophiles. Actually, Earle had objected strenuously to that particular design, which she found much too stylized for her taste; she probably would have preferred something that used actual historical devices. She finally consented, however, after a flurry of persuasive letters from her editor at Scribner's.[44] Earle's dedication, "To the Society of Colonial Dames of the State of New York This Book is Dedicated by a Loyal and Loving Member," perhaps explains Scribner's willingness to invest in such an expensive production, since sales were guaranteed to a group well able to pay.[45]

Critical reception of Earle's work may be assessed in numerous reviews, in both scholarly and popular venues, including *The Dial, The Nation, London Quarterly Review,* the *Journal of American Folk-Lore,* the *American Historical Review,* the *English Historical Review,* and *DAR Magazine.* The *American Historical Review* published reviews of four of her books, beginning with a brief "Minor Notice" about *Margaret Winthrop* in 1896. The first substantive review was published about *Home Life in Colonial Days,* Earle's most important book to date, and in some ways a departure from her previous work. According to reviewer Edward G. Porter, a prominent Massachusetts minister and antiquarian, the book benefited greatly from its "150 illustrations which shed much light upon the text." He contextualized Earle's work historiographically, citing "a new method of writing history, adopted by [John Richard] Green, [John Bach] McMaster, [John] Fiske and others," which reflected a new interest in social history, as well as a rising interest in "patriotic orders and local historical societies," and an ensuing demand for knowledge about growing "collections of relics." Earle, he continued, "has happily caught this spirit." Moreover, "while she would doubtless consider herself the product of the new period, she is to be credited with being one of its chief promoters."[46]

Other critics for the *American Historical Review* praised Earle equally highly, citing her scholarship, her creative use of sources, her ability to organize and make sense of widely disparate materials, and her pleasant literary style. The historian William B. Weeden praised *Child Life in Colonial Days* for its use of portraits, as well as its analysis of the influence of John Locke's *Thoughts on Education* upon eighteenth-century child-rearing practices. Blanche Evans Hazard, a professor of home economics at Cornell University, praised Earle for her originality within the emerging field of professional history. "In her studies of colonial institutions, whether of homes, taverns, gardens, amusements, or dress," wrote Hazard, "Mrs. Earle has brought many byways into the view of students of American history." As Hazard noted, however, Earle offered abundant scholarly support for those "byways" by her inclusion of "quotations from letters, orders, and diaries of men like Governor John Winthrop and George Washington."[47] John Ward Dean, a founding member of Boston's intellectually prestigious Prince Society, an early historical organization, deemed Earle's *Diary of Anna Green Winslow* "a valuable contribution to the personal and public history of provincial Massachusetts."[48]

Macmillan commonly used reviews as promotional devices, binding excerpts into Earle's books as back matter. At the end of *Stage Coach and Tavern Days*, for instance, Macmillan reproduced four reviewers' comments about *Home Life and Colonial Days*. As might be expected, since these excerpts were included to promote the book, the comments were all positive. This excerpt from another scholarly journal, *Education*, self-described as "A Monthly Magazine Devoted to the Science, Art, Philosophy, and Literature of Education," offers a clear sense of the attributes of Earle's work that her reviewers found most appealing: "Mrs. Earle has made a very careful study of the details of domestic life from the earliest days of the settlement of the country. The book is sumptuously illustrated, and every famed article, such as the spinning-wheel, the foot-stone, the brass knocker on the door, and the old-time cider mill, is here presented to the eye, and faithfully pictured in words. The volume is a fascinating one, and the vast army of admirers and students of the olden days will be grateful to the author for gathering together and putting into permanent form so much accurate information concerning the homes of our ancestors."[49] This reviewer stressed topic (domestic life), illustrations, appeal to scholars and collectors, scope, and accuracy of information. "Quaint," "curious," and "original"—words that should have pleased Earle—also appeared regularly in reviewers' commentaries. With the brisk sales of her books, Earle's authority grew. *The Sabbath in Puritan New England*—her first book—had gone through eight editions by 1896. As early as 1894, one reviewer, Daniel Rollins, was able to comment that "the author . . . needs no introduction to the American public."[50] By 1901, George Ellwanger, an eminent horticulturalist, had elevated Earle to the status of a "learned antiquarian."[51]

Earle enjoyed widespread popularity in mass-market publications as well. In 1899 the *New York Times* ran an article titled "American Historical Novels," in which the author noted "something of a revolution in the tastes and sympathies of readers of books of the day," with a resultant proliferation of books in which "American historical scenes and personages have a prominent place." The article cited a number of historical novels, but also noted the popularity of "Mrs. Alice Morse Earle's books on the social customs and every-day life of the Colonial period." Other articles geared toward recommending books to readers frequently endorsed Earle as a good choice. Her success in the bookstores was reflected in a report on the New York Christmas book market in 1898, which listed the best-sellers at each of the major bookstores and noted that *Home Life in Colonial Days* had had "very large sales" in the "finely illustrated and gift book" market. That same year Mrs. Morris P. Ferris, a prominent New York Colonial Dame, wrote to the editor of the *Times* to recommend a list of books that, she declared, "in my humble opinion, give the best ideas of early life in the New England Colonies," including six books by Earle.[52]

Another measure of Earle's prestige was the extent to which she was called upon to comment on the work of others. During 1894–95 she wrote four reviews for *The Dial* on topics as varied as Edwin Atlee Barber's study of American pottery and porcelain, Ludwig von Hohnell's African explorations, *The Mountains of California* by John Muir, and an esoteric study of New England fast days.[53] In 1902 Earle reviewed another book for *The Dial*, this time the recently published *Writings of Colonel William Byrd, of Westover in Virginia, Esqr.*, edited by John Spencer Bassett. By 1904 Frederick Browne, editor of *The Dial*, was entreating her to review another book for him. She responded, "You are quite right in believing that I would like to review the Horace Walpole Letters," continuing: "I have made a very careful study of Walpole—and his surroundings—I have written upon him—and them—and at one time contemplated a book upon the subject. . . . At any rate, I am ready—I am eager—and I believe I am fitted to write a sympathetic and an informed and scholarly monograph upon his letters—this new edition." Earle wanted to know what the requirements were for a review of this twelve-volume work. "Shall I write it upon the first 4 vols—if you send them to me?" she inquired, "or shall I write a short notice—with the long review later?" She noted that she was inclined toward the former, but only if Browne was willing to give her enough space: "I want to do something I can be proud of." Furthermore, she had already taken matters into her own hands. She informed Browne that she had "been so much interested in this new edition that I have decided to correspond with the publishers and editors about it. I want to learn a little about Mrs. Paget Toynbee—and her work."[54] Her comment does not make it clear whether she viewed Toynbee as a rival or as a potential colleague. In the small world of professional women historians, perhaps she simply sought intellectual companionship.

These glimpses of Earle's personality reveal that she was conscious of her role as a cultural arbiter. In that role she sought to construct new interpretations of the past, new forms of evidence, and new modes of presentation that would buttress her authoritative voice. Earle's significance as a writer lies in her development of a new historical domesticity, her vehicle for social transformation. Her work expanded the boundaries of traditional formal conceptions of civilization to include the intimacy of the domestic sphere. She responded to a growing sense of cultural urgency by churning out an enormous body of literature that would serve her larger progressive agenda. The focus of that agenda, her audience, was two-pronged. She, like other progressive reformers, sought to provide social models for newly arrived Americans; she also sought to confirm the power of her white, Anglo-Saxon, middle-class heritage. In this dual role, however, Earle had to conform to her society's assumptions about gender roles, class position, and especially family values. But in order to exert any degree of widespread influence, she had to step outside those expectations and become a professional. The resulting tension between her mind and her heart was not new to the 1890s, as Mary Kelley and other historians of women have demonstrated, but was exacerbated by a growing reliance on professional solutions, which imposed new standards of performance on both men and women.[55] That tension was poignantly expressed in an inscription Earle wrote on the cover of her personal copy of *Sun-Dials and Roses of Yesterday*. Beneath her name, stamped in gold, she penned, "her Book and Heart."

Earle's absolute commitment to her dual career as a writer and a wife and mother ultimately took its toll on her health. In 1899 she wrote to John Wolff Jordan, librarian of the Historical Society of Pennsylvania, "In a day or two I go to Dansville, N.Y., the Jackson Sanatorium, for baths, massage, &c."[56] The Jackson Sanatorium, founded in the late 1850s by the health evangelist and entrepreneur James C. Jackson, and still flourishing at the turn of the century, offered patients "all forms of baths, massage, Swedish movements, and electricity given by skilled attendants," as well as "tennis, golf, croquet, charming drives, [and] out-door life on the great asphalt roof of the Main building."[57] Chronic insomnia had prompted Earle to seek relief at "Our Home on the Hillside," as it was called. "I cannot sleep," she wrote to Jordan, "I never sleep two hours a night, and I am going there for treatment before I have nervous prostration or some kindred abomination."[58] Insomnia, however, was one symptom of a new disease that was afflicting many urban middle-class Americans during the late nineteenth century. George Miller Beard introduced nervous prostration, or neurasthenia, to Americans in 1881 with the publication of his book *American Nervousness: Its Causes and Consequences.* Beard described neurasthenia as a disease of the modern age, a result of the shift from handwork to brainwork. Unlike their ancestors, whose lives had been defined by physical labor, men and women of the post–Civil War era more often than not worked at desks, with their minds, rather than out of doors, with their bodies. Beard and many of his contemporaries interpreted the rise of neurasthenia as a sign of the decline of Anglo-Saxon culture.[59]

Earle's fear of "nervous prostration" suggests yet another cultural explanation for her work. Throughout her career she described experiences that seemed somehow more authentic than those known to her own urban society. Guided by a faith in the power of heredity to prevail in a world characterized by massive social change, Earle sought to identify and classify the attributes that had shaped her ancestors, and the ancestors of all established white Americans. Puritan men and women, as she presented them, had been rugged, constant, brave, and pious. They had been thrifty and inventive, not captive to modern consumer culture. They had appreciated the beauty in simple things, but they had also loved color and whimsy. Most important, they had loved liberty, and even more, they had valued family and community. Familiarity with their behavior and with the material structures that typified their lives provided a tangible and culturally therapeutic link with the past. The historical evidence and interpretations that Earle offered her readers both signified and reinforced class values, and the possibilities of historical continuity helped to alleviate cultural fears about the present.

"I am *mortal* and cannot write more than *one* big book a year," complained Earle to a fellow author, the Bostonian Elizabeth Porter Gould, in 1903.[60] It seems ironic that the work of "domesticating" history nearly drove Earle to nervous collapse. She may have felt oppressed by the new pace of reform, but through her writing, with its distinctive focus on domesticating history, she seems to have found a means of reconciling her heart, and the demands it exacted, with her mind. In this context, she created a method and form for a new kind of historical writing.

CHAPTER 6

Home Life and History

W RITING HISTORY, FOR ALICE MORSE EARLE, involved more
than assembling carefully researched facts into an appealing
narrative. Her emphasis on domestic life and its material culture, both as historical evidence about the past and as agency for shaping the future, placed Earle at the cutting edge of historical scholarship.
Her career coincided with the passing of the age of Francis Parkman and
George Bancroft, when the first generation of academically trained historians was transforming historical writing into something more rigorously "scientific." Within this scholarly context, Earle found the freedom
to explore social and cultural subjects—particularly the worlds of women
and the home, using artifacts as evidence and drawing on the methods of
folklorists and anthropologists, as well as art historians, antiquarians, and
domestic advice writers.

Earle's selection of home life as a favorite topic related closely to her faith
in the formative power of material environments and must have drawn
some of its inspiration from domestic advice literature, published from the
1830s on. Lydia Maria Child, beginning with her earliest work on child
rearing, published in 1831, as well as many others who followed her, saw
the American home as an institution to be scrutinized and utilized for its
potential to reform society by shaping individual behavior from one's earliest moments. Catharine Beecher's *Treatise on Domestic Economy*, which
appeared in 1841, approached the problem of the domestic environment

with the same scientific rationality that her contemporaries employed to define the structure of other institutions: prisons, asylums, schools, cities.[1] Sixteen years later Elizabeth Fries Ellet, who shifted gears from history to domesticity, wrote *The Practical Housekeeper*, which followed a similar pattern. Both authors provided their readers with thoughtfully conceived plans for improving their homes, bringing up their children, cooking, gardening, and myriad other details of housekeeping. Their emphasis on the domestic environment reflected a deep underlying faith in the perfectibility of the individual through the agency of a moral home and women as purveyors of that morality.[2]

In 1870, four years before Earle married and began housekeeping herself, Harriet Beecher Stowe and her sister Catharine Beecher collaborated on a domestic advice book, *The American Woman's Home*. Beecher and Stowe dedicated their book "To the Women of America, in whose hands rest the real destinies of the republic, as moulded by the early training and preserved amid the mature influences of home." This dedication, and much of the rhetoric within, reiterated the importance of the domestic sphere to the future of the United States. In particular, Beecher and Stowe believed that the way a house was furnished and adorned could have tremendous power over its inhabitants. They commented extensively on "the important subject of beauty in reference to the decoration of houses," arguing that "while the aesthetic element must be subordinate to the requirements of physical exercise, and, as a matter of expense, should be held of inferior consequence to means of higher moral growth; it yet holds a place of great significance among the influences which make home happy and attractive, which gives it a constant and wholesome power over the young, and contributes much to the education of the entire household in refinement, intellectual development, and moral sensibility."[3] Earle, writing twenty years later, elaborated on the environmentalist domestic philosophy of Beecher, Ellet, and Stowe, but with a new emphasis on history, and its impact on the home, as a much-needed instrument of social reform.

Although Earle identified herself as a historian and her scholarly products as history, she fit rather uneasily into the emerging historical mainstream. Aside from the fact that she was one of only a handful of women writers of history, what set her work apart from much other historical writing of the period was not so much its prescriptive tone as her choice of topics, her use of evidence, and, most important, her audience. Her main predecessors as writers of women's history were Martha J. Lamb, Sarah Bolton, Frances Willard, Louisa Moulton, Phoebe Hannaford, and, above all, Elizabeth Ellet.[4] Ellet had published a three-volume work, *The Women of the American Revolution* (1848–1850), utilizing a biographical approach to her subject. Each chapter was organized around the life of an individual woman, beginning with George Washington's mother, Mary, and focusing heavily on genealogy, heroic deeds, and the influence of women as wives and mothers. Ellet departed from the realm of male historians by placing women at the center of her writing, as well as by establishing a firm scholarly place for women and domesticity in the larger American historical narrative.[5]

This type of home-centered history—employing established families and their material settings as behavioral models—was familiar to Earle's readers. Since the second quarter of the nineteenth century, a spate of popular books had been published which scrutinized the homes and families of famous men and women. *Homes of American Authors* (1852) illustrated the domestic roots of William Jennings Bryan, James Fenimore Cooper, Nathaniel Hawthorne, and Washington Irving, among others, followed by a sequel, *Homes of American Statesmen. The Life of Mary Lyon,* published in 1852, illustrated Lyon's birthplace, a picturesque cottage surrounded by trees at the bottom of a steep ravine; Mount Holyoke Female Seminary, which Lyon founded; and her burial monument.[6] This genre attempted to provide behavioral and environmental explanations for the greatness of particular individuals in order to serve middle-class readers as guides through the social and cultural vagaries of a world in transition. George Washington was scrutinized especially thoroughly. Benson J. Lossing's widely read *Home of Washington and Its Associations, Historical, Biographical, and Pictorial,* published in 1859 and reissued in a revised post–Civil War edition in 1866, analyzed not only Washington's life but also his genealogical lineage, particularly his English progenitors. Earle wrote to Lossing, extending her gratitude for his scholarship: "I cannot close without expressing to you the debt I owe to you—my interest in historical study, my patriotism, my literary ambition have all been fostered and deeply aided by reading your books." Fifty years after the publication of Lossing's *Home of Washington,* interest in the English branch of the Washington family still ran high. Earle collected material on this family and indicated to Lossing that she was interested in writing a book about them, noting that she was "preparing a magazine article upon George Washington's Table Ware &c. and of course wish to be very accurate." She referred to Lossing's mention of a set of china that he claimed had been presented to Washington by French officers, asking about his sources for that claim.[7]

Philadelphia writer and Colonial Dame Anne Hollingsworth Wharton was also busily collecting Washington material for a proposed book, exploring his English ancestry and homestead.[8] By 1900, when Thomas Allen Green published *Some Colonial Mansions and Those Who Lived in Them*, the formula was established.[9] Each section of Green's book began with a family history, augmented by illustrations of the family homestead and its furnishings, as well as the family coat of arms; this was followed by a detailed genealogical chart for each family discussed. Green began, of course, with the Washingtons.

Folklore and folk life studies, in particular, offered Earle another connection to professional women, as well as a focus on domestic life. Early women reformers—whether at settlement houses in American cities, among freedmen and women in the South, in the remote mountain communities of Appalachia, or among Native American peoples on the Great Plains and in the West—had found significance in traditional women's crafts as evidence of cultural endurance and as a means of cultural renewal. Newly published research about folk customs, as well as a burgeoning crafts revival, suggested redeeming links between cultural survival and social uplift, especially (though not exclusively) to women. By actively making traditional artifacts—whether baskets, clay pots, woven rugs, or needlework embroideries—women could model ideal American behavior while at the same time restoring their own native vigor and cultivating a richer appreciation of past cultures.[10] For Earle, an amateur painter as well as a writer of history, the relationship between cultural ideas and their material embodiments was clear. Through her writings she determined to reveal the mentalities of her predecessors by carefully examining their goods.

Earle was also strongly influenced by the multiplicity of "pastkeeping" activities that were reshaping both the American countryside and its urban centers and were focused as much on families and domestic life as on the world of military heroes and political leaders. By the 1890s these took the form of historical societies and house museums; libraries and athenaeums; monuments; exhibitions of art, decorative arts, and historical paintings; and various other forms of institutionalized collective memory. One of the earliest, Deerfield's Memorial Hall, was the work of the antiquarian and local historian George Sheldon. It offered visitors an array of historical relics through which they could experience the village's past in intimate detail. The most prominent relic at Memorial Hall, the famous door from the so-called Old Indian House, commemorated the 1704 raid by French and Native American forces on the English settlement at Deerfield, known widely as the "Deerfield Massacre." For visitors to the museum, the door's physical presence transformed an abstract historical event into a romantic narrative of family and community survival.[11]

Memorial Hall quickly expanded into a series of community-wide historical activities, largely engineered by Sheldon and C. Alice Baker, a seasonal town resident, author, and educator who restored the antique Frary House and opened it to the public in 1892. Meanwhile, in 1886, the town had established the Deerfield Summer School of History and Romance, which offered a lecture series aimed at indoctrinating attendees in the importance of local and regional history as a hedge against moral decline. The Summer School, largely attended by women, also successfully promoted a moral and cultural renaissance for Deerfield, as well as the restoration of the town's architectural heritage. Another energetic reformist stream followed the settlement house model, pursuing arts and crafts as a therapeutic and aesthetic activity for women, one that also had economic benefits. Collectively these "common parlors," as Baker termed them, served to unify and invigorate Deerfield's historical culture and village community in a particularly gendered way. Although Sheldon had launched the Pocumtuck Valley Memorial Association, it was the local women who developed the town's "pastkeeping" activities to their fullest extent.[12]

Earle made her first visit to Deerfield in September 1892, visiting Memorial Hall with George Sheldon, followed by tea and an evening at Frary House. "For the treasures of Memorial Hall," she wrote to Sheldon following that visit, "I can find no sufficient words of praise." Her letter brimmed with enthusiasm about what she had seen, marking the beginning of a collegial friendship between Earle and Sheldon. She continued to correspond with him for the next ten years, exchanging research queries, articles of interest, and tidbits of gossip. She must have returned to Deerfield again and again, seeking evidence and illustrations for her books among the collections housed at Memorial Hall and the photographs of Frances and Mary Allen.[13]

Folklorists, antiquarians, and social reformers alike all emphasized the importance of the relationship between history and its cultural embodiments, as did Earle. In keeping with this growing focus on historical material culture, she made certain that all of her later books and many of her magazine articles were fully illustrated. One book, *Curious Punishments of Bygone Days,* was illustrated entirely with woodcuts created by the artist Frank Hazenplug, perhaps in an attempt to soften and romanticize the harsh and gloomy subject matter.[14] Her extensive and authoritative use of a wide variety of material evidence, as well as her domestic emphasis, set her apart from her peers in the historical profession.

The widespread popular appeal of Earle's books and articles indicates that she had tapped into the mainstream of middle-class culture, a culture that was pulled by the competing currents of scientific modernism, a national nostalgia for "the golden age of homespun," and a sense of mission to restore American society by reinvigorating traditional values.[15] Earle drew heavily from the last of these currents, with its implicit critique of contemporary society. She was interested not only in the forces that shaped what she presented as the heroic character of early Americans, those seventeenth-century Puritans who braved hardship to settle a new land and the eighteenth-century patriots who made it America, but also in the ways in which that heroic character expressed itself, once released from the bonds of colonialism. The century surrounding the signing of the Constitution was most certainly for Earle the golden age. As the age of her parents and grandparents, it was the era that was most closely linked to her own historical memory as well as to that of most of her readers.

As we have seen, in the 1890s a new, scientific standard of intellectual endeavor came to define the field of history, and this was the scholarly context in which Earle worked. That standard required total objectivity and a rigorous commitment to empirical analysis.[16] Beginning with *The Sabbath in Puritan New England,* Earle focused not on the roles that specific individuals or events had played in determining the course of the nation's history, but on institutions, and particularly the institutions that shaped the lives of ordinary American men, women, and children: religion, home, family, food, education, travel, clothing, recreation, and punishment.[17] In this sense she conformed to the standards of the new, scientific history. Belief in institutions as instruments of social reform and in the shaping power of material environments was not new in the 1890s.

Earle and her readers were the recipients rather than the initiators of a legacy that had been building throughout the nineteenth century. Since the earliest decades after the creation of the new American republic, planners, policymakers, and reformers had been tinkering with a variety of new institutional forms, customizing them to address an assortment of social problems ranging from education and criminal behavior to poverty, mental illness, and urban crowding. Many of the solutions presented, whether a penitentiary, an insane asylum, a school, or a new urban plan, reflected a newfound faith in the therapeutic power of environment.[18] Once environments were identified as having social power, planners, writers, and social critics subjected them to intense scrutiny from all sides.

Rather than relying solely on existing archival evidence of social and cultural customs, as did most of her academic peers, Earle expanded the scope of historical examination into the realm of material evidence, specifically the artifacts and activities of womanhood and the home. She believed that material objects, especially those with the patina of past ownership, had the power to inform as well as reflect human behavior and values; historical objects exerted a special kind of potency, conveying the power and heredity of their owners across time, in a sense shaping the future. For Earle and her peers, control not just over these objects but over their interpretation through history itself assumed a critical new importance as an antidote to the uncertainty of the late-nineteenth-century present.[19]

In constructing her historical narratives, Earle did not limit herself to the scholarly methods of academic historians. As a collector, she was naturally drawn to the newly emerging scholarship on the connoisseurship of American decorative arts, especially ceramics, silver, and furniture. Both *The Ceramic Art* by Jennie J. Young and *The China Hunter's Club* by Annie Slossen had appeared in 1878, right after the Centennial. The Gorham Manufacturing Company published John H. Buck's *Old Plate*, the earliest study of American silver, in 1888. Theodore S. Woolsey's *Old Silver* followed in 1896. Perhaps the most influential of all, Irving Whitall Lyon's *Colonial Furniture of New England* (1891), would have afforded Earle a model for rigorously researched information about artifacts.[20] Lyon's book was published the same year as Earle's *Sabbath in Puritan New England*. A reviewer for the *Atlantic Monthly* considered it "the first thoroughly scientific examination of one interesting corner of this field."[21] In *The Dial*, another reviewer commented on the timeliness of Lyon's topic, predicting, "If only those families who show with pride a bit of furniture that 'came over in the Mayflower' will purchase his volume, it will quickly be out of print."[22]

Earle wove the artifacts that she had discovered through her research and travels into her histories. In her discussion of colonial schools, she noted that "if girls were not taught much book-learning, they were carefully instructed in all housewifely arts," including spinning, knitting, sewing, and embroidery. Fortunately for scholars, Earle continued, "many of the fruits of these careful lessons of colonial childhood remain to us." She went on to include a shopping list of "quaint samplers, bed hangings, petticoats and pockets, and frail lace veils and scarfs," available for study in numerous repositories.[23] In a chapter titled "Home Furnishings," Earle explored the physical world of the Puritan home. She moved from probate inventories to Lyon's *Colonial Furniture of New England* to the objects themselves. Throughout her discussions of household furnishing, and all other aspects of ordinary life in colonial New England, Earle interjected comments about the location of study objects. For readers who wanted to see real specimens of New England furniture, she identified the Connecticut Historical Society as the owner of the colonial chests described by Lyon and pointed readers of her discussion of fireplaces toward Deerfield, noting, "In the Deerfield Memorial Hall there lives in perfection of detail one of these old fireplaces—a delight to the soul of the antiquary."[24]

Scientific history, the prevailing methodological doctrine of the 1890s, developed out of a modern interest in applying evolutionary theories to historical events. Its rise paralleled the shift toward professionalization, and may be interpreted as part of a broad attempt to attain professional legitimacy. The new scientific method required total objectivity of its practitioners. The romantic literary tradition that had characterized much previous historical writing, with its emphasis on heroic acts and the force of individual personality, was to be discarded by professional historians in favor of a new emphasis on impersonal external structures. Imagination and historical narrative were to give way to realism and the arrangement of historical events within a developmental model of progress.[25]

Earle's work did not fit comfortably into the category of scientific history. She seems to have been unwilling to subject her writing, especially her romantic narratives, entirely to the orthodox standards imposed by the new professional criteria. It would seem that she incorporated only those aspects of scientific history that reinforced her essentially conservative outlook. The institutional focus must have appealed to her conceptions about social order, and the developmental model, with its implications about the value of the past, confirmed her personal sense of heritage and family continuity.

Like many of her academic counterparts, Earle was more concerned with general categories of behavior than with specific individuals. When she did write about individuals, as in her biography of Margaret Winthrop or her edited diary of Anna Green Winslow, she was careful to represent them in a more anthropological sense—as products of their social and cultural environment—thus making the historical lessons of their lives more broadly applicable. Her theory of historical change was shaped by her assumptions about material forces and genetic continuity. Because Earle actively directed her work at a broad audience rather than an audience of professional historians, she found it difficult to sustain the impersonality and objectivity that the historical profession demanded. Her tone was frequently personal, and she sometimes committed the cardinal sin (at least in terms of standards of historical objectivity) of using her own voice, even identifying with her subjects. Blanche Evans Hazard's review of Earle's last book, her 1903 two-volume *Two Centuries of Costume in America,* confirmed the distance between Earle and her academic peers. Hazard cited Earle's strategy of studying the history of colonial Americans through the lenses of housing, gardens, social rituals, and especially, their clothing as praiseworthy for opening up new fields of inquiry to scholars. Hazard noted further that Earle had wisely supported her studies with detailed evidence from archival sources and authoritative voices of significant historical actors, lest traditional historians trivialize her emphasis on social history and material culture.[26]

The domestic objects with which Earle fleshed out her colonial world collectively offer a vision of her educational goals and theoretical assumptions. If we survey these objects as a group, it becomes clear that she selected carefully to reinforce her larger agenda. All 1,285 illustrations in Earle's books were captioned, providing her readers with descriptive information about the object as well as frequent references to provenance, current ownership and/or location, artist or maker, country of origin, and date. The captions also acknowledged twenty-five different photographers who provided her with illustrations. The number of illustrations varied from book to book, and seems to have been determined both by the subject matter and the availability of material evidence, as well as the intentions of author and publisher with regard to audience and format. *China Collecting in America*, the only illustrated book Earle wrote for Scribner's, contained sixty-seven images of ceramic objects, most of them associated with the rituals of formal food service.[27] The book was apparently not the commercial success that Earle and William C. Brownell, her editor at Scribner's, had hoped. In February 1893 he sent her a royalty report for *China Collecting* and *The Sabbath in Puritan New England*, commenting that he hoped the enclosed check for $158.10 would alleviate whatever disappointment she might feel about lagging sales. "Of course we have done the best we could, in our judgment, for the 'china book,'" wrote Brownell, explaining, "The 75 illustrations & the paper they involved naturally increased the plant cost so as to force the price up to $3.00 and that limited the sale no doubt!" He sounded optimistic about the long-term success of *China Collecting*, however, feeling it to be a book "that will work its way up, percolate as it were," although he concluded with the caveat that "nothing special seems to go so well as what is general," citing the success of her first book—which had gone through seven editions in the first two years it was in print—as evidence for that observation.[28]

With a few exceptions, Earle completely decontextualized the objects she illustrated in *China Collecting*. Most of the illustrations in this book, and in many of her other books, depicted isolated artifacts, surrounded by white space or a gray background, providing no indication of their original function, the people who might have owned them, or the environment in which they existed. By divorcing these objects so fully from any recognizable context, Earle employed the formalist methods of art history, focusing on aesthetic value, style, and national origin, freeing the objects from any possible constraints that context might have imposed. The exclusion of context, furthermore, would have enabled her china-collecting readers to envision those artifacts in any context they desired—presumably their own collections.[29]

Home Life in Colonial Days, issued by Macmillan in November 1898, represented a permanent departure for Earle from her longtime relationship with Scribner's, and, more important, a continuation of her earlier exploration of the use of material as well as literary evidence. *Home Life*, through both its text and illustrations, constructed a tale of rapid progress from wilderness settlements to houses and living patterns that would have been clearly recognizable—despite an overlay of strange detail—to most of Earle's late-nineteenth-century readers. Here, as in her earlier works, Earle employed an anthropological rather than a chronological or aesthetic organizational structure, beginning with shelter, and considering successively food, clothing, transportation, religion, and community.

She clearly recognized the importance of the illustrations both as devices to engage her audience more fully and as affirmation of her own worth as a historian. "The illustrations for this book are in every case from real articles and scenes," she stated in the foreword, immediately establishing an aura of authenticity for the text that would follow and defining the illustrations as bearers of that authenticity. At the same time, Earle established her own essential role as a cultural interpreter of evidence that would otherwise have remained obscure and indecipherable. "Many a curious article as nameless and incomprehensible as the totem of an extinct Indian tribe has been studied, compared, inquired and written about," she commented, "and finally triumphantly named and placed in the list of obsolete domestic appurtenances."[30] Earle's heroic conception of herself as rescuer of the past was securely buoyed by the success of her previous nine books and was closely linked to her progressive social mission: to rescue the present.

Much in the manner of a folklorist, Earle described the process of saving this cultural inheritance "from the lofts of woodsheds, under attic eaves, in dairy cellars, out of old trunks and seachests from mouldering warehouses," as well as from "the treasure stores" of Deerfield Memorial Hall, the Bostonian Society, the American Antiquarian Society, and countless other state historical societies.[31] Often the mere physical presence of a historic artifact was not sufficient evidence for Earle. She sought to retrieve not only the object itself but also its underlying intellectual essence, as expressed symbolically through the medium of language. "An article would be found and a name given by old-time country folk," Earle related, "but no dictionary contained the word, no printed description of its use or purpose could be obtained, though a century ago it was in every household." She viewed the loss of nomenclature as seriously as she viewed the loss of material culture, and consciously expanded her collecting activities to include the retrieval of this rapidly disappearing "homespun vocabulary."[32]

The intellectual structure of *Home Life in Colonial Days*, and the nature of material evidence presented, focused on the mundane and ordinary rather than the extraordinary. Earle employed humble objects such as trade signs, goose baskets, toasting forks, tankards, brooms, bed warmers, well sweeps, niddy noddys, and pipe tongs to invoke this sense of ordinariness. She looked at custom rather than at individual behavior, traditional practice rather than specific success stories. In so doing, she extended her message broadly to society at large rather than the more limited audience of wealthy individuals who might have been able to relate to silver shoe buckles, silk tapestries, and Chippendale chairs. Her localistic rather than national focus added to the accessibility of her lessons. This was a conscious decision, grounded in her ideas about learning and current educational theory (particularly the teachings of John Dewey). As she advised her DAR sisters in 1899, "A new and interesting method of studying history is to begin with the history of the immediate surrounding of the individual, the town or village, local government, etc., then the county, the State, the nation; making the individual observe for himself."[33]

Earle exhorted her audience to study and write about historical events of the Revolutionary period, but rather than entire military campaigns, she urged them to address "a single detail," for example, to write about the clothing or food of a Revolutionary soldier, or about "the health of women and children at that time," or about education, household furnishings, fireplaces, bedrooms, and every domestic occupation—"wool-spinning, cheese making, candle dipping, soap-boiling, quilt-piecing, sewing, preserving."[34] Viewing history in this way "is just as necessary to grown persons as to children," she continued, "and it would almost seem that the narrower our field the greater our interest."[35] Through exhaustive research about these or any other minute topics, amateur scholars, Earle believed, would make an inestimable contribution to the empirical data that could form the basis of broader historical interpretation. She cited the papers of a long-deceased New Englander, recently culled by a well-meaning descendant of all but the man's diaries—tedious accounts of "one hundred dull New England sermons." Earle lamented the loss of his account books, records of the education of his children, and other papers reporting the ordinary events of his life rather than rarified thoughts. "His individual sentiments should have perished with him, pious though he was," she remarked, dismissing his orthodox Puritan beliefs as repressive rubbish, "but his every-day life was that of his fellow-men and so has an ever-living interest."[36]

In using home life as her focus, Earle was not completely alone. As she had seen in Deerfield with the restoration of Frary House, by the 1890s the historic preservation movement had begun to gain momentum, resulting in the establishment of numerous house museums and period rooms. In common with many of these, Earle's version of everyday life, as constructed in *Home Life in Colonial Days,* was idealized, intended to incorporate and conform to prevailing middle-class values and expectations about community behavior. Because the objects and customs she depicted typically had disappeared from common use, they implied a certain status through a patina of longevity and inheritance, and so served to shore up class boundaries.[37] Earle, however, was consciously using status symbols reflective of values other than wealth, although wealth could improve access to these symbols, and in some cases may have been required to do so. The houses and lives she described in *Home Life* were not typically those of the colonial elites. Rather than representing the material excesses of great wealth, Earle's reconstruction of colonial home life was defined by simplicity, industry, family, and ancestry. She may have been making a comment about the values of the newly rich in late-nineteenth-century America, but it seems clear that her republican focus was also an intentional attempt to improve access across class lines and thus broaden the scope of her progressive agenda.

If that agenda can be defined generally as affirming and securing Earle's own white middle-class world, the objects and behavior she chose to praise or criticize provide insight into the mentality and values of that world. Earle's vision of colonial life, for example, was one that emphasized cleanliness: tablecloths were "spotless," Southern plantations were always "pleasant," and the interior timbers of Rhode Island houses were "sanded in careful designs" with clean beach sand.[38] As a self-proclaimed "antiquarian," Earle was careful to separate herself (and her audience) from her less elevated contemporaries. In a discussion of the appearance and social meaning of front doors, she referred to a discarded door from an old Falmouth house that was reused on a henhouse, commenting dryly, "The hens and their owner were not of antiquarian tastes and relinquished the windows for a machine-made sash more suited to their plebeian tastes."[39] While the "plebeians"—and the implications of ignorance expressed in this anecdote—were her ultimate social target, Earle seems to have been more concerned with shoring up and even rescuing the culture of her own class, in order that it might withstand the ever-increasing pressures from those who did not share her vision.

Earle's work represented not a sentimental rejection of modern culture, however, but rather a desire to improve it by providing historical domestic models, and to that end she worked hard to set herself apart from those who would present the past as a more highly civilized product of the present. She validated her modern identity by relegating her predecessors to the realm of "quaintness" when she saw them behaving in ways that were mildly embarrassing to her, or with which she did not wish to identify. "Quaint" provided a cue to her readers that what they were about to witness could be subject to some degree of critical interpretation. Colonists who did not understand how to consume tea, for example, and who made the mistake of buttering the brewed tea leaves and eating them instead of drinking the liquid, were "quaint." When confronted with behavior that was clearly incompatible with her own modern values, however, Earle resorted to a class-based explanation. For instance, she found the practice of having children stand behind adults during meals analogous to throwing food to dogs, and could envision this "animalistic" behavior occurring only among people of "low station."[40]

If the institutional structures of civilization and social maintenance (roads, inns, shelter, food, clothing, education, punishment) provided Earle with historical evidence of human progress, she also found the roots of decline in institutional forces, particularly in the culturally debilitating effects of the rise of factory production. In *Home Life* she referred to "that great monster, the mill-machinery. Riots and misery were the first result of the passing of hand weaving and spinning."[41] This was an ironic sentiment for the daughter of a machinist, whose family inheritance included a healthy measure of early-nineteenth-century industrial prosperity. Earle resorted to mythmaking in an attempt to counter her perception of decline, characterizing the historical changes rendered by industrialization as a "revolution in domestic life," precipitated by the transition from "mother and daughter power to water and steam power." In Earle's view, the clothing of colonial times was "strongly and honestly made" because it was "sewed by hand" and "lasted long," and since "fashions did not change from year to year," it "could be passed from generation to generation."[42] By contrast, the implied "now" to this idealized "then" was severely weakened and effete. The new materialism, which Earle was attempting to counter through her explication of the material life of the past, was an insidious culprit, a softening agent against which she and many of her peers felt compelled to sound an alarm.

Although class conflict had no place in the society Earle depicted in *Home Life,* her work implicitly endorsed a class system as an agent of social stability and family security. And one of the chief vehicles for class segmentation and group identification in this and other books by Earle was the material world she depicted. The objects constituting this world conveyed social cues that were readily recognizable to Earle's status-conscious readers. Objects communicated their class connections through their materials, their ownership, their historical associations, their national origin, their scarcity or survival rate, and their current ownership. Each of these factors had the capacity to add to the intrinsic value of an object and, for those who chose to follow Earle's roadmap and collect objects similar to those she depicted, to convey that status to the modern homeowner.

While a wide variety of objects appeared throughout the full range of Earle's work, paintings, prints, and specifically portraits far outnumbered any other type of material evidence.[43] Although Earle was well aware of the cultural power of art objects, and even envisioned her costume book as an art history as well as a costume history, she analyzed paintings primarily as documentary evidence of domestic life and social customs. She was concerned not with formal academic or aesthetic trends but rather with the presentation of the sitters themselves—their posture, clothing, hairstyles, children, and environment, as well as the myriad identifiable details of lace, collars, buttons, shoes, cloaks, hats, gloves, and so forth. Earle's heavy reliance on portraits established an implicit class dimension: only certain members of colonial society had the means to afford formal depictions of themselves and their families. Earle did not need to state this explicitly; the portraits spoke for themselves through their rich silks and satins, lace collars, and elegant surroundings.

Other domestic objects acquired class dimensions through their historical associations with high-ranking members of colonial society such as John Winthrop and George Washington. Winthrop's stoneware jug was featured prominently in two of Earle's books. The jug, even without its Winthrop connections, would have expressed social power through its rich silver mounts and engraved depiction of Adam and Eve on the lid. In case her readers did not understand the social significance of the design and materials, Earle quoted a sixteenth-century French source, Estienne Perlin, who stated, "The English drink beer not out of glass but from earthen pots, the cover and handles being made of silver for the rich. The middle classes mount them with tin."[44] Twenty-five of the objects she illustrated had some association with either George or Martha Washington. These associations with famous people endowed certain objects with ancestry of the most impressive sort, in an age when genealogy and ancestral heritage had assumed important political dimensions.

An artifact's age could also increase its instructive value for Earle, but certain ages were more highly valued than others, if the aggregate of her selections can be accepted as an indication. Earle carefully dated thirty-three of the objects illustrated in *Home Life in Colonial Days,* either in the text or in the captions. The Winthrop jug, which was made in 1607, had the honor of being the most senior object, while a photograph of the kitchen fireplace in the poet John Greenleaf Whittier's home, taken about 1895, was the most junior. (Whittier's fireplace, however, was surely redeemed from such a lowly status by the fact that the *objects* in the photograph had a much longer pedigree.) The second half of the eighteenth century generated the largest number of objects—a period of enormous significance in American history, which could have conveyed heroic associations to any object made or used within its scope. This pattern was not unique to *Home Life in Colonial Days.* Almost 33 percent of the dated objects illustrated in all of Earle's books were associated with the fifty-year period between 1750 and 1800.

The second-most-frequent date cluster for objects depicted in Earle's books, however, fell entirely outside the realm of "colonial" America: about 21 percent of her dated illustrations depicted material culture produced between 1800 and 1850. Earle's extension of American history into the nineteenth century conforms to a wider cultural notion of "the age of homespun." The agent of American decline was apparently not independence from the British so much as the social and economic expansion wrought by industrialization and urbanization.

This fact was underscored by the large number of artifacts (a majority) illustrated by Earle that had originated in British North America, which is hardly surprising considering the subject matter of her books. The objects that fell outside the scope of the American-made, then, provide more suggestive clues about the value of foreign associations. Earle's extensive reliance on British artifacts was a reflection of the resounding Anglophilia with which middle-class Americans were increasingly smitten during the last years of the nineteenth century and particularly the early years of the twentieth century.[45] The ratio among her illustrations of American-made to British-made objects during the years 1751–1800, however, seems skewed toward the American, probably more so than could be explained by the phenomenon of war. This likely was a result of Earle's patriotic political agenda, which would have influenced her choice of images.

In addition to England, China, and France, Earle illustrated small numbers of objects made in Holland (eleven), Scotland (nine), Germany (six), and Italy (three), and one object each from Austria, Flanders, Japan, Mexico, Persia, Portugal, Russia, and Spain. Their geographic scope arguably paralleled the ideal demographic profile that Earle and her nativist colleagues would have endorsed for the country. The group included heavy representation from northern Europe and minimal if any representation from the rest of the world. Earle's almost total exclusion of African American material culture from her reconstruction of early America suggests a late-nineteenth-century social vision that had little room for the inheritors of African culture. She wrote several times about the African American custom of Pinkster, an annual holiday event characterized by eating, drinking, storytelling, song, and dance. In *Old New York,* Earle noted that "the week following Whitsunday has been observed with great humor and rejoicing in many lands, but none more curiously, more riotously, than in Old New York, and to some extent in Pennsylvania and Maryland; and, more strangely still by an alien, a heathen race, —the negroes." She went on to describe Pinkster as "one of our few distinctively American folk-customs," offering rich details about the variant practices of this holiday in Albany, Long Island, and New England.[46] In addition to Pinkster, Earle briefly discussed African American religion, citing the presence of voodoo and other magic-based practices in Rhode Island and elsewhere. She presented Cuddymonk, "a typical Narragansett negro," as evidence. Cuddymonk, according to Earle, was "deeply and consistently superstitious, and knew a thousand tales of ghosts and spirits and witches and Manitous, old traditions of African Voodooism and Indian pow-wows. He was profoundly learned in the meaning of dreams and omens and predictions, and he did not hesitate to practise—or attempt to practise— all kinds of witch-charms and 'conjures' and 'projects,' though he was a member in good standing, as he proudly stated of 'de Pistikle Church.'"[47] In both this and the previous account, Earle's words—despite their implicit racism—reflected her strong interest in folklore and folkways and her desire to see the descendants of slaves as curious relics of an authentic American past.

In Earle's books, the current ownership of the objects she depicted established a crucial link between implied class distinctions and living members of specific social groups. She carefully delineated the owners of these vehicles of cultural heritage, ostensibly to document her research methods. The perhaps unintended result, however, was to provide a list of names of the living descendants of the colonial elite, the successful inheritors of a legacy of power and wealth. Earle constructed subtle devices that would reinforce those connections. When describing an illustration of a garden, for example, she frequently referred to its location as "the Seat of," creating an impression of aristocratic lineage.

Her illustrations reinforced class linkages not only by their content but also by their size. Certain illustrations were reproduced as full-page images, while others were incorporated into the text as half- or quarter-page images. While the size and number of illustrations was ultimately determined by the budget allocated to the book by the publisher, Earle had a great deal of control over the selection process as well as placement. She certainly would not have failed to exercise her authority as author to identify those images that merited full-page status. Certain ones were selected because of the photographic quality of the original image; not all of Earle's sources produced photographs of equal proficiency. But other images were most certainly positioned and sized to reinforce and elaborate on some textual theme.

The subtext of *Home Life in Colonial Days*, as conveyed through its material culture as well as through the literary and archival evidence presented, had much to do with the disputed vision of woman's role in late-nineteenth-century America. Earle's selection of home life in general as a topic for analysis, and her specific identification of the demise of "mother and daughter power" as evidence of social and cultural decline, raises the issue of gender for scholars today, as it surely must have for Earle's largely female audience during the book's heyday.[48] Earle used gender consciously as a means of promoting her social vision. She reinforced her myth of the pre-industrial past, which assumed that the women of colonial America had led relatively contented lives, with a wide array of material evidence that was specifically associated with women and women's work. Of the 142 objects illustrated in *Home Life in Colonial Days,* three-quarters of them clustered around tasks and domestic roles traditionally assigned to women. Chief among these were the production and service of food and the domestic production of textiles.[49]

Four years before the publication of *Home Life,* in January 1894 *The Outlook,* a magazine that was generally conservative on the issue of suffrage, had reviewed Earle's *Customs and Fashions in Old New England.*[50] In addition to deeming it "a most interesting book" that would "offer many evenings of delightful entertainment to the family reading circle," the reviewer regarded Earle as something of a revisionist. "We think of those early days as days of hard work and little pleasure," the author stated. But Earle had provided evidence to the contrary in her description of the personal choices involved in dress. "Though simplicity of dress was one of the corner-stones of the Puritan Church," noted the reviewer, "the individual members did not yield their personal vanity without many struggles."[51] Reinforcing the message that had begun with *The Sabbath in Puritan New England,* Earle humanized Puritan culture through anecdotes about the problem of vanity for Puritan women, rendering the model of early New England society far more appealing to her readers. The idea of a society composed of individuals struggling for self-expression was considerably more palatable to an increasingly consumer-oriented middle class than the traditional sober, orthodox version, which saw individuals as subsumed by society. This subtle revision provided a matrix into which middle-class Americans could fit themselves more comfortably, thus helping them accommodate their own modern values to an ideological structure that venerated Puritan ideals of family and domesticity, ultimately making the Puritan myth a more effective socializing device. That process, which the *Outlook* reviewer had documented as early as 1894, was in full bloom by 1898, when *Home Life* was published. When viewed in the context of rising levels of consciousness among women about the issue of suffrage and, more broadly, the role of women in society, Earle's work assumed a significant place in the debate, reflecting one of its central questions: What should woman's function be?[52]

Earle's employment of such carefully explicated material evidence reinforced her overall goal of using historical writing as a tool for reshaping modern American family life. In order to use the past to achieve that goal, she had to mold it carefully, employ evidence selectively, and convince her readers that what they were receiving was true. Earle's adoption of history as her lens lent the imprimatur of truth to her work, while her departure from traditional forms of historical evidence provided her with a new realm in which to construct a useful vision of the past. In this departure, particularly in her embrace of the material culture of domestic life as evidence of the culture and society of early America, she was unique in the 1890s. Her primary intention was not to present her readers with a decorating guide to quaintness through the integration of antiques into their homes. Instead she offered up the domestic history of the past as a prescription for the problems of the present. The resonance of her vision was confirmed by the widespread popularity of her books; its utility coincided with her personal assumptions about "the greatest lesson which history can teach." This lesson she conveyed to her Chicago DAR audience in 1899: "that it may be a training in patriotism."[53]

CHAPTER 7

Remembering the Garden

❦

FROM THE TIME SHE MARRIED AND MOVED to Brooklyn Heights in 1874, where she soon established a garden of her own, Alice Morse Earle repeatedly used the metaphor of the garden as a means both of affirming her gender identity and of reconciling her ambivalence about urban life. A garden, Earle believed, was an essential component of "home," and thus an important female domain. Moreover, gardens, and especially "old-fashioned" gardens, had the power to connect the present to the past in tangible ways, which made them an important means of transmitting historical values and ensuring social and cultural continuity—even in modern cities. Her two garden books, *Old-Time Gardens, Newly Set Forth: A Book of the Sweet o' the Year,* published by Macmillan in 1901, and *Sun-Dials and Roses of Yesterday,* published by Macmillan in 1902, offered readers a dual agenda (fig. 19). First, Earle intended to present a clear, scholarly history of gardens in America, along with an examination of plant materials and other garden material culture. But *Old-Time Gardens* also offered a sentimental, gendered overlay, closely drawn from Earle's own childhood, her experience as a mother, and her theories about education, all of which she intended to be useful to her readers in their present-day lives.

Earle was not the only person for whom the idea of an old-fashioned garden seems to have had mythic appeal. Garden writing had paralleled the growth of reform ideology in antebellum America. As early as 1830, Thomas Fessenden wrote in *The New American Gardener* that ornamental

FIGURE 19. With the publication of *Old-Time Gardens* in 1901, Earle entered the world of garden writing in earnest. She quickly followed with S*un-Dials and Roses of Yesterday* in 1902. Author's collection.

gardening was "one of the most innocent, the most healthy, and to some the most pleasing enjoyment in life."[1] Improving the American landscape became a national obsession by mid-century, reinforced by a proliferation of books and articles about gardens, trees, plants, seeds, and their relation to the ideal American home.[2] The extent to which this idea had permeated popular culture by the 1840s is suggested by the work of America's best-known landscape gardener of the day, Andrew Jackson Downing. He had already achieved great literary success with *A Treatise on the Theory and Practice of Landscape Gardening* (1841) and *Cottage Residences; or, A Series of Designs for Rural Cottages and Cottage-Villas, and Their Gardens and Grounds* (1842), and he began to publish a new periodical in July 1846. *The Horticulturist,* a "Journal of Rural Art and Rural Taste," proclaimed on its opening page that it afforded readers "all that can most interest those whose feelings are firmly rooted in the soil, and its kindred avocations." The promised offerings included thoughts on "the garden and the orchard; the hot-house and the conservatory; the park and the pleasure grounds . . . blooming trees, and fruitful vines . . . good gardens, fair flowers . . . the humblest cottage garden, as well as the most extended pleasure grounds."[3] Downing was certain that his new venture would prove successful, largely because of the high level of interest he had personally witnessed in all things horticultural. He commented:

> Fewer, perhaps, are there, who have watched as closely as ourselves, the zeal and enthusiasm which the last five years have begotten in American Horticulture. Every where, on both sides of the Alleghenies, are our friends rapidly turning the fertile soil into luxuriant gardens, and crying out loudly for more light, and more knowledge. Already do the readers of rural works in the United States number more than in any cisatlantic country, except gardening England. Already do our orchards cover more acres than those of any other country. Already are the banks of the Ohio becoming famous for their delicate wines. Already are the suburbs of our cities, and the banks of our broad and picturesque rivers, studded with the tasteful villa and cottage, where a charming taste in ornamental gardening is rapidly developing itself.

In a final burst of patriotic pride, Downing concluded, "The patient toil of the pioneer and settler has no sooner fairly ceased, than our people begin to enter with the same zeal and spirit into the refinements and enjoyments which belong to a country life, and a country home."[4]

Downing was accurate in his prediction about the appeal of gardening. Books on gardens and gardening abounded during the later nineteenth cen-tury, in part a reflection of the economic growth that was occurring, in part a product of the formation of large country estates and new suburban landscapes—both with gardens. In the post–Civil War era, the popularity of Anna Warner's *Gardening by Myself* (1872) and *The Home Garden* by Ella Rodman Church (1881) confirmed the increasing allure of gardening as a wholesome, productive, and emotionally stimulating activity for middle-class women.[5] It was during these years, when Alice Morse Earle was busy rearing her young family, that in the architectural critic Mariana Griswold Van Rensselaer (Mrs. Schuyler Van Rensselaer) began writing articles about landscape gardening for the new periodical *Garden and Forest*, then went on to become a leading theorist of landscape design. Her articles were collected and published in 1893 as *Art Out-of-Doors: Hints on Good Taste in Gardening.*[6] Another book, published the following year, also captured the popular imagination of women interested in creating gardens. Celia Thaxter's *Island Garden,* with illustrations by Childe Hassam, charmed readers with the history and ongoing activities in Thaxter's own garden on Appledore Island, off the coast of New Hampshire.[7]

By 1899 the practice of landscape gardening had become professionalized into landscape architecture with the formation of the American Society of Landscape Architects. Most of the founding members were male, including Frederick Law Olmsted, and the early training programs at Harvard, MIT, and the University of Pennsylvania were not open to women. Beatrix Jones Farrand, the lone woman among the founding members of the association, had trained informally under Charles Sprague Sargent, founder of the Arnold Arboretum.[8]

Earle was not the first person to link gardening explicitly with larger gender issues. Another Macmillan garden book, *Elizabeth and Her German Garden,* a memoir published in 1898, had reiterated the romantic notion of the garden as a place of refuge and solace for women—in this case an expatriate Englishwoman, married to a count and living in Germany.[9] Almost twenty years earlier, Sarah Orne Jewett's "From a Mournful Villager" had appeared in the *Atlantic Monthly.* Here Jewett introduced the theme of loss associated with certain types of gardens, specifically in this instance the "front yard." Her narrative began with a lament: "Lately I have been thinking, with much sorrow, of the approaching extinction of front yards, and the type of New England village character and civilization with which they are associated."[10]

Jewett's sketch captured a sentiment that would become a recurrent theme in the works of Alice Morse Earle: the link between gardens of the past and a cultural heritage that seemed to be rapidly disappearing. For Jewett's mournful villager, the front yard served as an expressive outlet for early American women held captive by prevailing gender conventions. Even if a fence marked the boundaries of her world, the colonial housewife could develop that confined space to its full potential—or not. As Charles Dickens, who visited New England in 1842 and then again in 1867–68, commented, "The well-trimmed lawns and green meadows of home are not there; and the grass compared with our ornamental plots and pastures, is rank, and rough, and wild."[11] In the wake of advancing suburbanization, front yards as Jewett had known them seemed doomed. "The disappearance of many of the village front yards may come to be typical of the altered position of woman," she suggested, "and mark a stronghold on her way from the much talked-of slavery and subjection to a coveted equality." Jewett further observed that a woman "used to be shut off from the wide acres of the farm, and had no voice in the world's politics; she must stay in the house, or only hold sway out of doors in this prim corner of land where she was queen. No wonder that women clung to their rights in their flower-gardens then," she wrote, adding as a final point, "and no wonder that they have grown a little careless of them now, and that lawn mowers find so ready a sale. The whole world is their front yard nowadays!" Here Jewett was echoing other voices of ambivalence toward the changing conceptions of gender during the last quarter of the nineteenth century. Front yards, she observed, had lent strength to early American communities, as places where people saw one another on a daily basis and shared bits of news. She did not miss the irony of women's sphere being contained within a fence, but she seems to have felt that the benefits—neighborliness, family security, and what she termed "quaintness and pleasantness"—were worth the tradeoff. "People do not know what they lose," she concluded, "when they make way with the reserve, the separateness, the sanctity of the front yard of their grandmothers."[12]

Alice Morse Earle certainly agreed with Jewett's assessment of the value of front yards; in fact she wrote about them extensively in the second chapter of *Old-Time Gardens*, titled "Front Dooryards." Earle cited Jewett's story as a source for her readers, and her discussion drew heavily on Jewett's arguments. Like Jewett, Earle mourned the passing of the dooryard. "I cannot doubt," wrote Earle, "that the first gardens that our foremothers had, which were wholly of flowering plants, were front yards, little enclosures hard won from the forest."[13] As such, dooryard gardens were worthy of veneration because they provided a tangible link to the strength of character and Puritan values that had created the New England settlements. She described the contents of these old-fashioned gardens in detail, citing peonies, lemon lilies, phlox, tiger lilies, pinks, and box as admirable occupants. Part of the appeal of the peony lay in its "Brahmin" associations, as well as its longevity. The phlox, she specified, should be white—so as not to clash with the other blossoms. The tiger lily, which Earle admitted was not really all that old, was included because of its charm. Annuals, however, "were few in number." Instead, "perennial plants of many years' growth were the most honored dwellers in the front yard, true representatives of old families."[14] The notion of continuity and long-established

families resounded through these descriptions of "grandmother's garden."
Only those who had lived in one place long enough could have full access
to this type of garden. The plant materials that had been carried across the
ocean as seeds and slips by Puritan women in the seventeenth century had
been tended for generations and thrived in the American soil. Indeed, the
enduring success of these gardens was related to their very Englishness.
Earle celebrated "these old English garden flowers" as "such gracious things;
marvels of scent, lavish of bloom, growing so readily and hardily, spread-
ing so quickly, responding so gratefully to such little care"—not unlike the
people who first cultivated them.[15]

By the time she wrote *Old-Time Gardens,* Earle had already developed
a successful formula for publishing works about history and material culture. This book, like *Home Life in Colonial Days, Child Life in Colonial Days,*
and *Stagecoach and Tavern Days,* employed a loosely chronological topical
structure heavily illustrated with photographic evidence. She had written
about gardens and landscape previously, as portions of earlier books and
articles, but this was her first book fully dedicated to plants and gardens.
As with her earlier books, Earle relied on a varied array of primary sources,
beginning with John Josselyn's 1672 *New England Rarities Discovered.* Of
Josselyn, Earle wrote, "we should have scant notion of the gardens of these
New England colonists" but for him. She went so far as to transcribe his
flower lists to make them more accessible to her readers. Earle knew her
audience and understood that they, as gardeners and prospective gardeners, were shaped as much by consumerist motivations as by intellectual
curiosity. Her book was one of the first to detail the consumer possibilities in historic gardening. She identified the material culture of colonial
gardens for her readers, who, after perusing *Old-Time Gardens,* could con-
fidently choose from among a knot, a maze, or a parterre, with various
configurations of walks, edgings, and accouterments. An old pump or well
sweep could be an interesting focal point, as could a fountain, a water
garden, or even a sunken garden (which Earle did not recommend without the assistance of an architect). Old-fashioned garden furnishings might
include arbors, arches, pergolas, stone or marble seats, wrought-iron gates, a
dovecote, or that "conventional emblem of industry," a beehive (fig. 20). She
described different types of boundaries for gardens, ranging from box
hedges to bricks, boards, plant materials, railings, or her favorite, a full-

The Homely Back Yard.

FIGURE 20. "The Homely Back Yard," from *Old-Time Gardens,* 1901. Photograph by Henry Troth. This garden, with its grape arbor, brick walk, flower border, vegetable beds, and half barrel planted with sweet peas, appealed to Earle's perception of a wholesome past, in particular the old pump. "Why," she inquired, "are all the old appliances for raising water so pleasing?"

blown wall. "An ideal flower garden must be an enclosed garden," she wrote, harking back to the old dooryard.[16]

Earle discussed the latest trend in fashionable gardening, the "formal" or "Italian" garden. European travel and publications about the art and material culture of the Old World had generated among Americans a growing interest in replicating the grand gardens of England, France, and especially Italy. "Within the past five or six years," she noted, "there have been laid out in America, at the country seats of men of wealth and culture, a great number of formal gardens—Italian gardens, some of them are worthily named."[17] As an example Earle cited Drumthwacket, the extensive garden of M. Taylor Pyne in Princeton, New Jersey. She found this garden particularly admirable because of its classicism and its restrained design. Another Italian garden she admired was the one created for Hollis H. Hunnewell in Wellesley, Massachusetts (fig. 21). In her discussion of the Hunnewell garden, Earle cited the influence of Vernon Lee.

FIGURE 21. Italianate garden of Hollis H. Hunnewell, on the shores of Lake Waban, Wellesley, Mass. Metropolitan News Company postcard, 1909. Earle used a similar image of this elaborate garden, begun by Hunnewell in 1843, in *Old-Time Gardens* as evidence of the influence of garden designer Vernon Lee. The garden today is part of the Wellesley College campus. Photograph courtesy of Wikipedia Commons.

Lee, whose real name was Violet Paget, had grown up in Italy as an expatriate, and had been a childhood friend of the painter John Singer Sargent. Lee's circle included Oscar Wilde, Henry James, and Edith Wharton. In 1880 she published *Studies of the Eighteenth Century in Italy,* which introduced many new readers, including Earle, to the possibilities of Italian design.[18]

Despite their ancient origins, however, Italian gardens, though worthy—even sometimes splendid—were not typically "old-fashioned," according to Earle. She regarded them as "new," perhaps equating them with the new money that had created them—a not too subtle comment on the growing conflict between established Americans, like Earle herself, and the burgeoning ranks of wealthy industrial capitalists, who had no roots. Old-fashioned components, however, could redeem a formal garden. Earle illustrated two such gardens: Yaddo, in Saratoga Springs, New York, which had a charming rose garden, and Avonwood in Haverford, Pennsylvania, designed in 1896 by Percy Ash and bordered with boxwood.[19] Earle devoted an entire chapter to the virtues of boxwood, which she considered one of

FIGURE 22. Box-edged garden at Duck Cove, Wickford, R.I. The formal boxwood parterre garden, planted by Earle's grandmother-in-law at her summer home on Narragansett Bay in the early nineteenth century, confirmed Earle's belief in the longevity of box, as well as family persistence. Photograph by the author.

the most important features in any old-time garden (fig. 22). Box had ancient origins, according to Earle; Pliny had used it in the gardens of his favorite villa in Tuscany. Moreover, she found the distinctive scent of box to be "hypnotic," evoking deeply held memories whenever she smelled it. A well-clipped box edging could enliven the most prosaic landscape, even the county jail in Fitchburg, Massachusetts, where the warden's wife had installed a box-edged garden. Presumably the hypnotic scent had a redeeming effect on the inmates who tended the grounds.[20]

Old-Time Gardens also gave Earle a platform for expressing her views on urban society and progressive education. Using her parents' garden as a metaphor, she presented her ideal model for social relations, envisioning that garden as an established, harmonious community, where every plant had a personality and a purpose. "I like a garden in which plants have been growing in one spot for a long time, where they have a fixed home and surroundings," she remarked. Her vision of this community did not, however, preclude the possibility of change. "In our garden the same flowers shoulder each other comfortably and crowd each other a little, year after year," in much the same manner as human populations grow, organically and naturally. This garden community, however, unlike Earle's urban community, grew from within, not as a result of the incursion of strangers. Flowers in this garden looked "like long-established neighbors, like old family friends, not as if they had just 'moved in,' and didn't know each other's names and faces." Like people, Earle asserted, "plants grow better when they are among flower friends."[21]

Earle's descriptions of her parents' garden epitomized her new approach to history. She presented a history of real life, of nature in a garden, of small things in domestic settings, invested with broader meanings through which she judged her whole culture. Her historical writings generally, but particularly her garden writings, inspired a very different method and subject for history, as well as a new theoretical vision through which to criticize urban culture.[22]

Plants in the Morse garden readily accepted new neighbors, as long as they came with an acceptable pedigree and did not threaten the status quo. "Beloved Ambrosia," for example, "which filled my mother's garden in every spot in which it could spring, and which overflowed with cheerful welcome into the gardens of our neighbors," wrote Earle, had been transplanted from the garden of a great-aunt in Walpole, New Hampshire.[23] Aquilegia, a red and yellow columbine, "had been brought from a rocky New England pasture when the garden was new." In 1870 a newer variety of aquilegia, "California Columbine," was introduced to its eastern-born "sister," apparently with harmonious results, despite its western origin.[24]

Earle's vision of the garden reflected her vision of the urban society in which she had lived since her birth. Certain flowers in the Morse garden always had higher status than others. This status was usually defined in terms of associations, age, or personal attributes such as scent or color, rather than on economically based characteristics such as expense or exoticism. For example, the arethusa, she recalled, "was one of the special favorites of my father and mother, who delighted in its exquisite fragrance."[25] Other plants—fritillaria, violets, lilacs, bluebells, and roses—conveyed a "sense of long-continued friendship and acquaintance."[26]

Box occupied a hallowed position in Earle's hierarchy of plants. "To the many of us," she wrote, "the bitter aroma of the Box, cleanly bitter in scent as in taste, is redolent of the eternal past." According to Earle, however, the ability to savor box was not accessible to all; in fact, she construed the appreciation of box as a measure of taste and class distinction, describing its power as "an hereditary memory, half-known to many, but fixed in its intensity in those of New England birth and descent, true children of the Puritans." To that elect few, "box breathes out the very atmosphere of New England's past."[27]

In contrast to the venerable box, more modern plants, and particularly annuals, were rarely given bed space in the Morse garden. Through her characterization of modern plants and annuals as newcomers, Earle confirmed her commitment to hereditary transmission and exclusion as a means of social limitation and class definition. Earle remarked condescendingly of Dutchman's-pipe that it "had a leafage too heavy save to make a thick screen or arch quickly and solidly. It did well enough in gardens which had not had a long cultivated past, or made little preparation for a cherished future; but," she continued, "it certainly was not suited to our garden, where things were not planted for a day." Dutchman's-pipe, in fact, was a favorite planting around the front porches of the urban middle classes, perhaps even on Chatham Street in Worcester, because it served their desire for privacy. It grew quickly and thickly, and was often trained up wires to form leafy curtains, which would screen city families from their neighbors.[28]

The idea of continuity was paramount to Earle, as it certainly had been for her parents. Their own quest for continuity expressed itself in a concern with transmitting values from one generation to the next, as well as an emphasis on child rearing as a vehicle for that process. The notion of having been "garden-bred" provided Earle with a framework for envisioning her own childhood and carried broader implications about her social vision. She believed that her childhood in a garden had endowed her with a acuteness not available to other children, enabling her to "recall perfectly every flower I saw in pasture, swamp, forest, or lane when I was a child."[29] Earle and her sister, Frances, had honed their horticultural skills as teenagers by painting botanical images of plants in watercolor. These paintings required close observational skills as well as artistic sensibilities on the part of both girls. In this activity the Morse sisters were typical of young women of their social class: painting with watercolors was carefully inculcated through educational curricula beginning in the eighteenth century as an appropriate activity for well-bred young women (fig. 23).

Yet Earle's garden vision was not one of simple pastoralism. Juxtaposing her own experience with that of a farm-bred child, she found the

FIGURE 23. Botanical painting by Mary Alice Morse or her sister, Frances Clary Morse, about 1870. As a young woman, Earle aspired to be a poet and an artist as well as a writer. She and her sister, Frances, painted a series of watercolor images of flowers, an activity that confirmed class and gender expectations. This unsigned painting came from a folder labeled "Paintings by Mary Alice Morse and Frances Clary Morse." Collection of Matthew and Laura Post and family.

latter wanting. Earle summarily dismissed any assumption that "a love of Nature and perception of her beauties and a knowledge of flowers, are the dower of those who are country born and bred; by which is meant reared upon a farm." In her view, "farm children have little love for Nature and are surprisingly ignorant about wild flowers, save for a very few varieties," while "the child who is garden bred has a happier start in life, a greater love and knowledge of Nature."[30] The irony of this view lay in its implicit indictment of her own rural inheritance. Earle was drawing her vision of a golden age not from the hardscrabble New England frontier but rather from the genteel civility of eighteenth-century towns and cities.

In her repudiation of frontier history as a usable past at the same moment when Frederick Jackson Turner was elevating the idea of the American frontier to a role as the defining influence on national character, Earle reflected an ongoing cultural controversy.[31] She perceived the frontier, which included much of rural America in the East as well as the West, as a source of disorder. Earle's urban background had conditioned her to look to cities as the centers of civilization and culture—whether or not she always admitted it. Several of her books offered nostalgic visions of an urban as well as a rural past. The urban past she admired, however, was not that of Brooklyn, or even Worcester, but rather that of the colonial era, which she adopted as her standard for a good material existence and a cultured life.

Earle's preference for cultivated gardens and her assumptions about the formative power of those gardens reflected her interest in modern conceptions about child rearing. "It is a principle of Froebel," she explained to her readers, "that one must limit a child's view in order to coordinate his perceptions." Friedrich Wilhelm August Froebel (1782–1852), the nineteenth-century German philosopher, educator, prophet, and pioneer in the kindergarten movement, seems to have been an important influence on Earle. His theories about early childhood education centered on the idea of removing young children to a protected place—a *Kindergarten*, or children's garden—where they could be guided through the process of exploration by trained adults. Reflecting Froebel's philosophy, Earle continued, "In a garden [the child's] view is limited and he learns to know garden flowers and birds and insects thoroughly when the vast and bewildering variety of field and forest would have remained unappreciated by him."[32] Within the confines of their parents' garden, the Morse children had been shaped by this cultivated environment, as in turn were Earle's own children (see fig. 10). They learned to use their imaginations to fashion toys and create games from plants and flowers; to transmit flower lore from child to child, perpetuating a flower-centered angle of vision about the world around them; and, more generally, to master the skills of civilized social interaction.

Earle characterized those children who were not reared in a garden as irrevocably deprived: "The sober teachings of science in later years can never make up the loss to children debarred of this inheritance."[33] In a world increasingly dominated by Darwinian notions of mutability, she clearly preferred to rely on more traditional notions of family influence and environment, perhaps as a means of stabilizing her own power and position in a rapidly changing universe.

Although Earle spent her entire adult life in Brooklyn Heights, a "garden community," albeit one lacking in old-fashioned charm, she did have a garden of her own.[34] Sitting in the late afternoon sun in a second-floor room at the rear of her house on Henry Street, she would have been able to contemplate her garden, lying below her in the shadow of the great bridge, with Manhattan looming beyond. An episode with a lost kitten, described by Earle in her book, suggested the shape and form of her Henry Street garden. "One evening last May I walked down the garden path," she wrote, "then by the shadowy fence-side toward the barn. I was not wandering the garden for sweet moonlight, for there was none; nor of love of flowers, for it was very cold; we even spoke of frost, as we ever do apprehensively on a chilly night in spring. The kitten was lost. She was in the shrubbery at the garden end, for I would hear her plaintive yowling; and I thus traced her."[35] This passage reveals a long narrow garden, geographically defined by a path, a barn, a fence, and shrubbery at the "end." The "shadowy fence-side" conveys a tension, even a sense of danger, probably emanating from the city lurking unmentioned on the other side of it, even though Earle felt safe enough to venture out alone in pursuit of her lost pet. Both the fence and the shrubbery provided a reasonably adequate, though penetrable, barrier against intrusions. Her choice of the word "barn" to describe her outbuilding, instead of the more fashionable "carriage house," is also significant. Even in the heart of Brooklyn, which had a population of more than 250,000 people by 1900, Earle had attempted to create a rural sanctuary, much as her parents had in Worcester. Since the 1840s, urban Americans, inspired by the writings of reformers such as Andrew Jackson Downing, had been concerned with invoking nature to create urban forms and spaces that would counter the deleterious effects of the city.[36] Her references to specific location in the garden suggest that this sanctuary was large enough to contain destinations, and to be geographically complex. Although she did not mention specific flowers, their presence was implicit; this was not one of those "poor little strips of back yard . . . too densely shaded for flower blooms" which typified the city, and which Earle disdained.[37] Nor did she mention the presence of gardeners, although she must have had help to maintain her backyard retreat. Gardening help would have been readily available in urban Brooklyn in the 1890s—a period of severe economic recession. Earle, of course, would have supervised the process, as well as donned her gloves to do light weeding and deadheading, but it is unlikely that she did much of the hard physical labor in her garden.

Old-Time Gardens, though on the surface a simple garden reverie, upon closer analysis seems in every respect to be a tangible representation of Alice Morse Earle's rising anxiety about urban life. Embedded in her flowery descriptions was a system for criticizing an alien world. In the complex environment of the city, where there was little space for real gardens, Earle's book enabled the reader to cultivate a garden in the mind, and she fortified her intellectual message with visual prompts. The book was profusely illustrated with photographs of gardens, flowers, trees, architectural settings, and such garden accouterments as sundials, benches, and beehives. Some of the gardens illustrated were famous. In addition to those mentioned earlier, Earle included scenes from Mount Vernon, Bartram House in Philadelphia, Van Courtland Manor, and Bishop Berkeley's house in Newport.

In fact, her illustrations offered a visually unified geography of the original thirteen colonies, a geography infused with longing for a simpler, more organic past. One of the reviewers of *Old-Time Gardens,* writing for *The Dial,* expressed this notion rather succinctly, which suggests that it had a certain cultural resonance for the early twentieth century, still suffering from the ravages of war thirty-five years earlier: "It is with gardens 'in the good old Colony days when we lived under the King' that Mrs. Earle is concerned. . . . New England and the Old Dominion join in her tale, and now and again she permits something from the loveliness of the present to intrude gracefully upon the ordered beauty of the past."[38]

The photographs of gardens included in the book not only helped to heal the wounds of a nation too recently strained by civil war but also catered to a growing interest in tourism as a celebration of America's greatness. Since the earliest decades of the nineteenth century, Americans and Europeans had been traveling around the United States, visiting the places that had seen important events enacted, or that offered awe-inspiring landscapes. Faneuil Hall and Niagara Falls alike attracted visitors who wanted to see these sights with their own eyes. By the end of the century, the custom of touring and the tourist industry itself were well established. Americans, particularly those of the middle class, could use their newly acquired summer vacations to visit scenic landmarks in the mountains or at the seashore, or to return from their largely urban lives to the "home places" of their past.[39] As tourists began to descend on the towns and villages of northern New England each summer, they became increasingly selective about the places they preferred, eventually settling on specific sites for their vacations, whether in tourist hotels, available rooms on farms, rented cottages, or, ultimately, houses of their own.

New Ipswich, the small town on the Souhegan River in the Monadnock region of New Hampshire where the family of Alice Morse Earle's mother had originally lived, became a summer destination for vacationing Boston families during the 1890s. The town, which was the site of the first textile mill in New Hampshire at the beginning of the nineteenth century, had begun to lose its mills and its economic base, as well as its population, by mid-century. By the end of the century, outsiders with leisure time and money were purchasing the abandoned houses and farms as summer residences. One by one the dilapidated buildings were restored to a colonial glory that many of them had never possessed. Summer residents scoured the countryside for antiques with which to create authentic-feeling interiors: rocking chairs, cast-iron stoves, whale oil lamps, mahogany center tables, spool beds, and more. These rejuvenated goods were supplemented with newly made but old-looking rugs, tables, sofas, and other "colonial" style furnishings that were readily available in any major city.[40]

In addition to the interior spaces of their summer homes, the summer people worked to refurbish the surrounding landscape—of the town at large and their own houses as well.[41] Caroline Barr Wade, whose family had lived in a prominent house in the center of New Ipswich for several generations, created elaborate gardens at the end of the century, with

brick walkways, rustic groves, bridges and water features, and rectilin-
ear beds of perennials, shrubs, and roses. Henry Trowbridge Champney
hired a Boston landscape gardener to create his New Ipswich garden. The
result included paved walkways, roses climbing over wooden arbors, and a
large cast-iron fountain imported from the prestigious Mott Iron Works
of New York City. Earle herself wrote lovingly of her family's summerhouse and garden in Wickford, Rhode Island, with its box hedges and
sundial (see fig. 22).[42] The old seaport on the west side of Narragansett
Bay became a thriving summer colony in the 1870s largely because of its
proximity to Newport and its situation as a rail and steamship depot for
summer travelers.

Whether in coastal Maine, Massachusetts, Rhode Island, or summer
colonies elsewhere, restored summerhouses, along with their gardens, provided a setting for all sorts of social activities that often included a historical element. In New Ipswich, as in many other small summer vacation
towns, the new village gentry formed a "historical society," which was in
effect a social club that met on a regular basis at the houses of different
members, who would show off relics and present research papers about the
history of the town or of their own families. These local historical societies
helped summer residents feel established in the town, as well as endorsing
the historical authenticity of their summer experiences.[43] The gardens, too,
nourished the spirits of work-weary urban dwellers on vacation. Caroline
Barr Wade and her family and friends held elaborate outdoor teas in the
shade of a landmark willow tree. Many families in places like New Ipswich
had annual reunions at the old homestead (whether theirs or someone
else's). The blending of indoor and outdoor activities, an essential part of
summer in New England, created lasting memories and a nostalgic sense
of historical continuity with a past that existed only in the mind. Docu-
menting summer vacations through photography was an important part of
the process. Countless photo albums exist even today, with black paper
pages and lovingly inserted and labeled images of summer residents dressed
up in old-fashioned clothing, picnicking, playing croquet, dancing, spinning, and taking tea. Staged photographs were not unlike other popular
forms of theatrical reenactment—parades, colonial teas, balls, and pageants. Gifted (and not so gifted) amateurs took many of these photographs, while others were the work of professionals. Earle used such photographs as illustrations in a number of her books.[44]

The form and structure of *Old-Time Gardens*—its illustrations, its cover design, and its thematic organization—were calculated to appeal to this new audience of colonial revivalists, as well as to reinforce Earle's underlying progressive intentions. Her attention to detail and historical accuracy would have resonated with those who were restoring colonial summerhouses and gardens. While this was not explicitly an advice book, she clearly believed in the power of influence. Her words and images were calculated to uplift her readers as well as shape their behavior. The *Dial* reviewer praised her book for its "congenial subject" and "pleasant pages," and was generally delighted with the volume, "from its lovely cover to the ferny end-papers," finding that it "abounds in kindliness and sunny serenity,—altogether a book to be loved."[45]

The cover of *Old-Time Gardens* conveyed an impression of modern artistic taste, made accessible by its explicitly colonial iconography. The design included an embossed depiction of a stylized drapery of pink, white, and blue hollyhocks that formed a backdrop for a white sundial on an attenuated neoclassical stand. The title and author's name, stamped in gold in a quaint but at the same time modern typeface, confirmed the combi-nation of memory and modernity. Even the color of the cloth— a soft dove gray—managed to communicate a sense of age and organic earthiness. It suggested the color of old weathered clapboards, against which the hollyhocks—a favorite flower of generations of children—grew freely up the side of a barn.[46]

In selecting a sundial as the primary image for her cover, Earle made a statement about content, which she reiterated a year later in *Sun-Dials and Roses of Yesterday*. The sundial, emblem of organic time, was also, according to Earle, an important early vehicle for literacy. She described sundials as part of a "Literature of the Bookless," which she defined as "inscriptions and legends and mottoes, which were placed, not only on buildings and walls, and pillars and bridges, but on household furniture and table utensils." Earle noted that she had collected more than two hundred sundials, as well as photographs of others, and copies of many more inscriptions and mottoes. Furthermore, the symbolic use of the sundial on paper money during the Revolution imbued this image with heroic associations. Its use on the cover would have linked Earle's book and social vision explicitly to the golden age of late-eighteenth-century America.[47]

The designer's art was evident on the dedication page of *Old-Time*

FIGURE 24. Dedication page, *Old-Time Gardens* (1901), designed after a Renaissance knot garden. The inscription reads, "To my daughter, Alice Clary Earle, to whose knowledge of flowers and flower lore I owe many pages of this book." Author's collection.

Gardens as well. Here Earle chose a "knot" as the device for her inscription (fig. 24). This was a baroque garden form characterized by internal complexity and external regularity. Earle explained that knots "were not flower beds edged with Box or Rosemary" but rather "square, ornamental beds, each of which had a design set in some close-growing, trim plant, clipped flatly across the top, and the design filled in with colored earth or sand; and with no dividing paths."[48] Her design, adapted from a seventeenth-century garden plan book, contained an inscription to her daughter Alice Clary Earle. Her use of this puzzle device to open her book presaged a complex layering of meaning throughout the volume, weaving memory and illusion with tangible reality, overlapping the life cycles of different generations, and using the past as a means of exploring and perhaps shaping the future. Earle's faith in the power of inheritance permeated her writing. For her, family was the strongest mechanism for continuity. "I knew what flowers they played with and how they played," she wrote of her ancestors, explaining her intuitive access to history, "for they were my great-grandmothers and grandfathers, and they played exactly what I did, and sang what I did when I was a child in a garden."[49]

Earle recognized change at work all around her and was searching the past for ways to counter some of its impact. The domestic and family life of colonial America—stripped of Puritan theological overtones—repeatedly emerged in her writings as a useful cultural corrective for contemporary problems. Enclosure was one solution. "Every garden," she commented, "must have boundaries, definite and high."[50] The gardens of her grandmothers always had an enclosure, a fenced area, around the front door. In colonial times, Earle declared, the enclosure preserved a certain standard of intimacy: only friends were invited to enter the enclosed space. The compact size of these enclosures made them easy to maintain; weeds were a sure sign of social and moral decay.

The idea of socially defined spaces as exclusionary devices was particularly important in an urban setting, where the potential for intrusion by strangers was high. J. B. Jackson, in his discussion of the imaginative structure of gardens, has pointed out that the word "garden" has always carried with it implications of enclosure.[51] An enclosed garden in the city would protect its occupants from "street imps." Earle illustrated as an example the Worcester garden of Miss Harriet P. F. Burnside, describing its secret portion, sequestered from all but intimate friends.[52] For Earle, the enclosure paralleled the front hall of a house. "Everyone who had enough social dignity to have a front door and a parlor and visitors thereto," she wrote," also desired a front yard with flowers as an external token of that honored standing."The power to exclude certain visitors and to embrace others properly was a visible means of communicating status. According to Earle, having an enclosed garden at the front door "was like owning a pew in church; you could be a Christian without one, but not a respected one."[53]

Old-Time Gardens suggests that Earle was ultimately concerned with social and cultural survival. She feared that the power of her class, as well as her colonial heritage, was being eroded, both from without and from within. Unlike her ancestors, her contemporaries—and particularly their children—seemed to her to have been softened by the advances of civilization. To express her dissatisfaction, she used the voice of a disgruntled Crown Imperial fritillaria, now sequestered away in her garden, out by the barn—"Here I am . . . torn away from the honored border by the front door path, and even set away from the broad garden beds, and thrust with sunflowers and other plants of no social position whatever"—merely because its odor had become disagreeable to the modern nose of the lady of the house. "Smell to heaven, indeed!" the plant exclaimed. "I wish her grandfather could have heard her! He didn't make such a fuss about smells when I was young, nor did anyone else; no one's nose was so over-nice."[54]

Civilization, however, could not completely eradicate the power of the past. Earle evoked lilacs, peonies, and daylilies—all hardy survivors—to demonstrate the irrepressible nature of heredity. She found a certain comfort in the sight of old lilac bushes growing out of the cellar holes of abandoned farms in the country, or in the image of a lonely but tenacious box plant twisting its way up through the hard-packed earth of a tenement yard.[55]

Gardens, Earle believed, could yield both models for living and models for learning. The study of the minute details of pruning and planting, culling and gathering conformed to her progressive notions about the educational process. Throughout the remainder of her career, the metaphor of the garden continued to serve her as a means for expressing her anxiety about social and cultural change. Her "home garden," as she called it— the Worcester garden of her parents—offered Earle and her children a symbolic refuge from the urban present as well as a palpable link with the values of a golden age.

CHAPTER 8

Genealogy and the Quest for an Inherited Future

❧

D ESPITE HER CONTINUED ALLEGIANCE TO THE RURAL traditions of New England, New York City was the backdrop against
which Earle operated for most of her life. For at least nine months
of every year, she and her family lived in an urban neighborhood, surrounded by unfathomable numbers of strangers. The Earle house in Brooklyn Heights stood on a block of Henry Street amidst almost fifty other
houses. That one block was a minuscule section of an enormous grid that
spread relentlessly—northwest into Manhattan, pausing briefly at the East
River, south to the Atlantic Ocean, and eastward on Long Island. In a
world of such indeterminate physical boundaries, new social and cultural
boundaries had to be developed and continually reinforced from within.
Earle's strategy for constructing those boundaries involved an emphasis
on roots and ancestry, real or imagined. Genealogical connections could
offer a sense of virtual family and long-standing community ties, even
where there were none. Moreover, social and cultural boundaries, Earle
believed, could be maintained through physical proximity to symbolic
forms that would stand in for real ones. Ancestral artifacts, as well as ancestors themselves, could help to bolster families against the insecurity of
the present (fig. 25).

For Earle and most other members of the urban middle class, the process
of establishing and maintaining new social boundaries had begun several
generations before—in Earle's case, with the generation of her father and

FIGURE 25. Earle's family in Worcester, like many other families, expressed their ancestry visually through their domestic settings. Her sister, Frances Clary Morse, included this photograph, taken in the Morse family dining room, in her 1902 book *Furniture of the Olden Times*. The handsome mahogany sideboard and knife boxes, the array of silver tea wares and decanter trolleys, and the blue and white historical transfer-printed plates hanging on the wall all suggest deep American roots and give evidence that collecting and connoisseurship were a Morse family enterprise.

mother. The quest for new forms of social security expressed itself in inward-looking families, clustered in selective groups. These groups were typically defined by status (determined by class and race) and familial links (genealogy), not by local proximity and communitarian values as in earlier times. Social and urban historians have identified a process of turning inward, away from traditional community values and toward an increasingly atomized nuclear family and more individually centered social attitudes. This separation of public from private life became the dominant middle-class behavioral system during the first half of the nineteenth century.[1] In this privatized world, individual families—to the extent that they were able—remained the basic nuclear social unit that they had been since the earliest Puritan days. In contrast with the Puritan model, however, late-nineteenth-century middle-class families tended to insulate themselves from the world around them, relying instead on internal structural supports that operated within carefully defined small groups of like-minded "respectable" people.

In antebellum towns and cities especially, families began to employ architectural and behavioral strategies to reinforce their economic and social distinctions rather than interacting seamlessly with the community at large. Through careful genealogical screening, backed up by increasingly selective neighborhoods, clubs, vacation spots, and other social devices, they were able to create a new social nexus that was the product of personal selection, genteel behavior, and individual will, rather than being determined, as the Puritans saw it, by the will of God.[2]

Two important forces, one demographic and one intellectual, helped shape the choices people now made about their social identities and their ideas of community. Since the earliest years of the nineteenth century, demographic forces had been eroding the ability of most Americans to predict with any certainty what the future might hold for themselves and their children. Rural communities found themselves squeezed by increasing numbers of newcomers competing for limited prime acreage.[3] The fertility of their marginal farmland was not always adequate to support large numbers of in-migrants or to compete with the potential of newly accessible, highly fertile acreage in lands to the west. That situation was exacerbated by improvements in transportation that made it possible for farmers in these newly settled regions to ship their agricultural produce to eastern markets. In the face of declining agricultural opportunity for newcomers, the lure of the frontier and the rapidly developing industrial cities offered an irresistible future to many rural New Englanders—in particular those at the fringes rather than the center of society. The growth rate of Vermont, whose population had increased sevenfold, from 30,000 inhabitants in 1781 to 217,000 in 1810, dropped precipitously between 1810 and 1820 to a mere 8 percent.[4] By 1885 the Massachusetts state census reported that those currently residing in the place where they had been born numbered only slightly more than one-third of the population. The large number of immigrants who had entered Massachusetts during the decade, seeking employment in the industrial cities, skewed this figure downward; even among native-born Americans, however, fewer than 50 percent were living in the city of their birth. Whatever its causes, the pattern of dispersion of families, which came to be a defining characteristic of life in much of New England during the nineteenth century, interrupted the orderly transmission of community and family values from one generation to the next.[5]

In this transitory social context, families had to devise new means of ensuring some degree of continuity. As their lives became increasingly less place-bound, Americans began to rely more heavily on symbolic structures, as embodied in both social rituals and material forms, to perpetuate their traditional values and maintain their collective identities.[6] Kinship networks, which had provided a functional structure for political authority as well as business and social activities, diminished in their effectiveness as geographic mobility increased. For many families, legal inheritance, a traditional means of passing power and social order from one generation to the next, became displaced by new class-based sources of power grounded in commercial and economic success, which undermined long-standing family and community structures. The resulting discontinuity required a reworking of the linked concepts of kinship and inheritance. By the end of the century, increasing numbers of middle- and upper-class Americans, including Alice Morse Earle, were attempting to reconsolidate their eroded family power base by invoking the institution of ancestry. Bolstered by genetic theory and reconstructed through the quasi-scientific discipline of genealogy, ancestry could function metaphorically to help shore up social boundaries and reaffirm eroded family power.

As a hedge against the dispersion and disruption of family continuity, families had long relied on their family Bibles, where they could record births, marriages, and deaths. Schoolgirls and young women also frequently stitched records of elite families into samplers, family trees, and heraldic emblems. As the needlework scholar Betty Ring has pointed out, these works helped genteel families both to proclaim and to maintain their elite status. That they required not only a pedigree to proclaim but also the leisure time to depict it would not have been lost on visitors to fashionable parlors and chambers.[7] Some families might have their important events recorded on the surface of a redware pie plate or charger, or some other visual mnemonic device that would ensure the perpetuation of family memory. Family heirlooms of all kinds reinforced genealogical connections between generations, especially for women. Monogrammed silver, linens, even furniture conveyed female identity through successive generations, especially at a time when women were prohibited from owning real estate (fig. 26).[8] Trunks laden with clothing lovingly packed by grandmothers descended into the hands of granddaughters, who delighted in trying on the gowns, hats, gloves, and lace collars of their foremothers. For Earle,

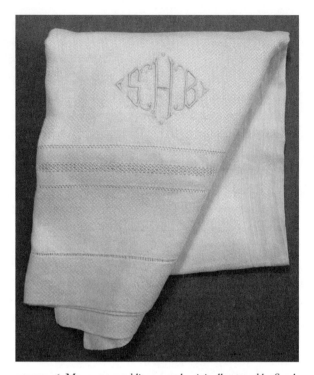

FIGURE 26. Monogrammed linen towel, originally owned by Sarah Bean Hadden, great-grandmother of the author. Sarah Tyler Bean married Archibald Hadden in 1881, and this was probably a wedding gift or part of her trousseau. Marking possessions with monograms offered women a means to construct a historical identity. These items could be passed down from mother to daughter through time, keeping the original owner alive throughout a family's history. Collection of the author.

collecting ancestors and collecting material goods were closely analogous. If her ancestors represented a genetic inheritance, their goods—or goods that were temporally or spatially associated with them—embodied a cultural inheritance. Genealogy clarified tribal bonds, and material goods helped to maintain tribal boundaries. In both instances, collecting offered a means of reclaiming that inheritance, of keeping it in safe hands so that it might be transmitted to future generations.

Distance from the ancestral hearth elevated the importance of record-keeping, especially for those on the periphery. By 1800, geographic proximity to one's family could no longer be assumed or expected. More abstract methods of maintaining family continuity had to be devised. In addition to families' maintaining their Bibles and other memory totems, towns carefully recorded the movement of their members, publishing an-nual reports that detailed the increase and decrease of the population. Events that typically would have been witnessed by a wide circle of family and longtime friends had now to be carefully reconstructed in letters to those who, with increasing frequency, were rendered absent by geographic distance. Although distance had been a disruptive factor for American families since the seventeenth century, the accelerated rate of migration by the turn of the nineteenth century made the idealized constructs of home and family loom larger than ever before in the cultural imagination.

The settlement patterns represented among Earle's direct ancestors reveal a combination of persistence and dispersion typical of the New England experience.[9] The first two generations settled in a geographic ring that, not surprisingly, clustered around Boston, extending west to Marlborough, north to Woburn, and south to Medfield. The next two generations, who lived between 1601 and 1740, persisted in the original settlement towns but also migrated to some of the other outlying towns, including Sherborn, Lexington, and Concord, as well as north to Ipswich. The fifth generation persisted in Sherborn, Sudbury, and Watertown but expanded into Wayland and southwest to Framingham. During this generation the new immigrants from Scotland, via Northern Ireland, settled in Londonderry, New Hampshire, around 1720. The sixth and seventh generations, who lived until 1822, persisted in Sudbury and Wayland throughout the entire eighteenth century until 1793, pushing northward as well into north-central Massachusetts and into the New Hampshire frontier, settling in Lunenburg, Massachusetts, and New Ipswich, Peterborough, and Dublin, New Hampshire. The agricultural crisis of the early nineteenth century drove the eighth generation farther out onto the frontier, to Andover, Vermont, and Jackson, Maine, and finally, by the ninth and tenth generations, south to the industrial cities of Worcester and, ultimately, Brooklyn.

In 1858 the genealogist Andrew Ward, whose professional credentials included membership in the New England Historic Genealogical Society (founded in 1845), the Connecticut Historical Society, the State Historical Society of Wisconsin, and the Pennsylvania Historical Society, briefly summarized the history of the field of genealogy in the United

States, noting, "A greater degree of interest on the subject has prevailed throughout New England the last twenty years than during the whole previous period since its settlement, and is rapidly increasing." Ward attributed this new interest in part to the publication in 1829 by John Farmer, whom Ward termed a "genealogical pioneer in the New England States," of the names of many of the first New England settlers. The major force for genealogical activity, however, seems to have been the recent formation of the New England Historic Genealogical Society in Boston, whose publications both answered and advanced the quest for ancestral information.[10] Ward also cited the prevalence of family gatherings as an added stimulus to genealogical interest. In the case of the Rice family, the subject of an 1858 study by Ward, several generations of descendants had been convening annually at the homestead of their ancestor Edmund Rice in Wayland. According to Ward, these gatherings were "chiefly of a social character" and were attended by descendants who lived in the immediate vicinity of Wayland as well as those who had to travel from "remote places" to attend.[11] These events were hardly unique to the Rice family.

Despite its rapid rise in popularity in the later years of the nineteenth century, genealogy had a much older history. Biblical genealogies, with their succession of "begats," provided a chronicle of tribal connections, as well as a means of measuring historical time. Classical literature also employed genealogies to establish the descent of aristocratic families from the gods.[12] Birth order has always been an important means of structuring the transmission of power, and ancestry has long been used to authenticate personal claims to status and recognition, particularly in periods of social stress. Benvenuto Cellini's autobiography, written amid the turmoil of early Renaissance Florence, cited his family's descent from Caesar's generals as evidence of the validity of his credentials.[13] The institution of the British monarchy, despite some notable interruptions in succession, was governed by a basic presumption that power is inheritable.

In the newly created United States, birth order, as well as the hierarchical system it represented, became tainted by its associations with an essentially anti-egalitarian Old World order. The new order, reflected in the American constitutional structure, replaced inheritance with the principle of representative democracy. By the second half of the nineteenth century, however, especially in urban society, flourishing capitalism and a seemingly fluid class system made the earlier equalitarian reluctance to

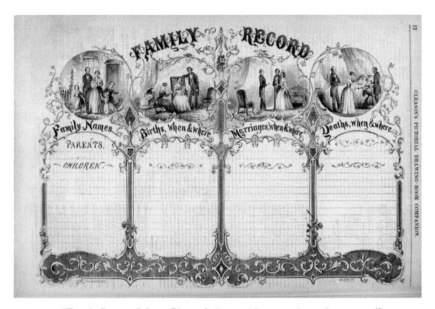

FIGURE 27. "Family Register" from Gleason's *Pictorial Drawing Room Companion* (January 7, 1854). By the mid-nineteenth century, genealogy had become increasingly popular among families who had been in America long enough to have "ancestors," as well as among families living far from their ancestral hearths, lest they lose track of their forebears. According to the accompanying article, this document "will afford those of our readers who desire to do so, an opportunity to register there all those sacred family matters, which every domestic circle should preserve; and when bound, it will form a record which our descendants will particularly value." The Internet Archive; original in Boston Public Library.

invoke ancestry seem naïve. Once again, Americans sought to consolidate their power, this time class power, through the ancient tribal vehicle of genealogical verification. Anglo-Saxon theorists expanded the horizons of ancestry from individual family to nation and ultimately to human progress in general, investing genealogy with added importance as a mechanism for securing social order. The rising popularity of genealogy, both as a scholarly pursuit and as a hobby, stimulated publishers to produce lithographed charts on which individuals could record their own family trees. The inclusion of these charts in such widely read magazines as *Gleason's Pictorial Drawing Room Companion* helped to spread the interest in personal ancestry, which was further nourished by the rise of public libraries and historical societies (fig. 27). There amateur and professional genealogists could find the collections of deeds, wills, parish records, family Bibles, and other historical records they needed to satisfy their quest for complete documentation of their family histories. In 1900 an anecdotal article about the genealogical community described three categories of researchers: "First may be found the amateurs—generally ladies—who admit in moments of relaxation from the severe mental strain that it is 'most bewitching,' and their delight in finding 'another ancestor' is often un-bounded." The second group was composed of the "kind enthusiast" doing a favor for a friend. Expert genealogists made up the third.[14]

By the second quarter of the nineteenth century, the cultural demand for genealogical documentation also resulted in the publication of formal family histories intended for widespread distribution among descendants of the early emigrants. Perhaps inspired by the bicentennial of the Puritan Great Migration in the 1630s, these family histories began with a founding couple, usually of British heritage—and ideally with aristocratic connections—and developed the family tree structure from the patrilineal descent of that couple's children. When Andrew Ward published his history of the Rice family, dedicated "to the descendants of Edmund Rice," he remarked that a number of family histories had already been traced and published, although many of these had been printed privately. "Others are being so," he continued, prophesying that "the time is coming, when a library will not be considered properly furnished, unless it contains a history of the family to which it belongs."[15]

That time had already arrived for the Morse family. In an 1849 letter to his son Edwin, Benjamin Morse, Alice Morse Earle's grandfather, inquired "how cousin Abner gets along with his genealogy of the Morses." Cousin Abner was the Reverend Abner Morse, an early member of the New England Historic Genealogical Society, founded in Boston in 1845. *The Memorial of the Morses* was published in 1850, just five years after the society's founding. The linkage that genealogies of this kind established to a far-off aristocratic ancestor provided families with a possible means of social distinction, sometimes complete with a coat of arms, a visible symbol of superiority. The importance of that linkage in terms of community stature was indicated by the genealogical appendices that often appeared at the back of local histories. Abner Morse's work provided detailed documentation of the Morse pedigree for the genealogical appendix to Levi Leonard's 1855 history of Dublin, New Hampshire.[16]

The popularity of these family histories lay partly in the high levels of geographic mobility that characterized nineteenth-century America and partly in the exponential increase in the numbers of descendants in families that had been in North America for eight or nine generations. The Rice family history documented the existence of 1,400 families and almost 7,000 descendants of Edmund Rice. Ward explained that the Rice history had been necessitated by the fact that branches of the family were "now in all parts of the land." Furthermore, "those living very remote from the 'Homestead,' whence the dispersion of the race began, cannot, in the nature of things, possess much knowledge of their ancestry, and perhaps have, for townsmen and neighbors, relatives that are unknown to them as such."[17]

The idea that one was living among strangers who might be relatives would surely have resonated among the many Americans who, by the 1850s, inhabited a world in which most of the people around them were unknown to them. Perhaps the most profound social transformation of the nineteenth century was the metamorphosis from a society characterized by family connections and face-to-face interactions to one in which interactions were conducted through the intermediaries of formalized legal and behavioral codes and bureaucratic structures.

The publication of Darwin's evolutionary theories in 1859 lent a new intellectual credence to these genealogical investigations. Darwin had posited that all species were subject to random variation and natural selection, and that only those best suited to their environment would survive. Popular acceptance and application of Darwin's ideas varied: many Americans felt that natural selection and random variation were true for species in wild nature, but that humans were separated from the beasts by consciousness (thinking) and conscience (morality). Moreover, the long period of nurture granted to human young seemed to confirm that heredity could be influenced through environmental agency. Earle's position on this principle, as expressed through her materialist emphasis, was a mediating one: she believed firmly in the power and importance of heredity—as her focus on genealogy demonstrated—but she also recognized the power of institutions and human nurture to shape human behavior. Her scholarly concentration on the history of American customs and social institutions, then, may be interpreted as an attempt to determine the sources of American strength—both hereditary and environmental.

Genealogy, however, could be employed as a means of discerning fitness: those families and individuals who had survived could be viewed in both historical and scientific terms as embodying genetic success. In this sense, genealogical evidence could provide a comforting level of predictability about the future in a world where traditional boundaries and rules seemed to have vanished. Earle's invariable use of both of her family names, Morse and Earle, can be interpreted as evidence of the extent to which she embraced this genealogical belief system. Of course, sterling ancestry was not a requirement for success, as it had been in the Old World. One important aspect of middle- and upper-class culture during this period was its emphasis on codified behavior. Regardless of birth, men and women who had achieved a requisite degree of economic prosperity could move up socially, provided they were willing to learn and accommodate the behavioral norms that governed all areas of middle-class life. The way one dressed, or educated one's children, or dined in public, or decorated one's parlor could all serve to confirm one's acceptance by social peers or one's betters, or, less happily, to undermine that hard-won economic success with social rejection. For example, middle-class Americans, noted Earle, were no longer "blissfully ignorant of the existence or presence of microbes, germs, and bacteria." They now understood these phenomena in social as well as scientific terms and could no longer drink "contentedly in succession from a single vessel, which was passed from hand to hand, and lip to lip, around the board," as had their "sturdy and unsqueamish forebears."[18]

DAR founder Ellen Hardin Walworth considered "the forms of society" "as essential to the good order of society as are the forms of law to the administration of justice." For Walworth, "the bit of pasteboard that we call a visiting card establishes a barrier in social intercourse as effectual as if it were a bar of steel." To her mind, as to the minds of her readers, "this little thing, lightly thrown about, is really a symbol of the sacredness of home." Furthermore, "like many forms it may be abused," but "it cannot be spared." Walworth's recognition of the calling card, and the behavior that it commanded, as symbolic raised the institution of home to a level that could be achieved only by those with the proper training, intuitive sensibilities, and background. Its very ephemerality formed the basis for a conscious attempt to restrict social entry to those who had either inherited or somehow assimilated an understanding of the proper symbolic modes of behavior.[19]

The historical discontinuity of social acceptance based on behavioral grounds alone was evident in its disputed reception. Social satirists such as William Dean Howells, Edith Wharton, and other literary commentators amused their middle-class readers with comic tales about the social ineptness of the self-made bourgeoisie. In Howells's novel *The Rise of Silas Lapham,* a newly elevated Bostonian recently transplanted from the country can make an appropriate social statement by building a grand house in the Back Bay, but his lack of appropriate ancestry leaves him ill-equipped to deal with the social scrutiny of his Brahmin hosts at a dinner party.[20] Such works contested the prevailing American mythology about equal access to power, reflecting a generally conservative discourse about refinement, social fitness, and inherited attributes which formed the foundation of social Darwinism.

The rapidly changing demographic complexion of American cities during the last decade of the nineteenth century, a result of the recent arrival of massive numbers of immigrants from southern and eastern Europe, further nurtured a tribal urge for self-preservation among the urban middle class.[21] Genealogy offered the twin parameters of biology and history to raise a secure boundary around those Americans who felt particularly assaulted by the influx of newcomers. In her conclusion to *Margaret Winthrop,* Earle analyzed the culture of New England in terms of its immigration history, focusing on the significance of the Great Migration of 1634–1639 and the cessation of immigration after 1640 for almost a hundred years. "Thus," wrote Earle of her fellow New Englanders, "we were, to use Lord Bacon's words, 'built up from within, not pieced out from without.'" "The result," she concluded "was the establishment of a homogeneity which has afforded and perpetuated a distinct type, almost a race, only ... that would be claiming for ourselves too great a place among the nations of the earth."[22] This statement did not merely assert Earle's vision of New England homogeneity; it completely obliterated the existence of black and Native American New Englanders, two groups who, it seems, had no place in Earle's racial scheme.

Despite her professed reluctance to use the term "race" to describe herself and her New England peers, Earle was expressing a common late-nineteenth-century social conception. Racial theories dominated the popular discourse about immigration, as they shaped most other post-Darwinian social discourse. In a world that had been "built up from within," genealogy became an important mechanism for establishing one's position in the social network, the one true measure of character and entitlement. Earle's faith in the power of blood—a euphemism for genetic makeup—was tellingly expressed at the conclusion of *Margaret Winthrop*, where she included a brief account of Winthrop's children and descendants. Her purpose, other than to satisfy the curiosity of her readers, seems to have been to make a point about the illustrious array of progeny generated by the Winthrop union, including the then–duke of Norfolk. "Thus," Earle proclaimed, "the blood of the Puritan mother runs in the veins of the most prominent Roman Catholic nobleman in England," a discovery that, in the context of the extreme anti-Catholic sentiment of the 1890s, expressed the prevailing faith in the subtle power of ancestry to influence even the pope.[23]

Genealogy, furthermore, offered the added benefit of educational uplift to those who chose to participate. In addition to the DAR and the Society of Colonial Dames, Earle was a member of the recently organized (1895) National Society of New England Women, New York City's largest patriotic club, with 325 active and 174 associate members by 1899.[24] The stated purpose of the New England Society was threefold: philanthropic ("to promote the interests of all women of New England origin, either socially or in the line of professions and trades"), educational (to advance "the study of American history, religious, political, and social, beginning with the landing of the Pilgrims"), and social ("whereby the bond of union and fellowship will hold a far-reaching power and influence").[25] The group maintained strict membership classifications that were dependent on bloodlines. It defined an active member as "one who is a native of New England, or both of whose parents or one parent and husband were born there." Associate members—"having one parent, or one or more grandparents, or a husband, who were native New Englanders"—were not eligible to hold the highest offices of the organization, according to the bylaws: "This method will always keep the governing power of the society in the hands of its genuine New England members."[26]

The more pressing agenda of all three organizations, however, was the Americanization of immigrants through influence, example, and outreach. American attitudes toward immigrants had shifted gradually over the course of the nineteenth century from a position of grudging acceptance to one of open hostility. Newcomers had always been viewed with suspicion, but as demographic and economic pressures placed mounting stress on conceptions of community and nationality, the resulting tensions shaped an increasingly restrictive immigration policy. The ideology of assimilation, grounded in the notion that the American experience would obviate cultural and ethnic differences, gave way to fears that the "new" immigrants—largely from southern and eastern Europe—were inassimilable and therefore a threat to the Anglo-Saxon stock. The disappearance of the American frontier, which was made official by the federal census of 1890, coupled with reports of declining fertility among established white Americans, exacerbated urban middle-and upper-class fears about the impact of unchecked immigration. Social Darwinist notions of "survival of the fittest" made ancestry increasingly important as a means of differentiating between old and new Americans, and excluding the latter from elite circles. Ancestral organizations, including the Daughters of the American Revolution and the Colonial Dames of America, both founded in 1890, worked to collect data and define standards that would scientifically establish American hereditary lines.

The scientific theories that reinforced the ideology of racial nationalism drew heavily on the work of historians. Beginning in the 1840s with the publication of an American edition of Sharon Turner's *History of the Anglo-Saxons* and George Perkins Marsh's *Goths in New England,* and continuing after the Civil War with the work of John Fiske and Herbert Baxter Adams, American historians had developed quasi-scientific theories about the progress of civilization, interpreting American civilization squarely with-in a northern European context. Fiske pronounced federalism to be America's unique contribution to the Saxon form of self-government, and Adams's "germ theory" posited America as the culmination of a process of civilization that had begun in the Teutonic forests of Germany and been transmitted racially by the Saxons to England and then to America.[27]

By perpetuating the memory of the Revolutionary heroes through monuments, street names, house restoration, and historic site preservation, as well as archival research and documentation of the past, ancestral organizations (including those to which Earle belonged) hoped to offer useful lessons in patriotism. They also lobbied for and organized public celebrations and pageants to commemorate important historical events, and attempted to reach students directly by donating history books to school libraries and reproductions of historical paintings to school classrooms.[28]

The rhetoric of Americanization permeated the publications of the DAR, particularly the writings of Ellen Hardin Walworth. In 1892, in the inaugural issue of *American Monthly Magazine,* the DAR house organ, Walworth proclaimed that "the main motive of the Society . . . is love of country, and the leading object of its effort is to perpetuate a spirit of true Americanism." The magazine invoked the words of two American presidents, Grover Cleveland and George Washington, to sanction the mission of the organization.[29] Washington, in his Farewell Address, had urged all Americans "to promote as an object of primary importance institutions for the general diffusion of knowledge." Such institutions, he believed, would develop "an enlightened public opinion" and afford "to young and old such advantages as shall develop in them the largest capacity for performing the duties of American citizens."[30] Washington's words imbued education with a clear patriotic mission, one that permeated the DAR itself and its mouthpiece journal.

Grover Cleveland, a Democrat whose reform philosophy won him enough Republican support to return him to the White House in 1892, exhorted "the descendants of the Pilgrims" not to "fail in the discharge of their highest duty," for American culture was doomed, said Cleveland, "if, yielding to the temptation of an un-American tendency, they neglect to teach persistently that in the early days there was, and that there still ought to be, such a thing as true and distinctive Americanism." Furthermore, he warned, "our government is not suited to a selfish and sordid people, and . . . in their hands, it is not safe." Cleveland concluded these remarks by acknowledging the sacred function of generational transmission: "This heritage of ours has been confided from generation to generation to the patriotic keeping and loving care of true Americanism, and . . . this alone can preserve it to shelter a free and happy people."[31]

In an attempt to reinforce federalism as the ideal model of good government, which could be transmitted through subsequent generations, the National Society of the Colonial Dames of America and National Society of the Daughters of the American Revolution each adopted structural models that were designed to accommodate both local self-government and national order.[32] Walworth explained this to her DAR sisters, justifying the emphasis on individualism in terms of the gender of the organization's membership when she hypothesized that intuition was a more powerful force than logic, citing a comment made by Senator George Hoar (a distant relation of Earle's) about "the combined wisdom of juries, which in so many cases puts the jury in the place of judgment rather than the judge," as evidence of "the superiority of instinctive and intuitive judgment over the logical method." For "as women are admitted to possess this intuitive and instinctive judgment in an extraordinary degree," Hardin continued, "it may be found that there is wisdom in their selection of this most democratic principle of Americanism, the sovereignty of the individual, as the keystone of the organization."[33] To that end, the DAR organized itself into a loose confederation of local chapters, ensuring that the power of the institution would remain collective rather than centralized. The chapters conducted their business independently throughout the year, albeit following prescribed procedures for admitting new members, and gathered once a year in Washington, D.C., for a "Continental Congress," where they could collectively determine the course of the institution for the next year.

Walworth's emphasis on intuition over logic was perhaps a reaction against the excesses of the business community, which seemed to many Americans by the 1890s to be driven solely by the cold logic of capitalism. Walworth warned her readers about the mixed blessing of economic opportunity for women. "Now when so many avenues of business, so many opportunities of effort are open to women," she advised, "it is important for [them] to make a just estimate of the relation between the business world and the social world." For if a woman partook of the opportunities offered her by the business world, she might "lose sight of her rightful position in society" and ultimately be rendered unfit to exercise her social power. Walworth perceived this threat as disastrous for the future of American society. Without the guiding influence of women, society in general, and in particular what Walworth termed "our race," was doomed "to return to a semi-barbaric condition."[34] Walworth's words seem to embody a fairly rigid notion of essentialism with regard to what women (that is, white middle-class women) should be. It was an attitude that would have put her at odds with her pro-suffrage sisters, who were less willing to view womanhood as genetically restricted.

Earle was thoroughly familiar with this rhetoric, and she would have agreed with Daniel Webster's definition of society as "the more cultivated portion of the community in its social relations and influences."[35] Her own ancestry, as well as that of her husband—who, with two *Mayflower* emigrants among his forebears, was more highly bred than his wife in terms of the number of "quality" ancestors in his pedigree—planted her firmly in that "cultivated portion," and provided her with a large genetic pool of positive ancestral traits to fall back on. From her earliest writings, Earle incorporated her own ancestors where appropriate, establishing a broad historical community of Americans to which she had direct, inherited links.

Earle's membership application for the DAR provides specific access to some of the inhabitants of that community. While the Colonial Dames required prospective members to provide evidence that they were descended from Revolutionary officers or people who had held positions of some political or social importance in colonial America, the DAR merely stated that membership in the organization was open to all women who were at least eighteen years old and "descended from a man or woman who with unfailing loyalty to the cause of American independence, served as a sailor, a soldier or civil officer in one of the several Colonies or States, or in the United Colonies of States, or as a recognized patriot, or rendered material aid thereto."[36] The added proviso "provided the applicant is personally acceptable to the Society" could be invoked to ensure that the organization's homogeneous membership would not be subjected to racial, ethnic, or class diversity.[37]

Both organizations required their members to trace their immediate lineage back at least four generations, so as to establish a permanent historical record that could facilitate genealogical research for generations to come. The names of both husbands and wives were to be provided, because, as the DAR historian Mary Lockwood pointed out to the membership, it was frequently the wife's name that helped distinguish her husband from many others with the same name. "John Adams would have stood for naught in Massachusetts genealogy," commented Lockwood dryly, without the contextual clarifier of his wife, Abigail. "There were forty-nine John Adamses who fought in the Revolution."[38]

Earle, whose family tree embraced several Revolutionary officers, selected Captain the Honorable Richard Heard to establish her lineage. Heard had represented Middlesex County at the Massachusetts Provincial Congress, which, according to Earle's application papers, "was composed of the most influential patriots in the Commonwealth." The congress, "under the spirited leadership of John Hancock," Earle wrote, formed Committees of

Safety and Correspondence and sent "messages of defiance" to Governor Gage, and as a result, "the War of the Revolution was materially hastened." Heard, who was fifty-two years old in 1774, enlisted in the Company of Minute Men after the congress adjourned, for the purpose, according to Earle, of showing "by his example to his fellow citizens that the rank and file should be composed of men of honor and dignity in the community." He served eight months, was present at the battles of Concord, Lexington, and Bunker Hill, and for his services received "the highest sum paid any Sudbury man," £132.[39]

Heard, born in Wayland, Massachusetts, in 1720, was the son of Zachariah Heard and Silence Browne. Zachariah Heard had emigrated from England sometime before 1707, the year he purchased a homestead and shop in Cambridge. The deed listed him as a clothier, although according to family tradition he had also served in the British navy. Silence Browne was the daughter of Captain Thomas and Patience Foster Browne, one of Sudbury's wealthiest and most notable gentry families. After their marriage, the Heards moved to Wayland, a town adjacent to Sudbury, where Zachariah served as a selectman in 1710, surveyor in 1714, and constable in 1716. Richard, their second son, married Sarah Fiske in 1746. Fiske, born in Sudbury, was also descended from a prominent Massachusetts family. Her great-great-grandfather David Fiske had emigrated in about 1637 from Suffolk, England, to Watertown, Massachusetts, where his landholdings totaled 227 acres. Jonathan Fiske, Sarah's father, was characterized by family tradition as "a man of importance and wealth."[40] It was he who moved from Lexington, where several generations of Fiskes had settled, to Sudbury sometime after 1711.

The marriage of Richard Heard and Sarah Fiske, by uniting two prosperous and civic-minded Middlesex County families, further consolidated several generations of local power and landownership. It was a pattern that would continue, at least in this particular family, for only one more generation. In 1773 their daughter Sarah Heard married Jonathan Hoar, son of another prominent Sudbury family. By the time Sarah and Jonathan's daughter Betsey was ready to marry in the late 1790s, however, post-Revolutionary New England was a dramatically different place. The geographic network that had retained its localistic character throughout much of the eighteenth century had expanded dramatically, north into Vermont, New Hampshire, and Maine, and even more forcefully west into New York State and Ohio. In 1798 Betsey Hoar left Sudbury for Andover, Vermont, to marry a young man newly arrived from New Hampshire, Benjamin Morse—Alice Morse Earle's paternal grandfather.[41]

Despite the geographic and cultural distance from Middlesex County, the community of settlers in Andover re-created the same strong kinship networks they had known in Massachusetts and Connecticut. Benjamin Morse, Betsey Hoar's husband, was reared in Dublin, New Hampshire, where his grandfather Thomas Morse had been one of the original proprietors in the 1760s. Thomas Morse's family had lived in Sherborn, Massachusetts, about eight miles southeast of Sudbury, for three generations prior to his northward migration. The Hoar family had also made forays into New Hampshire beginning in the mid-eighteenth century. The circumstances that brought the two together can only be surmised, but strong kinship networks existed in both families—as they did in many New England families—and these would have sustained ongoing communication between the established family centers in Massachusetts and the satellite communities in New Hampshire and beyond.[42]

Few families were exempt from the effects of dispersion into the frontier, and Alice Morse Earle's own immediate family was no exception. Her father, Edwin Morse, had been born one of a pair of twins. His twin brother, Edward, left for Ohio in the 1830s—a parting that must have been particularly difficult for an identical twin.[43] He settled in Cincinnati, combining the practice of law with real estate speculation. Although he certainly made enough money to travel back east for periodic family visits, Edward's life in what was then still considered the West must have seemed strange and distant to his New England relatives. The disruptive effects of distance are evident in a letter written to Earle by her paternal uncle Reuben Morse in 1894. Edwin Morse had died in 1891, and Earle had apparently written to Reuben for genealogical details about his family and those of his brothers and sisters. Although Reuben—Edwin and Edward's brother—was able to relate that Edward had four children, and even provided their names (Helen, Edith, Jessie, and Harry), he was unable to recall the name of Edward's wife.[44] He was quite elderly at the time, but he also clearly had not had a close or continuous relationship with his brother's family.

Unlike her elderly uncle, Earle was very interested in the names and details of all members of her family, past and present. In a letter to

William C. Brownell, her editor at Charles Scribner's Sons, she discussed a proposed dedication to her current work in progress, *Colonial Dames and Good Wives*. She had already identified members of ancestral organizations as a potential market for the book, suggesting to Brownell that "in these days of Colonial Dames Societies and Daughters of all dates and wars, I think this book would have a good sale—if treated properly." "Properly" included advertising the book in the DAR's *American Monthly Magazine,* the magazine of the Daughters of Revolution, and the *American Historical Register,* which Earle joked was "devoted to the exploitation and edification of all the 'Patriotic-Heredity' Societies of America," and of which she was an honorary associate editor. In addition to advertising, she added, "I should cater a little by binding it in Col. Dames Soc colors, blue and buff."[45]

The dedication Earle proposed, "To the Colonial Dames, whose blood runs in my veins, whose spirit lives in my work," listed thirteen of her female ancestors—"in rather fine italic type," she suggested, "so not to take up too much room." In her letter to Brownell, Earle cited Elizabeth Morse, Alice Hoar, Mary Clary, Margaret Adams, Deborah Atherton, Judith Thurston, Hannah Phillips, Barbara Sheppard, Abigail Mason, Sarah Wyeth, Elizabeth Brown, Silence Heard, and Sufference How. "These names dominate the ancestors of our very best Massachusetts stock," she commented. "I don't suppose you, being an insular Rhode Islander, know enough about these names to appreciate that they are very good names in Massachusetts," she added jokingly.[46] Actually the list in Earle's letter contained several inaccuracies and did not completely conform to the dedication published in the book; this may have been of a piece with the informal tone of her letter, or may indicate (yet again) a willingness to embroider her personal genealogical history when she chose. Earle had no ancestor named "Mary Clary"; her grandmother Clary's first name was Persis, and her great-grandmother's name was Catherine Clary. She was probably referring to Mary Adams, wife of George Fairbanks. Furthermore, the blood of Elizabeth Brown and Barbara Sheppard definitely did not run through her veins. "Alice" Hoar (was Earle transposing her own identity here?) was actually Joanna Hoar, to whom Earle eventually did dedicate *Margaret Winthrop*. Hoar had been characterized by Charles Francis Adams as the mother of much of New England, including the Quincy family, Abigail Adams, John Quincy Adams, and others. "Indeed, it may fairly be questioned whether, in the whole wide field of American genealogy, there is any strain of blood more fruitful of distinguished men," wrote Adams, completely disregarding the distinguished women who produced the blood.[47]

As we have seen, an important link between genealogy and modern life for many women, Earle included, resided in the popular colonial revival activity of dressing up in the clothing of one's ancestors. These events often revolved around a tea party, an evening ball, a staged photograph, or a historic pageant, but whatever their mode, they transformed genealogy into a physical embodiment. As a form of historical play, they offered women a chance to inhabit, albeit it only in an imaginative sense, the world of their ancestors (fig. 28).[48] Earle's final book, *Two Centuries of Costume in America,* catered to this popular activity. The two-volume work tied together genealogy, ancestry, and material culture through its examination of one of the most traditional means of establishing, transmitting, and demonstrating social boundaries: clothing. In the preindustrial world that Earle described, social order was customarily maintained through physical appearance. Clothing served as a means for elites to differentiate themselves from all others, and was accordingly protected through the legal system by sumptuary laws.[49] Earle understood this system well, and throughout her study of costume, she attempted to explicate the social significance of the items she was describing. "A regard for dress was then, as now, an indication of due respect for the proprieties of life," she wrote. "It was then also a symbol of social distinction," she added, citing the existence of sumptuary laws as her evidence.[50] Her presentist tone in this passage confirms a larger purpose to this work, as in her other works: to educate and reform her own society through exposure to and instruction about the "customs and fashions" of the past.

Clothing, as one of the basic structures of tribal definition, served as a particularly potent social mechanism for Earle. In *Two Centuries of Costume* she supplemented a varied array of archival sources—letters, journal notations, household accounts, probate inventories, and literary evidence—with three basic forms of material evidence: portraits, surviving items of clothing, and photographs of her contemporaries wearing their ancestors' costumes.[51] An advertisement published in *American Monthly Magazine* in the spring of 1903 (the year the two-volume work was published) suggests Earle's method of gathering evidence, as well as the defining criteria

The Romance of Old Clothes.

FIGURE 28. "The Romance of Old Clothes," from *Two Centuries of Costume in America* (1903), Mrs. Eva E. Newell, Plantsville, Conn., photographer. For Earle and her readers, ancestral clothing offered a tangible and highly romantic link to the past. These items could not only be touched, smelled, and admired but also be worn, enabling the wearer literally to embody her family history.

for that evidence. "Alice Morse Earle is soon to bring out a book entitled 'Two Centuries of Dress in America,'" the notice began. "She is seeking to secure photographs of quaint, unusual or beautiful articles of dress, old portraits and miniatures with the history thereof. For this purpose she has sent out a circular asking for information, as she wishes to make the book valuable as well as interesting. Many of the Daughters of the American Revolution will be able to supply much needed information."⁵² The notice's specific reference to the DAR confirms the book's genealogical focus. Who better than the Daughters themselves to confer ancestral authenticity?

Earle had proposed a new book on costume in a letter to George Brett, president of Macmillan, in January 1903. She had been totally consumed with her previous book, *Sun-Dials and Roses of Yesterday,* up to its publication the previous November, and as she indicated to Brett, had not been certain that she wanted to undertake another big project so quickly. "Mr.

Booth [Macmillan editor W. S. Booth] wrote me a short time ago about another book," she reported, and "I did not answer being so uncertain of my coming year. But now I find I can see my future, and it has been changed by recent events." Perhaps she had intended to rest a bit, or even travel, but the death of her first grandchild, the newborn son of her daughter Mary Earle Moore, had precipitated a personal and family crisis. "His life was sacrificed I suppose by the operation for appendicitis my daughter endured last summer," she continued. "We are most unhappy over this loss—and my daughter is indeed in a grievous state." Consequently, "I am disinclined to social life at present, and naturally turn to book writing." She intended to spend all of her time with Mary for the immediate future and instructed that Brett should write to her there—with the implication that spare hours between nursing and emotionally supporting her daughter could be spent writing.[53]

The book, as she envisioned it, would be a history, to include, in addition to New England dress, Quaker, Huguenot, and Dutch clothing customs, as well as "the influence of the Indians in the picturesque hunting-shirt, &c.," as illustrated "by reproductions of contemporary portraits and photographs and drawings from existing articles of dress."[54] The period covered by the book, 1620–1820, she intentionally extended into the early nineteenth century in order to include "the picturesque dress" of that era. She also specified a format that called exclusively for inset photogravure plates—no halftone images—in which she intended to classify different articles of clothing (shirts, neckwear, embroidered gloves, purses, and the like), all of which could offer tangible links to people of the past.

Earle had already written one book on the history of costume, *Costume of Colonial Times*, published by Charles Scribner's Sons in 1894. That book was not illustrated, however, and she assured Brett that Scribner's had always intended to bring out an illustrated edition—although it never did. She concluded her proposal with the comment "I am sure of this—that *someone* will write a book on Costume if I do not—there is such a constant demand for it."[55]

Brett was intrigued by Earle's new plan and sent her a contract immediately, along with two recent books that had been illustrated in color, anticipating that the forthcoming book might also be a candidate for color illustration. Earle, however, was troubled by the quality of the color reproductions. "I cannot make them seem natural to me," she complained of the landscape and sea views, although "when we turn to interiors, especially to costume it is different. The more definite cut line of the parts of costume, its less subtle shadows, all are more suited to the mechanical effects of the colour process." Despite offering her grudging acquiescence, she admitted to Brett, "I do not care for colored illustrations in a book, mixed with illustration in black and white because they give a spotty look." She felt that "studies in browns" "would be a much more elegant book," nevertheless conceding, "I suppose the colored illustrations would *sell* well, in the trade I mean."[56] Ultimately, whether out of deference to Earle or because of their high production cost, Macmillan discarded the idea of color illustrations.

By the end of January, Earle reported to Brett that the book was progressing. "I have made queries in important quarters," she wrote, "and can secure not only the best but *all* the fine portraits existing in Virginia, Charleston, Baltimore, Annapolis, and New York, and I can always get everything in New England." She also noted that her friend and fellow writer Ogden Codman Jr. was preparing a book on the portrait painter John Singleton Copley. Codman's book would provide historical information about each portrait, including biographies of the sitters. He had promised Earle free Copley photographs for the costume book if she wanted them.[57] Although Earle claimed that her works addressed what scholars a century later would term vernacular culture, her delight at finding "the best" portraits, as well as her preoccupation with the physical appearance of her books, suggests impression management as a conscious goal.[58] Earle, a performer of relatively high status, frequently presented herself, or her subjects, in an egalitarian mode, veiling their actual standing with a veneer of universality. Despite the appearance of universality, however, the values represented remained class-bound, representative of Earle's upper-middle-class social expectations.

In addition to ten Copley portraits, Earle located 208 other portraits to use as illustrations in her costume book.[59] The sitters (almost all of whom were identified) represented a highly recognizable array of seventeenth- and eighteenth-century American gentry families. The Adamses, Beekmans, Bowditches, Bowdoins, Boylstons, Browns, Byrds, Cadwaladers, Carrolls, Carters, Cottons, Custises, Clintons, Edwards, Ellsworths, Hamiltons, Holyokes, Izards, Livingstons, Madisons, Mathers, Penns, Pinckneys, Ridgleys, Saltonstalls, Waldos, Websters, Winslows, and

Gold-covered Brocade Gown of Mrs. Eliza Lucas Pinckney.

FIGURE 29. "Gold-covered Brocade Gown of Mrs. Eliza Lucas Pinckney," from *Two Centuries of Costume in America* (1903). According to family legend, Madam Pinckney spun the silk for this gown, had it woven into a brocade fabric, and then made the dress herself. Here, Pinckney's descendant Alice Rutledge Reese wears her great-great-great-great-grandmother's costume. Dressing up in ancestral clothing could offer descendants tangible confirmation of their ancestors' inheritable attributes.

Winthrops were all presented as generic exemplars of American clothing customs, with little comment about class, economic status, or region.

The articles of clothing Earle used to supplement her portraits were authenticated through genealogical connections. In this sense they assumed the status of relics. Because all of these relics had clearly defined associational linkages with real people, they served Earle as physical manifestations of the departed ancestors. Relics have a mystical power to conjure up the past, and Earle consciously invoked that power to inflate the potency of her message.[60] The power of relics and the power of genealogy intersected when descendants appeared wearing the clothing of their ancestors. Earle reproduced a photograph of the great-granddaughter of Alice Rutledge Reese dressed in her ancestor's gown (fig. 29). The profusion of historical pageants at the turn of the twentieth century provides further testament to the popularity of dressing up. David Glassberg has suggested that part of the appeal of historical pageants lay in their enabling participants to get inside the past and see how it felt.[61] The act of dressing up represented more than nostalgic reenactment for Earle and her peers, however. If one wore one's ancestor's clothing, and behaved—even briefly— as one's ancestors had behaved, that activity might influence contemporary behavior. Earle's strong faith in the associational power of artifacts supported that conclusion.

This line of inquiry may be taken one step further, with the suggestion that the act of dressing up in old clothes demonstrated that the Anglo-Saxon race was still capable of "fitting into" them, both physically and culturally. Reenacting the genteel behavior of the past provided proof that the roots had survived over time.[62] By the turn of the century, the style of dressing up had evolved from representing dour Puritans to a more humanized depiction of Puritan life. In contrast to stereographs published at the time of the Centennial and even as late as 1891—which presented colonial American social life and domestic activities as a rather serious business—those published at the turn of the century illustrated scenes such as "Blindman's Buff in Old Boston" and other tableaus with titles such as "When Our Great Grandparents Were Young," "The Forfeit" (which depicted a kiss), "The Revelation" (the kisser unmasked), and "Our Great-Grand-Parents Were Young Once Too" (fig. 30). Participants in these scenes, though garbed as their ancestors had been garbed, displayed modern sensibilities with regard to social and sexual behavior. They

FIGURE 30. "A Ball-Room Scene in Colonial Days," 1900, Underwood & Underwood, Ottawa, Kans. Humorous stereograph views presented models dressed as eighteenth-century Americans being distinctly friskier than Puritan stereotypes had previously suggested. Courtesy of Library of Congress Prints and Photographs Division, Washington, D.C., 20540 USA.

renounced the Puritanism of their ancestors as too repressive of the natural forces that were, as Frederick Jackson Turner had suggested, the true source of American strength. Earle's costume book, as with all of her books, would guide these descendants to a more accurate and authentic re-creation of the past. The act of dressing up, then, could provide a concrete means of measuring the past against the present. This book would confirm that the descendants, while well grounded in their biological past, had evolved into a new race, one that would carry the nation into the future.

For Earle and her contemporaries, the genealogical imperative and all of its associated activities served as a conservative force for social and cultural stability and yet also an engine for social reform. Those with "roots" felt entitled to positions of social and cultural power. Through her club work, her lecturing, and, most important, her writing, Earle engaged in a mission that was both personal and political. Her ancestry gave her admission to a select society: the inheritors of the Revolution and perpetuators of the republican experiment. Within that sheltered group, she could socialize comfortably and gain satisfaction from "doing good." In a larger sense, however, these genealogical and ancestral organizations were engaged in a new kind of social engineering as well, using history—through a variety of public outreach mechanisms—to restore the Union to what they perceived as its historically "American" character.

CHAPTER 9

Toward a New Public History

※

A LICE MORSE EARLE'S FINAL BOOK, *Two Centuries of Costume in America*, rounded out an illustrious career as a writer. She had written seventeen books—all of which had been well received by the public—as well as some forty-two articles, Moreover, she had accomplished this enormous output in the space of only fourteen years. The body of work she produced created a lasting legacy—a new kind of democratized history of American life. Material culture, as Earle knew well, abounds in symbolic meanings. The corpus of her work served in both public and private settings as a guide for Americans eager to insert themselves into a new national creation narrative, one that she had fleshed out with props, settings, costumes, and activities. Using her books and articles as a script, readers could insert themselves directly into that narrative—reinventing their own identities, but authenticated by the presence of real things.

Earle's histories, aimed at popular audiences, served to provide an alternate paradigm to the formal vision presented by academic historians, who were increasingly writing primarily for their peers, and the nostalgic yearning among popular readers for a new national history that would allow them entry into the story.[1] For Earle and her peers, a history that embraced the harsh Calvinist doctrine of Puritanism was of limited utility; they lived in a world that was governed far more by consumer values than by piety. They sought a history that seemed authentic, that salvaged the Puritan attitudes toward family, duty, integrity, and industry, but also

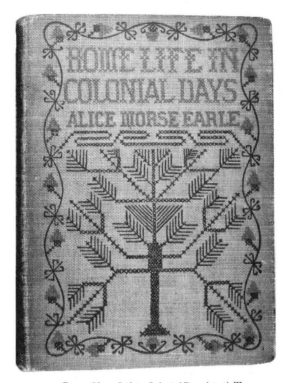

FIGURE 31. Cover, *Home Life in Colonial Days* (1898). The cover design's evocation of a cross-stitch sampler reinforced the book's message about the power of the past to domesticate the present and future. The book itself could easily serve as a "quaint" decorative accessory in a Colonial Revival home, conveying Puritan values to successive generations. Author's collection.

a history that was romantic, emotionally satisfying, and, most important, relevant to their present. Earle's best-selling *Home Life in Colonial Days*, as well as her other books, provided useful templates by which readers could reconstruct their lives, both privately and publicly (fig. 31). Through her writing, Earle expanded the scope of the American story, allowing participation by a broad range of people. Her vision of history embraced a new theatricality, delineating props that could accessorize private and public historical stage sets. Her influence found expression in the decoration of private parlors, bedrooms, and kitchens, as well as historic house and garden restorations and re-creations, museums' period room settings, historical pageants, colonial balls and teas, and the proliferation of other Colonial Revival forms that appeared at the turn of the twentieth century.

For its practitioners, this new type of history, supported by Earle's scholarship, clearly held enormous educational as well as cultural potential. It embraced a greatly enlarged field of evidence, expanding access beyond professional scholars and other well-educated readers. Its advocates—ranging from educators and women organizers of house museums and historic gardens, to suffrage and anti-suffrage activists, and members of local historical societies—believed that vernacular artifacts and anecdotes about ordinary life were just as important a means of cultural transmission as the words and biographies of the famous.[2] Earle enriched her historical vision through the conscious assignment of symbolic meaning to many of the objects she discussed in her texts, and by her extensive reliance on metaphor. In this way she was able to invest the most ordinary colonial artifacts with a significance that would help her readers find meaning in their own lives. This strategy further confirmed the underlying cultural complexity of Earle's work, as well as its utility as a vehicle for examining divergent social and cultural agendas.[3]

Earle's immediate success coincided with the emergence of a growing antiquarian outlook among middle- and upper-class Americans, and more specifically with the widespread colonial revival. The developing interest in re-creating colonial environments as an educational mechanism afforded an arena in which Earle came to exert a significant amount of cultural power. After the national Centennial celebration, a surge of permanent installations began to appear in widely disparate regions of the country. George Sheldon, a native of Deerfield, Massachusetts, had received the charter for the Pocumtuck Valley Memorial Association in 1870, "for the purpose of collecting and preserving such memorials, books, records, papers and curiosities as may tend to illustrate and perpetuate the history of the early settlers of this region and the race which vanished before them."[4] The invocation of the rhetoric of race here and elsewhere in Sheldon's writings provides confirmation of the extent to which racial theories dominated popular historical discourse during the late nineteenth century.

Ten years later, in 1880, Sheldon moved his collection into newly acquired quarters in Memorial Hall and installed a gallery with three period rooms, a bedroom, parlor, and kitchen.[5] The kitchen presented a now familiar array of artifacts, including a fireplace with crane and kettle, a musket and a string of

OLD FIREPLACE

FIGURE 32. "Old Fireplace," from Clifton Johnson, *The New England Country* (1893). Photographer Clifton Johnson produced numerous images for Earle's books. This one, however, came from his own book and depicts the iconic "New England Kitchen" installed by George Sheldon at Memorial Hall in Deerfield, Mass.

dried apples hanging on the chimney breast, a hearth equipped with myriad iron, copper, and brass cooking implements, a wooden firkin, gourds, a brass warming pan, a bellows, a pierced tin lantern, and a tinderbox and candle. Assorted other furnishings completed the scene, a picture of which was reproduced by the New England writer, photographer, and artist Clifton Johnson in his book *The New England Country,* published in 1893 (fig. 32).[6] These included a wooden cradle, a settle, several plain ladder-back chairs, a simple Windsor chair, a tripod candle stand, and a cupboard containing pewter plates and porringers. Johnson, who came from Hadley, Massachusetts, used the Deerfield kitchen just sixteen miles to the north to illustrate his romantic pictorial tour through the New England past, confirming the appeal of Sheldon's fabrication. Moreover, these illustrations reinforced the widespread perception that the world Sheldon's kitchen portrayed was somehow generically representative of all of New England, and therefore all of the American historical past.[7]

Earle expressed a similar sentiment about Sheldon's creation in her "Home Interiors" chapter in *Customs and Fashions in Old New England.*

"In Deerfield Memorial Hall there lives in perfection of detail one of these old fireplaces," she wrote, "a delight to the soul of the antiquary. Every homely utensil and piece of furniture, every domestic convenience and inconvenience, every home-made makeshift, every cumbrous and clumsy contrivance of the old-time kitchen here may be found, and they show to us, as in a living photograph, the home life of those olden days."[8]

Also in Deerfield, Frary House had just been restored by its owner, C. Alice Baker, a Boston educator, avid collector of antique furnishings, and pioneer in the field of architectural and historical restoration. Earle's first visit to Sheldon and Deerfield in September 1892 naturally included a visit to Baker's project. Later writing to Sheldon, she noted, "I enjoyed my tea and evening at Frary House."[9] Baker had purchased Frary House in 1890 and spent two years creating a world in which the past could be literally revisited, experienced, and enjoyed (fig. 33). In the summer of 1892, Baker opened her completed house with a grand ball, to which all guests came in period costume, clothed theatrically in the garb of their ancestors. Baker, who was, like Earle, a progenitor of modern experiential education, believed strongly in the necessity of making history accessible and envisioned historical artifacts and houses as a means of transmitting traditional values to the present.[10] Embarking on a campaign to rescue their village from social and economic decline by resurrecting its historical past and the values it implied, Baker and her circle of women friends formed "common parlors," where they advocated for the restoration of Deerfield's houses, produced Arts and Crafts embroidery, held meetings, lectures, and teas, and raised money to support their agenda through the sale of their hand-produced products. Through their agency, along with that of George Sheldon, Deerfield was transformed from a dying village into a thriving tourist destination.[11]

Earle visited Deerfield many times and developed a close personal relationship with Sheldon. She urged him to publish his history of Deerfield and offered to share her experience with him to help him get the book into print. "I should like to sort out and arrange and plan with you," she told him. "I think a great deal of 'literary shape'—and the sequence of chapters, the comparative prominence given to subjects, the rounding out of a symmetrical whole, and those qualities have been much praised in my books." Sheldon may or may not have needed her assistance, but they remained friends and correspondents. She clearly held Sheldon in high

FIGURE 33. Frary House kitchen, restored by C. Alice Baker in 1892. After Baker opened her museum house, visitors could literally step back into the past and experience the domestic lives of their ancestors. As with George Sheldon's period kitchen at Memorial Hall, Frary's room is far more cluttered that it would have been in the 1700s. The goods serve as romantic suggestions of the room's original occupants, mainly genteel and industrious women and children. The array of pewter on the mantle shelf, however, confirms a male presence, implying an intersection with the outside world of commerce and goods. Courtesy of Historic Deerfield, Deerfield, Mass.

regard and had nothing but praise for "the treasures of Memorial Hall." In 1901 Earle sent Sheldon a photograph of a Deerfield house that she wanted to use in *Old-Time Gardens,* asking him to identify it. That summer she and her sister, Frances, went "prospecting" to Memorial Hall in search of artifacts for Frances's new book on furniture. Earle regarded Memorial Hall as an important research collection and returned there whenever she needed more material for her books.[12]

Other institutions followed Sheldon's lead at Deerfield, confirming a growing focus on public history and a regional community of pastkeepers that would ultimately be served by Earle's authority. The Concord, Massachusetts, Antiquarian Society opened its exhibits in 1887, organized by a local stationer, Cummings Davis, and twenty years later George Francis

Dow opened what scholars have traditionally credited as the first period rooms in New England at the Essex Institute in Salem.[13] Dow's rooms reflected a level of environmental authenticity that had not character-ized the period rooms of his predecessors. He banned artifact labels from the exhibit space and incorporated specific architectural detailing, using building fragments and reproductions of existing examples, even recon-structing a timbered ceiling to enhance the visitor's sense of place.[14]

On the West Coast, Charles Wilcomb created his first colonial room settings, albeit an exhibit focused on New England rather than New Spain, when he set up a colonial kitchen and bedroom in 1896 at San Francisco's newly founded Golden Gate Park Museum. In a report to the park commissioners he clearly stated his educational objectives: "I pro-pose to illustrate in a simple but effective manner the modes of life of our forefathers and ancestors." And in order "to accomplish this successfully," he added, "the interior of the exhibition room should be made to harmo-nize with the exhibits. All I require is a low ceiling with rafters; ceiling and walls covered with plain pine boards; two or three windows, and an imitation fireplace."[15]

Like Sheldon and Dow, Wilcomb, who had been born in Weirs, New Hampshire, in 1868, believed in the expressive power of domestic artifacts to evoke the essence of New England values and community on the West Coast. Although his first period rooms opened two years before the pub-lication of *Home Life in Colonial Days,* Wilcomb was so impressed with Earle's scholarship that he cut out illustrations and portions of her text and incorporated them as label copy into his later colonial exhibits at the Oakland Public Museum in 1910.[16] Without a detailed comparative analy-sis of both of Wilcomb's exhibits, it is impossible to measure the extent to which *Home Life* may have reshaped his interpretation of the colonial past. The parallel, however, between Earle's presentation of colonial life and that depicted in all of the early period rooms provides a measure of the degree to which Earle's work was a product of what was going on around her. Her conception of the artifactual array that constituted a "New England kitchen" was a product not only of her own family origins and rural relatives but also of the flurry of other writings and installations that appeared during the decades surrounding and following the Civil War.

Earle's writings facilitated the work of furnishing the historic house

museums and interpreting the growing volume of historical society collections during the first decades of the twentieth century. In addition to
guiding public institutions, her numerous books and articles served as
a resource for restoring and furnishing many private residences as well.
Within these theatrically constructed neocolonial settings, both wealthy
urban and suburban dwellers and those of more modest means could display their personal collections and reenact the social dramas of the past,
treating their modern malaise with doses of romanticized authenticity.

Since at least the mid-nineteenth century, the creation of genteel environments had been an important middle-class social strategy, and one
that was increasingly executed by women as domestic consumers.[17] By the
turn of the century, the colonial idiom had become the mode of choice.
The process had begun with the inclusion of antiques—spinning wheels,
grandfather clocks, Windsor chairs, iron cookware—anachronistically inserted into a modern "French" or "Renaissance" parlor. In 1880 Kate Taylor
of Norwalk, Connecticut, wrote to her sister in Rochester, New York,
about her newly colonialized dining room: "This week we expect to have
up in the dining room a genuine old Franklin stove. Jim has found one at
last, with brass pieces on the top, and brass trimmings in the front. I don't
think he can ever pay for the wood to burn in it, but he is delighted with
his purchase. . . . With our old clock and spinning wheel, the dining room
will have quite an antique appearance."[18] These objects provided their
owners with symbolic reminders of a preindustrial culture and the passage
of time. Preserved as relics, they affirmed a myth of collective identity that
had existed in the past and continued to exist metaphorically in the present. The narrative content of the colonial revival underscored its appeal. A
reconstructed colonial hearth, or, increasingly, a newly made rocking chair
or sideboard in the "colonial" style, provided a point of access into the intimacy of family stories or, through writers like Earle, generic stories in
which anyone could participate.

At a time of expanding popular interest in using the materials of the
colonial past to invent new scenarios for the present, Earle's work was both
culturally shaped and culturally shaping. Her book sales certainly benefited from the burgeoning antiques trade and the colonial revival desire
for historically accurate domestic reconstructions. Even antique dealers
took advantage of her expertise, setting up their shops as period rooms
to enhance the salability of their goods—much as Earle contextualized

historical artifacts in her books.[19] Earle helped to educate collectors, guiding their taste for and understanding of the artifacts of the past. She appealed to a readership that was as interested in collecting antiques as in history. Although she used her own collections to illustrate her books when possible, she was less important as a collector herself than as an arbiter of collectibles.

In addition to her influence as a wellspring of information for the creators of museum and historical society exhibits and as a proponent of the colonial revival among individuals in their homes, Earle's work had a public impact as a resource for those producing historical pageants after the turn of the century.[20] These pageants provided a conventionalized vision of domestic life in colonial America. Women, who were usually seen as confined to the home unless they were Revolutionary heroines, spun and wove and generally reinforced preconceptions about appropriate gender roles. Esther Willard Bates, author of *Pageants and Pageantry,* a how-to guide for planning and producing historical pageants, tableaux, and amateur theatricals, certainly recognized the value of Earle's work. Bates's book, published in 1912, offered detailed information about set design, props, costumes, scripts, and music, and included a lengthy bibliography that listed thirteen of Earle's books as useful references for pageant makers. In fact, Earle was the only colonial American history authority cited. According to Bates, an educator, "Colonial history makes a particularly good field for exploration, and furnishes a great variety of incident, costumes, and manners." Any one of Earle's books could have served as a roadmap for re-creating a colonial kitchen, a tea, a wedding, a tavern scene, or other representation of colonial society. Many of her books were held in public libraries, research archives, or school libraries, such as that of the Girls' Department at P.S. 1 in Manhattan. There, students could consult a copy of Earle's *Costume of Colonial Times* for accurate information about colonial dress should they wish to perform in theatrical or patriotic events. According to Bates, spectacles such as these offered considerable educational value: "Our schools can teach patriotism and give an understanding of the genius of our institutions most effectively by bringing into life again the scenes and the men who laid the foundation of the United States and assured its permanence. Such a setting in pageantry," she stressed, "will impart something of the glamour and romance that attached to the events of Old World History, and

FIGURE 34. Schoolchildren dressed up for historical pageant (around 1900). The audience for Earle's writings included teachers and pageant planners, as well as museums, collectors, and homemakers. These children in their historical garb represent the ultimate achievement for Earle: shaping the future by inculcating values of the past. Courtesy of Laurel Historical Society, Laurel, Md.

thereby increase the interest, particularly of youth, in the records of this land" (fig. 34).[21]

Earle's books and articles would indeed have provided useful references for pageant planners. For instance, the colonial wedding, a topic about which Earle had written a chapter in *Customs and Fashions in Old New England* (1893), as well as an article for the *Journal of American Folklore* (1893), became a favorite pageant scene, affirming the values of continuity and community.[22] Pageants and pageant-like activities provided women in particular with an avenue for public expression. As a popular form of entertainment for women's clubs, they enabled participants to "get inside of the past and see how it felt."[23] The National Society of New England Women, that Brooklyn club for New England expatriates (in which Earle was a member and frequent presenter of historical programs), produced a number of staged "entertainments" that attempted to reproduce such old

New England customs as quilting bees, corn-husking bees, and an event held at the Metropolitan Opera House in 1897 titled "The Carnival of History."[24] Surely Earle's fellow clubwomen appreciated the usefulness of Earle's books as a source for staging these events.

Turn-of-the-century popular interest in the colonial had begun to be expressed not only in an antiquarian sense but also in the creation of new architectural interiors and exteriors that people were choosing as a public face for twentieth-century family homes. Houses, and especially household furnishings, assumed the forms and details of their seventeenth-, eighteenth-, and early-nineteenth-century counterparts. Earle had commented on this trend as early as 1892 in *China Collecting,* remarking that "it is a matter of course that this old china should show to its best advantage in an old-fashioned house, or in a new house built in the 'American colonial' style of architecture."[25] While some architects and manufacturers strove for historical authenticity, the great majority used historical details in a referential manner, combining Queen Anne or Windsor chair backs, paw feet, carved shells, fanlight windows, and neoclassical pillars indiscriminately to achieve a stylistic mélange that was generically "colonial."[26]

When the Boston photographer Charles Plumer documented houses and furnishings in New Ipswich, New Hampshire, in the early 1900s, he found loving re-creations of "colonial kitchens, parlors, and chambers." These "stages" offered settings where inhabitants could reenact the rituals of domesticity and gentility that they felt had been lost in the hubbub of modern urban life. One of these Colonial Revival living rooms captured by Plumer contained an assortment of cues that could transport the family into the realm of "bygone days" (fig. 35). The ancestor portraits hanging over the mantle, photographically reproduced so that they could be shared by geographically dispersed descendants, and the needlework sampler on the wall brought people and patterns of work from the past into the present. The rag rugs scattered around the room offered further tribute to the simplicity, durability, and inherent nobility of handmade goods. The steeple clock on the mantle—redundant in an age of wristwatches—offered a romantic reference to the passage of time, as did the cast-iron "potbellied" stove, a remnant of the 1840s. The chairs in this living room represented several different ages and social levels, the aristocratic Queen Anne coexisting peacefully with the democratic ladder-back and two Windsors, the chairs of Washington and Jefferson. These chairs suggest another clue to

FIGURE 35. Living room of Mrs. Ethel McKown Parker, New Ipswich, N.H., 1912, Charles Plumer, photographer. Mrs. Parker carefully furnished her "Little Red House," a summer residence in a colonial-era village, with antiques and family heirlooms, including Windsor and ladder-back chairs, and an Empire style center table with Argand lamp, a steeple clock and transfer-printed jug on the mantle, and rag rugs on the floors. As a piece, the interior represents pastkeeping activities and the colonial revival at its peak. Courtesy of the New Ipswich Historical Society, New Ipswich, N.H.

the popularity of the style: its broad accessibility. Oliver Coleman, author of *Successful Homes* (1902), described the colonial style as occupying "the middle ground between rich and poor, the great and small; it stretches either way, and can enter freely either class and do no harm to properness and art."[27]

That the rage for Colonial Revival furnishings coincided with the popularity of Earle's books further confirms the extent to which her work was influenced by as well as influential in the movement. As an antiquarian, a collector, and an arbiter of taste, Earle served the colonial revival throughout her own era and well beyond it. Her progressive agenda, however, demanded more than a new decorative style. She, like other reforming women of the late nineteenth century, sought a better world, and she believed that the transformative power of artifacts was a means to that end. Her influence and attention, naturally, extended to the lives of her own children, especially her daughters, Alice Earle Hyde and Mary Earle Moore. Both daughters followed their mother's example and joined the Fort Greene chapter of the Daughters of the American Revolution, Moore in 1897 and Hyde in 1918.[28] Hyde, the elder daughter, assumed the responsibility of continuing her mother's genealogical pursuits after Earle's death in 1911. Hyde's research was detailed and thorough, and she was diligent about making copies for her children, her sister and brother, and subsequently their children, maintaining the tradition of passing the family heritage along to the next generation.[29]

After Mary Earle married the New York stockbroker David Thomas Moore in 1902, they moved to a house in Westbury, Long Island. Before the newlywed couple arrived home, Earle went to the house and prepared what she considered a suitable reception for them. "Have you ever had candles of bayberry wax—pale green and fragrant?" Earle later asked *Dial* editor F. F. Browne. "When my daughter was married . . . I ordered a gross of these candles and when she entered her home—her country house—one hundred and fifty years old—I had every candle-stick filled with them, and a candle-box full of them waiting."[30]

With this act, Earle combined her faith in the shaping power of environment with that in the shaping power of historical presence. Although there was probably no specific historical precedent for her gesture, she no doubt believed that she was acting in a historically accurate manner, a belief that was buttressed by her use of two important historical material references—bayberry, a traditional eighteenth-century candle ingredient, and the candles themselves. The quality of the light strengthened the metaphor: what Earle presented to her daughter and new son-in-law was not merely candles but a gift of the light from what she envisioned as a softer, gentler era.

Earle's wedding gift to the Moores conveyed the same historicized prescription for gentility. A household inventory prepared for D. Thomas Moore in 1915 listed, as part of the dining room furnishings, "1 Tiffany, Young and Ellis six piece old American coin silver floral repoussé tea service." The service included a hot water kettle and stand, a teapot, a covered sugar bowl, an open sugar basket with handle, a covered cream pitcher, and a waste bowl. Each piece in the set was engraved on the bottom "Mary from Father and Mother, April 15th 1902," the date of their wedding.[31]

The style and material of wedding gifts typically embodied, in physical form, the hopes and aspirations of the giver for the future of the new couple.[32] Silver, with its intrinsic value as a metal as well as its associations with wealth and luxury, was a traditionally desirable material for any gift. In colonial America, families who could afford silver tried to provide their daughters with dowries of "plate." In its substance, then, the Earles' gift conveyed generations of expectations about the perpetuation of family status through material goods. In its function, it expressed an underlying agenda of gentility. Tea, a luxury beverage during the eighteenth century, quickly came to signify an entire repertoire of elite social behaviors related to its service and consumption, along with expectations of hospitality, behavior that, by 1902, when the Moores were married, had been fully internalized by socially aspiring Americans of all classes.[33]

American silver manufacturers by the turn of the twentieth century were producing tea services at every level of price and elaborateness, and Tiffany & Company led the field in terms of elite consumer appeal. Earle, however, chose a tea service made not by Tiffany & Company but by Tiffany, Young & Ellis fifty or more years earlier.[34] In a culture that had valued progress for almost a century, this choice must be understood as a conscious rejection of newness. While this may have been a family service, Earle might easily have purchased the tea service from any of a number of antique dealers in New York, or from Tiffany & Company itself, which maintained an "antiques" department. For Earle, the age of this item added to, rather than detracted from, its value; in fact, the only component missing that could possibly have made it even more valuable was a family provenance.[35]

Mary Earle entered an upper-class world when she married Thomas Moore, a world of yachts and polo ponies and governesses for the children. A peek into her living and dining rooms via the household inventory, reveals a furnishing scheme that was heavily indebted to her mother's influence. Much of the furniture dated from the eighteenth and early nineteenth centuries, including many pieces with family connections, as well as objects purchased as antiques.[36] In the library, presumably on a mantel shelf, there were "7 pair Old English and Colonial assorted brass candlesticks . . . (one pair fitted for electricity)"; a pair of English brass andirons with an "old wrought brass handled shovel" and fuel tongs to match; an "old mahogany mantel clock" from the shop of Eli Terry of Plymouth, Connecticut; a collection of seventeen "early embroidered needle work samplers, dating from 1733 to 1835"; assorted Nanking and Canton porcelains, like those George Washington had at Mount Vernon; and, in an even more explicit reference, on the wall a pair of oval hand-colored portraits of George and Martha Washington.[37]

While Earle was clearly pleased with her daughter's marriage, she felt some degree of discomfort over the variance between her own expectations, shaped by her middle-class upbringing and life experience, and the more lavish upper-class lifestyle enjoyed by the Moores. She commented to Francis Browne that she thought her daughter's home was "lovely— save for one thing—her neighbors are too rich. Mrs. Mackey, William C. Whitney and the like are ill company for young folk."[38] Earle may have felt that her daughter and son-in-law were not old and wise enough to fend off the potentially corrupting effects of great wealth. In the face of this ambivalence, Earle's gifts to her grandchildren were an important means of countering the corporate ethic of the wealthy business community to which D. Thomas Moore belonged. The Tiffany silver milk jug inscribed "Susan Moore from her Grandmother Alice Morse Earle, Christmas 1909," and especially the silver porringer, also made by Tiffany & Company, that Earle presented to her granddaughter Susan to commemorate her birth on September 9, 1908, had, Earle believed, symbolic as well as intrinsically expressive powers that would shape her granddaughter's future.[39]

Earle discussed her philosophy concerning the symbolic functions of objects in *Sun-Dials and Roses of Yesterday*. Sundials, for Earle, functioned in an emblematic way as well as in a practical way (fig. 36). When she used the word "emblem," she defined it for her readers to mean "Emblem in the highest, the specific, the Shakespearian sense of the word, Emblem with a moral lesson to suggest or even tell in detail." In order for an emblem to function, "it must have some implied meaning in addition to its actual presentation or it is not an Emblem." Moreover, "there is no doubt that any object or any deed which has or has had a symbolic meaning receives through this a certain charm, a charm occult and often scarcely formulated, yet nevertheless present." The idea that objects have multiple levels of meaning was not a new one in 1902, nor was it one with which Earle, reared in the wake of New England transcendentalism, would have been unfamiliar.[40]

Captain Bailey's Seasons'-dial.

FIGURE 36. Seasons' dial made by John S. Bailey, from *Sun-Dials and Roses of Yesterday* (1902). This unusual sundial indicates not only the time of day but also the lines of latitude and signs of the zodiac. Author's collection.

Earle explained that sundials functioned as "an absolute symbol of the progress of time," and as such could operate on multiple levels of human consciousness. Likewise, the humble spiderwort, *Tradescantia virginiana*, as a plant of "American nativity" that had penetrated the soil of England, "being carried there from Virginia by the botanical explorer, Tradescant," communicated far more than its mere botanical presence might suggest.[41] In an American garden, tradescantia served to represent persistence and hardiness, thus reminding those who viewed it of the hardiness of their forebears.

A large part of the intrinsic power of artifacts was derived from extrinsic sources. On choosing a sundial for a garden, Earle mused, "I have a fancy that a sun-dial should ever have some extrinsic value; an object yields more readily to the power of association." She recommended that readers have their sundials made "from stone taken from some historic or memorable spot." The resulting sundial "fairly speaks to you" of a lost ancestor, in the instance she discusses a blacksmith who had fought at the battle of Bennington, and "of the certainty of the blows with which he made his way through life, conquering Time because he fearlessly and cheerfully filled it with honest and dignified work."[42] Earle believed that the intrinsic qualities of even the most ordinary objects served to express deeply rooted cultural meanings: "We feel it in sign-boards, in sign-posts or guide-boards; let us see why. Whence is the word *sign*? Think of the very word, and you have the key to the secret—and to the interest."[43] Mundane artifacts communicate their messages, according to Earle, not only through language but also in their forms: "All architectural erections conspicuous for height and slenderness, such as obelisks, steeples, minarets, tall towers, and upright stones and monuments, under the assertion that they represent the pyramidal forms of fire, . . . have had symbolic meaning ever since the days of fire-worshippers."[44] In our post-Freudian world, Earle's analysis seems obvious. In 1902, however, her insight probably grew out of her long-standing interest in folklore and ethnography. What seems significant here is that she was attempting to penetrate the mystical realm of intrinsic meaning as a way of understanding the communicative power of these artifacts. In linking objects—whether historical or of her own time—with cultural archetypes, Earle seemed to be seeking some essential nature, the ultimate prime object, which, if understood, could somehow legitimize the patrimonial claims of her class and facilitate the construction of hegemonic devices that would perpetuate that class's moral codes.

The artifacts she selected, including the porringer she bestowed on her granddaughter, expressed Earle's conceptions of the ideal order. Porringers seem to have been a particularly potent icon in the colonial era (and

FIGURE 37. Silver porringer made by Paul Revere (1735–1818) and acquired by the Salisbury family of Worcester to commemorate the birth of Stephen Salisbury II in 1798. Earle herself, who presented her granddaughter Susan Moore with a silver porringer made by Tiffany & Co., continued the tradition of the porringer as a gift to newborn children. Worcester Art Museum, Gift of Stephen Salisbury III.

remain so to this day); they were a standard feature in nineteenth-century re-creations of colonial kitchens, though usually made of pewter rather than silver (fig. 37).[45] Earle described an old-time dresser in *China Collecting in America* "with narrow ledges of shelves hung with old pewter porringers."[46] She also included an illustration of porringers in *Home Life in Colonial Days,* with a poetic caption which suggested that their appeal was somehow related to their visual impact: "The porringers that in a row/ Hung high and made a glittering show" (fig. 38).[47] The popularity of porringers cannot be fully explained by their materials, function, or historical associations alone. Their ubiquitous presence confirms that they

86 ′   Home Life in Colonial Days

" The porringers that in a row
Hung high and made a glittering show "

These porringers were in many sizes, from tiny little ones two inches in diameter to those eight or nine inches across. When not in use many housekeepers kept them hanging on hooks on the edge of a shelf, where they formed a pretty and cheerful decoration. The poet Swift says: —

FIGURE 38. "The porringers that in a row / Hung high and made a glittering show," from *Home Life in Colonial Days* (1898). Porringers, and other artifacts that came in graduated sizes, appealed to collectors in part because of the challenge of completing the set. These might also have been used as measuring devices for preparing or serving food; their material and highly decorative form, however, suggests a higher function than mere cookery.

resonated with some deeper chord of cultural meaning. There seems to have been something intrinsically affecting about the formal qualities of these objects and the metaphoric messages they embody.[48]

Earle's porringer, made of silver but in its design explicitly referring to its more humble pewter predecessors, displays the typical shallow round bowl form, with an elaborately pierced handle applied to the upper edge of one side.[49] Earle discussed the form and function of porringers, as she understood them, in *Home Life in Colonial Days*, where she illustrated a cupboard shelf containing four blue and white "States" plates in graduated sizes and five pewter porringers, also in graduated sizes, hanging in front of the plates.[50] In her description of the usage of porringers, Earle ignored the possibilities implied by the availability of graduated sizes, noting only that "porringers were much used at the table, chiefly for children to eat from."[51] Her assignment of this form to children reflects her willingness to draw conclusions that were sometimes grounded more in imaginative speculation than in historical documentation. She offered no explanation for her assertion, and had either overlooked or chosen to ignore evidence provided by Samuel Sewall, one of Earle's frequent sources for information on colonial customs, who wrote that he had "drunk a porringer of Sage Tea" as a cold remedy in 1704, when he was fifty-two.[52]

To understand the deeper level of meaning of the porringer for Earle, it is necessary to move beyond its functional aspects and probe its poetic dimensions.[53] In terms of the poetic structure of the porringer, there seem to be two separate discourses, one centered on the bowl and the other on the handle. Porringer bowls are plain, smooth, gently rounded, and essentially nest-like in both shape and size. The image of the nest is an archetype, representing the most elementary form of habitation.[54] Nests also evoke birth and female nurturing, along with a sense of life's rhythms and renewal. The nest image would have endowed the porringer with special life-giving powers, a poetic image particularly significant in light of Earle's association of it with child rearing, and would have enhanced its potency as a domestic icon. The interest in collecting "nested" sets of porringers gave these objects additional force as embodiments of replication and renewal. The porringer could thus have functioned imaginatively for Earle and her generation of domestic historians as a reference to the power of genealogy and racial purity. Its intrinsic femaleness confirmed women as the primary bearers of that cultural mission.

The handle, with its tree-like form and pierced decoration, must also have contributed to the affective power of the porringer for Earle, as it had since its inception and still does today—though within rather different cultural contexts. The virtuosity of its execution provided a metaphoric reference to artifice and culture (in the highest meaning of the words), and the thirteen piercings, the uppermost of which was a quatrefoil (an explicitly religious motif), could be perceived as a symbolic representation of the thirteen original colonies and the religious conviction of their founding. The tree of life, another primal archetype, added yet another dimension to the imaginative reconstruction of this artifact, further endowing it with mystical powers, which would have strengthened and perpetuated the cultural values that led to its initial construction.

Finally, Earle's conscious selection of this form to commemorate her granddaughter's birth reaffirmed her antimodern predilections as well as her progressive intentions. The porringer was an anachronism in 1908, having long since been supplanted for eating and drinking by specialized modern glass and ceramic forms. Its lingering presence reflected the pursuit of an idealized community that many Americans believed had disappeared, a cultural longing that could not be fully satisfied by all that modern technology had to offer. In their quest for that community, Earle and other Americans who were writing about, reinterpreting, and actively collecting remnants of the colonial past were formed by the modern world around them. The new progressive paradigm that their cumulative production represented—a paradigm that drew heavily on the past to try to shape the future by reconstructing the present—was the product of a dialectical interaction between a deeply rooted faith in progress and a growing uncertainty about their ability as individuals to cope with social and cultural change.

CONCLUSION

✣

A FTER A PROLIFIC WRITING CAREER THAT LASTED fourteen years, Earle stopped writing in 1904. Though she lived until 1911, there is no sign that she felt any urgency to produce more books. The abruptness of this conclusion raises questions about Earle's motives as a historian and an author. Was she driven by personal motives: the gratification of widespread acclaim, or perhaps the financial rewards of successful literary production, which, once achieved, no longer impelled her to continue? Or can her high rate of production be attributed to more idealistic motives: to a desire to reform her society, to provide a vision for the future constructed from a particular set of standards from the past? Alternatively, once her husband had died (1904), perhaps she felt free to travel and focus on her now married children and her grandchildren (fig. 39).

There is no way to single out any one explanation as dominant. The significance of Earle's work lies in its enduring impact. Her multiple messages, shaped by the intersecting realms of her personal context and her professional agenda, as well as the discrepancies between her social vision and the reality of her own everyday life and family experiences, continue to appeal to popular audiences. Earle envisioned colonial society as characterized generally by stability and traditional country values. In reality, the American past had not been a particularly stable place, as evidenced by the history of colonial New England, including that of Earle's own ancestors. Her depictions of stability nevertheless generated widespread

FIGURE 39. Alice Morse Earle with her grandchildren, 1910. By that year she was almost sixty years old, had authored seventeen books and many magazine articles and book reviews, and was doubtless tired and ready to retire from the grind of historical writing. Collection of Donald J. Post Jr.

popularity for her published work. In her own era of great social disruption, her reconstruction of colonial American society as a golden age tapped into a shared yearning for the values of honesty, simplicity, and self-sufficiency.

It was the city, however, that furnished Earle's country vision with much of its context and content. Earle's parents had embraced the city of Worcester as a place of excitement and opportunity, and had moved there eagerly from the country in the 1830s and 1840s. Earle herself lived in Brooklyn Heights for her entire adult life and appreciated her urban setting as an important source of civilization. Urban settings in the past, too, represented for her the height of civilization. In colonial New York, Boston, and Philadelphia she found the ideal urban scale and degree of gentility, and she offered these societies to her modern readers as "a stick to beat the present."[1]

Earle's urban roots had molded not only her vision of the past but also her philosophy of social evolution. She learned strategies from her mother and father that enabled her, as it had them, to cope with the social cost of urban living. Especially in her books that focused on urban life, *Colonial Days in Old New York* and *Diary of Anna Green Winslow: A Boston Schoolgirl of 1771*, Earle carefully emphasized the importance of family as a civilizing agent, and particularly the importance of child rearing and education in an urban society.

As a member of a generation that felt increasingly ambivalent about the impact of industrial capitalism, Earle embraced the quest for progressive solutions to the disorder of her present. That quest expressed itself in her books and articles as a search for a new history, one that would reject the harshness of Calvinist determinism and would endorse individualism and the power of the human spirit—even in Puritan New England. Earle rejected the theology of the Puritans but embraced their civilization, which she discovered in their material environments, family life, customs, and social institutions. She documented the existence of a culture of resistance to the ideology of determinism: Puritans were not passive, nor should her modern readers be so.

As a historian, Earle operated within a newly professionalized intellectual context. Her work, however, was distinctive in its anthropological emphasis on the domestic lives of ordinary people, especially her reliance on material evidence. Like many of her professional colleagues, Earle viewed historical change as a social process rather than the result of a sequence of isolated individual actions. She saw history as the past of a culture, and her particular methodological slant devolved from her definition of that process specifically in terms of domestic life and social relations. Her perspective was formed in part by her interest in education and her own child rearing experience, in part by her personal fondness for collecting antiques, and in part by her understanding of an audience that valued ancestry as a means of contending with the present. Once she developed her basic method, subjects abounded—which helps to explain her prolific output.

Her literary mission comes into even sharper focus when viewed through the lens of gender. As a woman, Earle felt all of the traditional pressures to provide for her husband and family while conforming to middle-class expectations about genteel feminine behavior. She sought the company of other women who, like her, were seeking to stretch their cultural and intellectual boundaries through shared activities in clubs and organizations run by women. And like many other women of her generation, Earle felt a feminist sense of moral duty to help care for society at large; her decision to step out into the public realm and become a cultural critic stemmed from that belief. Although she was ambivalent about what woman's proper political role in the United States should ultimately be, Earle knew that women, especially native-born white middle-class women, could collectively preserve the values they admired, have an impact on the shape of modern society, and ensure a more hopeful future.

Earle was widely admired, both by her peers and by professional historians. At her death in 1911, Mrs. Field's Literary Club paid tribute to Earle's work on childhood with "An Appreciation of Childhood: An Appreciation of Mrs. Alice Morse Earle's Literary Work." The "Literary Notes from London" editor of the *New York Times* wrote a wrote a lengthy eulogy extolling her many virtues. Earle's death "removes from our literary activities a writer of authority in her special line," the writer declared.

> Her many books on Colonial life, customs, manners, dress, and furniture are recognized as the best, the most accurate and the fullest descriptions that have been written of the paraphernalia and the methods of life of our forefathers. She was a painstaking and conscientious investigator, and never described articles which she had not herself examined. But her work, along with its accuracy, won its place also because of the interest with which she clothed her descriptions of the people and the life of Colonial days. Notwithstanding her many volumes her pen never lost its freshness; and her power of recreating the old-time manners and customs knew no abatement. Not a little of the charm of her pages is due to the simplicity of her style. But her own keen personal interest in the life of which she wrote was perhaps the chief source of the appeal her books have long had, and will doubtless long continue to have, for young and old.[2]

The high regard for Earle's scholarship did not diminish in the years following her death. During the early twentieth century, she was frequently cited as an authority on a variety of subjects ranging from colonial portraits to teapots to foodways.[3] In the mid-1930s a *New York Times* journalist rediscovered Earle and published two articles on historic foodways in which she was cited as a source. In 1951, one hundred years after her birth, the Reading, Massachusetts, Antiquarian Society held a special meeting in observance of Earle's centennial. The speaker, Mrs. Roland J. Sawyer, was charged to "tell something of the life of the writer whose works so thoroughly describe colonial life and customs in New England."[4]

In 1991 Michael Pollan, then executive editor of *Harper's* magazine, made Earle and several other early female garden writers the focus of an article about nature writing. Pollan expressed "fresh respect and admiration" for these women, for their modesty, "their attachments to small, unspecial places, their gentle humor in response to nature's indignities—these things, which had seemed before so minor, now shone forth as the considerable virtues they are," adding, "So much of what I needed to learn about nature, I realized, they simply took for granted."[5]

Earle's assumptions remain a powerful force even today. Many of her books have been continuously reprinted and are still available. *Home Life in Colonial Days*, her most popular book, went through more than twenty-five editions from the time Macmillan first published it in 1898, and is in print today in a 2011 replica edition published by the New York Public Library.[6] Earle is still regarded as an authority on colonial American life by professional historians, both academic and popular.[7] Over one hundred years after its initial publication, customers of Amazon.com gave the book a high rating. One reader-reviewer commented enthusiastically: "Alice Morse Earle has written several books on life in Colonial America. This is the first of her books I've read, and I am eager to move on to another volume. . . . Mrs. Earle's 'Home Life' is a fascinating description of everyday life." Another reviewer declared: "In her wonderfully readable narrative, Earle conveys life in the colonies with vividness missing from most conventional texts. . . . Earle's work is a feast of enjoyable information for history readers, collectors, and anyone else who wants to know how the early settlers lived."[8] Both of these late-twentieth-century reviewers captured the continuing appeal of Earle's books: they are full of well-researched historical detail, and they are written in a thoroughly accessible manner.

Earle's work grew out of, as well as fed (and continues to feed), a passion for material things. The widespread interest in collecting the relics of the American past stemmed in part from an acquisitive desire to own these objects as distinguishing emblems of one's superior level of civilization and taste. Earle's texts suggest, however, that she viewed the material world of the past as a standard for contemporary society, just as the thinly veiled sense of cultural urgency which permeated her books and articles suggested that she saw her work as a vehicle for social education. Her emphasis on the intimate and the local and on the value of objects as educational devices reflected the influence of the progressive educational theorists Friedrich Froebel and John Dewey. Within that context, Earle's work must be viewed as critical to the transformation of American educational institutions to include museums, historical re-creations, and pageants as learning activities.

She understood the expressive potential of material artifacts, particularly, their power to communicate social values. Her final words, conveyed to her descendants in her will, expressed her continuing faith in the power of goods to embody broader meanings—in that case, Earle herself. Because of her fears that her heritage, her culture, and her children's future was in jeopardy, she used her popularity as an author as a means of transmitting the values implied by the material culture of colonial America to a mass audience. That her construction of colonial society limited its membership to white Americans of Anglo-Saxon origin did not trouble her. The social composition, like the social behavior she envisioned as ideal, was shaped by her agenda for the present and future.

The appeal of that vision was widespread and long lasting. Earle's work has influenced a century of historical interpretation of American domestic life. Because of their detailed material focus, her books and articles have guided countless reconstructions of historical settings, vignettes, pageants, dramatic productions, novels, period rooms, and Colonial Revival interiors, perpetuating her particular late-nineteenth-century values of quaintness and homogeneity through several generations of popular historical consciousness. Moreover, those material remnants of the colonial past, when wrenched from Earle's scholarly context and deposited without explanation in public settings, assumed their own tangible reality that further reinforced prevailing impressions of a homogeneous past. Museums and historical societies would spend much of the twentieth century under the spell of Alice Morse Earle's progressive legacy. Her memory of the Garden and her thinly veiled longing for that lost Edenic past have retained their power to influence popular American conceptions of social and domestic order.

NOTES

AAS   American Antiquarian Society, Worcester, Mass.

Earle-Hyde Papers   Earle-Hyde Family Papers, collection of
                            Donald J. Post Jr., Middlebury, Conn.

Earle-Moore Papers   Earle-Moore Family Papers, collection of
                            Thomas S. Powers, South Royalton, Vt.

Macmillan Papers   Macmillan Company records, Manuscripts
                            and Archives Division, New York Public Library,
                            Astor, Lenox, and Tilden Foundations

Morse-Earle Genealogy   Family genealogy compiled by Alice Earle Hyde,
                            ca. 1920, Earle-Moore Family Papers

PVMA   Collection of the Pocumtuck Valley Memorial
                            Association, Deerfield, Mass.

Scribner Papers   Archives of Charles Scribner's Sons, Manuscripts
                            Division, Department of Rare Books and Special
                            Collections, Princeton University Library

PREFACE

1. Esther C. Averill, "Alice Morse Earle, a Writer Who Popularized Old New England," *Old-Time New England* 37 (January 1947): 73–78. Twenty-five other biographical entries are listed in various biographical dictionaries published during Earle's lifetime; most of the published biographical material has been summarized in Wendall Garrett's entry on Earle in *Notable American Women, 1607–1950: A Biographical Dictionary*, ed. Edward T. James et al., vol. 1 (Cambridge: Belknap Press of Harvard University Press, 1971), 541–42.

2. The town records and histories of Dublin, New Hampshire, and Andover, Vermont, provided information about Earle's grandfather and his ancestors. The town history of New Ipswich, New Hampshire, recorded the settlement history of Earle's mother's family. Frederic Kidder and Augustus A. Gould, *The History of New Ipswich* (Boston: Gould and Lincoln, 1851). Versions of Alice Earle Hyde's genealogy, as well as her research notes and numerous family photographs, are in both the Earle-Hyde Papers and the Earle-Moore Papers. Since the copy in the Earle-Moore Papers is more complete, I cite from it throughout this book.

3. Frances C. Morse, *Furniture of the Olden Time* (1902; repr., New York: Macmillan, 1927).

4. Julia Pane, a resident of 242 Henry Street, graciously allowed me to examine the interior of the house in March 1992.

5. So far I have unearthed 287 letters to, from, or related to Earle. I believe that more exist, possibly uncatalogued, in the holdings of historical societies or libraries with whom Earle may have corresponded before she died in 1911.

INTRODUCTION

1. Customer reviews of *Home Life in Colonial Days* and *Customs and Fashions in Old New England,* www.amazon.com (May 19, 2011).

2. Mary R. Beard, ed., *America through Women's Eyes* (New York: Macmillan, 1933), 550. The feminist historian Bonnie Smith has argued that Beard, generally cited as the initiator of the "new women's history," was actually the "inheritor of an older tradition" that featured Earle prominently. See Bonnie G. Smith, "The Contribution of Women to Modern Historiography," *American Historical Review* 89.3 (June 1984): 709–10.

3. Harvey Wish, *Society and Thought in Early America: A Social and Intellectual History of the America People* (New York: David McKay, 1950), 580–81.

4. Elizabeth Stillinger, *The Antiquers* (New York: Alfred A. Knopf, 1980), 61–68; Laurel Thatcher Ulrich, *Good Wives: Image and Reality in the Lives of Women in Northern New England, 1650–1750* (New York: Alfred A. Knopf, 1980), xiii; Linda K. Kerber, "Separate Spheres, Female Worlds, Woman's Place: The Rhetoric of Women's History" (1988), in *Toward an Intellectual History of Women: Essays by Linda Kerber* (Chapel Hill: University of North Carolina Press, 1997), 166.

5. Karal Ann Marling, *George Washington Slept Here: Colonial Revivals and American Culture, 1876–1986* (Cambridge: Harvard University Press, 1988), 164; John F. Kasson, *Rudeness and Civility: Manners in Nineteenth-Century Urban America* (New York: Hill and Wang, 1990), 17; Michael Kammen, *Mystic Chords of Memory: The Transformation of Tradition in American Culture* (New York: Alfred A. Knopf, 1991), 148. There are doubtless hundreds of other such references. A cursory search of Google Books (http://books.google.com) performed in March 2010 for books published since January 1980 mentioning Alice Morse Earle resulted in 785 hits. A year later (May 2011), a search for books by Alice Morse Earle in the abebooks.com database drew 2,993 hits (editions old and new, in existence and for sale).

6. Joseph A. Conforti, *Imagining New England: Explorations of Regional Identity from the Pilgrims to the Mid-Twentieth Century* (Chapel Hill: University of North Carolina Press, 2001), 214–34, quotations on 205; Ellen Fitzpatrick, *History's Memory: Writing America's Past, 1880–1980* (Cambridge: Harvard University Press, 2002), 32–33.

7. In *The Culture of Professionalism: The Middle Class and the Development of Higher Education in America* (New York: W. W. Norton, 1976), Burton J. Bledstein has characterized the rise of this "culture of professionalism" as an integral aspect of Victorian middle-class culture, reflective of a new, vertically categorized world-view (80–92, 107). John Higham suggested that the trend toward professionalization "represented a profound reaction against the democratic openness and rawness of the pre–Civil War era," and that academic historians and amateurs alike "felt a common mission to civilize the masses on the one hand and subdue the upstart *nouveau riches* on the other." John Higham with Leonard Krieger and Felix Gilbert, *History: The Development of Historical Studies in the United States* (Englewood Cliffs, N.J.: Prentice-Hall, 1965), 9–10. Edwin T. Layton Jr., in a study of the engineering profession, *The Revolt of the Engineers: Social Responsibility and the American Engineering Profession* (Baltimore: Johns Hopkins University Press, 1986), asserted that "professionalism derives from the mere possession of esoteric knowledge, not its specific content." He identified the underlying values of professionalism as "autonomy, collegial control of professional work, and social responsibility" (4–6).

8. Julie Des Jardins, *Women and the Historical Enterprise in America: Gender, Race, and the Politics of Memory, 1880–1945* (Chapel Hill: University of North Carolina Press, 2003), 15–19.

9. Alice Morse Earle, "History as Loved and Hated," paper presented at a meeting of the Daughters of the American Revolution, 1899, Earle-Hyde Papers. Michael Hoberman, "The Names of the Flowers: Ruby Hemenway's Redemption of History," *Frontiers: A Journal of Women Studies* 25.1 (Winter–Spring 2004): 172–89, a study of Ruby Hemenway, a local color writer, interprets this emphasis on local historical detail as a proto-feminist act, albeit an unconscious one, of subverting the national perspective of professional history, a "collapsing of the public and private spheres," with a resulting inclusiveness that was previously impossible.

10. Many scholars have employed generational analysis to help elucidate American identity and experience. The inheriting generations often struggled to make sense of their forebears' values and experiences, as well as find ways to weave those ancestral histories into their own "modern" daily lives. Early work by Lois Banner and James McElroy employed generational models to explain the reform mentality of the antebellum period. John Mack Faragher's later study of changing community life in Sugar Creek, Illinois, employed a similar generational analysis to clarify increasing levels of independence for women after 1840. More recently, Joyce Appleby, *Inheriting the Revolution: The First Generation of Americans* (Cambridge: Harvard University Press, 2000), used the collective autobiographies of the generation who came of age after the Revolution to explain the rise of liberal individualism. A consideration of Earle as part of a generational cohort holds possibilities for fresh interpretations of the later nineteenth century as well, providing a means of moving beyond individual perceptions and strategies to generational patterns. Lois W. Banner, "Religion and Reform in the Early Republic: The Role

of Youth," *American Quarterly* 23.5 (1971): 677–95; James L. McElroy, "Social Control and Romantic Reform in Antebellum America: The Case of Rochester, New York," *New York History* 58.1 (January 1977): 16–46; John Mack Faragher, *Sugar Creek: Life on the Illinois Prairie* (New Haven: Yale University Press, 1986), 205–15.

11. Daniel Scott Smith's article "Family Limitation, Sexual Control, and Domestic Feminism in Victorian America," *Feminist Studies* 1.3–4 (Winter–Spring 1973): 40–57, identified the demographic changes and raised initial questions about their causes and effects. Historians of women began to devise explanations in an attempt to defuse the "woman as victim" view of history. Nancy Cott, for example, argued that the lower birthrates implied new power and autonomy for women in marriage relationships and, indeed, the rise of a marriage of affection—another source of female empowerment. See Nancy Cott, *The Bonds of Womanhood: "Woman's Sphere" in New England, 1780–1835* (New Haven: Yale University Press, 1977). The best starting point on the demographic transition remains Carl N. Degler, *At Odds: Women and the Family in America from the Revolution to the Present* (New York: Oxford University Press, 1980), 180–81, which summarized the competing arguments about its causes and effects. Since Degler, there has been a wealth of scholarship focusing on the changing shape of women's lives during these decades. More recent syntheses can be found in Steven Mintz and Susan Kellogg, *Domestic Revolutions: A Social History of American Family Life* (New York: Free Press, 1988); and Katherine Kish Sklar, "Victorian Women and Domestic Life: Mary Todd Lincoln, Elizabeth Cady Stanton, and Harriet Beecher Stowe," in *Women and Power in American History*, ed. Kathryn Kish Sklar and Thomas Dublin, 3rd. ed. (Upper Saddle River, N.J.: Prentice Hall, 2009), 122–33.

12. Barbara Miller Solomon, *In the Company of Educated Women: A History of Women and Higher Education in America* (New Haven: Yale University Press, 1985), 63, showed that the number of female students in higher education almost doubled between 1870 and 1910, to 39.8 percent of all students in college.

13. In 1981 Winterthur Museum organized a conference on the colonial revival in America, providing the first interdisciplinary survey of ongoing scholarship on that topic. That conference raised issues of gender, class maintenance, cultural communication, and the process of modernization, as well as expanding considerably the body of evidence related to the colonial revival—particularly in the realms of art, architecture, and literature. The papers were published in Alan Axelrod, ed., *The Colonial Revival in America* (New York: W. W. Norton, 1985). Three of the essays are particularly relevant to a study of Alice Morse Earle, shedding light on her significance and the colonial revival context. Melinda Young Frye, "The Beginnings of the Period Room in American Museums: Charles P. Wilcomb's Colonial Kitchens, 1896, 1906, 1910," 217–40, a study of Charles P. Wilcomb, an early museum educator in California, identified Earle as an important influence on Wilcomb's turn-of-the-century period room construction. Celia Betsky, who decoded and catalogued the prevailing tropes of Colonial Revival art and literature in an attempt to identify the "mental interiors" of late-nineteenth-century

Americans, provided in "Inside the Past: The Interior and the Colonial Revival in American Art and Literature, 1860–1914," 241–77, a helpful model for analyzing the symbolic content of that material world. Beverly Seaton, "A Pedigree for a New Century: The Colonial Experience in Popular Historical Novels, 1890–1910," 278–93, analyzed popular historical literature of the period, providing a useful summary of Earle's literary context—if not Earle herself—and speculated about the role that popular literature played in expressing national values. For more recent interpretations of the colonial revival, see Marling, *George Washington Slept Here,* 166 (identifying Earle as the "reigning queen" of the Colonial Revival literary genre); Harvey Green, "Looking Backward to the Future: The Colonial Revival and American Culture," in *Creating a Dignified Past: Museums and the Colonial Revival,* ed. Geoffrey L. Rossano (Savage, Md.: Rowman & Littlefield, 1991), 1–16; Sarah L. Giffen and Kevin D. Murphy, *"A Noble and Dignified Stream": The Piscataqua Region in the Colonial Revival, 1860–1930* (Old York, Me.: Old York Historical Society, 1992), a study that includes numerous quotes from Earle related to her garden scholarship; James M. Lindgren, *Preserving Historic New England: Preservation, Progressivism, and the Remaking of Memory* (New York: Oxford University Press, 1995); William H. Truettner and Roger B. Stein, eds., *Picturing Old New England: Image and Memory* (Washington, D.C.: National Museum of American Art; New Haven: Yale University Press, 1999); Conforti, *Imagining New England,* which offers the most comprehensive analysis of Earle's context and impact, classifying her work as "local color history" (217); Thomas Andrew Denenberg, *Wallace Nutting and the Invention of Old America* (New Haven: Yale University Press, 2003); Michael C. Batinski, *Pastkeepers in a Small Place: Five Centuries in Deerfield, Massachusetts* (Amherst: University of Massachusetts Press, 2004); and Richard Guy Wilson, Shaun Eyring, and Kenny Marotta, *Re-creating the American Past: Essays on the Colonial Revival* (Charlottesville: University of Virginia Press, 2006), a volume in which Earle makes only minor appearances.

14. Earle's assumptions about social responsibility and the need for new strategies to counter massive social changes position her squarely within the camp of progressivism. In his classic interpretation of progressive thought, *The Search for Order, 1877–1920* (New York: Hill and Wang, 1966), Richard Wiebe defined progressivism as a quest for bureaucratic solutions to socio-structural problems. For a generational analysis of progressivism, see Robert M. Crunden, *Ministers of Reform: The Progressives' Achievement in American Civilization, 1889–1920* (New York: Basic Books, 1982), 276–77. Solomon, *In the Company of Educated Women,* furthered Crunden's argument in her assessment of the impact of college education on Earle's generation (of whom Jane Addams was a member). Solomon found that these college women assumed that they would encounter new kinds of obligations and opportunities as educated adults, but that they would somehow maintain the standards of traditional gender roles.

15. Solomon, *In the Company of Educated Women,* 109–11. On women writers of history in particular, see Nina Baym, *American Women Writers and the Work of History,*

1790–1860 (New Brunswick: Rutgers University Press, 1995); and Fitzpatrick, *History's Memory,* especially her discussion of Earle (30–33).

16. For a discussion of the changing notions of individualism, see Raymond Williams, *Keywords: A Vocabulary of Culture and Society,* rev. ed. (New York: Oxford University Press, 1983), 161–65. Herbert G. Gutman raised the issue of the role of individualism in shaping American historical narratives in "Historical Consciousness in Contemporary America," in *Power and Culture: Essays on the American Working Class* (New York: Pantheon, 1987), 395–402. More recently, Linda K. Kerber has considered individualism through the lens of gender in her essay "Can a Woman Be an Individual? The Discourse of Self-Reliance," in *Toward an Intellectual History of Women,* 200–23.

17. Mary Beth Norton, *Liberty's Daughters: The Revolutionary Experience of American Women* (Boston: Little, Brown, 1980); Linda Kerber, *Women of the Republic: Intellect and Ideology in Revolutionary America* (New York: W. W. Norton, 1980); Kerber, "'History Can Do It No Justice': Women and the Reinterpretation of the American Revolution," in *Women in the Age of the American Revolution,* ed. Ronald Hoffman and Peter J. Albert (Charlottesville: University Press of Virginia, 1989), 3–42; Degler, *At Odds,* 8, 189–96; Margaretta M. Lovell, "Reading Eighteenth-Century American Family Portraits: Social Images and Self-Images," *Winterthur Portfolio* 22.4 (Winter 1987): 243–64.

18. Raymond Williams, *Keywords,* 164–65, noted the distinction between the idea of individuality, which implied uniqueness within a broader unifying group or species, and individualism, which connoted separateness.

19. Much has been written about the historical relationship between domesticity and gender. A traditional interpretation of "separate spheres" argued that in the early nineteenth century, women lost status because of industrialization and turned to domesticity as a result. Barbara Welter, "The Cult of True Womanhood, 1820–1860," *American Quarterly* 18.2 (1966): 151–74, offered an early explication of the ideology of separate spheres. She interpreted separate spheres, however, as a mechanism for the oppression of women rather than as a source of collective female power. Nancy Cott, in *The Bonds of Womanhood,* countered Welter, arguing that domesticity did not victimize women but rather increased women's power, at least at home, and that separateness bolstered collective "bonds," through which women ultimately could engage in social and political power. About that same time, Carl Degler summarized the ways in which women's lives were changed by industrialization, reinforcing the linkage to the rise of domesticity as a female ideology in the nineteenth century. See Degler, *At Odds,* 8–9, 26–29. More recently, however, scholars have refuted the notion of separate spheres entirely, arguing that domesticity has always been woman's lot, but also that the view of women must employ multiple lenses of race, class, gender, ethnicity, region, occupation, and more. In their edited volume *No More Separate Spheres! A Next Wave American Studies Reader* (Durham: Duke University Press, 2002) Cathy N. Davidson and Jessamyn Hatcher have gathered together many of these arguments, and their introduction summarizes

the changing attitudes towards the "separate spheres" metaphor (7–26). Both Mary Beth Norton and Laurel Ulrich have presented compelling evidence about women's roles in colonial America that links women to home and family—and have argued against the notion that colonial society was somehow a "golden age" for women in terms of gender equality. See Norton, *Liberty's Daughters;* and Ulrich, *Good Wives,* 35–39. Mary Kelley, *Learning to Stand and Speak: Women, Education, and Public Life in America's Republic* (Chapel Hill: University of North Carolina Press, 2006), clearly maps the transformative impact of education for women, propelling them into increasingly public arenas and actions.

20. See Kelley, *Learning to Stand and Speak;* and Solomon, *In the Company of Educated Women,* chap. 4, "The Push into Higher Education," for detailed discussions of this trend in women's education. Solomon links the movement for educational reform to other forms of women's activism, including the suffrage movement and the rise of women's clubs such as Sorosis and the New England Women's Club (46). Karen Blair, in *The Clubwoman as Feminist: True Womanhood Redefined, 1868–1914* (New York: Holmes & Meier, 1980), has argued that women's clubs, especially literary clubs, were important feminist instruments, that they enhanced female autonomy, expanded the influence of women beyond the domestic sphere, and generally espoused a new ideology of "Domestic Feminism."

21. The most important study of the rituals and material forms used to define social order and collective identities in early America is Richard L. Bushman, *The Refinement of America: Persons, Houses, Cities* (New York: Alfred A. Knopf, 1992). Bushman's work is doubly important for any understanding of Earle because it addresses both her subject (eighteenth-century America) and her own context in the later nineteenth century.

22. For an assessment of the state of historical studies during the later nineteenth century, see Peter Novick's classic work *That Noble Dream: The "Objectivity Question" and the American Historical Profession* (Cambridge: Cambridge University Press, 1988), 47–50; and Ellen Fitzpatrick's more recent *History's Memory,* especially chap. 2, "Industrial Society and the Imperatives of Modern History," 13–50. For a specific analysis of changing interpretations of the Puritan past, see Conforti, *Imagining New England.*

1. FAMILY MATTERS

1. William Gilmore, *Reading Becomes a Necessity of Life: Material and Cultural Life in Rural New England, 1780–1830* (Knoxville: University of Tennessee Press, 1989), offers a rich interpretative backdrop for the lives of Earle's parents, both born during the half century after Independence. Gilmore's study area, Windsor County, Vermont, included the town of Andover, where Edwin grew up.

2. W. J. Rorabaugh has described the changing nature of the master-apprentice

relationship and the rising popularity of advice books, often written by ministers or educators, which became increasingly important for young men during this transition, offering them both moral guidance and practical information about their new urban situation. Without ready access to his father and mother for advice, Edwin Morse may well have turned to William Alcott's *Young Man's Guide* (1835), or any number of other similar volumes, published specifically for young men wishing to succeed in the business world. He would have learned the importance of early rising, of self-improvement, temperance, self-denial, and self-discipline, as well as how to dress, care for his health, and address his superiors in both speech and writing, and how to relate to the opposite sex. These advice books served both the needs of the master, who relied on their wisdom as a means of guiding the behavior of his workforce, and of the apprentice, for whom they offered important strategies for getting ahead. Rorabaugh noted that this new advice literature expanded upon the eighteenth-century model offered by Benjamin Franklin's autobiography, giving a much wider range of advice about how to function in the city and in the world of business. W. J. Rorabaugh, *The Craft Apprentice: From Franklin to the Machine Age in America* (New York: Oxford University Press, 1986), chap. 5, esp. 158–60. See also Paul Johnson, *The Shopkeeper's Millennium: Society and Revivals in Rochester, New York, 1815–1837* (New York: Hill and Wang, 1978), 53, 57.

3. John Morse to Abigail Mason Goodhue, August 23, 1844, Earle-Hyde Papers.

4. Abigail Goodhue, Jackson, Me., to Edwin Morse, Worcester, Mass., July 15, 1845, Earle-Hyde Papers.

5. Ibid.

6. Ibid.

7. Abigail Clary Goodhue, Troy, Me., to Edwin Morse, Worcester, Mass., September 14, 1846, Earle-Hyde Papers.

8. Ibid.

9. Edwin Morse, Worcester, Mass., to Abigail Goodhue, Jackson, Me., February 9, 1845, Earle-Hyde Papers.

10. Ibid.

11. Abigail Clary Morse, Jackson, Me., to Edwin Morse, Worcester, Mass., May 10, 1847, Earle-Hyde Papers.

12. Allen was "a mechanic and inventor of superior quality" who "invented a double-barreled breech-loading sporting gun, and was probably the first to use steel shells in connection with such an arm; these shells could be reloaded indefinitely. He was the pioneer, in this country, in the manufacture of double-barreled shot guns and fowling pieces." Charles G. Washburn, *Industrial Worcester* (Worcester: Davis Press, 1917), 204–6.

13. In addition to Washburn's early study *Industrial Worcester,* two other important sources trace the history and dynamics of Worcester's growth during the nineteenth century. See Robert W. Doherty, *Society and Power: Five New England Towns, 1800–1860* (Amherst: University of Massachusetts Press, 1977); and Roy

Rosenzweig, *Eight Hours for What We Will: Workers and Leisure in an Industrial City* (New York: Cambridge University Press, 1983).

14. Doherty, *Society and Power*, 24–26, 33.

15. Sam Bass Warner Jr. identified this pattern in Philadelphia during the same time period in *The Private City: Philadelphia in Three Periods of Its Growth*, 2nd ed. (Philadelphia: University of Pennsylvania Press, 1987), 56–59. Other studies of nineteenth-century urban life offer more subtle interpretations of the nuances of these changing residential patterns, especially Christine Stansell, *City of Women: Sex and Class in New York, 1789–1860* (Urbana: University of Illinois Press, 1982); and Stuart M. Blumin, *The Emergence of the Middle Class: Social Experience in the American City, 1760–1900* (New York: Cambridge University Press, 1989).

16. U.S. Census, Manuscript Schedules, Worcester County, Mass., 1850, 305, Boston Public Library (microfilm).

17. Ibid. To reconstruct the Morse family's immediate neighborhood, I compared the census data with information in *The Worcester Almanac, Directory, and Business Advisor for 1850* (Worcester: Henry J. Howland, 1850).

18. U.S. Census, Worcester County, Mass., 1850, 304–7.

19. Occupations of the boardinghouse residents included iron founder, clerk, harness maker, jobber, card maker, car builder, physician, insurance agent, and architect—a microcosm of the larger neighborhood. The gender ratio of the boarders (fourteen men, eleven women) was also close to that of the neighborhood at large, but unlike ratios in the rest of the neighborhood, only one of the twenty-four boardinghouse residents was married. Ibid., 304.

20. Ibid. Persis Thorndike was the daughter of Abby Morse's sister Betsy Clary and Ebenezer Thorndike of Dixmont, Maine; Olive Snow was the daughter of another sister, Catherine Clary, and Aaron Snow of Jackson, Maine. Morse-Earle Genealogy. Christine Stansell described the importance of kinship networks, as well as regional and village connections, as mechanisms for community formation among urban, largely immigrant women during this period. Although Stansell was discussing the urban poor, her observations about urban social strategies seem equally applicable to more middling in-migrants like Abby Morse. Stansell, *City of Women*, 55–58.

21. Although Edwin and Abby Morse named their daughter Mary Alice, she was called Alice by her family, and always referred to herself as Alice Morse, later Earle.

22. At the very least, Edwin Morse received a one-sixth share of $2,500 in proceeds from the sale of his father's four hundred acres of land in Andover. Since Benjamin Morse's will cannot be located, the exact distribution of his estate is unknown. Edwin may have received more, as his mother joined him in Worcester following her husband's death. Andover Book of Deeds, Andover, Vt., vol. 1, 487–89.

23. Washburn, *Industrial Worcester*, 120. It is not clear exactly what year Morse began his association with the company. The Worcester City Directory first listed him as employed by Shepherd, Lathe & Co. in 1853. The credit reports of R. G. Dun

& Co., however, recorded the formation of Shepherd, Lathe & Co. in early 1854. Russell R. Shepherd, one of the partners, had previously been doing business with Clarence Wheeler under the name S. C. Coombs & Co. The Dun reports described Shepherd & Lathe as a highly reliable manufacturer of machines and tools, consistently doing good business. Massachusetts, Vol. 104, pp. 599, 632, 902, R. G. Dun & Co. Credit Report Volumes, Baker Library Historical Collections, Harvard Business School.

24. Henry J. Howland, *The Worcester Almanac, Directory, and Business Advisor for 1853* (Worcester: H. J. Howland, 1853), 119; idem, *The Worcester Almanac, Directory, and Business Advisor for 1856* (Worcester: H. J. Howland, 1856), 144.

25. According to notes made by Mary F. Brightman, June 9, 1943, Frances Clary Morse died on March 22, 1933, and was buried at Worcester Rural Cemetery. Alice Morse Earle Biographical Information and Photographs, AAS.

26. Stuart Blumin has summarized the characteristics of that mentality as consisting of six fundamental strategies: limitation of family size, an emphasis on codified behavior, the extension of childhood, an emphasis on education, delay of marriage, and a reliance on purchased environments to express and inculcate perceived standards of civility. Blumin, *Emergence of the Middle Class,* 187–88. Mary Ryan, in *Cradle of the Middle Class: The Family in Oneida County, New York, 1790–1865* (New York: Cambridge University Press, 1981), demonstrated the importance of educating children as a critical strategy for middle-class mobility. Richard Bushman identified the desire for gentility as a driving force for middle-class "improvement." Families added parlors, picket fences, and gardens to their houses to provide the outward appearance of inner refinement and respectability. See Richard L. Bushman, *The Refinement of America: Persons, Houses, Cities* (New York: Alfred A. Knopf, 1992), chap. 11, "City and Country," 256–62, 273–79. For a reappraisal of the transformation of family strategies in the face of a transforming rural economy and an emerging urban domestic culture, see Catherine E. Kelly, *In the New England Fashion: Reshaping Women's Lives in the Nineteenth Century* (Ithaca: Cornell University Press, 1999).

27. Isaac Ferris, "Men of Business: Their Home Responsibilities," in *The Man of Business, Considered in His Various Relations* (New York, 1857), 24–25; quoted in Blumin, *Emergence of the Middle Class,* 138.

28. Thomas Bender, *Toward an Urban Vision: Ideas and Institutions in Nineteenth-Century America* (Baltimore: Johns Hopkins University Press, 1975), 132–34. See also Dolores Hayden, *Building Suburbia: Green Fields and Urban Growth, 1820–1900* (New York: Vintage Books, 2003), 21–44. For a study of the impact of market culture and urban influences on families during the antebellum period, see Kelly, *In the New England Fashion.*

29. F. W. Beers, *Atlas of the City of Worcester, Worcester County, Massachusetts* (1870; repr., Rutland, Vt.: Charles E. Tuttle, 1971), pl. 17; *Atlas of the City of Worcester Massachusetts from Official Records, Private Plans, and Actual Surveys* (Philadelphia: G. M. Hopkins, C.E., Publisher, 1886), pl. 8.

30. See Bushman, *The Refinement of America,* 354–65, on the social geography of urban space and the devices used by developers to impart elegance to city houses and public buildings.

31. Richard Sennett, "Middle-Class Families and Urban Violence: The Experience of a Chicago Community in the Nineteenth Century," in *Nineteenth-Century Cities: Essays in the New Urban History,* ed. Stephan Thernstrom and Richard Sennett (New Haven: Yale University Press, 1969), 386–420, described similar responses among middle-class families in the Union Park section of Chicago during a slightly later period. Sennett argued that the families he studied experienced conflicting desires to take advantage of the opportunities of the city, but at the same time to withdraw from its dangers into the sheltering nest of family and home. The Morses seem to have fit Sennett's pattern. Catherine Kelly draws similar conclusions about the tensions between rural values and urban necessities in *In the New England Fashion,* especially chap. 2, "All the Work of the Family," 19–63.

32. Marcus Whiffen, *American Architecture since 1780: A Guide to the Styles* (Cambridge: MIT Press, 1969), 102–8. Explicit allusions to elegant French taste, whether through architecture, furniture, modes of dining, clothing, or even language, were a common means for middle- and upper-class Americans to proclaim their worldliness during this era. See, for example, Susan Williams, *Savory Suppers and Fashionable Feasts: Dining in Victorian America* (New York: Pantheon Books, 1985), 24–25. Cookbooks of this period were laced with French words—*bon bons, déjeuner, consommé, liqueurs*—and sometimes even provided their readers with dinner party menus in both French and English. See also Bushman, *The Refinement of America,* 250–62, for a larger discussion of vernacular gentility.

33. For a general discussion of the ideals that defined the uses of household space during the Victorian era and the ways in which middle-class families commonly expressed their values, see Harvey Green, "Piano in the Parlor," chap. 4 of *The Light of the Home: An Intimate View of the Lives of Women in Victorian America* (New York: Pantheon, 1983), 92–111. Dining rooms began to appear in gentry houses by the mid-eighteenth century, but the term "dining room" was not used to any great degree until after the Revolution. See Mark R. Wenger, "The Dining Room in Early Virginia," in *Perspectives in Vernacular Architecture,* ed. Thomas Carter and Bernard L. Herman, vol. 3 (Columbia: University of Missouri Press, 1989), 156–58; Abbott Lowell Cummings, "Inside the Massachusetts House," in *Common Places: Readings in North American Vernacular Architecture,* ed. Dell Upton and John Michael Vlach (Athens: University of Georgia Press, 1986), 226. Dining rooms did not, however, appear regularly in published architectural plans for houses of the urban and suburban middle classes until the 1850s. Williams, *Savory Suppers,* 51–68.

34. Blumin, *Emergence of the Middle Class,* 138–39. See also Kenneth L. Ames, "When the Music Stops," chap. 4 of *Death in the Dining Room* (Philadelphia: Temple University Press, 1992), 150–84.

35. Earle's childhood coincided with a widespread increase in emphasis on the acculturation and education of children, both in schools and through carefully constructed

home environments and rituals. See, for example, Green, *Light of the Home*, especially chap. 2, "The Cult of Motherhood," 29–58; as well as Karin Calvert, "Cradle to Crib: The Revolution in Nineteenth-Century Children's Furniture," in *A Century of Childhood, 1820–1920*, ed. Mary Lynn Stephens Heininger (Rochester, N.Y.: Margaret Woodbury Strong Museum, 1984), 33–63.

36. Alice Morse Earle, *Old-Time Gardens, Newly Set Forth: A Book of the Sweet o' the Year* (New York: Macmillan, 1901), 159.

37. For specific references to Earle's parents' garden, see ibid., 25, 38, 47–48, 55, 74, 159, 165, 172, 199, 237, 299, 330, 340.

38. Ibid., 337, 340. Earle included a photograph of the Fawcett garden in her book. Edwin Fawcett, according to the 1860 federal census, was only twenty-eight years old, a merchant, with $12,000 worth of real estate and $2,100 in personal wealth. He lived on Chatham Street with his wife, Rosetta, and seventeen-year-old Malek A. Loring, one of his clerks. U.S. Census, Worcester County, Mass., 1860.

39. Edwin Augustus Morse, Annapolis, Md., to Alice and Frances Morse, December 21, 1861, Earle-Hyde Papers.

40. Edwin Augustus Morse to Abigail and Edwin Morse, May 13, 1864, Earle-Hyde Papers.

41. Alfred S. Roe, *Worcester Classical and English High School: A Record of Forty-seven Years* (Worcester: published by the author, 1892), 5–6.

42. Ibid., 101, 113, 126. Eighty-one students graduated in 1881.

43. Roe's history of Classical and English High School does not identify the textbooks used to teach history, except for a brief reference to Charles Goodrich's history of the United States. Ibid., 83–84.

44. Alice Morse Earle, "History as Loved and Hated," paper presented at a meeting of the Daughters of the American Revolution, 1899, Earle-Hyde Papers, 2. Robert M. Crunden, in *Ministers of Reform: The Progressives' Achievement in American Civilization, 1889–1920* (New York: Basic Books, 1982), discussed childhood reading as an aspect of the cultural background of those who became progressives. He listed *Our Young Folks, Pilgrim's Progress,* and the works of Jane Austen, William Thackeray, Charles Dickens, Tennyson, Robert Browning, Matthew Arnold, Emerson, Thomas Carlyle, and John Ruskin as common to the group, commenting, "All these works taught moral lessons; all were linear in their development; all seemed replete with Protestant assumptions on every subject from sex to salvation," and "all gave a spurious sense of permanence to a life increasingly in flux" (91).

45. City of Worcester, *Reports Concerning the Public Schools for 1869* (Worcester: Tyler & Seagrave, 1870), 47–56.

46. Earle, *Old-Time Gardens*, 120.

47. Crunden, *Ministers of Reform*, 276–77.

48. Roe, *Worcester Classical and English High School*, 113.

49. Sarah A. Leavitt, *From Catharine Beecher to Martha Stewart: A Cultural History of Domestic Advice* (Chapel Hill: University of North Carolina Press, 2002), 19.

Leavitt discussed the ambivalence many later Victorian domestic writers felt about suffrage, citing the works of Elizabeth Ellet, Catharine Beecher, Marion Harland, and Emma Churchman Hewitt, all of whom sent a clear message to their female readers: choose home. Each of these writers, however, believed that women's artistic abilities would strengthen their domestic potency.

50. Alma Lutz, "Elizabeth Ellet," in *Notable American Women, 1607–1950: A Biographical Dictionary,* ed. Edward T. James et al., vol. 1 (Cambridge: Belknap Press of Harvard University Press, 1971), 569–70. See Linda K. Kerber's analysis of Ellet's books in "History Can Do It No Justice": Women and the Reinterpretation of the American Revolution," in *Toward an Intellectual History of Women,* ed. Linda K. Kerber (Chapel Hill: University of North Carolina Press, 1997), 63–68.

51. "George Gannett," in *National Cyclopedia of American Biography,* vol. 1 (New York: James T. White Co., 1898), 390, cited in Virginia Lopez Begg, "Alice Morse Earle: Old Time Gardens in a Brave New Century," *Journal of the New England Garden History Society* 8 (Fall 2000): 13–21.

52. Edwin M. Bacon, *King's Dictionary of Boston* (Cambridge: Moses King, 1883), 379.

53. Barbara Miller Solomon, *In the Company of Educated Women: A History of Women and Higher Education in America* (New Haven: Yale University Press, 1985), 47, 56.

54. Probate inventory of Edwin Morse, case 12889, filed January 11, 1892 (County of Worcester, Commonwealth of Massachusetts), vol. 483, 267; *Historical Statistics of the United States: Colonial Times to 1970, Bicentennial Edition,* pt. 1 (Washington, D.C.: U.S. Bureau of the Census, 1975), 168, 213.

55. Roe, *Worcester Classical and English High School,* 9.

2. PARLOR CULTURE, PUBLIC CULTURE

1. Morse-Earle Genealogy.

2. Marla Miller and Anne Lanning have discussed the notion of a "common parlor," as used by women in Deerfield, Massachusetts, in the late nineteenth century. These were public spaces over which women presided—libraries, craft workshops and salesrooms, house restorations. Their purpose was to "restore 'traditional' moral values, to rehabilitate Anglo Saxon communal pride and cultural authority, and to revitalize white middle-class economic life." The blurring of lines between public and private spaces implied by club activities is related to this impulse. Marla R. Miller and Anne Digan Lanning, "Common Parlors: Women and the Recreation of Community Identity in Deerfield, Massachusetts, 1870–1920," *Gender and History* 6.3 (1994): 435–55.

3. Henry Earle was a direct descendant of Ralph Earle (not the painter). An Earle family genealogy, published in 1888, noted that Ralph Earle, born in 1606, was first recorded in North America in 1638 at Newport, Rhode Island, where he was a sawyer. At a town meeting in 1647 he was "chosen to keep an Inn to sell beer and

wine and to entertain strangers." He also served as the tax assessor for Newport and may have owned the Bristol ferry in 1655. Ralph Earle was married to Joan Savage, a woman ten or eleven years older than he, who was reputed to have lived to be over one hundred years old. At his death in 1678, Ralph left his wife as executrix; upon her death his land was divided in a two-to-one ratio between his son and grandson, both also named Ralph Earle. His movable estate was divided into five parts, with two parts distributed to his son and one to each of his three daughters, Mary, Martha, and Sarah. By the early eighteenth century, the Earle family fortunes had increased considerably. Oliver Earle, great-grandson of Ralph, was living in New York City in 1716, "engaged in the East India trade." His bequest to his wife, Rebecca, reveals a lifestyle that would have to be characterized as affording well beyond mere necessities. *The Earle Family: Ralph Earle and His Descendants,* comp. Pliny Earle (Worcester: privately printed, 1888), 3, 46–47, 340, 367.

4. New York, Vol. 418, p. 282, R. G. Dun & Co. Credit Report Volumes, Baker Library Historical Collections, Harvard Business School.

5. Tax assessors valued the business of Randall H. Green & Son, brokers located at 94 Wall Street in New York City, at $201,152 in November 1866. *Monthly and Special List, New York, District 32, IRS Tax Assessment List, 1862–1918,* www.ancestry.com.

6. George T. Lain, *The Brooklyn City and Business Directory* (Brooklyn: Lain & Company, 1877), 257.

7. In 1878 Henry Earle was listed in the Brooklyn directory as a broker, doing business in New York. Subsequently he always was listed alternatively as a banker or a broker, at two different addresses. The 1880 directory listed him as a banker at 18 Wall Street; the 1881 directory listed him as a broker at 5 Wall Street; and the 1882 directory listed him as a banker at 5 Wall Street. *Brooklyn City Directory* (1878), 260; (1880), 284; (1881), 302; (1882), 306.

8. *Brooklyn City Directory* (1880), iii.

9. Richard Edwards, ed., *An Historical and Descriptive Review of the City of Brooklyn* (New York: Historical Publishing Company, 1883), 64. Edwards edited the *Brooklyn Daily Eagle.*

10. Both houses occupied by the Earles have been described in Clay Lancaster, *Old Brooklyn Heights: America's First Suburb* (Rutland, Vt.: Charles E. Tuttle Company, 1961), 99, 103. At 277 Henry Street, a four-story house occupied by a widow in the 1850s, they possibly rented rooms prior to purchasing a house of their own.

11. Charles Lockwood, *Bricks and Brownstones: The New York Rowhouse, 1783–1929* (New York: Abbeville Press, 1972). A similar three-story brownstone at 434 Henry Street, in good condition on a full lot, was advertised in the *Brooklyn Daily Eagle* on December 14, 1902, as a "Bargain" at $7,500). By contrast, *The Manufacturer and Builder* reported on the construction of two-story Queen Anne style laborers' cottages in Brooklyn in 1879, selling for $500 apiece. "Building Intelligence," *The Manufacturer and Builder* 11.11 (November 1879): 257. The Earles' house, which was built in 1841, has been converted to four separate living quarters. Few interior details dating from the Earles' occupancy remain.

12. U.S. Census, Manuscript Schedules, King's County, N.Y., 1880, 21, New York Public Library (microfilm).

13. Ibid.

14. New York, Vol. 418, p. 282, R. G. Dun & Co. Credit Report Volumes.

15. "Charles Goodyear," *Scientific American Supplement,* no. 787 (January 31, 1891).

16. New York, Vol. 351, p. 1300a/35, R. G. Dun & Co. Credit Report Volumes.

17. Ibid., 1278, 1217, 1300m, 1300a/35.

18. Helen H. Greene to Alice Earle Hyde, April 15, 1925, Earle-Hyde Papers.

19. Carl N. Degler, *At Odds: Women and the Family in America from the Revolution to the Present* (New York: Oxford University Press, 1980), 101–3, 220–26; Mary Lynn Stephens Heininger, ed., *A Century of Childhood, 1820–1920* (Rochester, N.Y.: Margaret Woodbury Strong Museum, 1984), 1–63.

20. Copies of these images exist in the Alice Morse Earle Biographical Materials and Photographs, AAS; Earle-Hyde Papers; and Earle-Moore Papers.

21. Beverly Gordon, *The Saturated World: Aesthetic Meaning, Intimate Objects, Women's Lives, 1890–1940* (Knoxville: University of Tennessee Press, 2006), 179–87.

22. A number of scholars have written about the significance of Colonial Revival imagery, including Roger B. Stein, "After the War: Constructing a Rural Past"; and William H. Truettner and Thomas Andrew Denenberg, "The Discreet Charm of the Colonial," both in *Picturing Old New England: Image and Memory,* ed. William H. Truettner and Roger B. Stein (Washington, D.C.: National Museum of American Art; New Haven: Yale University Press, 1999), 15–41, 79–109; Thomas Andrew Denenberg, *Wallace Nutting and the Invention of Old America* (New Haven: Yale University Press, 2003), 63–67; Suzanne L. Flynt, *The Allen Sisters: Pictorial Photographers, 1885–1920* (Deerfield, Mass.: Pocumtuck Valley Memorial Association, 2002); and Gordon, *Saturated World,* 130–35.

23. Alice Morse Earle Biographical Materials and Photographs; Earle-Hyde Papers; Alice Morse Earle, *Old-Time Gardens, Newly Set Forth: A Book of the Sweet o' the Year* (New York: Macmillan, 1901), 350. The photograph is unattributed, but it is possible that Earle's sister, Frances Morse, may have dabbled in photography.

24. Catharine E. Beecher and Harriet Beecher Stowe, *The American Woman's Home: or, Principles of Domestic Science* (New York: J. B. Ford & Co., 1870), 294–96.

25. Alice Morse Earle to George Ellwanger, December 3, 1901, courtesy of the Trustees of the Boston Public Library / Rare Books.

26. Judge John Pitman (1785–1864) was a prominent Rhode Island jurist, and his two sons, Joseph (1819–1883) and John (1813–1892), started a silkworm plantation at Duck Cove in 1830. Randall Greene (1798–1878) married Judge Pitman's daughter Harriet (1817–1909) and turned the cocoonery into a summer cottage in 1850. Helen H. Greene to Alice Earle Hyde, April 15, 1925, Earle-Hyde Papers. Wickford, directly across Narragansett Bay from Newport, was easily accessible from Brooklyn via both rail and steamboat. The Earles could have taken the New York, New Haven, and Hartford Railroad to New London and then the New York, Providence, and Boston Railroad directly to Wickford Junction, about twenty

miles south of Providence. The journey by rail, according to Baedeker's 1893 guide to the United States, took between five and eight hours, and offered excellent views of the shoreline of Long Island Sound. With four small children, however, a more practical—and possibly more exciting—option might have been to travel to Wickford by overnight steamer. According to Baedeker, the steamers "all run at night, leaving New York about 5 or 6 p.m.," and passengers were not required to leave their staterooms until seven o'clock in the morning. In addition, Baedeker noted, "the steamers on all these lines are well fitted up and contain good restaurants, etc.; those of the Fall River Line"—the Plymouth, the Puritan, the Pilgrim, and the Providence—"are especially large and luxurious." Karl Baedeker, ed., *The United States, with an Excursion into Mexico: A Handbook for Travellers, 1893* (1893; facsimile ed., New York: Da Capo Press, 1971), 62, 66.

27. Information about the Pitman family was pieced together from Alice Earle Hyde's genealogical notes, and from a letter to Hyde from her aunt Nellie Greene, reminiscing about the family and Wickford. Helen H. Greene to Alice Earle Hyde, April 15, 1925, Earle-Hyde Papers. See also Earle-Moore Genealogy.

28. Alice Morse Earle, "A Baptist Preacher and Soldier of the Last Century," *New England Magazine* 18.4 (June 1895): 409. This may be the chair illustrated in the 1917 edition of Frances Morse's history of furniture, described as a "Transition Chair, 1785," and belonging to Earle's daughter Alice (Mrs. Clarence R. Hyde). Frances Morse, *Furniture of the Olden Time* (New York: Macmillan, rev. ed. (New York: Macmillan, 1917), 202, fig. 186.

29. Alice Morse Earle, "The Oldest Episcopal Church in New England," *New England Magazine* 13.5 (January 1893): 577, 582.

30. Ibid., 587.

31. Alice Morse Earle to George Ellwanger, December 3, 1901. Earle also mentioned Homogansett in *Home Life in Colonial Days,* describing a sundial that had "stood for years in the old box-bordered garden at Homogansett Farm, in Wickford, in old Narragansett." Alice Morse Earle, *Home Life in Colonial Days* (New York: Macmillan, 1898), 442–43. The boxwood garden is still extant at Duck Cove.

32. Details about this cottage are unclear, although family members have indicated that it was on the water, abutting the Greene and Pitman properties and connected to them by a narrow lane. In 1888 Joseph P. Earle (Henry's brother) transferred a large Duck Cove parcel to his sister Mary T. Earle. The deed suggests that there was much changing of hands of pieces of the property among the Greene, Earle, and Pitman heirs over the course of the last quarter of the nineteenth century. It seems always to have been a family compound. Deed, Joseph T. Earle to Mary T. Earle, June 29, 1888, recorded August 10, 1893, North Kingston, R.I., Land Records, vol. 41, 371.

33. Alice Morse Earle, "A Pickle for the Knowing Ones," *Christian Union* 41.4 (January 23, 1890): 140. Earle's literary output for 1890–1892 included seventeen articles (for these see the Chronological Bibliography at the end of this book), *The Sabbath in Puritan New England,* and *China Collecting in America.*

34. "The Clubs of Brooklyn," *Brooklyn Life* 17.421 (March 26, 1898): 15, 23. This article included a photographic portrait of Henry Earle, captioned "Club Member."

35. Ibid., 11–13, 21. The *Official Golf Guide* of 1899 reported that the Crescent Athletic Club had "about 200 golfing members," adding: "The course was laid out by George Straith in the fall of 1896 and there are now eighteen holes in play. 'Crescent' golfers have developed considerable skill during the past year and the club is fortunate in securing so good a course near the city." Dues and entrance fees were $25 each. Of Marine and Field, the *Guide* reported the addition of a nine-hole golf course in 1897, an entrance fee of $75, and annual dues of $50. The names of the holes were Park, Bridge, Marsh, Bowery, High Tee, Midway, Northeast, Ridge, and Home. Josiah Newman, comp. and ed., *The Official Golf Guide of the United States and Canada for 1899* (New York: privately printed, 1899), 212, 207.

36. "The Clubs of Brooklyn," 22.

37. "About Brooklyn Society," *Brooklyn Daily Eagle,* June 7, 1896.

38. A. E. Hewitt, *A History of Mrs. Field's Literary Club* (Brooklyn: privately published, 1909), 5–7; Mrs. Field's Literary Club Papers, Brooklyn Historical Society.

39. Hewitt, *History of Mrs. Field's Literary Club,* 31–48; L. E. Purcell, "Trilby and Trilby-Mania: The Beginning of the Bestseller System," *Journal of Popular Culture* 11.1 (1977): 62–76. See also "Making the Bestseller List," *Rave Reviews: Bestselling Fiction in America,* www2.lib.virginia.edu/exhibits/rave_reviews/list_making.html.

40. Hewitt, *History of Mrs. Field's Literary Club,* 58.

41. Abbe was also a suffrage activist who worked to gather petitions to eliminate the word "male" as a voting qualification in the New York State Constitution. To that end she served as Chairman of the Committee on Parlor Meetings, social gatherings organized by women in their homes to persuade men to sign the petitions. Several of these meeting were held at Abbe's house at 11 West Fiftieth Street, as well as at the homes of prominent friends. Abbe was quoted as saying: "It is the Lord's work. . . . We will get over 1,000 signatures of prominent men through social influences alone." "Society Women Want Votes," *New York Times,* April 11, 1894.

42. Anna Ware Winsor, "The City History Club," *Municipal Affairs* 2.3 (September 1898): 463–64; "A New Club," *The Outlook* 49.3 (January 20, 1894): 2, 114.

43. "Woman's Club: History of the Brooklyn Organization," *Brooklyn Daily Eagle,* February 10, 1890.

44. Friedrich Froebel was a pioneering educator in the kindergarten movement. Froebel academies appeared in many American cities during the late nineteenth century. Michael Steven Shapiro, *Child's Garden: The Kindergarten Movement from Froebel to Dewey* (University Park: Pennsylvania State University Press, 1983). Earle later incorporated Froebel's educational theories into *Old-Time Gardens,* a specific instance of the benefit to her professional work that club activities may have provided.

45. "Among the Women's Clubs," *New York Times,* October 22, 1893.

46. Leavitt cites household advice writers Lydia Maria Child, Catharine Beecher, Helen Hunt Jackson, and Sarah Josepha Hale (publisher of *Godey's Lady's Book*) as

"among the most influential women writers of the nineteenth century." Sarah A. Leavitt, *From Catharine Beecher to Martha Stewart: A Cultural History of Domestic Advice* (Chapel Hill: University of North Carolina Press, 2002), 11.

47. Earle, *China Collecting*, 18.

48. For a good introduction to the development of the suffrage movement, as well as opposition to it, see Ellen Carol DuBois and Lynn Dumenil, *Through Women's Eyes: An American History with Documents*, 2nd ed. (Boston: Bedford / St. Martin's, 2009), 326–29, 354–56, 471–72.

49. "Charge of the Anti Brigade: Orders Issued to the Clinton Avenue Division This Morning," *Brooklyn Daily Eagle*, May 3, 1894).

50. "Woman's Club: History of the Brooklyn Organization."

51. Karen Blair, *The Clubwoman as Feminist: True Womanhood Redefined, 1868–1914* (New York: Holmes & Meier, 1980), 3–5, 23, 111.

52. The link between suffrage and temperance had been forged by 1874, when the Women's Christian Temperance Union endorsed the woman's vote. In the process, however, the suffrage movement gained a powerful enemy, the liquor industry, which worked hard to protect its profits by fighting against suffrage.

53. "Woman's Club: History of the Brooklyn Organization"; "Suffrage in the Balance: Daughters of the Revolution Hear Both Sides," *New York Times*, May 1, 1894. Other members of the Putnam family were closely linked to Alice and Henry Earle. Henry's first business partner was Nathaniel D. Putnam, and Albert E. Putnam was a special investor in their firm for several years. The latter was also the son-in-law of David W. Morrison, who was in turn the son of the former president of the Manhattan Bank Company. David Morrison attended the symposium. New York, Vol. 418, p. 282, R. G. Dun & Co. Credit Report Volumes.

54. "An Anti-Suffrage Movement," *The Outlook* 49.17 (April 28, 1894): 738.

55. "A Woman's Protest Against Woman's Suffrage," *The Outlook* 49 (1894): 760.

56. Ibid.

57. Ibid. Mary Pitman Earle married David Thomas Moore at the Church of the Pilgrims on April 15, 1902. Moore's mother had been among those present at the anti-suffrage meeting. Twenty-four hundred people were invited to the wedding; among the names of those who were present at both events are Abbott, Beecher, Chittenden, De Silver, Ide, Leech, McKeen, Moore, Morrison, Putnam, Southard, and Stillman. The anti-suffrage protesters who lived in Brooklyn Heights resided at 70, 91, 101, and 143 Willow Street; 123 and 212 Columbia Heights; 43, 83, and 94 Remsen Street; 6 Clark Street; 43 Pierrepont Street; and 146 Henry Street. Wedding list, April 15, 1902, Earle-Moore Papers.

58. Katherine Kish Sklar, "Victorian Women and Domestic Life: Mary Todd Lincoln, Elizabeth Cady Stanton, and Harriet Beecher Stowe," in *Women and Power in American History*, ed. Kathryn Kish Sklar and Thomas Dublin, 3rd. ed. (Upper Saddle River, N.J.: Prentice Hall, 2009), 122–33.

59. Assistant editors, *St. Nicholas Magazine*, New York, N.Y., to Alice Morse Earle, February 19, 1901, PVMA.

60. Alice Morse Earle to George Sheldon, January 9, 1902, ibid.
61. "Equal Suffrage Their Aim," *New York Times,* April 12, 1894.
62. Alice Morse Earle, *Margaret Winthrop* (New York: Charles Scribner's Sons, 1895), 334–35.
63. See Karal Ann Marling's account of the rise of Betsy Ross as an iconic figure in *George Washington Slept Here: Colonial Revivals and American Culture, 1876–1986* (Cambridge: Harvard University Press, 1988), 17–20. For a far more detailed account of Ross's life and cultural significance, see Marla R. Miller's scholarly biography *Betsy Ross and the Making of America* (New York: Henry Holt, 2010).
64. Earle, *Margaret Winthrop,* 335. Earle devoted an entire chapter of *Margaret Winthrop* to the story of Anne Hutchinson. She speculated sympathetically about what the events surrounding Hutchinson's trial and subsequent exile might have cost Winthrop—wife of the governor but a woman and near neighbor of Hutchinson. Earle did not condemn Hutchinson but rather suggested the cost to the entire Puritan experiment of her individual choices and beliefs. Ibid., 269–87.
65. Gilman, born in 1860, was nine years younger than Earle. Both had long New England roots, but all biographical similarity stops there. For a more explicit analysis of Gilman and her radical context, see Ann J. Lane, *To Herland and Beyond: The Life and Work of Charlotte Perkins Gilman* (New York: Pantheon Books, 1990).
66. Jane Cunningham Croly, *The History of the Woman's Club Movement in America* (New York: Henry G. Allen & Co., 1898), 868.
67. Ibid., 898.
68. "The Clubs of Brooklyn," *Brooklyn Life* 17.421 (March 26, 1898): 22–29.
69. Earle's DAR ID number was 8538. Alice Morse Earle, application for membership, Daughters of the American Revolution, DAR Library, Washington, D.C.; *Daughters of the American Revolution Lineage Books* are available online at www.ancestry.com. Earle was also a member of the Long Island Chapter of the Daughters of the Revolution, formed in 1891, which had refused to become part of the larger national umbrella organization. The DAR has individual chapters but is governed by a federal structure, whereas each chapter of the Daughters of the Revolution retained its individual state-based autonomy. Earle, as regent of the Long Island Society of the Daughters of the Revolution, was active in the move to unite the two groups in 1896. "All Daughters May Combine," *Brooklyn Daily Eagle,* July 1, 1896; "Women's Clubs," *Brooklyn Daily Eagle,* June 11, 1899.
70. The term "Colonial Dames" refers to two separate organizations: the Colonial Dames of America and the National Society of the Colonial Dames of America. The CDA was formed first, in New York City. The NSCDA grew out of a Philadelphia spin-off of the CDA. Allegedly the CDA members were reluctant to accept the descendants of the illegitimate children of Benjamin Franklin as members.
71. Mary S. Lockwood and Emily Lee Sherwood, *Story of the Records, D.A.R.* (Washington, D.C.: George E. Howard, 1906), 24, quoted in Patricia West, *Domesticating History: The Political Origins of America's House Museums* (Washington, D.C.:

Smithsonian Institution Press, 1999), 44. The formation of hereditary groups like the DAR and the Colonial Dames must be viewed as part of a broader attempt by middle-class Americans to reconsolidate their power base. As Robert Wiebe has suggested in *The Search for Order, 1877–1920* (New York: Hill and Wang, 1966), however, this was not merely an attempt to regain the old community-based order, but rather an effort to construct a new national order, preempting the rampant power of business and industry by co-opting their bureaucratic and scientific methods to conservative moral ends. Wiebe argued that the decline of local community power ultimately resulted in a social and political realignment along class lines, bolstered, for the middle class, by a widespread faith in bureaucratic solutions to social and economic problems (52).

72. An early history of the Colonial Dames of America confirmed the educational mission of the organization, noting that "the Dames must make their own researches in family Bibles and old letters, and the pedigree-charts must be filled out in their own handwriting; this was considered too onerous and the rule was soon abandoned." *The Colonial Dames of America, 1890–1904* (New York: Irving Press, 1904), 4.

73. "Proceedings of the First Continental Congress," *American Monthly Magazine* 1.2 (1892): 130.

74. "Women's Club in London: The Lyceum Club Contemplates a Common Meeting Place for All Women," *New York Times*, July 26, 1904.

3. NEW ENGLAND KISMET

1. "Alice Morse Earle and Her Books," *New York Times Saturday Review of Books and Art*, July 21, 1900, 15; reprinted in "General Gossip of Authors and Writers," *Current Literature* 29 (September 1900): 286–87.

2. Thomas Bailey Aldrich (1836–1907) helped to define the literary genre of which Earle was a part. His fictionalized account of his own childhood in Portsmouth, New Hampshire, *The Story of a Bad Boy* (1868), and subsequent writings offered a nostalgic vision of the New England past. Other "local color" writers, including Harriet Beecher Stowe, John Greenleaf Whittier, and Sarah Orne Jewett, created narratives that offered readers a realistic vision of a serene and usable past, one that could provide a refuge from the problems of modernity. Joseph Conforti has called Earle's writings "local color history," which he described as "an evocative recreation of the past that incorporates the aesthetic sensibility of the regional literary realism that descended from Harriet Beecher Stowe to writers like Sarah Orne Jewett." Joseph A. Conforti, *Imagining New England: Explorations of Regional Identity from the Pilgrims to the Mid-Twentieth Century* (Chapel Hill: University of North Carolina Press, 2001), 217. For a general introduction to the uses of New England's past in the post–Civil War period, see Dona Brown and Stephen

Nissenbaum, "Changing New England: 1865–1945," in *Picturing Old New England: Image and Memory,* ed. William H. Truettner and Roger B. Stein (Washington, D.C.: National Museum of American Art; New Haven: Yale University Press, 1999), 1–8.

3. "Alice Morse Earle and Her Books," 15.

4. Ibid. Henry Van Dyke (1852–1933) was pastor of the Brick Presbyterian Church in New York City and author of many inspirational texts, including essays, poems, and several stories about the history of Christmas. "Van Dyke, Henry," in *The Columbia Encyclopedia,* 6th ed. (New York: Columbia University Press, 2002).

5. See Conforti, *Imagining New England,* an excellent study of the history and significance of Pilgrim-Puritan history in the construction of New England identity. Conforti argues that Earle "reflected and contributed to a new adaptation of Puritan-Pilgrim tradition" and that her work both humanized and "restored moral and physical strenuosity" to the Puritan story (220). See also Roger B. Stein's essay "Gilded Age Pilgrims," in Truettner and Stein, *Picturing Old New England,* 43–51, which carefully tracks the evolution of the Puritan story via literary and pictorial depictions, from the seventeenth century forward. By the late nineteenth century, as Stein has noted, visual artists were employing elaborate artifactual detail to make their depictions of Puritan life and piety more accessible to their contemporaries— in much the same way that Earle used anecdotes, humor, and artifactual evidence to humanize her historical studies.

6. See, by Alice Morse Earle, "The New England Meeting-House," *Atlantic Monthly* 67.400 (February 1891): 191–204; "A Pickle for the Knowing Ones," *Christian Union* 41.4 (January 23, 1890): 140; "Narragansett Pacers," *New England Magazine* 8.2 (March 1890): 39–42; "The Puritan Judge's Wooings," *Independent* 42.2172 (July 17, 1890): 5; "A Dying Narragansett Church," *Andover Review* 14.79 (July 1890): 43; "Pewter Bright," *Independent* 43.2228 (August 13, 1891): 4; "Tuggie Bannocks's Ghost," *Independent* 43.2246 (December 17, 1891): 35; "Ghost, Poet, and Spinet," *New England Magazine* 9.6 (February 1891): 778–84; "The Queen's Closet Opened," *Atlantic Monthly* 68.406 (August 1891): 215–27; and "China Hunter in New England," *Scribner's Magazine* 10.3 (September 1891): 345–58.

7. Mary Kelley has demonstrated that earlier women writers adopted this same posture; despite the fact that they were highly successful in the marketplace, they routinely characterized themselves as private, domestic women. Earle's continuation of this pattern after 1900 suggests either that she was constrained by a highly conservative personal ideology, or that cultural ambivalence about women's roles lingered well after social practices began to change. Mary Kelley, *Private Woman, Public Stage: Literary Domesticity in Nineteenth-Century America* (New York: Oxford University Press, 1984), chap. 8. Despite Earle's discomfort with being a "public" women, in reality women had been encouraged to read and write about history since the early republic, as a means of buttressing the values of home and domesticity. See Nina Baym, *American Women Writers and the Work of History, 1790–1860* (New Brunswick, N.J.: Rutgers University Press, 1995).

8. "Alice Morse Earle and Her Books," 15.

9. Edwin W. Morse to Alice Morse Earle, December 6, 1893, and January 22, 1894, E. W. Morse Letterbooks, vol. 2 (1883–1894), 389, 476, Scribner Papers (hereafter Morse Letterbooks). E. W. Morse (no relation to Alice Morse Earle) had explained to Samuel Clemens (who accepted his offer) that the magazine published a wood engraving of a famous author each month as the frontispiece, accompanied by a personal sketch of the author's literary career. E. W. Morse to Samuel Clemens, February 1, 1890, Morse Letterbooks, vol. 1 (1887–1890), 390.

10. Edwin W. Morse to Alice Morse Earle, August 24, 1900, Morse Letterbooks, vol. 5, 408; Alice Morse Earle to Charles Scribner's Sons, August 25, 1900, Scribner Papers.

11. Kelley, *Private Woman, Public Stage,* 28–29, 139–40, 184, 220, 288.

12. Alice Morse Earle, *Home Life in Colonial Days* (New York: Macmillan, 1898), 388.

13. Alice Morse Earle, *Child Life in Colonial Days* (New York: Macmillan, 1899), 349–50.

14. Alice Morse Earle to William C. Brownell, April 18, 1895, Scribner Papers.

15. Earle, *Colonial Dames and Good Wives,* 109.

16. Ibid., 87.

17. Alice Morse Earle, *Margaret Winthrop* (New York: Charles Scribner's Sons, 1895), 334–35.

18. The early Puritan social vision emphasized community order above all else; Puritan leaders sought to maintain that order through the regulation of every realm of human behavior. Individual will posed a serious threat to this organic conception of social order and, as Richard Bushman has demonstrated in *From Puritan to Yankee: Character and the Social Order in Connecticut, 1690–1765* (New York: W. W. Norton, 1967), 3–21, led to the social and economic transformations of eighteenth-century America.

19. Earle was not unique in feeling this malaise. See Richard Wiebe, *The Search for Order, 1877–1920* (New York: Hill and Wang, 1966), especially chap. 6, "Revolution in Values," 133–63; and Ellen Fitzpatrick, "Industrial Society and the Imperatives of History," in *History's Memory: Writing America's Past, 1880–1980* (Cambridge: Harvard University Press, 2002), 13–50.

20. Conforti, *Imagining New England,* 220–22. Earle's choice of the pastoral mode placed her in a literary context that dated back at least to the writings of Virgil. According to Raymond Williams, this literature looked to the countryside and the idealized values it represented—innocence, harmony, and virtue—as "a stick to beat the present." Moreover, Williams has suggested the importance of dichotomy, the counter-pastoral, in defining this "country" literature. Earle's pastoral was counterdefined by ideas of urbanity and mobility. Raymond Williams, *The Country and the City* (New York: Oxford University Press, 1973), 12, 16–17.

21. Alice Morse Earle, *The Sabbath in Puritan New England* (New York: Charles Scribner's Sons, 1891), 327.

22. See Laurel Thatcher Ulrich, *The Age of Homespun: Objects and Stories in the Creation of an American Myth* (New York: Alfred A. Knopf, 2001), 14–18.

23. Ibid., 18.

24. For a book-length study of Green's significance, see Anthony Brundage, *The People's Historian: John Richard Green and the Writing of History in Victorian England* (Westport, Conn.: Greenwood Press, 1994).

25. Earle examined the collection of communion tokens in the coin collection at the American Antiquarian Society in Worcester. Earle, *Sabbath in Puritan New England*, 123.

26. The Reverend Daniel Rollins, review of *The Sabbath in Puritan New England*, by Alice Morse Earle, *New England Historical and Genealogical Register* 46.183 (1892): 287–88.

27. Earle, *Sabbath in Puritan New England*, 14.

28. Ibid., 15. For a more thorough analysis of the evolution of Puritan meetinghouses, see Peter Benes, "Sky Colors and Scattered Clouds: The Decorative and Architectural Painting of New England Meeting Houses, 1738–1834," in *New England Meeting House and Church: 1630–1850. Dublin Seminar for New England Folklife: Annual Proceedings, 1979*, ed. Peter Benes (Boston: Boston University Scholarly Publications, 1980), 51–69.

29. Earle, *Sabbath in Puritan New England*, 18.

30. Ibid., 109.

31. Ibid., 327.

32. Ibid., 234.

33. The custom of singing by rule, or from words and notes written down, rather than "lined" aloud by the minister for the congregation to follow, was highly controversial, according to Earle. Some traditionalists felt that the act of writing down the notes was blasphemous. Ibid., 208–9, 212.

34. Alice Morse Earle, "A New England Kismet," *Scribner's Magazine* 11.3 (March 1892): 295–302 (all page references are from this version); reprinted in Earle, *China Collecting in America* (New York: Charles Scribner's Sons, 1892), 394–407.

35. Ibid., 295.

36. Ibid., 296.

37. Ibid., 297.

38. Ibid.

39. The theme of rural dispossession expressed by Earle in this characterization became a crucial component of country literature during the eighteenth century, injecting a note of protest into the nostalgic vision. Williams, *The Country and the City*, 76–78.

40. Earle, "New England Kismet," 298–99.

41. Ibid., 301.

42. Ibid.

43. Ibid., 302.

44. Raymond Williams has argued that this literary trope—the memory of a rural past—was used by successive generations to address current social problems. As he noted, the "resting places"—the cultural contexts selected to represent the ideal age—have historical significance. For Earle, that resting place seems to have been

the era of her grandparents and great-grandparents. Williams, *The Country and the City*, 12.

45. An 1886 history of the town of Andover claimed that Benjamin Morse arrived in the town in 1802; the town birth records, however, revealed that Morse's first child, Lawson, was born in Andover in 1799. Abby Maria Hemenway, ed., *The Local History of Andover, Vt.* (1886; repr., Chester, Vt.: S & S Printing, 1977), 48; Birth and Death Register, Office of the Town Clerk, Andover, Vt.

46. Thelma Kalinen and Lorraine Korpi, eds., *Historical Glimpses of Andover, Vermont, 1767–1961* (Andover, Vt.: privately printed, 1961), 4–5. It was Wentworth's practice to reserve five hundred acres from every township he chartered to provide missionary income for the Anglican Church; see George Aldrich, *Walpole as It Was and as It Is* (Claremont, N.H.: Claremont Manufacturing Co., 1880), 17.

47. Morse purchased the land from Major Smith and Abour Johnson, yeomen of Chesterfield, Vermont; two hundred acres of the Governor's Lot had already been sold off for taxes. Andover Book of Deeds, vol. 4, 286, Office of the Town Clerk, Andover, Vt.

48. Reuben Morse was reported to have served as a private in the company of Captain Salmon Stone and as a lieutenant in the company of Colonel Moses Nichols in 1780 and fought at the battles of Bennington and Stillwater. See Samuel Carroll Derby, *A List of the Revolutionary Soldiers of Dublin, N.H.* (Columbus, Ohio: Press of Spahr & Glenn, 1901), 15. Another source praised Morse's "quick discernment, deep penetration, and sound judgment. He early and zealously espoused the cause of his country, and, throughout the conflict which achieved our independence, evinced a patriotism rarely surpassed, and never questioned. He enlisted in the army of the Revolution, and fought with distinguished bravery in the battle at Ticonderoga." Levi W. Leonard, *The History of Dublin, N.H.* (Boston: John Wilson and Son, 1855), 371.

49. The house burned in 1915 and a much larger house was built on the property, north of the original farmhouse. The only remaining evidence of the scale and orientation of the house was provided by an archaeological survey of the site conducted in 1981. The remains of an old well, covered with a cut granite slab, suggested a location near the existing road, and trenches revealed a foundation wall about twenty feet long and the remains of what may have been a brick walkway. W. Dennis Chelsey et al., *Historical and Archaeological Assessment of Properties Located in the Proposed Extension of the Historic Harrisville District* (Durham, N.H.: University of New Hampshire, Archaeological Research Services, 1981), 58–61.

50. Benjamin Mason, who moved to Dublin in 1765 from Watertown, Massachusetts, also served on the first Dublin Board of Selectmen and was appointed chairman of the Committee of Inspection on March 7, 1774. The strength of the alliance between Mason and Thomas Morse, another important Dublin citizen, was confirmed through the intermarriage of two of their children: in addition to Reuben Morse's marriage to Abigail Mason, Sarah Morse married Thaddeus Mason. Morse-Earle Genealogy.

51. The rise of textile milling in Harrisville has been fully documented in John Borden Armstrong, *Factory under the Elms: A History of Harrisville, New Hampshire, 1774–1969* (North Andover, Mass.: Museum of American Textile History, 1985), 13–18. According to his estate inventory, Reuben Morse owned his home farm on lot 12, range 8, valued at $1,500; thirty-two acres of land at the northeast corner of lot 11 in the seventh range, valued at $266.67; lot 13 in the ninth range, $400; part of lot 18 in the ninth range, $440; and part of lot 10 in the seventh range, $220. Inventory of the Estate of Reuben Morse, October 10, 1810, Probate Records, Cheshire County Court House, Keene, N.H.

52. Leonard, *History of Dublin*, 371–72. The fate of Sarah Morse, youngest daughter of Reuben and Abigail, is unknown. Some details about the marriages and residences of this generation of Morses were provided by a letter written to Alice Morse Earle by her uncle Reuben. Reuben Morse to Alice Morse Earle, October 24, 1894, Earle-Hyde Papers. See also Martha McDonald Frizzell, *A History of Walpole, New Hampshire*, 2 vols. (Walpole, N.H.: Walpole Historical Society, 1963), 2:6, 139, 209–10.

53. Benjamin Morse and Darius Gassett ultimately purchased the remainder of the Governor's Lot from Reuben Morse's estate in 1811. Andover Book of Deeds, vol. 4 (1803), 250, 286; vol. 5 (1811), 364.

54. The tendency of parents to use land and inheritance to control their children was a pattern that dated from the seventeenth century, as Philip J. Greven Jr. has documented in "Family Structure in Seventeenth-Century Andover, Massachusetts," *William and Mary Quarterly*, 3d ser., 23.2 (1966): 234–56.

55. Hemenway, *Local History of Andover*, 48.

56. Andover Town Report, vol. 2, Office of the Town Clerk, Andover, Vt.

57. Hemenway, *Local History of Andover*, 86.

58. Kalinen and Korpi, *Historical Glimpses of Andover*, 12.

59. For a discussion of the pattern of decline that dominated the history of nineteenth-century Vermont towns, see Lewis D. Stilwell, "Migration from Vermont (1776–1860)," *Proceedings of the Vermont Historical Society* 5 (1937): 63–243.

60. Hemenway, *Local History of Andover*, 87.

61. Frederic Kidder and Augustus A. Gould, *The History of New Ipswich* (Boston: Gould and Lincoln, 1851), 22–49. The territory granted to the Ipswich proprietors in 1735 by the Province of Massachusetts had been part of a previous grant to John Mason by King James I in 1621. Subsequent title disputes between the original proprietors and the Mason heirs were finally resolved in 1749, after which settlement of the town began in earnest.

62. Ibid., 60–61. In terms of percentile of all tax rates listed in the 1763 list, Catherine McClary's rate ranked her in the third percentile, Daniel's in the seventeenth, and William's in the sixty-fourth percentile.

63. The town map in Kidder and Gould's history indicated two houses on the McClary land: one, occupied by William, was built in 1750 and was probably the original homestead; the other, occupied by Daniel, was built in 1762. Ibid., 271.

64. Ibid., 351.

65. Ibid., 352.

66. Ibid., 351. The Clary family's origins in Northern Ireland might explain their choice of Belfast, a town in Maine founded by Scots-Irish proprietors from Londonderry, New Hampshire.

67. Daniel and Persis Clary's first child, Betsy, was born in Dublin in 1800; all subsequent children were born in Jackson. Morse-Earle Genealogy.

68. Ibid.

69. Quoted in David Glassberg, *American Historical Pageantry: The Uses of Tradition in the Early Twentieth Century* (Chapel Hill: University of North Carolina Press, 1990), 11.

70. Warren Susman has laid out the terms of late-nineteenth-century ambivalence about the cultural significance of Puritanism, citing competing interpretations of Puritan ideology. See Susman, "Uses of the Puritan Past," in *Culture as History: The Transformation of American Society in the Twentieth Century* (New York: Pantheon, 1984), 41–46. See also Stein, "Gilded Age Pilgrims," 43.

71. Susman, "Uses of the Puritan Past," 20. See also Conforti, *Imagining New England*, 220–25.

72. The Reverend Daniel Rollins, review of *Customs and Fashions in Old New England*, by Alice Morse Earle, *New England Historical and Genealogical Register* 48 (1894): 97.

73. Conforti, *Imagining New England*, 221–22.

74. Alice Morse Earle, *Customs and Fashions in Old New England* (New York: Charles Scribner's Sons, 1893), title page. Appropriately—and perhaps ironically, in light of the sentiment expressed in this inscription—Earle dedicated this book "To the Memory of my Father," Edwin Morse, who had died in December 1891.

4. THE CHINA HUNTER

1. Alice Morse Earle, *China Collecting in America* (New York: Charles Scribner's Sons, 1892), 2.

2. The classic study of antimodernism is T. J. Jackson Lears, *No Place of Grace: Antimodernism and the Transformation of American Culture, 1880–1920* (New York: Pantheon Books, 1981). For a more recent interpretation that places the sentiment directly into the context of gender and material culture, see Laurel Thatcher Ulrich, *The Age of Homespun: Objects and Stories in the Creation of an American Myth* (New York: Alfred A. Knopf, 2002), especially the introduction, "The Age of Homespun," 12–40. On the emergence of antique collecting in the 1890s, see Briann G. Greenfield, *Out of the Attic: Inventing Antiques in Twentieth-Century New England* (Amherst: University of Massachusetts Press, 2009). Greenfield links the rise of collecting and marketing

antiques with the reinvention of regional culture and American historical memory. For the history of women's china collecting activities, see J. Samaine Lockwood, "Shopping for the Nation: Women's China Collecting in Late-Nineteenth-Century New England," *New England Quarterly* 81.1 (March 2008): 63–90.

3. Greenfield, *Out of the Attic*, 4–6; Karal Ann Marling, *George Washington Slept Here: Colonial Revivals and American Culture, 1876–1986* (Cambridge: Harvard University Press, 1988), 176–82.

4. Benson J. Lossing, *The Home of Washington* (New York: W. A. Townsend, 1866), 7. The history of Mount Vernon and the house museum movement is summarized in Patricia West, *Domesticating History: The Political Origins of America's House Museums* (Washington, D.C.: Smithsonian Institution Press, 1999), especially chap. 1, "Inventing a House Undivided." The cultural importance of conceiving Washington as a symbolic figure and the changing manifestations of that impulse have been discussed in Marling, *George Washington Slept Here;* and Barry Schwartz, *George Washington: The Making of an American Symbol* (New York: Free Press, 1987). See also James M. Lindgren's review essay *"Pater Patriae:* Washington as Symbol and Artifact," *American Quarterly* 41.4 (December 1989): 705–13.

5. For a history of "New England kitchens" as they were presented at sanitary fairs (fundraising events organized to support the U.S. Sanitary Commission's care for sick or wounded soldiers), see Rodris Roth, "The New England, or 'Old Tyme,' Kitchen Exhibit at Nineteenth-Century Fairs," in *The Colonial Revival in America,* ed. Alan Axelrod (New York: W. W. Norton, 1985), 159–83. See also Marling, *George Washington Slept Here,* 37–50.

6. Roth, "The New England, or 'Old Tyme,' Kitchen Exhibit," 165. Earle probably never saw the Brooklyn display of the New England kitchen. She was only thirteen years old when the Brooklyn Sanitary Fair was held, and did not move to Brooklyn until after her marriage in 1874.

7. Earle, *China Collecting in America*, 317.

8. Marling, *George Washington Slept Here,* 26–30. In her analysis of the ways that representations of Washington changed over time, Marling identified the Centennial Exhibition as a beginning point for much of the domestic emphasis that came to characterize American historical interpretations.

9. Roth, "The New England, or 'Old Tyme,' Kitchen Exhibit," 175.

10. "Catalogue of New England Farmers' Home of 1776" (Philadelphia, 1876), 1. photocopy. I am grateful to Rodris Roth for this reference.

11. Ibid., 4.

12. Ibid., 5.

13. See Marla R. Miller and Anne Digan Lanning, "Common Parlors: Women and the Recreation of Community Identity in Deerfield, Massachusetts, 1870–1920," *Gender and History* 6.3 (1994): 436, for a discussion of late-nineteenth-century Deerfield as a compelling example of the economic and social effects of industrialization on New England towns and villages.

14. "Catalogue of New England Farmers' Home," 6–7.

15. Ibid., 7.

16. In May 1893 Earle wrote to William C. Brownell at Charles Scribner's Sons that she was "on the eve of leaving for Chicago," where she would be staying at the Hyde Park Hotel. She did not stay long enough to hear Frederick Jackson Turner deliver his famous address in July of that year. Alice Morse Earle to William C. Brownell, May 19, 1893, Scribner Papers.

17. Many scholars have discussed the Centennial New England Kitchen, beginning with Roth, "The New England, or 'Old Tyme,' Kitchen Exhibit"; and Marling, *George Washington Slept Here,* 37–44. In *The Antiquers* (New York: Alfred A. Knopf, 1980), 14–16, Elizabeth Stillinger argued that the objects exhibited were valued less as examples of fine American craftsmanship than as indications of American progress since colonial times; and Greenfield, *Out of the Attic,* 19–21, asserts that the exhibit's connections to the stories of the past were far more compelling to the fair's visitors than their artistic attributes. A drawing of this kitchen by H. W. Pierce is reproduced in Marling, *George Washington Slept Here,* 18, fig. 1.19.

18. For important perspectives on the rise of antiquing in the United States, see Stillinger, *The Antiquers;* Greenfield, *Out of the Attic;* and Beverly Gordon, *The Saturated World: Aesthetic Meaning, Intimate Objects, Women's Lives, 1890–1940* (Knoxville: University of Tennessee Press, 2006), especially chap. 6, "Collecting."

19. For a theoretical discussion of antiquarianism, see Susan Stewart, *On Longing: Narratives of the Miniature, the Gigantic, the Souvenir, the Collection* (Baltimore: Johns Hopkins University Press, 1984), 140–41. William Hesseltine, in explaining the difference between antiquarians and historians, commented: "The antiquarian collects facts much as the museum curator collects artifacts—for themselves. He displays them, much as the suburban housewife displays her antique furniture—for their patina, their lines, or their design. The historian, however, gathers facts for their meaning and for their utility in reconstructing a viable narrative of mankind's past." William B. Hesseltine, "The Challenge of the Artifact," in *Material Culture Studies in America,* ed. Thomas J. Schlereth (Nashville: American Association for State and Local History, 1982), 100. The history of early American antiquarians, beginning with William Bentley in Salem in 1783, has been well documented in Stillinger, *The Antiquers;* see also Greenfield, *Out of the Attic,* 4–28.

20. Anne Hollingsworth Wharton, *Through Colonial Doorways* (Philadelphia: J. B. Lippincott, 1893), vii.

21. Robert and Elizabeth Shackleton, *The Quest of the Colonial* (Philadelphia: Century Co., 1907), 3–10. The history of collecting American decorative arts was surveyed by Richard H. Saunders in "Collecting American Decorative Arts in New England, Part I: 1793–1876," and "Part II: 1876–1910," *Antiques* 109 (May 1976): 996–1003, and 110 (October 1976): 754–63. More recently, Beverly Gordon has positioned collecting—especially collecting antiques and "curios"—as part of an emerging aesthetic sensibility, one that served an important social agenda of nurturing "good taste." Gordon, *Saturated World,* 168–70.

22. Shackleton and Shackleton, *The Quest of the Colonial,* 10.

23. Earle, *China Collecting*, 189.

24. Alice Morse Earle, *Sun-Dials and Roses of Yesterday* (New York: Macmillan, 1902), 432, 435.

25. The idea of a living informant relates to the methodology of ethnographers and folklorists, who were active at the same time that Earle was recording the New England past. Writing about the folklorist Charles Godfrey Leland (1824–1903), Richard Dorson described Leland's reliance on "chance meetings with folk personalities" as an important source of data; see Richard M. Dorson, "American Folklorists in Britain," in *Folklore: Selected Essays* (Bloomington: Indiana University Press, 1972), 262–63.

26. Earle, *China Collecting*, 122.

27. Advertisement, Manhattan Antique Store, New York, *Old China* 1.1 (October 1901): iii.

28. Advertisement, Arthur True & Co., New York, *Old China* 1.6 (March 1902): 95.

29. Advertisement and photograph, Boston Antique China Exchange, Boston, *Old China* 1.3 (December 1901): 18 facing.

30. Ibid., ii.

31. Advertisement, Frederick Forehand, Boston, *Old China* 2.6 (March 1903): ii.

32. Alice Morse Earle to Charles Scribner's Sons, May 2, 1900, Scribner Papers. A penciled notation at the bottom of this letter, dated May 10, indicates that Scribner's checked Earle's assertions about the competition; in addition to Barber's *Anglo-American Pottery* (1899), it notes the existence of his *Pottery and Porcelain of the U.S.*, published by George Putnam and available for five dollars a copy.

33. Edwin W. Morse to Alice Morse Earle, May 10, 1900, E. W. Morse Letterbook, vol. 5, 294, Scribner Papers.

34. Alice Morse Earle to George Brett, February 6, 1901, Macmillan Papers.

35. Irving Whitall Lyon (1840–1896) was a Hartford physician and early collector of American decorative arts. Lyon stated in his book that he had begun to collect old furniture "early in the year 1877," and that the activity of collecting was widespread in New England. See Rodris Roth, "American Art: The Colonial Revival and Centennial Furniture," *Art Quarterly* 27.1 (Spring 1964): 70. Lyon's study of colonial furniture utilized estate inventories, newspaper advertisements, and cabinetmakers' price books as well as direct comparative study of English examples. E. P. Dutton reprinted the book in 1977. See Elizabeth Stillinger, "Irving W. Lyon: The Hartford Patriarch," in *The Antiquers*, 69–78; see also the annotation in Kenneth L. Ames and Gerald W. R. Ward, eds., *Decorative Arts and Household Furnishings in America, 1650–1920: An Annotated Bibliography* (Winterthur, Del.: Henry Francis DuPont Winterthur Museum, 1989), 97.

36. Earle to Brett, February 6, 1901.

37. Singleton's book was essentially a geographic and chronological survey of furniture, beginning with "Early Southern" and "Later Southern," and continuing with "Early New England." At this point, however, the structure broke down, as Singleton began to defer to chronology over geography, with the injection of "Dutch and English

Periods." Book 5, "New England from 1700 to 1776," reverted to the original plan, but book 6, "Chippendale," adopted a stylistic model, and books 7 and 8 continued in that vein. Within each part, Singleton adopted a quasi-topological scheme, shaping her chapters around prominent owners and functional types of objects. Esther Singleton, *Furniture of Our Forefathers* (Garden City, N.Y.: Doubleday Page & Co., 1900).

38. Alice Morse Earle to George Brett, February 23, 1901, Macmillan Papers.

39. Alice Morse Earle to George Brett, March 14, 1901, Macmillan Papers. Earle continued to berate Singleton's work: in September she wrote to Brett, "When Part IV—on Dutch furniture appeared, I at once recognized in the illustrations a good many pieces of furniture from the houses of some of my friends, which I *know* had been bought in Holland within ten years. For the two handsomest pieces I wrote to the owner and she answered me that it was as I thought. They had been recently bought. She (Miss S.) would argue that they are old pieces such as Dutch-Americans had, but even that is not so. Some of the pieces are new, made within thirty years." Still, Earle conceded, "I would not undervalue her book—the illustrations are, many of them, beautiful. But to me her text is a dreary waste of page after page of meaningless inventories. She has no idea of values; commonplace things are made prominent & rare things unnoticed." Alice Morse Earle to George Brett, September 27, [1901], Macmillan Papers.

40. Memorandum, W. S. Booth to George Brett, n.d. [after April 7, 1901], Macmillan Papers. The formula for determining the retail price of the book was suggested by the penciled notation "10%/15%/1500/$250." Apparently Macmillan planned to offer Morse a 10 percent royalty, which would increase to 15 percent after the sale of 1,500 copies, and a $250 royalty advance. Earle had projected that her sister's book should sell for five or six dollars, a figure that would have grossed Macmillan between $7,500 and $9,000 for the first 1,500 copies. Ultimately Morse's book was priced at three dollars.

41. Advertisement, *Old China* 1.8 (May 1902): i.

42. For a comprehensive survey of the books published about furniture and furnishings, see Ames and Ward, *Decorative Arts and Household Furnishings,* especially 139, 159, 215, 222, 267, 274, 291, 304.

43. Ibid., 222, 97. Kirk Nelson, annotator of Barber's book for the Ames and Ward volume, identified it as the first one written for collectors of American glass. Lockwood (1872–1951) went on to install the period rooms at the Brooklyn Museum and the Museum of the City of New York.

44. Advertisement, *Old China* 1.12 (September 1902): iii. Published by Doubleday, Page & Co., *Country Life in America* cost twenty-five cents per copy or three dollars a year.

45. Greenfield, *Out of the Attic,* 6.

46. Shackleton and Shackleton, *The Quest of the Colonial,* 381.

47. Earle, *Sun-Dials and Roses,* 446.

48. Ibid.

49. Karen Halttunen in *Confidence Men and Painted Women: A Study of Middle-Class*

Culture in America, 1830–1870 (New Haven: Yale University Press, 1982) first raised the issue of hypocrisy as a defining feature of middle-class life. Other scholars have since linked the rise of collecting with the social disruptions that ensued from industrialization and modernization. See William H. Truettner and Roger B. Stein, *Picturing Old New England: Image and Memory* (Washington, D.C.: National Museum of American Art, Smithsonian Institution; New Haven: Yale University Press, 1999); Peter Benes, ed., *New England Collectors and Collections. The Dublin Seminar for New England Folklife: Annual Proceedings, 2004*, ed. Peter Benes and Jane Montague Benes (Boston: Boston University Scholarly Publications, 2004), in particular sec. 2, "Forming Early Collecting Institutions (Mid- and Late Nineteenth Century)"; and sec. 3, "Specialty Collectors: China and Furniture."

50. For a discussion of Hartford's important place in the development of china collecting specifically, and collecting in general, see William N. Hosley, "Hartford's Role in the Origins of Antiques Collecting," in Benes, *New England Collectors and Collections,* 102–16.

51. Henry Wood Erving to W. L. McAtlee, January 31, 1940, Gurdon Trumbull file, Registrar's Office, Wadsworth Atheneum, Hartford, Conn., quoted in Stillinger, *The Antiquers,* 68; Annie Trumbull Slossen, *China Hunter's Club* (New York: Harper & Brothers, 1878), 255, quoted in Stillinger, The *Antiquers,* 64. See also Gordon, *Saturated World,* 168.

52. William C. Prime, *Pottery and Porcelain of All Times and Nations* (New York: Harper & Brothers, 1878), 5. See also Hosley, "Hartford's Role in the Origins of Antiques Collecting," 106–9.

53. Earle, *China Collecting.*

54. Ibid., 1.

55. Beverly Gordon, "Intimacy and Objects: A Proxemic Analysis of Gender-Based Response to the Material World," in *The Material Culture of Gender, the Gender of Material Culture,* ed. Katharine Martinez and Kenneth L. Ames (Winterthur, Del.: Winterthur Museum, 1997), 237–52. Gordon draws on the proxemic theories of Edward T. Hall, *The Hidden Dimension* (New York: Anchor Books, 1969), to argue for a relationship between gender and the social distances from which artifacts are perceived and experienced. Russell Belk and Melanie Wallendorf have taken this a step further, arguing that collecting itself is an activity that shapes gender identity at the same time that it is shaped by gender concerns. See Russell W. Belk and Melanie Wallendorf, "Of Mice and Men: Gender Identity in Collecting," in Martinez and Ames, *The Material Culture of Gender,* 7–26.

56. Wedgwood and others involved in creating the demand for ceramic wares have been studied extensively by Neil McKendrick in McKendrick, John Brewer, and J. H. Plumb, *The Birth of a Consumer Society: The Commercialization of Eighteenth-Century England* (Bloomington: Indiana University Press, 1982), especially chap. 3, "Josiah Wedgwood and the Commercialization of the Potteries," 100–45. McKendrick described a British "china mania" that formed the basis for the surge of ceramic collecting in America a hundred years later. Grant McCracken has

discussed the specific process through which culturally constituted values are transferred to consumer goods in *Culture and Consumption* (Bloomington: Indiana University Press, 1990), 80–83.

57. Sarah A. Leavitt, *From Catharine Beecher to Martha Stewart: A Cultural History of Domestic Advice* (Chapel Hill: University of North Carolina Press, 2002), 9. Patricia West, writing about the founding of the Mount Vernon Ladies' Association, made explicit the connection between women's "aesthetic moralism" and the enshrinement of history and domesticity together in public house museums. See Patricia West, *Domesticating History: The Political Origins of America's House Museums* (Washington, D.C.: Smithsonian Institution Press, 1999), 2–5. On the development and cultural agenda of Frary House as a showcase for traditional domestic values, see Miller and Lanning, "Common Parlors," 443–44; and Michael C. Batinski, *Pastkeepers in a Small Place: Five Centuries in Deerfield, Massachusetts* (Amherst: University of Massachusetts Press, 2004), 177–85.

58. Gordon, *Saturated World,* 179–87.

59. Prime, *Pottery and Porcelain,* 415; Earle, *China Collecting,* 423.

60. Earle, *China Collecting,* 2–3.

61. On the emotional aspects of collecting, see Walter Benjamin, "Unpacking My Library: A Talk about Book Collecting," in *Illuminations: Walter Benjamin,* ed. Hannah Arendt (New York: Schocken Books, 1969), 59–67. Both Susan Stewart and Grant McCracken have written suggestively about the intellectual process and cultural meanings of collecting in ways that might shed new light on Earle's commentary about collecting. See Stewart, *On Longing,* 151–69; McCracken, *Culture and Consumption,* 45–50, 113–16.

62. Earle, *China Collecting,* 11.

63. Ibid., 417.

64. Since mid-century, Americans had been exposed to an ongoing debate in the British press about the deteriorating quality of manufactured goods. Best known was Charles Locke Eastlake's *Hints on Household Taste.* In critiquing modern furniture, Eastlake wrote: "Joinery is neither so sound nor so artistic as it was in the early Georgian era. A cheap and easy method of workmanship—an endeavor to produce a show of finish with the least possible labour, and, above all, an unhealthy spirit of competition in regard to price, such as was unknown to previous generations— have combined to deteriorate the value of our ordinary mechanic's work." Charles Locke Eastlake, *Hints on Household Taste: The Classic Handbook of Victorian Interior Decoration* (1878; repr., New York: Dover Publications, 1969), 4.

65. Fred L. Israel, ed., *1897 Sears, Roebuck Catalogue,* facsimile ed. (Philadelphia: Chelsea House Publishers, 1968), 105.

66. Earle, *China Collecting,* 258–59, 262. Prime's catalogue started with the same item, but Earle's list is far more extensive and reflects her American focus and the advantage of twelve years' hindsight since Prime first began his manuscript. See Prime, *Pottery and Porcelain,* 358.

67. Earle, *China Collecting,* 316.

68. Ibid., 318–19, 324.

69. Ibid., 324–31.

70. Ibid., 412.

71. Earle here was responding to a larger impulse across both the museum world and the antiques trade, as the value of narrative was displaced by the values of connoisseurship. Greenfield, *Out of the Attic*, 25–27, addressed the moral dilemma posed by collectors—whose activities severed objects from their contexts, destroying the stories and associations that had once enhanced their value. On the history of American collecting and connoisseurship in general, see Stillinger, *The Antiquers;* and Benes, *New England Collectors and Collections.* Edward Alexander's essay on Henry Watson Kent's efforts at the Metropolitan Museum of Art sheds light on the professionalization of museum curatorial practices at the beginning of the twentieth century; see chap. 3 in Edward P. Alexander, *The Museum in America: Innovators and Pioneers* (Walnut Creek, Calif.: AltaMira Press, 1997), 51–66.

72. Ronald P. Rohner, "Franz Boas: Ethnographer on the Northwest Coast," in *Pioneers of American Anthropology,* ed. June Helm (Seattle: University of Washington Press, 1966), 151. For a history of the rise of folklore and material culture studies in the 1880s and 1890s, see Simon Bronner, *American Material Culture and Folklife: A Prologue and a Dialogue* (Ann Arbor: UMI Research Press, 1985), 3–9; see also Jane S. Becker, *Selling Tradition: Appalachia and the Construction of an American Folk, 1930–1940* (Chapel Hill: University of North Carolina Press, 1998), 3–4.

73. The early fieldwork success of anthropologists Erminnie Smith, Alice Cunningham Fletcher, and Matilda Stevens confirmed this view of the gendered aspects of anthropology. Nancy Oestreich Lurie, "Women in Early American Anthropology," in Helm, *Pioneers of American Anthropology,* 33–38. The link between women missionaries and folk/craft revivals has been thoroughly discussed in Henry D. Schapiro, *Appalachia on Our Mind: The Southern Mountains and Mountaineers in the American Consciousness, 1870–1920* (Chapel Hill: University of North Carolina Press, 1978); and David E. Whisnant, *All That Is Native and Fine: The Politics of Culture in an American Region* (Chapel Hill: University of North Carolina Press, 1983).

74. William Wells Newell, "On the Field and Work of a Journal of American Folk-Lore," *Journal of American Folklore* 1.1 (April 1888): 3–7.

75. Alice Morse Earle, "Query," *Journal of American Folklore* 4.15 (October–December 1891): 354; "Waste-Basket of Words," *Journal of American Folklore* 5.16 (January–March 1892): 61; "The Queen's Closet Opened," *Atlantic Monthly* 68.406 (August 1891): 215–27. Earle's membership in the Society of Folk-Lore was noted in the 1900 edition of the British version of *Who's Who.* See Henry Robert Addison et al., *Who's Who,* vol. 52 (London: Adam & Charles Black, 1900), 361. Her first full-length article for the society was published in 1893, "Old-Time Marriage Customs in New England," *Journal of American Folklore* 6.21 (April–June 1893): 97–102.

76. Earle, *China Collecting in America* (New York: Charles Scribner's Sons, 1892), 22.

77. Alice Morse Earle, "History as Loved and Hated," paper presented at a meeting of the Daughters of the American Revolution, 1899, Earle-Hyde Papers, 8–9.

78. Earle, *China Collecting,* 2.

79. Francis W. Shepardson, "Studies in Early American History," *Dial* 54.21 (November 1896): 251. The authors mentioned by Shepardson all had written popular histories of colonial towns, biographies of important people, or romanticized accounts of historical events, including Lodge's *Boston,* part of the Historic Town series (1891); Weeden's *Hero Tales from American History* (1895; co-authored with Theodore Roosevelt); Bliss's *Side Glimpses from the Colonial Meeting House* (1894), *Quaint Nantucket* (1896), *and Colonial Times on Buzzards Bay* (1888); Brooks's *Olden Time Series: Gleanings Chiefly from Newspapers of Boston and Salem, Massachusetts* (1886); Wharton's *Through Colonial Doorways* (1893), *Colonial Days and Dames* (1894), *A Last Century Maid* (1895), and *Life of Martha Washington* (1897); and Maude Wilder Goodwin's *Colonial Cavalier, or, Southern Life before the Revolution* (1894), *White Aprons: A Romance of Bacon's Rebellion* (1896), and *The Half Moon Papers* (1897), which included Alice Morse Earle's essay "The Stad Huys of New Amsterdam." Green's *Short History of the English People* (1874) was reportedly the best-selling history book in America during the last quarter of the nineteenth century. See John Higham, with Leonard Krieger and Felix Gilbert, *History: The Development of Historical Studies in the United States* (Englewood Cliffs, N.J.: Prentice-Hall, 1965), 156.

80. For a sampling of what readers favored during the 1890s and the first decade of the twentieth century, see Beverly Seaton, "A Pedigree for a New Century: The Colonial Experience in Popular Historical Novels, 1890–1910," in Axelrod, *The Colonial Revival in America,* 278–93. Seaton listed six works of historical fiction on the best-seller lists, including S. Weir Mitchell's *Hugh Wynne, Free Quaker;* Winston Churchill's *Richard Carvel;* Paul Leicester Ford's *Janice Meredith;* Mary Johnston's *To Have and to Hold;* and Maurice Thompson's *Alice of Old Vincennes.* She observed an anti-Puritan bias in popular historical fiction that paralleled Earle's views. She also commented on gender depictions, arguing that women in historical fiction were typically portrayed as minxes, whereas Earle, Seaton noted, sought "historical precedents for the roles taken by her contemporaries" (285). Seaton concludes, "In the pages of these novels, readers found a spiritual ancestry for liberal religion, patterns for social behavior, comforting reminders of our 'racial purity,' and delightful glimpses of a sumptuous style of life" (293).

81. Susan Coultrap-McQuin, *Doing Literary Business: American Women Writers in the Nineteenth Century* (Chapel Hill: University of North Carolina Press, 1990), 194–97.

82. Earle, "History as Loved and Hated," 15.

83. Ibid., 16.

5. WRITING THE PAST

1. For an extended discussion of the rise of literature about the moral home and the role of women in its creation and maintenance, see David P. Handlin, *The American*

Home: Architecture and Society, 1815–1915 (Boston: Little, Brown, 1979), 4–21. For a more recent discussion of the rise of domestic advice literature in the 1830s, see Sarah A. Leavitt, *From Catharine Beecher to Martha Stewart: A Cultural History of Domestic Advice* (Chapel Hill: University of North Carolina Press, 2002), 9–39. On the class implications of this phenomenon, see Richard L. Bushman, *The Refinement of America: Persons, Houses, Cities* (New York: Alfred A. Knopf, 1992), 256–79.

2. Karal Ann Marling, "The Good Dames of the Colonial Revival," in *George Washington Slept Here: Colonial Revivals and American Culture, 1876–1986* (Cambridge: Harvard University Press, 1988), 174–70. For an analysis of the cultural imperatives of history and domesticity as expressed through the re-creation of Louisa May Alcott's Concord home, Orchard House, see Patricia West, *Domesticating History: The Political Origins of America's House Museums* (Washington, D.C.: Smithsonian Institution Press, 1999), 78–91; and Joseph A. Conforti, *Imagining New England: Explorations of Regional Identity from the Pilgrims to the Mid-Twentieth Century* (Chapel Hill: University of North Carolina Press, 2001), 225.

3. For a discussion of typical financial arrangements between authors and publishers during the period when Earle was writing, see John Tebbel, *A History of Book Publishing in the United States*, vol. 2, *The Expansion of an Industry, 1865–1919* (New York: R. R. Bowker, 1975), 132–43. Although Earle seems not to have mentioned her overall literary income directly with any of her correspondents, she spent much time discussing royalty figures with her editors at both Scribner's and Macmillan. In 1896, for example, she received a $750 advance for *Colonial Days in Old New York*, based on a 15 percent royalty. When she moved over to Macmillan in 1898, her advances increased to $1,000. William C. Brownell to Alice Morse Earle, May 20, 1896, Brownell Letterbook, vol. 4, 183, Scribner Papers; Alice Morse Earle to George Brett, November 30, 1899, Macmillan Papers. Butter in 1895 retailed for 24.9 cents a pound. *Historical Statistics of the United States, Colonial Times to 1970*, vol. 1 (Washington: U.S. Dept. of Commerce, Bureau of the Census: U.S. Govt. Print. Off., 1975), 213. Wage data obtained from the "Historical Census Browser," University of Virginia Library (http://fisher.lib.virginia.edu/collection/stats/histcensus/).

4. That same year Earle collaborated with Emily Ellsworth Ford on another volume, part of the Distaff Series intended for the Columbian Exposition, *Early Prose and Verse*, which detailed the historical contributions of New York women writers to American literature.

5. Alice Morse Earle, "History as Loved and Hated," paper presented at a meeting of the Daughters of the American Revolution, 1899, Earle-Hyde Papers, 9. This paper offers evidence that Earle was familiar with the leading historians of her day. In addition to Ranke and Herbert Baxter Adams, she praised the newly adopted use of the seminar method in American universities.

6. Ibid.

7. Alice Morse Earle to George Sheldon, September 14, 1892, PVMA. Obituary, Henry Earle Jr., *New York Times*, May 26, 1892; Alice Morse Earle, *Child Life in Colonial Days* (New York: Macmillan, 1899), dedication.

8. Alice Morse Earle to Mr. Nathaniel Paine, January 4, 1895, Correspondence File, 1890–1899, AAS. Thanks to Thomas Knoles, Marcus A. McCorison Librarian of the American Antiquarian Society, for identifying Paine for me.

9. Alice Morse Earle to Mr. Paine, January 8, 1895, ibid. Earle had already used this particular artifact as an illustration in *China Collecting in America*, published in 1892. In that instance she referred to the jug as "the oldest and most authentic piece of stoneware in the country. . . . It was the property of Governor Winthrop, who died in 1649, and was given to the Society by a descendent, Adam Winthrop." Alice Morse Earle, *China Collecting in America* (New York: Charles Scribner's Sons, 1892), 54, 55. This erroneous attribution had probably been pointed out to Earle by some conscientious researcher, and having got her facts wrong once, she was eager to remedy the situation in her new book.

10. Alice Morse Earle to Mrs. [Morris P.] Ferris, September 14, 1895, Alice Morse Earle Collection (#9040), Clifton Waller Barrett Library, Manuscripts Division, Special Collections Department, University of Virginia Library (hereafter Barrett Collection). Mary Lanman Douw Ferris was involved in founding a Colonial Dames museum at the Van Cortlandt mansion in the Bronx. A Van Cortlandt descendant, she also authored several books and numerous articles about Dutch New York, including a history of the Van Cortlandt mansion. John W. Leonard, ed., *Who's Who in America, 1901–1902* (Chicago: A. N. Marquis, 1901), s.v. Ferris, Mary Lanman Douw, 371.

11. Alice Morse Earle to Mrs. Ferris, August 16, [1895], Barrett Collection; Earle to Mrs. Ferris, September 14, 1895.

12. Alice Morse Earle to W. C. Brownell, November 27, 1896, Scribner Papers.

13. For the recollections of Alice Earle Hyde, see the Morse-Earle Genealogy, entry for "Mary Alice Morse." The Long Island Historical Society at 123 Pierrepont Street opened in 1863 and later became the Brooklyn Historical Society. It exists today as a major research library with "the most comprehensive collection of Brooklyn-related materials in existence," according to the its website. See "Overview of History of the Brooklyn Historical Society," www.brooklynhistory.org/about/history. html. The Mercantile Library Association of Brooklyn was established in Brooklyn Heights in 1857 and is now a branch of the Brooklyn Public Library.

14. Alice Morse Earle to J. Thomson Willing, July 27, [1902], Earle Letters, Charles Deering McCormick Library of Special Collections, Northwestern University Library (hereafter Earle Letters, NUL), originally laid into Alice Morse Earle, *Old-Time Gardens, Newly Set Forth: A Book of the Sweet o' the Year* (New York: Macmillan, 1901). Earle recycled material from *China Collecting* a number of times. For the *Ladies' Home Journal* she wrote "Stamps and Marks on Old China" (11.2 [January 1894]: 10), and "My Delft Apothecary Jars" (11.6 [May 1894]: 9–10). She also wrote a lengthy piece on china for the *Monthly Illustrator* the following year, "Old English Pottery and China in America," 3.9 (January 1895): 116–19. These are all available online at Google Books, http://books.google.com.

15. Alice Morse Earle to J. Thomson Willing, June 18, 1902, Earle Letters, NUL,

originally laid into Alice Morse Earle, *Sun-Dials and Roses of Yesterday* (New York: Macmillan, 1902).

16. Earle to Willing, July 27, [1902].

17. Morse-Earle Genealogy.

18. Alice Morse Earle to Frederick F. Browne, January 29, 1904, Miscellaneous Manuscripts, Sophia Smith Collection, Smith College, Northampton, Mass.

19. Miles Orvell has argued that an emphasis on authenticity was one element in a significant late-nineteenth-century shift away from a culture that valorized imitation, toward a culture that valued "the real thing." Miles Orvell, *The Real Thing: Imitation and Authenticity in American Culture, 1880–1940* (Chapel Hill: University of North Carolina Press, 1989), xv. Jackson Lears viewed the cultural emphasis on authenticity, particularly with regard to the Arts and Crafts movement, as part of a "crisis of cultural authority." T. J. Jackson Lears, *No Place of Grace: Antimodernism and the Transformation of American Culture, 1880–1920* (New York: Pantheon Books, 1981), xiv, 60, 61, 70, 73.

20. Earle to Paine, January 4, 1895. In 1890 the Danish-born photographer Jacob Riis had demonstrated the power of photography as a documentary medium with his stark images of the slums of New York City. His book *How the Other Half Lives: Studies among the Tenements of New York* (1890), which documented life in the slums of New York City, was an early example of photojournalism. Alan Trachtenberg, *Reading American Photographs: Images as History: Matthew Brady to Walker Evans* (New York: Hill & Wang, 1989), 170–71.

21. Two of Johnson's photographs appeared in *Home Life:* "Making Soap," and "Wire Ferry on the Connecticut"; Earle also used Sewell's "Weaving Rag Carpet" as an illustration in that book. Alice Morse Earle, *Home Life in Colonial Days* (New York: Macmillan, 1898), 254, 330, 238. For information about Earle's use of images by the Allen sisters, see Suzanne L. Flynt, *The Allen Sisters: Pictorial Photographers, 1885–1920* (Deerfield, Mass.: Pocumtuck Valley Memorial Association, 2002), 14, 37, 39, 41. "The Romance of Old Clothes" by Newell appeared in Earle, *Two Centuries of Costume in America*, 2 vols. (New York: Macmillan, 1903), 2:806. In her foreword to *Home Life,* Earle also acknowledged two other photographers, William F. Halliday of Boston and George F. Cook of Richmond, Virginia. Earle, *Home Life,* vii–viii.

22. Alice Morse Earle to George Sheldon, February 26, 1898, PVMA.

23. Flynt, *Allen Sisters,* 22–23.

24. Karal Ann Marling has argued that these Colonial Revival photographs of women served not only as a roadmap for decorating but also as a reinforcement of prevailing notions about both gender and racial purity in the colonial era. Marling, *George Washington Slept Here,* 164–76. On the emergence of women as photographic artists, see Flynt, *Allen Sisters,* 12–13.

25. Mary Electra Allen to Frances Benjamin Johnson, August 13, [1898], quoted in Flynt, *Allen Sisters,* 37.

26. Alice Morse Earle to George Sheldon, January 18, 1901, PVMA. Earle was apparently referring to Mary, but both Allens worked on the images for *Home*

Life, according to a letter from Mary Electra Allen to Frances Benjamin Johnson, June 4, 1900, quoted in Flynt, *Allen Sisters,* 39.

27. Alice Morse Earle, "The Queen's Closet Opened," *Atlantic Monthly* 68.406 (August 1891): 215.

28. Alice Morse Earle, "Ghost, Poet, and Spinet," *New England Magazine* 9.6 (February 1891): 778–84, and "Top Drawer in the High Chest," *New England Magazine* 10.4 (July 1891): 649–55.

29. Earle, "Ghost, Poet, and Spinet," 778.

30. Frances Clary Morse, *Furniture of the Olden Time* (New York: Macmillan, 1903), 248–55. Morse described a spinet as "a tiny instrument, in shape similar to our modern grand piano. The body of the spinet was entirely separate from the stand, which was made with stretchers between the legs, of which there were three and sometimes four, so placed that one leg came under the narrow back end of the spinet, one under the right end of the front, and one or sometimes two at the left of the front. The instrument rested upon this table or trestle" (251).

31. Ibid., 260.

32. Earle, "Top Drawer in the High Chest," 649.

33. Alice Earle Hyde's genealogy revealed Story ancestors in Henry Earle's family, thus reinforcing the Wickford connection. Alice Morse Earle, however, never lived in Wickford until after she was married. Morse-Earle Genealogy.

34. Earle, "History as Loved and Hated."

35. Alice Morse Earle, *Customs and Fashions in Old New England* (New York: Charles Scribner's Sons, 1893), 1.

36. Alice Morse Earle, *Curious Punishments of Bygone Days* (Chicago: Herbert S. Stone, 1896). Earle had previously published an article about New England marriage customs in the *Journal of American Folklore,* although she was not listed as a member of the American Folklore Society in 1893. Alice Morse Earle, "Old-Time Marriage Customs in New England," *Journal of American Folklore* 6.21 (April–June 1893): 97–102. The bylaws of the society stated its objective to be "the study of folk-lore in general, and in particular the collection and publication of the folk-lore of America." "By-laws," *Journal of American Folklore* 6.21 (April–June 1893): 4.

37. Earle, *Curious Punishments,* 11–13. François Maximilien Misson's *Memoirs and Observations in His Travels over England* was published in 1698.

38. Earle, *Curious Punishments,* 17.

39. Alice Morse Earle to Mary Sowles Perkins, May 21, 1898, Elizabeth Perkins Papers, Old York Historical Society, York, Me.

40. Alice Morse Earle to J. Thomson Willing, June 18, 1902, Earle Letters, NUL.

41. Ibid.

42. Ibid.; Earle, *Two Centuries of Costume,* 1:v.

43. Prospectus for *Old-Time Gardens* and *Sun-Dials and Roses of Yesterday* (New York: Macmillan, 1902), courtesy of the Trustees of the Boston Public Library/Rare Books, inserted in copy of *Home Life in Colonial Days* originally owned by author and Earle correspondent Elizabeth Porter Gould (1848–1906). The photogravure

process, developed during the second half of the nineteenth century, provided a method of reproducing original photographs on a printing press by means of an etched copper plate. The process was hampered by an inability to print text and image on the same page; the photogravure prints had to be mounted and bound into the book separately, which limited their flexibility and increased production costs significantly. The halftone process, invented in the 1880s, enabled printing of text and image on the same plate, greatly altering the economics of illustrated book production, as well as the public expectation for images along with words. The regular edition of *Old-Time Gardens,* produced entirely with halftones, sold for $2.50, according to Macmillan's advertisement in *The Dial.* See Beaumont Newhall, *The History of Photography* (New York: MOMA, 1964), 98, 175–76; *Dial* 32.373 (January 1, 1902): 3.

44. Francis W. Shepardson, "Studies in Early American History," *Dial* 21.249 (November 1, 1896): 251–53, quotation on 252. William C. Brownell to Alice Morse Earle, August 4 and September 21, 1896, Scribner Papers. I am indebted to Neville Thompson for the Margaret Armstrong attribution.

45. For a discussion of the post–Civil War development of book cover design as a marketing strategy, see Tebbel, *History of Book Publishing,* 2:164. An appealing cover would have augmented the book's potential in the gift market as well. *Home Life in Colonial Days,* for example, with its polychrome cover design resembling a cross-stitch sampler, was given to the writer Elizabeth Porter Gould as a Christmas present in 1898. Gould's copy of *Home Life in Colonial Days* was inscribed on the title page, "Elizabeth Porter Gould. Boston, Massachusetts. Christmas 1898." Courtesy of the Trustees of the Boston Public Library / Rare Books.

46. Edward G. Porter, review of *Home Life in Colonial Days,* by Alice Morse Earle, *American Historical Review* 4 (April 1899): 544–47.

47. William B. Weeden, review of *Child Life in Colonial Days,* by Alice Morse Earle, *American Historical Review* 5 (July 1900): 765–66; Blanche Evans Hazard, review of *Two Centuries of Costume in America,* by Alice Morse Earle, *American Historical Review* 10 (October 1904): 170–72.

48. John Ward Dean, review of *Diary of Anna Green Winslow: A Boston School Girl of 1771,* by Alice Morse Earle, *New England Historical and Genealogical Register* 49.193 (January 1895): 96.

49. Macmillan Company, advertisement for *Home Life in Colonial Days,* bound in Alice Morse Earle, *Stage Coach and Tavern Days* (New York: Macmillan, 1900).

50. Daniel Rollins, review of *Customs and Fashions in Old New England,* by Alice Morse Earle, *New England Historical and Genealogical Register* 48 (1894): 97.

51. George Ellwanger, review of *Old-Time Gardens,* by Alice Morse Earle, *The Dial* 31.372 (December 16, 1901): 515.

52. "American Historical Novels," *New York Times Saturday Review of Books and Art,* July 15, 1899); "Ten Favorite Books: Reports in Detail from the Large Book and Department Stores," *New York Times,* December 24, 1898; "To the Editor," *New York Times Saturday Review of Books,* August 6, 1898.

53. Alice Morse Earle, "American Pottery and Porcelain," *Dial* 16.187 (April 1, 1894): 212–13; "New Chapters of African Discovery," *Dial* 16.189 (May 1, 1894): 269–72; "The Mountains of California," *Dial* 18.207 (February 1, 1895): 75–77; "New England's Fast Days," *Dial* 19.218 (July 16, 1895): 41–43. This last review dealt with W. DeLoss Love Jr.'s *Fast and Thanksgiving Days of New England* (Boston: Houghton Mifflin, 1895), about which Earle commented that it was of limited appeal, except to antiquarians, but certainly not "Love's Labor Lost" (43).

54. Alice Morse Earle to Frederick F. Brown, January 22, 1904, Miscellaneous Manuscripts, Sophia Smith Collection. Paget Jackson Toynbee (1855–1932) edited and indexed *The Letters of Horace Walpole, Fourth Earl of Orford*. Clarendon Press published this sixteen-volume work in Oxford between 1903 and 1905.

55. Mary Kelley, *Learning to Stand and Speak: Women, Education, and Public Life in America's Republic* (Chapel Hill: University of North Carolina Press, 2006), 221–22.

56. Alice Morse Earle to John Wolff Jordan, March 4, 1899, Historical Society of Pennsylvania autograph collection [0022A].

57. Advertisement for the Jackson Sanatorium, Dansville, N.Y., in Leonard, *Who's Who in America, 1901–1902*, 1346. The placement of this advertisement in *Who's Who* suggests that Jackson's intended clientele were the urban bourgeoisie.

58. Earle to Jordan, March 4, 1899.

59. For interpretations of Beard's work and the cultural significance of neurasthenia, see Lears, *No Place of Grace,* 47–58.

60. Alice Morse Earle to Elizabeth Porter Gould, August 7, 1903, courtesy of the Trustees of the Boston Public Library / Rare Books.

6. HOME LIFE AND HISTORY

1. David J. Rothman, *The Discovery of the Asylum* (Boston: Little, Brown, 1971), 216–20; Katherine Kish Sklar, "Victorian Women and Domestic Life: Mary Todd Lincoln, Elizabeth Cady Stanton, and Harriet Beecher Stowe," in *Women and Power in American History,* ed. Kathryn Kish Sklar and Thomas Dublin, 3rd. ed. (Upper Saddle River, N.J.: Prentice Hall, 2009), 151–55.

2. Sarah Leavitt has argued that domestic advice literature "was a form of writing by women in the nineteenth century that allowed for women themselves to be in control of a collective, female moral destiny." This genre of women's writing was significant because it "gave white middle-class women a common vocabulary and a place to begin their own journeys with home (and moral) improvement." Sarah A. Leavitt, *From Catharine Beecher to Martha Stewart: A Cultural History of Domestic Advice* (Chapel Hill: University of North Carolina Press, 2002), 39. See also Elizabeth Fries Ellet, *The Practical Housekeeper: A Cyclopaedia of Domestic Economy* (New York: Stringer and Townsend, 1857).

3. Catharine E. Beecher and Harriet Beecher Stowe, *An American Woman's Home, or,*

Principles of Domestic Science; Being a Guide to the Formation and Maintenance of Economical, Healthful, Beautiful, and Christian Homes (New York: J. B. Ford, 1870), 84.

4. Julie Des Jardins, *Women and the Historical Enterprise in America: Gender, Race, and the Politics of Memory, 1880–1945* (Chapel Hill: University of North Carolina Press, 2003), 13–17.

5. According to Scott Casper, Ellet "defined the methods and purposes of women's history in the United States" with the publication of *Women of the American Revolution*. Like Earle, Ellet viewed herself as a professional and sought to present as accurate a picture as she could, but she also desired to interject an emotional understanding of the women of the past. Scott E. Casper, "An Uneasy Marriage of Sentiment and Scholarship: Elizabeth F. Ellet and the Domestic Origins of American Women's History," *Journal of Women's History* 4.2 (Fall 1992): 10–35.

6. In his study of American homes, David Handlin has discussed this literature extensively. According to Handlin, most authors of this genre of literature stressed the linkage between the childhood home and future greatness. David V. Handlin, *The American Home: Architecture and Society, 1815–1915* (Boston: Little, Brown, 1979), 19–26.

7. Alice Morse Earle to Benson Lossing, n.d., Benson Lossing Papers (M69–110:31), Syracuse University Library. I am indebted to Sandra Markham for this reference. The authoritative work about the craze for Washingtonia in the nineteenth century is Karal Ann Marling, *George Washington Slept Here: Colonial Revivals and American Culture, 1876–1986* (Cambridge: Harvard University Press, 1980).

8. Wharton's papers included an entire folder of research materials on Sulgrave, the Washington family's ancestral home in England. Anne Hollingsworth Wharton Papers, [1537], Historical Society of Pennsylvania.

9. Thomas Allen Green, *Some Colonial Mansions and Those Who Lived in Them, with Genealogies of the Various Families Mentioned* (Philadelphia: Henry T. Coates, 1900). Earle reproduced an illustration from this book in *Two Centuries of Costume in America*, vol. 1 (New York: Macmillan, 1903), 111.

10. David Whisnant has argued persuasively for the importance of cultural missionary workers and institutions in Appalachia as the genesis of the craft revival there. David E. Whisnant, *All That Is Native and Fine: The Politics of Culture in an American Region* (Chapel Hill: University of North Carolina Press, 1983), 11–12. A similar case could be made for the "industrial education" classes (basketry, pottery, needlework, and other "non-fine" arts) offered as early as 1890 by Jane Addams at Chicago's Hull House. See Mary Ann Stankiewicz, "Art at Hull House, 1889–1901: Jane Addams and Ellen Gates Starr," *Woman's Art Journal* 10.1 (Spring–Summer 1989): 35–39. For fresh insights into the gendered ways in which individuals experience the material culture of everyday life, see Beverly Gordon, *The Saturated World: Aesthetic Meaning, Intimate Objects, Women's Lives, 1890–1940* (Knoxville: University of Tennessee Press, 2006), 15–35. Gordon has argued that experiencing folk cultures or history in a sensory manner—through active making or reenacting—is an essential component of deep understanding.

11. Michael C. Batinski coined the term "pastkeeper" in his study of historical memory and its cultural meanings, *Pastkeepers in a Small Place: Five Centuries in Deerfield, Massachusetts* (Amherst: University of Massachusetts Press, 2004), 5.

12. Marla R. Miller and Anne Digan Lanning have thoroughly traced the gendered process of Deerfield's transformation into a historical community in "'Common Parlors': Women and the Recreation of Community Identity in Deerfield, Massachusetts, 1870–1920," *Gender and History* 6.3 (1994): 435–55. See also Batinski, *Pastkeepers in a Small Place,* 1–10.

13. Alice Morse Earle to George Sheldon, September 14, 1892, PVMA. Nineteen different artifacts used by Earle as illustrations in her various books were identified as having come from Memorial Hall or the PVMA (author's database).

14. In addition to *China Collecting in America,* the photographically illustrated books included *Home Life in Colonial Days* (1898), *Stage Coach and Tavern Days* (1899), *Child Life in Colonial Days* (1900), *Old-Time Gardens* (1901), *Sun-Dials and Roses of Yesterday* (1902), and *Two Centuries of Costume in America* (1903). Charles Scribner's Sons published *China Collecting;* Macmillan published the rest. The remainder of the books were illustrated either minimally—*Margaret Winthrop* and *Diary of Anna Green Winslow* each had a frontispiece illustration—or not at all.

15. Grant McCracken has posited that societies use a strategy of "displaced meaning" as a way of preserving cultural values from the corrosive effects of the present. Those values, and the objects and rituals that express them, are typically relocated or "displaced" onto a "golden age," identified as "a largely fictional moment in which social life is imagined to have conformed perfectly to cultural ideals." Moreover, the golden age validates those cultural ideals by implying that they once existed. Grant McCracken, *Culture and Consumption: New Approaches to the Symbolic Character of Consumer Goods and Activities* (Bloomington: Indiana University Press, 1990), 104–7. For an extended discussion of the origins of and context for the notion of an "age of homespun," as well as the cultural significance of homespun itself, see Laurel Thatcher Ulrich, *The Age of Homespun: Objects and Stories in the Creation of an American Myth* (New York: Alfred A. Knopf, 2001), 12–40.

16. Peter Novick, *That Noble Dream: The "Objectivity Question" and the American Historical Profession* (Cambridge: Cambridge University Press, 1988), 34–45. For a more gendered analysis, see Des Jardins, *Women and the Historical Enterprise in America,* 20–24.

17. By the late nineteenth century, the term "institution" was understood to include customs and practices that served to organize society, as well as organizations (including their physical manifestations) that focused their attention on particular groups. See Noah Webster, *An American Dictionary of the English Language,* 3rd. ed., rev. and enl. Chauncy A. Goodrich (Springfield, Mass.: George and Charles Merriam, 1860), 612; Raymond Williams, *Keywords: A Vocabulary of Culture and Society,* rev. ed. (New York: Oxford University Press, 1983), 168–69.

18. Changing institutional forms during the antebellum period have been studied in Rothman, *Discovery of the Asylum.* Gunther Barth, Kenneth Jackson, Sam Bass

Warner, and David Schuyler have all examined the role of urban environments in strengthening common social identities. See Gunther Barth, *City People: The Rise of a Modern City Culture in Nineteenth-Century America* (New York: Oxford University Press, 1980), 14–33; Kenneth Jackson, *Crabgrass Frontier: The Suburbanization of the United States* (New York: Oxford University Press, 1985), 14–17, 74–76; Sam Bass Warner, *The Private City: Philadelphia in Three Periods of Its Growth*, 2nd ed. (Philadelphia: University of Pennsylvania Press, 1987); and David Schuyler, *The New Urban Landscape: The Redefinition of City Form in Nineteenth-Century America* (Baltimore: Johns Hopkins University Press, 1986), chaps. 1–2. John Kasson found rising levels of ritual and ceremony governing American middle-class social behavior, which he has interpreted as being instrumental in the formation and maintenance of a middle-class hegemony. See John F. Kasson, *Rudeness and Civility: Manners in Nineteenth-Century America* (New York: Hill and Wang, 1990).

19. Many scholars have discussed the expressive power of artifacts. Richard L. Bushman, *The Refinement of America: Persons, Houses, Cities* (New York: Knopf, 1992), offers an extended analysis of the relationship between houses, gardens, and their accouterments, as they reflected constructions of social identity and changing aspirations for gentility (see chap. 4, "Houses and Gardens," 100–38). In *George Washington Slept Here*, Karal Ann Marling focuses specifically on the objects of the colonial revival and the particular power of images and artifacts associated with Washington. She points to the evocative power of George (and Martha) Washington's clothing as an impetus for much of the "dressing up" activity engaged in by women and men in the name of history (44–51).

20. Kenneth L. Ames and Gerald R. Ward, *Decorative Arts and Household Furnishings in America, 1650–1920: An Annotated Bibliography* (Winterthur, Del.: Henry Francis du Pont Winterthur Museum, 1989), 79, 97, 139, 212, 215.

21. Lyon had difficulty finding a publisher for his study of New England furniture. The manuscript was rejected by Harper's and Putnam's and finally published by Houghton Mifflin. For further discussion of Lyon's life and work, see Elizabeth Stillinger, *The Antiquers* (New York: Alfred A. Knopf, 1980), 74, 76.

22. C. A. L. Richards, "Old-Time Furnishings," review of *The Colonial Furniture of New England*, by Irving Whitall Lyon, *Dial* 12.143 (March 1892): 387.

23. Alice Morse Earle, *Customs and Fashions in Old New England* (New York: Charles Scribner's Sons, 1893), 29–30.

24. Ibid., 111, 128–31.

25. On scientific history, see John Higham with Leonard Krieger and Felix Gilbert, *History: The Development of Historical Studies in the United States* (Englewood Cliffs, N.J.: Prentice-Hall, 1965), 92–103.

26. Blanche Evans Hazard, review of *Two Centuries of Costume in America*, by Alice Morse Earle, *American Historical Review* 10.1 (October 1904): 170.

27. The illustrations in *China Collecting* included fifty-seven food service items (primarily pitchers, plates, and tea wares, but also punchbowls, coffeepots, a relish dish, ewer, mug, custard cup, platter, porringer, two tankards, and a tureen), as well as six

art objects (figurine groups, vases, a garniture set, and a print), two pieces of furniture (a chest of drawers and a corner cupboard), and an apothecary jar.

28. William C. Brownell to Alice Morse Earle, February 21, 1893, William C. Brownell Letterbook, vol. 2, 90, Scribner Papers. Brownell was wrong about the precise number of illustrations in *China Collecting*, but his expectations for the slow, steady increase of its sales were correct; after almost ten years on the market, *Old China*, a collectors' journal, reported to its readers that the supply of *China Collecting in America* was exhausted. *Old China* 1.11 (1902): i.

29. With the exception of *Margaret Winthrop*, which had a facsimile of a letter written by Winthrop to her husband as its frontispiece, the remainder of the books Earle published with Scribner's were completely devoid of illustrations. Perhaps the sluggish sales of the china book had induced Scribner's to adhere to the highly successful formula of *The Sabbath in Puritan New England*, which, with its plain gray cover and lack of illustrations, sold for $1.25. Her next book, *Customs and Fashions in Old New England*, published in 1893, had an identical cover and similar design layout, so that it might be seen, as Brownell indicated to Earle during their contract negotiations, as "a companion to 'The Sabbath in P.N.E.'" William C. Brownell to Alice Morse Earle, February 20, 1893, William C. Brownell Letterbook, vol. 2, 87.

30. Alice Morse Earle, *Home Life in Colonial Days* (New York: Macmillan, 1898), vii.

31. Ibid.

32. Ibid., viii.

33. Alice Morse Earle, "History as Loved and Hated," paper presented at a meeting of the Daughters of the American Revolution, 1899, Earle-Hyde Papers, 5.

34. Ibid.

35. Ibid., 8.

36. Ibid., 12.

37. For more on patina, see David Lowenthal, *The Past is a Foreign Country* (Cambridge: Cambridge University Press, 1985), 155–63; and McCracken, *Culture and Consumption*, especially chap. 2, "'Even Dearer in Our Thoughts': Patina and the Representation of Status before and after the Eighteenth Century," 31–43.

38. Earle, *Home Life in Colonial Days*, 20.

39. Ibid., 29.

40. Ibid., 102.

41. Ibid., 231.

42. Ibid., 281.

43. Earle's illustrations included 509 communication artifacts, 212 buildings, 137 tools and pieces of scientific and technological equipment (predominantly sundials), 137 tools and pieces of equipment for materials, 112 personal artifacts, 62 natural objects, 21 furnishings, 16 distribution and transportation artifacts, 14 recreational artifacts, and 5 unclassifiable artifacts (mostly lace fragments). Earle's illustrated objects classified according to James R. Blackaby, Patricia Greeno, and others, *The Revised Nomenclature for Museum Cataloging: A Revised and Expanded Version of Robert G. Chenhall's System for Classifying Man-Made Objects* (Nashville: American Association for State and Local History, 1974).

44. Earle did not identify her source other than by name and date, 1558. Alice Morse Earle, *China Collecting in America* (New York: Charles Scribner's Sons, 1892), 54.

45. Kristin Hoganson has considered the resonance of the national origin of consumer goods for American women and found a long-term trend toward "cosmopolitan domesticity," which came under attack at the end of the nineteenth century. Hoganson points out the irony of Colonial Revival goods that were perceived by their owners as "American" but that in fact frequently originated in England, China, and elsewhere. Kristin L. Hoganson, *Consumers' Imperium: The Global Production of American Domesticity, 1865–1920* (Chapel Hill: University of North Carolina Press, 2007), 39–43.

46. Alice Morse Earle, *Colonial Days in Old New York* (New York: Charles Scribner's Sons, 1896), 196–202. See also Earle, "Pinkster Day," *Outlook* 49.17 (April 28, 1894): 743–44.

47. Alice Morse Earle, *In Old Narragansett: Romance and Realities* (New York: Charles Scribner's Sons, 1898), 92–93. Catherine L. Albanese cited this passage and Earle's work as an important source on African American spirituality in *A Republic of Mind and Spirit: A Cultural History of American Metaphysical Religion* (New Haven: Yale University Press, 2007), 92–93.

48. See Patricia West's discussion of the disputed visions of ideal womanhood held by suffrage and anti-suffrage women in Concord, Massachusetts, during the restoration of Louisa May Alcott's Orchard House, in *Domesticating History: The Political Origins of America's House Museums* (Washington, D.C.: Smithsonian Institution Press, 1999), 68–78.

49. The most frequently occurring classification, documentary artifacts, was more gender-neutral, but its neutrality was skewed by the presence of nineteen photographs almost all of which depicted women performing various types of domestic work. Another category of illustrations, objects related to building, consists of seventeen items, nine of which were depictions of houses built by men but maintained by women. Of the next eighteen categories, four (land transportation equipment, advertising media, regulative and protective tools and equipment, and metalworking tools and equipment) represented spheres of activity traditionally assigned to men. Three seemed to be gender-neutral and could represent either male or female activity (personal gear, building components, and woodworking tools and equipment). The remaining eleven categories implied gender conventions traditionally associated with women. The objects have been classified and named according to the system detailed in James R. Blackaby, Patricia Greeno, and the Nomenclature Committee, *The Revised Nomenclature for Museum Cataloging: A Revised and Expanded Version of Robert G. Chenhall's System for Classifying Man-Made Objects* (Nashville: AASLH Press, 1988).

50. "Some Pages from the Past," review of *Customs and Fashions of Old New England*, by Alice Morse Earle, *Outlook* 49.1 (January 6, 1894): 25–26.

51. Ibid., 26.

52. The climate of debate had become increasingly heated during the 1890s, beginning with the formation of the National American Woman Suffrage Association

in 1890. For a discussion of the political climate surrounding the issue of suffrage during this decade, see Nancy Cott, *The Grounding of Modern Feminism* (New Haven: Yale University Press, 1987), 13–23. Theodora Penny Martin has examined the impact of education and changing expectations among women in her study of late-nineteenth-century women's clubs, *The Sound of Our Own Voices: Women's Study Clubs, 1860–1910* (Boston: Beacon Press, 1987), 40–47, 134–38, 167–69.

53. Earle, "History as Loved and Hated," 16.

7. REMEMBERING THE GARDEN

1. Cited in Christie H. White, "Reform and the Promotion of Ornamental Gardening," in *Dublin Seminar for New England Folklife Annual Proceedings, 1995: Plants and People,* ed. Peter Benes (Boston: Boston University Press, 1996), 103 n. 1.

2. The movement to "improve" the American landscape was part of a larger movement to refine and improve the new American nation by ordering and "cleaning up" its outdated social and material forms. Jack Larkin, "From 'Country Mediocrity' to 'Rural Improvement': Transforming the Slovenly Countryside of Rural Massachusetts, 1775–1840," in *Everyday Life in the Early Republic,* ed. Catherine E. Hutchins (Winterthur, Del.: Henry Francis DuPont Winterthur Museum, 1994), 175–200. Christie White has connected this movement to women and girls in particular, as well as to ornamental gardening as an appropriate activity for female improvement, in "Reform and the Promotion of Ornamental Gardening," 103–15.

3. *The Horticulturist* 1.1 (July 1846): 9.

4. Ibid., 10.

5. For a brief discussion of the rise of literature about gardening aimed at middle-class women, see Mac Griswold and Eleanor Weller, *The Golden Age of American Gardens: Proud Owners, Private Estates, 1890–1940* (New York: Harry N. Abrams, 1991), 16. See also Leslie Rose Close, "A History of Women in Landscape Architecture," introduction to Judith B. Tankard, *The Gardens of Ellen Biddle Shipman* (Sagaponack, N.Y.: Sagapress/Abrams in association with Library of American Landscape History, 1996), xiii–xix.

6. Her "Landscape Gardening" series began to appear in the journal in 1888. For more information about Van Rensselaer and the landscape art movement, see Ethan Carr, "*Garden and Forest* and 'Landscape Art,'" www.loc.gov/preserv/gardfor/essays/carr.html.

7. Celia Thaxter, *Island Garden* (Boston: Houghton Mifflin, 1894).

8. For a discussion of women's early professional involvement in landscape architecture, see Griswold and Weller, *Golden Age of American Gardens,* 19.

9. The author, Marie Annette Beauchamp, is better known as Elizabeth von Arnim. See Marie Annette Beauchamp [Elizabeth von Arnim], *Elizabeth and Her German Garden* (New York: Macmillan, 1898). This book has a strong following even today.

A later book of hers, also set in a garden, is *The Enchanted April* (1922), which was made into a popular film in 1992.

10. Sarah Orne Jewett, "From a Mournful Villager," *Atlantic Monthly* 48 (November 1881): 664–72, reprinted in *Sarah Orne Jewett: Novels and Stories* (New York: Library of America, 1994), 585. On the history of front yards and their transmission from Europe to North America in the seventeenth and eighteenth centuries, see Virginia Scott Jenkins, *The Lawn: A History of an American Obsession* (Washington, D.C.: Smithsonian Institution Press, 1994), 14–20.

11. Charles Dickens cited in Jenkins, *The Lawn,* 19. According to Jenkins, the appearance of grass lawns coincided with the rise of suburbs, as a safe place for children to play (20–33). The advent of the lightweight push lawnmower in 1870 made it possible to create a park-like swath of green grass, replacing the dooryard gardens of the past.

12. Jewett, "From a Mournful Villager," 587, 591.

13. Alice Morse Earle, *Old-Time Gardens, Newly Set Forth: A Book of the Sweet o' the Year* (New York: Macmillan, 1901), 40.

14. Ibid., 48.

15. Ibid., 4.

16. Ibid., 5, 391, 63.

17. Ibid., 75.

18. Vernon Lee, *Studies of the Eighteenth Century in Italy* (London: W. Satchell & Co., 1880; repr., Chicago: A. C. McClurg & Co., 1907). For more on Lee, an English "woman of letters" who spent much of her life in Italy, see Peter Gunn, *Vernon Lee: Violet Paget, 1856–1935* (New York: Oxford University Press, 1964); and Vineta Colby, *Vernon Lee: A Literary Biography* (Charlottesville: University of Virginia Press, 2003).

19. Earle, *Old-Time Gardens,* 75, 79–80. The Yaddo rose garden was created by Spencer Trask for his wife, Katrina, in 1899, on their Saratoga Springs estate. "Yaddo Garden Association: About the Yaddo Gardens," www.yaddo.org. The gardens at Avonwood Court, the estate of Charles E. Mather, were extensively illustrated in John Cordis Baker, ed., *American Country Homes and Their Gardens* (Philadelphia: House & Garden, John C. Winston Co., 1906), 26–31.

20. Earle, *Old-Time Gardens,* 93, 96, 101.

21. Ibid., 161–62.

22. In this Earle was part of a larger movement that linked horticultural pursuits with morality. See Tamara Plakins Thornton, "Horticulture and American Character," in *Keeping Eden: A History of Gardening in America,* ed. Walter T. Punch (Boston: Little, Brown, 1992), 189–203.

23. Earle, *Old-Time Gardens,* 237. This great-aunt was Esther Crafts (b. 1816), who was married to Dr. Ebenezer Morse, Earle's grandfather's brother. Levi Leonard, *The History of Dublin, N.H.* (Boston: John Wilson and Son, 1855), 370–71.

24. Earle, *Old-Time Gardens,* 260.

25. Ibid., 299.

26. Ibid., 165.

27. Ibid., 91.

28. Ibid., 185. Earle seems to have been suggesting that Dutchman's-pipe was somehow nouveau riche; actually, this leafy vine had a venerable eighteenth-century heritage in America. Ann Leighton, *American Gardens in the Eighteenth Century* (Amherst: University of Massachusetts Press, 1986), 417.

29. Earle, *Old-Time Gardens*, 267.

30. Ibid., 288.

31. Warren Susman identified this "revolt against the frontier" as a major contemporary theme in *Culture as History: The Transformation of American Society in the Twentieth Century* (New York: Pantheon Books, 1984), 29–36.

32. Earl, *Old-Time Gardens*, 288–89. See also Michael Steven Shapiro, *Child's Garden: The Kindergarten Movement from Froebel to Dewey* (University Park: Pennsylvania State University Press, 1983).

33. Earle, *Old-Time Gardens*, 327–28.

34. At the time when Henry and Alice Earle moved to Brooklyn and established their own garden, Brooklyn was already a thriving gardeners' community. Perusal of the *Brooklyn Eagle* reveals numerous local plantsmen, as well as ongoing planning to create a botanic garden. As early as 1872 the *Eagle* reported on a fundraising meeting of gentlemen who wanted to build a "Winter Garden, where all sorts of flowers and plants could be kept, and out of which a superior botanical school could grow." "Exotic and Botanic Garden," *Brooklyn Eagle*, March 30, 1872. Planning continued through the 1880s and 1890s, with the Brooklyn Botanic Garden finally opening in 1910.

35. Earle, *Old-Time Gardens*, 321.

36. David Schuyler, *The New Urban Landscape: The Redefinition of City Form in Nineteenth-Century America* (Baltimore: Johns Hopkins University Press, 1986), 4–6, 28. See also Thornton, "Horticulture and American Character," 190–92.

37. Earle, *Old-Time Gardens*, 154.

38. Review of "Old-Time Gardens," by Alice Morse Earle, *Dial* 31.372 (December 16, 1901): 515.

39. Dona Brown's *Inventing New England: Regional Tourism in the Nineteenth Century* (Washington, D.C.: Smithsonian Institution Press, 1995), an important study of the rise of regional tourism in New England, traces the development of these activities during the nineteenth century. Of particular interest to students of Earle's view of the rural past is chap. 5, "That Dream of Home: Northern New England and the Farm Vacation Industry, 1890–1900," and chap. 6, "The Problem of Summer: Race, Class, and the Colonial Vacation in Southern Maine, 1890–1900."

40. Brown has traced this process in Kittery and York, Maine, where William Dean Howells and his family established themselves as summer residents in 1898. Ibid., 179–83.

41. For an extended analysis of the Colonial Revival garden movement, see Lucinda A. Brockway, "'Tempus Fugit': Capturing the Past in the Landscape of the

Piscataqua," in *"A Noble and Dignified Stream": The Piscataqua Region in the Colonial Revival, 1860–1930*, ed. Sarah L. Giffen and Kevin D. Murphy (Old York, Me.: Old York Historical Society, 1992), 81–112. For narratives of a similar process in Deerfield, Massachusetts, see Michael C. Batinski, *Pastkeepers in a Small Place: Five Centuries in Deerfield, Massachusetts* (Amherst: University of Massachusetts Press, 2004); and Marla R. Miller and Anne Digan Lanning, "'Common Parlors': Women and the Recreation of Community Identity in Deerfield, Massachusetts, 1870–1920," *Gender and History* 6.3 (1994): 435–55.

42. The box garden at Earle's family estate in Wickford, planted (according to Earle) by Daniel Webster and Justice Joseph Story, was still standing when I visited the garden in August 2009, testament to the longevity of this plant.

43. See Brown's discussion of the importance of historical accuracy for summer visitors in *Inventing New England*, 184. In Kittery, as in New Ipswich, summer people were active in "producing" the local history of the area.

44. Beverly Gordon has described these staged photographs as "two-dimensional versions of the tableaux, pageants, and other costumed enactments" that constituted popular entertainment, in *The Saturated World: Aesthetic Meaning, Intimate Objects, Women's Lives, 1890–1940* (Knoxville: University of Tennessee Press, 2006), 130–35.

45. Review of "Old-Time Gardens," 515.

46. The shape and size of hollyhock blossoms, with their narrow necks and broad, flaring petals, made it easy for children to transform them into tiny women, with toothpicks for arms and fancy ruffled skirts.

47. Earle, *Old-Time Gardens*, 361, 365. The sundial appeared on Fugio bank notes, issued by the Continental Congress in 1776, as well as on the Continental dollar and the so-called Franklin cent, issued in 1787. See also R. S. Yeoman, *A Guidebook of United States Coins*, 39th rev. ed. (Racine, Wis.: Western Publishing Company, 1985), 30, 56.

48. Earle, *Old-Time Gardens*, 55–56.

49. Ibid., 36.

50. Ibid., 399.

51. J. B. Jackson, "Nearer Than Eden," in *The Necessity for Ruins and Other Topics* (Amherst: University of Massachusetts Press, 1980), 19–21.

52. Earle, *Old-Time Gardens*, 64.

53. Ibid., 50. For the significance of the front hall as a ritualistic space in Victorian America, see Kenneth L. Ames, "Meaning in Artifacts: Hall Furnishings in Victorian America," in *Common Places: Readings in American Vernacular Architecture*, ed. Dell Upton and John Michael Vlach (Athens: University of Georgia Press, 1986), 240–60.

54. Earle, *Old-Time Gardens*, 321.

55. Ibid., 96.

8. GENEALOGY AND THE QUEST FOR AN INHERITED FUTURE

1 Kenneth T. Jackson explored this public-private dichotomy in "Home Sweet Home: The House and the Yard," in *Crabgrass Frontier: The Suburbanization of the United States* (New York: Oxford University Press, 1985), 45–72. Stuart Blumin detailed these changing expressions of social identity through housing in *The Emergence of the Middle Class: Social Experience in the American City, 1760–1900* (New York: Cambridge University Press, 1989), especially chap. 5, "'Things are in the saddle': Consumption, Urban Space, and the Middle-Class Home," 138–90. Feminist historians have traced the process of turning inward to a shift in women's roles within the household, from productive contributors within the family economy to consumers and moral guardians. In that new capacity, women worked to transform their homes into genteel private spaces that would protect, nurture, and civilize their families. See, for example, Nancy Cott's classic work *The Bonds of Womanhood* (New Haven: Yale University Press, 1977); and Stephanie Coontz, *The Social Origins of Private Life: A History of American Families, 1600–1900* (New York: Verso, 1988).

2. In *The Refinement of America: Persons, Houses, Cities* (New York: Vintage Books, 1992), Richard Bushman has argued that "vernacular gentility" became an important strategy for establishing middle-class respectability in the nineteenth century, shaping the public and private faces of houses as well as urban landscapes; see especially chaps. 2 and 8–12. Bernard Herman's work on the evolution of urban housing confirms the use of material culture as well as social rituals to reinforce class assumptions and aspirations. See Bernard L. Herman, *The Town House: Architecture and Material Life in the Early American City, 1780–1830* (Chapel Hill: University of North Carolina Press, 2005).

3. Demographic change in rural New England, as Caroline Merchant has demonstrated in *Ecological Revolutions: Nature, Gender, and Science in New England* (Chapel Hill: University of North Carolina Press, 1989), chap. 5, effected sweeping changes for farm families in terms of productive networks, gender relations, and environmental consciousness.

4. Lewis D. Stilwell, "Migration from Vermont (1776–1860)," *Proceedings of the Vermont Historical Society* 5.2 (1937): 95. In *Those Who Stayed Behind: Rural Society in Nineteenth-Century New England* (Cambridge: Cambridge University Press, 1984), Hal S. Barron updated Stilwell's thesis by reexamining the demographic patterns of out-migration and persistence, finding that those who remained tended to be established farmers and merchants, typically married and native-born. Those who left were more likely to be artisans and laborers, a fact that shaped the character of rural New England for generations. Moreover, population decline tended to be more a product of declining in-migration rather than one of excessive out-migration. For a case study of one family's geographic dispersion through out-migration from Vermont, see Lynn A. Bonfield and Mary C. Morrison, *Roxana's Children: A Biography of a Nineteenth-Century Vermont Family* (Amherst: University of Massachusetts Press, 1995).

5. Stephan Thernstrom, *Poverty and Progress: Social Mobility in a Nineteenth-Century City* (New York: Atheneum, 1964), 199.

6. The idea of community as a culturally defined construct supplanted the traditional notion of community as spatially defined in the work of the anthropologist Robert Redfield, who suggested in 1930 that community is the product of communication systems, internal and external. See Richard R. Beeman, "The New Social History and the Search for 'Community' in Colonial America," *American Quarterly* 29.4 (Fall 1977): 422–33. David Hall, in his discussion of Calvinism as a symbolic order, maintained that ritual "represents and acts out a myth of collective identity. It is a process that affirms the social bond," as well as being "expressive of contradictions and alternatives." See David Hall, "Religion and Society: Problems and Considerations," in *Colonial British America: Essays in the New History of the Early Modern Era*, ed. Jack P. Greene and J. R. Pole (Baltimore: Johns Hopkins University Press, 1984), 336.

7. See Marla R. Miller's discussion of early American needle art, especially family coats of arms, in *The Needle's Eye: Women and Work in the Age of Revolution* (Amherst: University of Massachusetts Press, 2006), 96–101. See also Betty Ring, "Heraldic Embroidery in Eighteenth-Century Boston," *Antiques* (April 1992): 622–31, cited in Miller, *The Needle's Eye,* 259 n. 22. For essays on the artifacts that helped families record and convey family history, see Peter Benes, "Decorated Family Records from Coastal Massachusetts, New Hampshire, and Connecticut," in *Families and Children,* ed. Peter Benes (Boston: Boston University Press, 1987), 91–147.

8. For an extended discussion of this idea, see Laurel Thatcher Ulrich, "Hannah Barnard's Cupboard," in *The Age of Homespun: Objects and Stories in the Creation of an American Myth* (New York: Alfred A. Knopf, 2001), 108–41.

9. The Morse family settlement patterns may be compared with the settlement patterns of all American colonists for the period 1660–1775; see James Henretta, *The Evolution of American Society* (Lexington, Mass.: D. C. Heath, 1973), 11.

10. Andrew H. Ward, *A Genealogical History of the Rice Family Descendants of Deacon Edmund Rice, Who Came from Berkhamstead, England, and Settled at Sudbury, Massachusetts, in 1638 or 9* (Boston: C. Benjamin Richardson, 1858), iv.

11. Ibid., viii.

12. Oswald Barron, editor of *The Ancestor,* 1902–1905, and genealogist to the Honourable Society of the Baronetage, summarized the history of genealogy in *Encyclopaedia Britannica,* 11th ed., s.v. "Genealogy."

13. I am indebted to Michael Kucher for this observation.

14. R. Wilberforce, "Family Trees," *American Monthly Magazine* 16.6 (June 1900): 1168.

15. Ward, *Rice Family,* iv.

16. Benjamin Morse, Andover, Vt., to Edwin Morse, Worcester, Mass., February 15, 1849, Earle-Hyde Papers; Abner Morse, *Memorial of the Morses* (Boston: William Veazie, 1850); Levi W. Leonard, *The History of Dublin, N.H.* (Boston: John Wilson and Son, 1855), 370.

17. Ward, *Rice Family,* vi.

18. Alice Morse Earle, *Home Life in Colonial Days* (New York: Macmillan, 1898), 93–94.

19. Ellen Hardin Walworth, "American Society," *American Monthly Magazine* 1.4 (December 1892): 301–14. For a discussion of the social power of calling cards and card receivers, see Kenneth L. Ames, "First Impressions," in *Death in the Dining Room and Other Tales of Victorian Culture* (Philadelphia: Temple University Press, 1992), 7–43.

20. Lapham even purchases an etiquette book to determine what he should do with his gloves at a dinner party hosted by the Coreys, a Boston family with very long roots. His lack of familiarity with the established social forms—a familiarity that Howells seems to indicate results from long acculturation—leads ultimately to his demise. William Dean Howells, *The Rise of Silas Lapham* (1885), in *William Dean Howells: Novels, 1875–1886* (New York: Literary Classics of the United States, 1982), 1034–54.

21. I am using the term "tribal" in an anthropological sense, to suggest that the urban middle class relied on multigenerational family, kin, and community networks to maintain a sense of inclusiveness or group cohesion at the same time that they promoted exclusiveness.

22. Alice Morse Earle, *Margaret Winthrop* (New York: Charles Scribner's Sons, 1895), 319–20.

23. Ibid., 330–31, 333.

24. "Women's Club Notes," *Brooklyn Daily Eagle,* October 1, 1899.

25. Jane Cunningham Croly, *The History of the Woman's Club Movement in America* (New York: Henry G. Allen & Co., 1898), 897.

26. Ibid.

27. A brief summary of the development of racial nationalism may be found in Philip Gleason, "American Identity and Americanization," in *Harvard Encyclopedia of American Ethnic Groups,* ed. Stephan Thernstrom (Cambridge: Belknap Press, 1980), 41–43. For a more detailed analysis, see John Higham, *Strangers in the Land: Patterns of American Nativism, 1860–1925* (New York: Atheneum, 1969), especially chap. 6, "Toward Racism: The History of an Idea." Higham, who viewed nativism as a continuum, changing in intensity during periods of social stress, developed a clear link between the late-nineteenth-century rise of racial theories and patrician fears of social and cultural decline, particularly in New England.

28. See, for example, the constitution of the New York chapter of the Daughters of the Revolution, cited in "Daughters of the Revolution: A New-York Chapter of the New Organization Formed," *New York Times,* February 24, 1891).

29. On Americanization, see William B. Rhoads, "The Colonial Revival and the Americanization of Immigrants," in *The Colonial Revival in America,* ed. Alan Axelrod (New York: W. W. Norton, 1985), 341–61. See also Patricia West, *Domesticating History: The Political Origins of America's House Museums* (Washington, D.C.: Smithsonian Institution Press, 1999), 44–46, on the DAR's Americanization agenda. Many Americanization activities were grounded in public history, for example, the preservation of historic sites, pageants and commemorative celebrations, and the creation

of historical societies and history museums. For more perspective on these activities, see Michael Kammen, *Mystic Chords of Memory: The Transformation of Tradition in American Culture* (New York: Alfred A. Knopf, 1991); and two books by James M. Lindgren, *Preserving the Old Dominion: Historic Preservation and Virginia Traditionalism* (Charlottesville: University Press of Virginia, 1993), and *Preserving Historic New England: Preservation, Progressivism, and the Remaking of Memory* (New York: Oxford University Press, 1995).

30. "Resolution," *American Monthly Magazine* 1.1 (1892): 5–6.

31. Quoted in Ellen Hardin Walworth, "Principle of Organization of the National Society of the Daughters of the American Revolution," *American Monthly Magazine* 1.1 (1892): 8.

32. For a description of the organizational model of the Colonial Dames, see Mrs. Joseph Rucher Lamar, *A History of the National Society of the Colonial Dames of America, from 1891 to 1933* (Atlanta: National Society of the Colonial Dames of America, 1934), especially chaps. 2–4.

33. Walworth, "Principle of Organization," 11.

34. Walworth, "American Society," 302.

35. Cited ibid.

36. Cited in Martha Strayer, *The D.A.R.: An Informal History* (Westport, Conn.: Greenwood Press, 1973), 45.

37. Ibid. Strayer described a "Committee of Safety," which functioned within the early DAR organization to "'keep out' plain people by the 'blackball method'" (49).

38. Ibid., 48.

39. Alice Morse Earle, application for membership, February 6, 1895, National Society of the Daughters of the American Revolution Library, Washington, D.C.

40. Ibid.

41. Morse-Earle Genealogy.

42. Philip J. Greven Jr., *Four Generations: Population, Land, and Family in Colonial Andover, Massachusetts* (Ithaca: Cornell University Press, 1970), chaps. 7 and 9.

43. According to family reminiscence, "Edwin and Edward looked exactly alike even in old age." Morse-Earle Genealogy.

44. Edward Morse was listed in the 1862 Cincinnati directory as a partner in Lynn & Morse, real estate brokers, doing business across the Ohio River in Covington, Kentucky. *Williams' Cincinnati Directory, City Guide and Business Mirror for Year Commencing June 1, 1862: Twelfth Annual Issue* (Cincinnati: Williams & Co., 1862), 243, 219. Reuben Morse to Alice Morse Earle, October 24, 1894, Earle-Hyde Papers.

45. Alice Morse Earle to William C. Brownell, April 18, 1895, Scribner Papers. Earle's cavalier tone is somewhat puzzling, since the date of this letter coincided exactly with the date of her admission to the National Society of the Daughters of the American Revolution. This comment may be a way of distancing herself from the DAR identification, indicating that she was aware that not everyone—quite possibly including Brownell—took these organizations as seriously as they took themselves.

46. Ibid.

47. The dedication in Alice Morse Earle, *Colonial Dames and Good Wives* (Boston: Houghton Mifflin & Co., 1895), listed fourteen, not thirteen women: Elizabeth Morse, Joanna Hoar, Esther Mason, Deborah Atherton, Sarah Wyeth, Anne Adams, Elizabeth Browne, Hannah Phillips, Mary Clary, Silence Heard, Judith Thurston, Patience Foster, Martha Bullard, Barbara Sheppard, and Seaborn Wilson. Earle, *Margaret Winthrop*, 244–45.

48. See Beverly Gordon, "Dressing-Up as Embodied Amusement," in *The Saturated World: Aesthetic Meaning, Intimate Objects, Women's Lives, 1890–1940* (Knoxville: University of Tennessee Press, 2006), 107–38. On Earle's use of costumed women as historical "props" for her book illustrations, see Karal Ann Marling, *George Washington Slept Here* (Cambridge: Harvard University Press, 1980), 165. Marling distinguishes, however, between the staged photographs in Earle's books, which aimed for authenticity, and those of Earle's contemporary Mary Northend, whose intention was to showcase the colonial revival as a modern decorative style (169).

49. In *A World of Strangers: Order and Action in Urban Public Space* (New York: Basic Books, 1973), Lyn H. Lofland theorized that the shift from a world where anonymity was virtually nonexistent to a world of strangers mandated the rise of new social codes that would make strangers known (and therefore tolerable) to one another. "City life was made possible," he speculated, "by an 'ordering' of the urban population in terms of appearance and spatial location such that those within the city could know a great deal about one another by simply looking." Clothing lost its potency, however, in the modern city, which was characterized by "masked heterogeneity of populace." The older appearance-based order was undermined by the rise of a bourgeoisie, who felt entitled by wealth to the rights of elite status display; by demographic expansion, whereby a "massive influx of rural persons . . . challenged the already weakening appearential order simply by being ignorant or disdainful of it"; and by such technological factors as the mass production of cloth and clothing. In this new world, spatial codes and segregated activities assumed an exaggerated importance in the minds of middle-class Americans, as they must have for Earle and her peers, as essential to the maintenance of social order (22, 28, 60, 63–65, 80). Grant McCracken has explored clothing as an expressive cultural form in his chapter "Clothing as Language: "An Object Lesson in the Study of the Expressive Properties of Material Culture," in *Culture and Consumption: New Approaches to the Symbolic Character of Consumer Goods* (Bloomington: Indiana University Press, 1990), 57–61.

50. Earle, *Margaret Winthrop*, 88.

51. On the cultural appeal for women of old clothing and dressing up, see Gordon, "Dressing-Up as Embodied Amusement."

52. Notice, *American Monthly Magazine* 23 (1903): 241.

53. Alice Morse Earle to George Brett, January 19, 1903, Macmillan Papers.

54. Ibid.

55. Ibid.

56. Alice Morse Earle to George Brett, n.d. [between January 19 and 24, 1903], Macmillan Papers.

57. Alice Morse Earle to George Brett, n.d. [late January 1903], Macmillan Papers. Codman's offer of free photographs would have delighted Earle, since her contracts with Macmillan never provided a photographic budget that was ample enough to suit her requirements, a condition about which she complained constantly in her correspondence with Brett.

58. Erving Goffman, *The Presentation of Self in Everyday Life* (New York: Anchor Books, 1959), 11, 26, 36, 41–43. Goffman has posited that contradictions between physical appearance, those factors that indicate social status, and the manner of presentation can serve to heighten an audience's interest.

59. Portraits accounted for 61 percent of the illustrations in *Two Centuries of Costume*. Other artists represented included Washington Allston, Joseph Blackburn, Ralph Earle, Robert Feke, Thomas Gainsborough, Chester Harding, John Haskins, Hans Holbein, Wenceslaus Hollar, Gerard Honthorst, Jacob Huysmans, Henrietta Johnson, Angelica Kaufmann, Sir Godfrey Kneller, Sir Peter Lely, Michiel Jansze van Mierevelt, Samuel F. B. Morse, Charles Osgood, Charles Willson Peale, Allan Ramsay, Rembrandt, Sir Joshua Reynolds, George Richmond, Saint Memin, John Smibert, Gilbert Stuart, Thomas Sully, Jeremiah Theus, John Trumbull, Anthony Van Dyck, Benjamin West, John Woolaston, and Federico Zucchero.

60. In *The Past Is a Foreign Country* (Cambridge: Cambridge University Press, 1985), 238–49, David Lowenthal defined relics as a "tangible past," recognizable through their age, embellishment, or anachronistic quality, whether real or contrived, and of varying degrees of utility for historical understanding. Grant McCracken argues in "Clothing as Language" that clothing is an important expressive medium, and one that may be consciously used to convey political and cultural values.

61. David Glassberg, *American Historical Pageantry: The Uses of Tradition in the Early Twentieth Century* (Chapel Hill: University of North Carolina Press, 1990), 67. See also Marling, *George Washington Slept Here*, 210–15; and Dona Brown, *Inventing New England: Regional Tourism in the Nineteenth Century* (Washington, D.C.: Smithsonian Institution Press, 1995), 182–83.

62. For different perspectives on the expressive power of clothing, see McCracken, "Clothing as Language"; and Linda R. Baumgarten, "Leather Stockings and Hunting Shirts," in *American Material Culture: The Shape of the Field*, ed. Ann Smart "Martin and J. Ritchie Garrison (Winterthur, Del.: Henry Francis DuPont Winterthur Museum, 1997), 251–76. Michael C. Batinski expands reenacting beyond dressing up, to include needlework, cookery, and other realms, in *Pastkeepers in a Small Place: Five Centuries in Deerfield, Massachusetts* (Amherst: University of Massachusetts Press, 2004), 177–93; as do Marla R. Miller and Anne Digan Lanning in "'Common Parlors': Women and the Recreation of Community Identity in Deerfield, Massachusetts, 1870–1920," *Gender and History* 6.3 (1994): 435–55. See also "Beverly Gordon's gendered analysis of dressing up in *Saturated World*, 107–9, 124–25.

9. TOWARD A NEW PUBLIC HISTORY

1. Michael Kammen has interpreted this nostalgic impulse as a response to social and cultural change, stating, "Because so much that genuinely mattered was new . . . people needed notions of the past that would define their national identities in positive ways, and required secure traditions to serve as strong psychological anchors." His interpretation builds on Robert Crunden's profile of the progressive personality and ensuing "innovative nostalgia." Michael Kammen, *Mystic Chords of Memory: The Transformation of Tradition in American Culture* (New York: Alfred A. Knopf, 1991), 294–95; Robert M. Crunden, *Ministers of Reform: The Progressives' Achievement in American Civilization, 1889–1920* (New York: Basic Books, 1982), 90.

2. For a thorough analysis of the history of the house museum movement, see Patricia West, *Domesticating History: The Political Origins of America's House Museums* (Washington, D.C.: Smithsonian Institution Press, 1999), especially chap. 2, "Gender Politics and the Orchard House Museum."

3. Grant McCracken offers a compelling analysis of the expressive meanings of artifacts in *Culture and Consumption* (Bloomington: Indiana University Press, 1990), 57–89.

4. Walter Muir Whitehill, *Independent Historical Societies: An Inquiry into Their Research and Publication Functions and Their Financial Future* (Boston: Boston Atheneum, 1962), 368–70.

5. J. P. Spang III, "Preservation Project: Deerfield's Memorial Hall," *Antiques* 94 (August 1968): 206–8.

6. Clifton Johnson, *The New England Country* (Boston: Lee and Shepard, 1893), 1. Johnson's pen and ink illustration seems to have been copied rather precisely from a photograph of the Old Kitchen in Memorial Hall by the Deerfield photographers Mary and Frances Allen. Their photograph is reproduced in Melinda Young Frye, "The Beginnings of the Period Room in American Museums: Charles P. Wilcomb's Colonial Kitchens, 1896, 1906, 1910," in *The Colonial Revival in America*, ed. Alan Axelrod (New York: W. W. Norton, 1985), 232.

7. In addition to *The New England Country,* Clifton Johnson (1865–1940) wrote many other books about the New England past: *The Country School* (1893), *The Farmer's Boy* (1894), *What They Say in New England* (1897), *The Story of Johnny Cake* (n.d.), and *Old-Time Schools and School-books* (1904), as well as his later *American Highways and Byways,* a twelve-volume automobile tour of the United States beginning in the South in 1904. Johnson also wrote about the rural cultures of other nations in *Among English Hedgerows* (1899), *Along French Byways* (1900), *The Isle of the Shamrock* (ca. 1900), and *The Land of the Heather* (1903). In addition, he collected agricultural implements and founded a museum in Hadley, Massachusetts. Johnson, a well-known photographer as well as a writer, sold five of his photographs to Earle for publication in both *Old-Time Gardens* and *Home Life in Colonial Days:* "Making Soap," "Wire Ferry on the Connecticut," "The Garden's Friend," "Garden Walk at the Manse, Deerfield," and "White Day Lilies." Alice Morse Earle, *Home Life in Colonial Days* (New York: Macmillan, 1898), 254, 330; idem, *Old-Time Gardens, Newly Set Forth: A Book of the Sweet o' the Year* (New York: Macmillan, 1901), 48, 281, 442.

8. Alice Morse Earle, *Customs and Fashions in Old New England* (New York: Charles Scribner's Sons, 1893), 131.

9. Alice Morse Earle to George Sheldon, September 7, 1892, PVMA.

10. For an extended discussion of C. Alice Baker's life and work in Deerfield, as well as her progressive agenda, see Michael C. Batinski, *Pastkeepers in a Small Place: Five Centuries in Deerfield, Massachusetts* (Amherst: University of Massachusetts Press, 2004), 177–85.

11. Marla R. Miller and Anne Digan Lanning, "'Common Parlors': Women and the Recreation of Community Identity in Deerfield, Massachusetts, 1870–1920," *Gender and History* 6 (1994): 435–55. See also Batinski, *Pastkeepers in a Small Place,* 184–93.

12. Alice Morse Earle to George Sheldon, September 14, 1892, February 10 1894, February 26, 1898, April 12, 1901, and July 8, 1901, PVMA.

13. For further information about both Davis and Dow, see Elizabeth Stillinger, *The Antiquers* (New York: Alfred A. Knopf, 1980), 22–26, 149–54. See also Karal Ann Marling, *George Washington Slept Here* (Cambridge: Harvard University Press, 1980), 162–70.

14. Frye, "Beginnings of the Period Room," 235–37.

15. Charles P. Wilcomb, typescript, August 7, 1896, Archives, M. H. de Young Memorial Museum, San Francisco, 1, quoted ibid., 224–25. Frye's study of Wilcomb's colonial kitchens remains the definitive work on early period rooms, and particularly the career and impact of Wilcomb.

16. Frye, "Beginnings of the Period Room," 237.

17. See Richard L. Bushman, *The Refinement of America: Persons, Houses, Cities* (New York: Alfred A. Knopf, 1992), 402–47, for an explication of the historical dynamics of gentility.

18. Kate Taylor, Norwalk, Conn., to Annjennet Huntington, Rochester, N.Y., November 3, 1880, Huntington-Hooker Papers, Department of Rare Books and Special Collections, Rush Rhees Library, University of Rochester. On the growing significance of "antiques" in domestic interiors, see Laurel Thatcher Ulrich, *The Age of Homespun: Objects and Stories in the Creation of an American Myth* (New York: Alfred A. Knopf, 2001), 20–25.

19. Briann G. Greenfield, *Out of the Attic: Inventing Antiques in Twentieth-Century New England* (Amherst: University of Massachusetts Press, 2009), 21–22.

20. Karal Ann Marling has surveyed the content and meaning of historical pageants as part of her larger study of George Washington and the colonial revival; see Marling, *George Washington Slept Here,* 196–215. In *American Historical Pageantry: The Uses of Tradition in the Early Twentieth Century* (Chapel Hill: University of North Carolina Press, 1990), David Glassberg has argued that "historical pageantry flourished at the intersection of progressivism and antimodernism and placed nostalgic imagery in a dynamic, future-oriented reform context" (5).

21. Esther Willard Bates, *Pageants and Pageantry* (Boston: Gibbs & Co., 1912), 4–6, 26, 281–87. A copy of *Costume of Colonial Times* in the author's collection is stamped inside the front cover "P.S. 1, Manhattan / Girls' Dept. / Mary R. Davis, Prin."

Doubtless a search for other of Earle's books would turn up many more copies formerly held in libraries.

22. Glassberg, *American Historical Pageantry*, 135–36, 139.

23. Ibid., 67.

24. Jane Cunningham Croly, *The History of the Woman's Club Movement in America* (New York: Henry G. Allen, 1898), 897.

25. Alice Morse Earle, *China Collecting in America* (New York: Charles Scribner's Sons, 1892), 417.

26. Early scholarship about Colonial Revival furniture can be found in Rodris Roth, "American Art: The Colonial Revival and Centennial Furniture," *Art Quarterly* 27 (Spring 1964): 57–81. For subsequent literature about furnishings, see "Decorative Arts, Furniture, Interiors," in *Colonial Revival in America: Annotated Bibliography*, http://etext.virginia.edu/colonial/texts/ColRevBiv.html. The literature on the colonial revival abounds in articles about specific architectural examples. See, for instance, William Butler, "Another City upon a Hill: Litchfield, Connecticut, and the Colonial Revival," in Axelrod, *The Colonial Revival in America*, 15–51; or Richard M. Candee, "The New Colonials: Restoration and Remodeling of Old Buildings along the Piscataqua," in *"A Noble and Dignified Stream": The Piscataqua Region in the Colonial Revival, 1860–1930*, ed. Sarah L. Giffen and Kevin D. Murphy (York, Me.: Old York Historical Society, 1992), 35–78. See also Marling, *George Washington Slept Here*, 176–84.

27. Oliver Coleman, *Successful Houses* (Chicago: Herbert S. Stone, 1899), 46–48.

28. Mary Pitman Earle Moore, application for membership, and Alice Clary Earle Hyde, application for membership, Daughters of the American Revolution, DAR Library, Washington, D.C. Moore's records reveal that like her aunt Frances Morse, she was dropped for nonpayment of dues, in 1908.

29. Copies of Hyde's genealogy exist in the families of two Earle descendants, Donald J. Post, Southbury, Conn., and Thomas S. Powers, South Royalton, Vt.

30. Alice Morse Earle to Francis F. Browne, May 4, 1904, Miscellaneous Manuscripts, Sophia Smith Collection, Smith College, Northampton, Mass.

31. International Appraising Company, New York, "Residence Appraisal, D. Thomas Moore, Westbury, L.I.," Earle-Moore Papers (hereafter Moore Residence Appraisal).

32. Susan Williams, *Savory Suppers and Fashionable Feasts: Dining in Victorian America* (New York: Pantheon, 1985), 9–10, 88.

33. Ibid., 187; Susan R. Williams, introduction to *Dining in America, 1850–1900*, ed. Kathryn Grover (Amherst and Rochester: University of Massachusetts Press and Strong Museum, 1987), especially 10–14.

34. Charles Lewis Tiffany, in partnership with John B. Young, founded the firm of Tiffany & Young in 1837—an inauspicious time to begin a business because of the serious depression that began the same year. J. L. Ellis entered the firm in 1841, and Tiffany, Young & Ellis remained a partnership until 1853, when Tiffany's two partners retired and the firm became Tiffany & Company. This business chronology

dates the Moores' tea set to the period 1841–1853. For a comprehensive history of Tiffany & Company and its products, see Charles H. Carpenter with Mary Grace Carpenter, *Tiffany Silver* (New York: Dodd, Mead, 1978), 6–14.

35. The tea service may well have been a family heirloom, since Earle's mother and father were married in 1848, during the period when Tiffany, Young & Ellis was doing business. If it was presented to the Morses as a wedding gift, however, it would have had to be *new*, not old—bringing into sharp relief the contrast between cultural expectations of antebellum and turn-of-the-century America.

36. Marginal notes throughout the appraisal indicated the original price paid for purchased objects, in contrast to the valuation assigned by the appraiser. Moore Residence Appraisal.

37. Ibid., 11, 13–14.

38. Earle to Browne, May 4, 1904.

39. Moore Residence Appraisal, 39, 45.

40. Alice Morse Earle, *Sun-Dials and Roses of Yesterday* (New York: Macmillan, 1902), 164, 180. For Ralph Waldo Emerson's views on the difference between the "economical uses of things" and their symbolic or emblematic content, see Henry Glassie, "Meaningful Things and Appropriate Myths: The Artifact's Place in American Studies," in *Material Life in America, 1600–1860*, ed. Robert Blair St. George (Boston: Northeastern University Press, 1988), 86.

41. Earle, *Sun-Dials and Roses*, 201. In fact, tradescantia is hardy to the point of invasiveness, even in the barren soil of a northern New England garden.

42. Ibid., 230.

43. Ibid., 181.

44. Ibid., 183.

45. In 1981 the Williamsburg Craft House was still offering reproduction pewter porringers in two sizes. "Price List of Williamsburg Reproductions from Craft House," Williamsburg, Va., January 1981, 10.

46. Earle, *China Collecting*, 418.

47. Earle, *Home Life in Colonial Days*, 86.

48. Robert Plant Armstrong has defined the notion of "affecting presence" as related to the realm of intended feeling in things or events. This presence is perceptible at universal, cultural, or particular levels, and may represent both continuity and discontinuity. Robert Plant Armstrong, *The Affecting Presence: An Essay in Humanistic Anthropology* (Urbana: University of Illinois Press, 1971), 17–55.

49. Charles Montgomery, a scholar of American pewter, defined these objects as "small bowls with flat handles used for eating and drinking," adding that "American pewterers made them in great quantity and variety throughout the colonial period." The bowl appeared in two basic forms, either as a gently flaring, flat-bottomed basin or as a "bellied-bowl," whose sides were nipped in near the rim and usually culminated in a short, straight flange. In lieu of a flat bottom, the bellied-bowl type had a raised boss or dome worked into its base. Although some porringers had tab handles, by far the preferred type for collectors was the pierced

or "flowered" handle porringer. By tradition, these handles assumed a pyramidal tree-like shape, penetrated by thirteen saw-cut openings, creating an overall effect not unlike the carved decoration on a rococo chair splat. Montgomery devoted an entire chapter to porringers; besides pitchers, they were the only objects to receive such intense focus. Charles F. Montgomery, *A History of American Pewter* (New York: E. P. Dutton, 1978), 145, 148–51, figs. 9.3–9.10.

50. Earle, *Home Life in Colonial Days,* 86. The "States" pattern was manufactured in England for the American market by the firm of James & Ralph Clews (1819–1836). Its design, which included a bordering ribbon inscribed with the names of fifteen states, which surrounded a portrait of Washington and the allegorical figures of America blindfolded and Independence kneeling, made it extremely desirable among American collectors of English historical transfer-printed ware. Ellouise Baker Larsen, *American Historical Views on Staffordshire China* (1939; repr., New York: Dover Publications, 1975), 54.

51. Ibid., 85.

52. *The Diary of Samuel Sewall,* vol. 2, *(1699–1714), Collections of the Massachusetts Historical Society,* 5th ser., vol. 6 (Boston, 1879), 116, quoted in Montgomery, *History of American Pewter,* 148.

53. Poetic images, as Gaston Bachelard has suggested, are related to cultural archetypes embedded in human consciousness, and are accessible through the analysis and interpretation of consciousness. Gaston Bachelard, *The Poetics of Space,* trans. Maria Jolas (Boston: Beacon Press, 1969), xiv.

54. Ibid., 90–104.

CONCLUSION

1. Raymond Williams, *The Country and the City* (New York: Oxford University Press, 1973), 12.

2. "Literary Notes from London: Alice Morse Earle," *New York Times Book Review,* March 5, 1911, 124.

3. A search for her using Google Scholar produced eighty-eight references to Earle and her work published between her death in 1911 and 1940 (August 28, 2009).

4. "Reading to Mark Earle Centennial," *Bay State Historical League Bulletin* (October 1951). I thank Jane Nylander for this reference.

5. Michael Pollan, "A Gardener's Guide to Sex, Politics, and Class War," *New York Times,* July 21, 1991.

6. Alice Morse Earle, *Home Life in Colonial Days* (New York: New York Public Library, 2011). A search of the WorldCat database shows a surge of interest in Earle's books during the 1970s, probably because of the Bicentennial. Between 1970 and 1976, thirty-three different editions appeared in print. The numbers declined somewhat during the 1980s, but began to climb again in the 1990s, when twenty new editions appeared. After 2000, thirty-three separate editions came into print,

but many of these, especially from 2005 on, were either internet or print-on-demand books, which might not be a reliable reflection of Earle's popularity.

7. A search of JSTOR for references to Earle appearing in journal articles published between 1950 and 2012 produced just over two hundred hits. Amazon.com, which lists over eight hundred links to books written by Earle, also lists related works by other authors who have used Earle as an authority, many of whom are established academic historians who have used Earle as an authority.

8. A search of Amazon.com in January 2012 for Alice Morse Earle yielded all of her book titles, many currently in print, as well as, more commonly, works that were out of print or of limited availability. Among these items were twenty-one different editions of *Home Life*. Ten of her books were available as Kindle publications (several in multiple editions): *The Sabbath in Puritan New England*, *Colonial Dames and Good Wives*, *Colonial Days in Old New York*, *China Collecting in America*, *Customs and Fashions in Old New England*, *Home Life in Colonial Days*, *Stage Coach and Tavern Days*, *Two Centuries of Costume in America*, *Curious Punishments of Bygone Days*, and *Diary of Anna Green Winslow*.

CHRONOLOGICAL BIBLIOGRAPHY OF ALICE MORSE EARLE'S WORKS

BOOKS

The Sabbath in Puritan New England. New York: Charles Scribner's Sons, 1891.

China Collecting in America. New York: Charles Scribner's Sons, 1892.

√ *Customs and Fashions in Old New England.* New York: Charles Scribner's Sons, 1893.

Early Prose and Verse. Distaff Series, ed. Alice Morse Earle and Emily Ellsworth Ford. New York: Harper & Brothers, 1893.

Costume of Colonial Times. New York: Charles Scribner's Sons, 1894.

Diary of Anna Green Winslow: A Boston School Girl of 1771. Boston: Houghton Mifflin & Co., 1894.

Colonial Dames and Good Wives. Boston: Houghton Mifflin & Co., 1895.

√ *Margaret Winthrop.* New York: Charles Scribner's Sons, 1895.

√ *Colonial Days in Old New York.* New York: Charles Scribner's Sons, 1896.

Curious Punishments of Bygone Days. Chicago: Herbert S. Stone & Co., 1896.

In Old Narragansett: Romance and Realities. New York: Charles Scribner's Sons, 1898.

Home Life in Colonial Days. New York: Macmillan, 1898.

Child Life in Colonial Days. New York: Macmillan, 1899.

Stage Coach and Tavern Days. New York: Macmillan, 1900.

Old-Time Gardens, Newly Set Forth: A Book of the Sweet o' the Year. New York: Macmillan, 1901.

Sun-Dials and Roses of Yesterday. New York: Macmillan, 1902.

Two Centuries of Costume in America. New York: Macmillan, 1903.

ARTICLES AND ESSAYS

"A Pickle for the Knowing Ones." *Christian Union* 41.4 (January 23, 1890): 140.

"Narragansett Pacers." *New England Magazine* 8.2 (March 1890): 39–42.

"The Puritan Judge's Wooings." *Independent* 42.2172 (July 17, 1890): 5.

"A Dying Narragansett Church." *Andover Review* 14.79 (July 1890): 43.

"Pewter Bright." *Independent* 43.2228 (August 13, 1891): 4.

"Query." *Journal of American Folklore* 4.15 (October–December 1891): 354.

"Tuggie Bannocks's Ghost." *Independent* 43.2246 (December 17, 1891): 35.

"The New England Meeting-House." *Atlantic Monthly* 67.400 (February 1891): 191–204.

"Ghost, Poet, and Spinet." *New England Magazine* 9.6 (February 1891): 778–84.

"Top Drawer in the High Chest." *New England Magazine* 10.4 (July 1891): 649–55.

"The Queen's Closet Opened." *Atlantic Monthly* 68.406 (August 1891): 215–27.

"China Hunter in New England." *Scribner's Magazine* 10.3 (September 1891): 345–58.

"Shoes Worn in Colonial New England." *Christian Union* 45.4 (January 23, 1892): 160.

"Waste-Basket of Words." *Journal of American Folklore* 5.16 (January–March 1892): 61.

"The First New England Thanksgivings." *Independent* 44.2295 (November 24, 1892, 1892): 3.

"Early New England Holidays." *Christian Union (1870–1893)* 46.25 (December 17, 1892, 1892): 1171.

"Child Life in Old New England." *Independent* 44.2299 (December 22, 1892): 3; 44.2300 (December 29, 1892): 2; 45.2301 (January 5, 1893): 9.

"A New England Kismet." *Scribner's Magazine* 11.3 (March 1892): 295–302.

"Funeral Customs in Early New England." *Independent* 44.2265 (April 28, 1892): 5.

"Old Colonial Drinks and Drinkers." *National Magazine* 16.2 (June 1892): 149.

"The Oldest Episcopal Church in New England." *New England Magazine* 13.5 (January 1893): 577–93.

"The First New England Thanksgiving." *Friends' Review* 46.26 (January 19, 1893): 412.

"Old-Time Marriage Customs in New England." *Journal of American Folklore* 6.21 (April–June 1893): 97–102.

"Travel in New England in Olden Times." *Independent* 45.2327 (July 6, 1893): 3; 45.2330 (July 27, 1893): 3.

"A Boston School Girl in 1771." *Atlantic Monthly* 72.430 (August 1893): 218–24.

"Pope Day in America." *Independent* 45.2344 (November 2, 1893): 7.

"Old-Time Church Music in New England." *Outlook* 48.22 (November 25, 1893): 933–34.

"Stamps and Marks on Old China." *Ladies' Home Journal* 11.2 (January 1894): 10.

"New Year's Eve and Day." *Independent* 46.2353 (January 4, 1894): 1.

"St. Valentine's Day in Olden Times." *Outlook* 49.6 (Feb 10, 1894): 271.

"The Crusoes of the Noon-House." *Congregationalist* 79.16 (April 19, 1894): 561.

"Pinkster Day." *Outlook* 49.17 (April 28, 1894): 743–44.

"My Delft Apothecary Jars." *Ladies' Home Journal* 11.6 (May 1894): 9–10.

"A Black Politician." *Independent* 46.2370 (May 3, 1894): 26.

"May Day in Olden Times." *Independent* 46.2372 (May 17, 1894): 4.

"Church Communion Tokens." *Atlantic Monthly* 74.442 (August 1894): 210–14.

"Courtship and Marriage in Puritan Days." *Ladies' Home Journal* 11.9 (August 1894): 2.

"An Old Thanksgiving Fireside." *Independent* 46.2400 (November 29, 1894): 1; 46.2401 (December 6, 1894): 3.

"Three Heroines of New England Romance." *Book Buyer* (December 1, 1894): 571.

"The Doctor's Pie Plates." *Independent* 46.2403 (December 20, 1894): 4.

"Old English Pottery and China in America." *Monthly Illustrator* 3.9 (January 1895): 116–19.

"Flower-lore of New England Children." *Atlantic Monthly* 75.450 (April 1895): 459–66.

"Fashions of the Nineteenth Century." *Chautauquan* 21.2 (May 1895): 131–38, 259–64.

"A Baptist Preacher and Soldier of the Last Century." *New England Magazine* 18.4 (June 1895): 407–14.

"Domestic Service in Revolutionary Days." *Independent* 47.2429 (June 20, 1895): 4.

"Householding in Old New England." *Ladies' Home Journal* 12.7 (June 1895): 8.

"Required Reading for the Chautauqua Literary and Scientific Circle." *Chautauquan* 21.3 (June 1895): 259; 24.3 (December 1896): 259.

"Candles in Old New England." *Christian Advocate (1866–1905)* 70.24 (June 13, 1895): 374.

"Domestic Service in Revolutionary Days." *Independent* 47.2428 (June 13, 1895): 4.

"Rhoda's Legacy." *Outlook* 51.25 (June 22, 1895): 1095–96.

"Daughters of Liberty." *Independent* 47.2431 (July 4, 1895): 5; 47.2432 (July 11, 1895): 7.

"New England's Fast Days." *Dial* 14.218 (July 16, 1895): 41.

"A Monument to the Prison-Ship Martyrs." *American Historical Register and Monthly Gazette* 12 (August 1895): 1423–37.

"Newspaper Women of Colonial Times." *Independent* 47.2437 (August 15, 1895): 3.

"The Sunday of the Puritan Colonies." *Independent* 47.2449 (November 7, 1895): 4.

"'The End of His Days,' in Colonial New York." *Independent* 48.2487 (July 30, 1896): 3.

"Correspondence." *Book Buyer (1867–1903)* 13.10 (November 1, 1896): 625.

"Degeneration." In *Essays from the Chap Book.* Chicago: Herbert S. Stone, 1896, 37–43.

"The Pleasures of Historiography." In *Essays from the Chap Book.* Chicago: Herbert S. Stone, 1896, 47–55.

"The Bureau of Literary Revision." In *Essays from the Chap Book.* Chicago: Herbert S. Stone, 1896, 59–63.

"Old-Time Flower Gardens." *Scribner's Magazine* 20.4 (April 1896): 161–78.

"The Bilboes." *Chap Book* 5 (August 1896): 289–95.

"The Ducking Stool." *Chap Book* 5 (September 1896): 353–63.

"Punishments of Authors and Books." *Chap Book* 5 (September 1896): 512–20.

"The Schoolmaster in Old New York." *Book Buyer* 13.9 (October 1, 1896): 531.

"The Pillory." *Chap Book* 5 (October 1896): 443–50.

"The Whipping Post." *Chap Book* 5 (November 1896): 561–68.

"The Scarlet Letter." *Chap Book* 6 (November 1896): 31–37.

"New Year's Day in Dutch New York." *Christian Observer* 84.53 (December 30, 1896): 20.

"Punishments of Authors and Books in Bygone Days." *Current Literature* 21.2 (February 1897): 180.

"Matrimonial Divinations." *Lippincott's Monthly Magazine* (April 1897): 554.

"Old Colonial Drinks." *Current Literature* 22.3 (September 1897): 256.

"Schools and Education in American Colonies." *Chautauquan* 26.4 (January 1898): 362–66.

"Colonial Household Industries." *Chautauquan* 26.5 (February 1898): 475–49.

"Indian Corn in Colonial Times." *Chautauquan* 26.6 (March 1898): 586–90.

"Colonial Times." *Chap Book* 8.8 (March 1, 1898): 329.

"Correspondence." *Chap Book* 9.1 (May 15, 1898): 8.

"St. Tammany's Birthday." *Independent* 50.2580 (May 12, 1898): 3.

"Black Jacks." *Chap Book* 9.1 (May 15, 1898): 21–22.

"Mead or Metheglin." *Chap Book* 8.12 (May 1, 1898): 482–83.

"Huff-cup and Nippitatum." *Chap Book* 9.3 (June 15, 1898): 83.

"Among Friends." *New England Magazine* 24.6 (August 1898): 18–23.

"Sunday in New Netherland and New York." *Atlantic Monthly* 78.468 (October 1898): 543.

"The Stad Huys of New Amsterdam." In *Historic New York, Being the First Series of the Half Moon Papers,* ed. Maud Wilder Goodwin, Alice Carrington Royce, and Ruth Putman. New York: G. P. Putnam's Sons, 1898, 41–73.

"The Rogerenes." *Independent* 51.2659 (November 16, 1899): 3078.

"A Gallant Silken Trade." *New England Magazine,* n.s., 22.5 (July 1900): 557–63.

"Coral Cactus and Rosy Cake." *New England Magazine,* n.s., 23.4 (December 1900): 470–74.

"Dancing Flowers and Flower Dances." *New England Magazine,* n.s., 26.5 (July 1902): 556–60.

"Sabbath-Day Posies and Noon House Fare." *Interior* 34.1737 (September 10, 1903): 1190.

"Sabbath-Day Posies and Noon-House Fare." *Congregationalist and Christian World* 88.37 (September 12, 1903): 360.

"Episodes of Thanksgiving Day in 1820." *Interior* 34.1747 (November 19, 1903): 1517.

"Sun-Dials Old and New." *New England Magazine,* n.s., 29.5 (January 1904): 563–77.

"Old-Time Drinking Habits." *Bonfort's Wine and Spirit Circular* 61.5 (January 10, 1904): 227.

"The Home." *Interior* 35.1774 (May 26, 1904): 683.

"Samplers." *Century Magazine* 83.3 (March 1912): 676–85.

REVIEWS

Review of *The Pottery and Porcelain of the United States,* by Edwin Atlee Barber. *Dial* 16.187 (April 1, 1894): 212–13.

Review of *Discovery by Count Teleki of Lakes Rudolph and Stephanie,* by Ludwig von Hohnell. *Dial* 16.189 (May 1, 1894): 269–72.

"Some Recent Books of Travel." Review of *Diary of a Journey across Tibet,* by Captain Hamilton Bower; *Among the Moors: Sketches of Oriental Life,* by Georges Montbard; *On the Wallaby; or, Through the East and across Australia,* by Guy Boothby; *The Gypsy Road,* by Grenville A. J. Cole. *Dial* 17.194 (July 16, 1894): 39.

Review of *The Mountains of California,* by John Muir. *Dial* 18.207 (February 1, 1895): 75–77.

"Travels in the Orient." Review of *A Corner of Cathay: Studies from Life among the Chinese,* by Adele M. Fielde; *Across Asia on a Bicycle,* by Thomas Gaskell Allen Jr. and William Lewis Sachtleben; *When We Were Strolling Players in the East,* by Louise Jordan Miln; *Wandering Words,* by Sir Edwin Arnold. *Dial* 18.211 (April 1, 1895): 210.

Review of *The Fast and Thanksgiving Days of New England,* by W. DeLoss Love. *Dial* 19.218 (July 16, 1895): 41–43.

Review of *A Puritan Pepys,* by Henry Cabot Lodge. *Bookman* 5.5 (July 1897): 425.

Review of *The Writings of "Colonel William Byrd, of Westover in Virginia, Esqr.,"* ed. John Spencer Bassett. *Dial* 32.381 (May 1, 1902): 308–10.

"In Garden Ways." Review of *Formal Gardens of England and Scotland,* by H. Inigo Triggs; *American Gardens,* ed. Guy Lowell; *Miniature and Window Gardening,* by Phoebe Allen and Dr. Godfrey; *A Garden in the Suburbs,* by Mrs. Leslie Williams; *Flowers and Gardens: Notes on Plant Beauty,* ed. Rev. Canon Ellsworth; *Garden-Craft, Old and New,* by John D. Sedding. *Dial* 32.383 (June 1, 1902): 374–77.

"Two Good Garden Books." Review of *In My Vicarage Garden and Elsewhere,* by Rev. Henry N. Ellecombe; *Stray Leaves from a Border Garden,* by Mary Pamela Milne-Home. *Dial* 33:386 (July 16, 1902): 32–33.

Review of *The Pleasures of the Table,* by George H. Ellwanger. *Dial* 33:396 (December 16, 1902): 460–61.

"English and Tuscan Gardens." Review of *Roses for English Gardens* by Gertrude Jekyll and Edward Mawley; *In a Tuscan Garden,* by Georgina S. Grahame. *Dial* 34.401 (March 1, 1903): 147.

"Gardens and Garden-Blooms." Review of *A Woman's Hardy Garden,* by Helena Rutherford Ely; *The Book of the Wild Garden* by S. W. Fitzherbert; *The Flower Beautiful* by Clarence Moores Weed. *Dial* 34.407 (June 1, 1903): 360.

"An Era of Flower Books." Review of *How to Make a Flower Garden,* ed. L. H. Bailey; *Bog Trotting for Orchids,* by Grace Greylock Niles; *Our Mountain Garden,* by Mrs. Theodore Thomas; *An Island Garden,* by Celia Thaxter; *Little Gardens,* by Charles M. Skinner. *Dial* 36:431 (June 1, 1904): 355–57.

INDEX

SUSAN R. WILLIAMS is a professor of history and women's studies at Fitchburg State University in Massachusetts. Previously, she curated the collections of household accessories and tablewares at the Strong Museum in Rochester, New York, specializing in glass, ceramics, and silver. She received a PhD in the history of American civilization from the University of Delaware in 1992 and is the author of two previous books, *Savory Suppers and Fashionable Feasts: Dining in Victorian America,* and *Food in the United States: 1820s to 1890.* She lives in New Ipswich, New Hampshire, with her husband, Harvey Green.